THE VOICE OF WITNESS READER

THE

VOICE OF WITNESS READER

*Ten Years of Amplifying
Unheard Voices*

EDITED AND WITH AN INTRODUCTION BY

DAVE EGGERS

VOICE OF WITNESS

VOICE OF WITNESS

MCSWEENEY'S BOOKS
SAN FRANCISCO

For more information about McSweeney's, see www.mcsweeneys.net
For more information about Voice of Witness, see www.voiceofwitness.org

Copyright © 2015 McSweeney's and Voice of Witness

Illustrations by Julien Lallemand

ISBN: 978-1-940450-77-3

2 4 6 8 10 9 7 5 3 1

CONTENTS

INTRODUCTION

This started in Sudan, in 2003. Valentino Achak Deng and I had traveled from the U.S. to his hometown of Marial Bai, in the Bahr al-Ghazal region of what is now South Sudan. During the twenty-year civil war between the north and south of Sudan, he and thousands of young boys and girls had fled the attacks of militias known as the *murahaleen*. With this group, known as the Lost Boys, Valentino had walked over a thousand miles through war-ravaged country to reach the relative safety of a refugee camp in Ethiopia. He spent two years there and later ten more years at Kakuma, a camp in northwest Kenya. Finally, in 2001, the United States resettled Valentino and thousands of the so-called Lost Boys and Girls, who were by then young men and women, in various parts of the U.S. Valentino was sent to Atlanta, and we met a few years later. He had asked me to write his biography, and to that end, we thought we should get back to Marial Bai. He had not been there in seventeen years.

Valentino and I boarded an old Russian plane and sat in the cargo hold, and after four stops where we landed on dirt airstrips and grain and bicycles were unloaded, we finally landed in his home town. He was reunited with his family, amid much celebration and many tears.

While we were in Marial Bai, Valentino and I spoke to many dozens of people about their lives, about their experiences during the civil war, which was then in the middle of a cease-fire. With the help of Save the Children, an NGO that helped reclaim and repatriate abductees, we were able to speak to three women who during the conflict had been abducted by the *murahaleen*. They'd been taken as children and had been sold as war bounty, held against their will for as long as ten years. One of the women had borne children by her captor; when she was freed from bondage, she was not allowed to take them with her. She and the other women we spoke to had recently returned to Marial Bai, but because they had been abducted at such a young age, they spoke none of the local language, Dinka. During their captivity, they had been made to forget their mother tongue, had been taught Arabic and made to accept new names and roles. We listened to their stories, astonished and horrified that this all had happened in the 1990s. Crimes and practices most of the world assumed were no longer possible—the abduction and slavery women and children—all had happened on a large scale during the Sudanese civil war.

Though Valentino and I knew there was much work ahead to put his own story on paper, we made a pact that we would find a way to get the stories of the women told, too. One of the established issues in the civil war in Sudan was a marked lack of reliable information coming from the conflict. Because the country was and is the least-developed nation in Africa, and because at the time there were no cellular phones, no electrical grid, few roads or services, there was spotty journalistic coverage of the war, and unconscionable atrocities were thus more possible.

When I got back to the U.S., I walked around with the faces and stories of the women from Marial Bai in my head. I looked in books and online for any record of stories like theirs, and found the information was scarce, and detailed narratives were nonexistent. There were a few exit interviews conducted by NGOs, but these accounts were very brief—sometimes as short as one paragraph. Making heard the stories of the women I'd met seemed a task uniquely suited to oral history.

At the time, oral history was on my mind. Studs Terkel, a hero of mine growing up in Chicago, had recently released *Hope Dies Last*, a collection of oral histories about 9/11. With that book Terkel had again demonstrated the power of a well-curated collection of first-person narratives—and the simple and central importance of listening to those who lived history in order to understand history. Terkel had been putting masterful collections together for years—from *The Good War*, his complicated exploration of World War II, to *Working*, his exploration of the lives of the employed, underemployed, and unemployed in the United States. He was, and remains, the person best able to bring oral history to a large, mainstream audience.

With Terkel as inspiration, I imagined a series of books that would use oral history to record and amplify the voices of the unheard—and as these things do, my hopes for the series leaped far ahead of any practical notions. It seemed that in addition to the book of women's voices from Sudan, there should be a book of voices from Sierra Leone, a book of narratives from Chechnya, a book from the former Yugoslavia. It would be a series devoted to illuminating human rights crises around the world, and naturally I embodied the typical well-meaning American in looking abroad, first, for instances of the human spirit being compromised.

That was until a chance meeting at an event honoring Terkel himself. In late 2003, Terkel was at the University of California, Berkeley, for an onstage interview. And though he was ninety-one years old, he was as sharp and funny and passionate as ever—he even wore his signature outfit, a red-checked shirt, a bow tie, and red socks. After the event, as the audience was milling in the lobby, I met Dr. Lola Vollen, and she and I began talking about the power of oral history, and in the course of conversation I mentioned the series I had in mind.

She was intrigued, but wondered why such a series had to start abroad. What about human rights issues here in the U.S.? She'd been working with the wrongfully convicted and exonerated in the U.S., and found their plight woefully underreported. We see stories in the newspaper about a man or women being freed after ten, twenty years in prison, and we believe that that's the end of the story. But there is so much more, she said. To fully understand the scope of the issue of wrongful incarceration and re-entry, we need to hear from the people who have experienced this— we need their stories.

So there in the lobby, just after a Studs Terkel event, Vollen and I conceived of a project to interview U.S. exonerees, to record and edit their stories into a collection of narratives. McSweeney's would be the publishing partner, and Publisher's Group West, a Berkeley distributor, would get the books out into the world. In a final bit of tidy happenstance, a few months later, Orville Schell, then the head of Berkeley's Graduate School of Journalism, asked if I might be interested in teaching a course. I asked if the course could be one on oral history, where the students learned interview techniques and from it a book might emerge. Being a man of great generosity and evident faith in the unproven, he agreed. It all came together.

A year or so later, we published *Surviving Justice: America's Wrongfully Convicted and Exonerated.* That book benefited from the hard work and passion of a platoon of Berkeley graduate students who interviewed twelve men and women who had served as many as twenty-seven years in prison for crimes they didn't commit. The process, which took two semesters, taught us all— the students, Vollen, and myself—an immeasurable amount about how best to conduct and edit the interviews, and most importantly how to partner with the narrators to be certain that the process left them feeling more, and not less, whole. And feeling that the experience, though it may be difficult, would be a positive one during the interviews, during publication, and after.

To that end, a number of key principles emerged from *Surviving Justice*, and still guide the project today, as Voice of Witness marks its tenth year and thirteenth publication. These principles have been tested and improved over the years, and have benefited from the constant refinement of the Voice of Witness staff, as well as the legion of editors, interviewers, and narrators the organization has worked with.

I. TO FEEL HEALED A PERSON NEEDS TO FEEL HEARD

The first principle insists that we provide the narrators the time and sense of control to tell their story in a way that makes them feel heard. When we began the process with our exoneree narrators, very often they told us that previous interviews they'd conducted made them feel less complete, less whole, than they'd felt before. We wanted to change that. We needed to do better. We wanted to give the control back to the narrators. Particularly for individuals who have had their narratives taken from them—individuals who have been wrongfully labeled as *murderer, terrorist, illegal, unwanted, unworthy*—it's essential that they know that they will control the process, that they can talk about anything they want to talk about, and they can avoid topics they want to avoid. And that at the end of it, because their narratives will read exactly as they happened, because they will reflect the truth of their lives, the process will leave them feeling more whole. They will feel that they have regained the narrative of their life. And that when the book is published, for once their names will be attached to a truth they recognize as accurate and complete.

It's important to note that we don't seek out individuals who have no interest in telling us their stories. The process is entirely voluntary. They can end any interview at any time, and terminate the process at their will. With any Voice of Witness book, there are narrators who, after being interviewed, ask to exclude their story from publication, and always their requests are honored. Whenever appropriate or requested, names are changed to protect the narrators and their families. And always the interviewers are instructed about the risks of re-traumatization. But because the undertaking is voluntary and controlled by the narrators, and because the end goal is only to publish one's truth, the narrators find the recording and publishing of their stories as therapeutic, empowering, even permanently transformative.

Lorena, a narrator featured in the book *Underground America: Narratives of Undocumented Lives*, had grown up in California as a typical American kid. It was only when she was a teenager that she was told she had been born in Mexico, and that she was undocumented. This severely limited her options in life, and she lived in the shadows, always fearful of being caught, imprisoned, even deported to Mexico, a country she barely knew. Finally, though, she had had enough of living in the shadows. "When I decided to share my story," she says, "I set out to change people's perspectives on undocumented immigrants. It turned out, however, that the biggest change of perspective happened to me. Publishing my life story with Voice of Witness gave me exactly that—a voice. Sharing my story made me visible. It made me a real person. I was 'documented' and accounted for, if only in a book. The book's success is something I am now able to tell my son I was part of."

II. A HUMAN IS MORE THAN HIS OR HER TRAUMA

The second principle that guides our books is that in every case we want the narratives to tell the whole story of the person—not just the story of the person at the moment of trauma or violation. Too often in media interviews with individuals who have lived through a human rights crisis, the person interviewed is reduced to a moment of victimization, and then that person can feel reduced. To be sure that we capture the entire person, our interviewers are encouraged to start at the beginning, to ask about childhood, adolescence, about narrators' lives before they were touched by crisis or injustice. For the narrators, telling their stories becomes far more complete and balanced, because, after all, any human is much more than the moment when his or her rights were compromised. And for the reader, knowing more about the arc of someone's life—watching narrators grow up, make mistakes, knowing who they loved and what they wanted— helps us identify with them, and of course to see them as fully human.

III. TO CHANGE MINDS WE NEED TO COMPLICATE THINKING

We are clear in that we want readers to come away from any Voice of Witness book with a greater understanding of an issue or crisis and those affected by it. Where there is injustice that can be rectified, very often it's the individual stories of the victimized that spur us to action. But first we need readers, or lawmakers, or anyone who in a position to make a difference, to understand a situation in a more nuanced, layered, and inclusive way. And this starts by complicating our thinking.

To believe any subject—immigration, the rights of workers, political upheaval in Zimbabwe—is simple, or can be simplified, is a grave mistake. But of course it's a tempting mistake to make, and it's made every day by presidents, legislators, media commentators, polemicists, and demagogues. Very often it serves them to make a complicated situation simple. To pretend there is black and white when there is only a spectrum of infinite gray. So the first step on the road to understanding is to take a breath and know that it's complicated and will take time to understand (and far longer to master).

The second step is to acknowledge that the issue does not exist in an abstract realm, but exists, and affects, individuals. That, for example, a prison's policy of restraining a woman when visiting a doctor's office will result in women being shackled during childbirth. Simplistic laws and regulations make for complicated, unforeseen, and barbaric results.

The third, and most often overlooked, part of all this, is recognizing not just the complexity of an issue or policy or historical moment, and its effect on real humans, but that these humans themselves are endlessly complex. They conform to no expectations and fit into no neat categories. To show the range of those affected by a policy or state of upheaval, it's essential then that we understand that those affected are not types of people, but actual people of incredible variety. In every book, then, we seek to represent as many different experiences as possible. When we interview exonerees, then, we want to hear from the young men of color who make up a disproportionate percentage of the wrongfully convicted, and we also want to hear from someone like Beverly Monroe, a suburban woman in her fifties with a degree in organic chemistry. In *Underground America*, we wanted to hear from the Latin American immigrants who make up the largest group of undocumented in the U.S., but it was crucial to also hear narrators from China, Pakistan, and Cameroon, because people come to this country from every part of the globe.

Being sure to tell not just the more emblematic, but also the more unusual stories, is crucial. To remember the complexity of human experience we have to represent that complexity in the books.

IV. IT TAKES AS LONG AS IT TAKES

Listening to and recording the full arc of a person's life takes time, so Voice of Witness interviewers and editors have to be prepared to spend as long as necessary to get it right. Some narrators are naturally linear and colorful storytellers, while others need to be drawn out a bit, to provide the kind of thoroughness and detail that allows their stories to come alive. Some interview sessions take only three hours, and during those three hours a narrator might tell a concise and vivid accounting of his or her life. Others can take months, even years of periodic interviews, to cover it all.

In all cases, though, interviewers allow the process to unfold organically. This is not a hit-and-run interview, where a microphone is placed in front of someone, the interlocutor disappearing once they get their quote. This is instead a process with no set timeline. Renowned oral historian Dave Isay has said, "Listening is an act of love," and we're guided by this maxim—that the act of one human sitting and listening to another, with no agenda and no timetable, can itself be a transformative and empowering experience. Peter Orner, editor of three Voice of Witness books, says, "In San Francisco, in Zimbabwe, in Haiti, people I've interviewed have said to me some variation of the same sentiment, which is: 'You know, nobody, even members of my own family, has ever asked me these sorts of questions.' It's a way of connecting to people across countries, cultures, languages. It brings people together in ways that aren't too common."

V. WE HONOR THEIR STORIES
BY MAKING THEM RIGHT

If after these interviews, we publish sterile accounts of trauma, we are not doing justice to the narrators. We do them justice by helping to make their stories heard, and to make their stories heard we need to make them right. And we make them right by ensuring the stories are told in the narrator's authentic voice, are correct, and are compelling and comprehensible.

About the first point, regarding authentic voice: we don't fit the narratives into rigid formats. If we asked the same questions of every narrator, or transformed each narrator's way of speaking into a standardized or formalized manner, we would lose much of what makes each person unique and what makes his or her story resonant. If we're hoping to portray the full humanity of an individual, we have to allow for that individual's unique way with words. We have to bring out the humor and hopes of narrators, we have to make room for their tangents and obsessions—even their flaws and contradictions.

The second point is one of the things that makes Voice of Witness very distinct. Because oral history, for many general readers, is a hard sell, we try to make these books approachable, and to offer a reader the same immersive and captivating experience they would get from great narrative fiction or nonfiction. Reading, moreso than any other art form, involves direct participation, in that the reader is actively imagining the world depicted on the page. This participation creates a profound and more internalized experience, and is the reason fiction, or great narrative nonfiction, has for a thousand years had an unparalleled power to change minds and hearts. We seek to find that same level of detail and depth of feeling. How do we get this level of detail? It's easier than you would think. Mainly, we ask questions. If a narrator says, "I grew up in rural Colombia," we ask, "What did it look like? Smell like? What were the sounds?" Every human has these sensory details catalogued; they only need to be asked for them. They also need to be slowed down. Often, we tell stories quickly; we cut to the main event, or we'd prefer to talk about the meaning of an event and we skip a clear narrative of the event itself. So our interviewers slow things down. "Tell me more about that," they say. "Let's pause and really remember that day." As with sensory details, narrators are usually quite capable of remembering all of these things; they only need to be given room.

VI. THEY OWN THEIR STORIES,
NOW AND ALWAYS

Through all of this, of course, the narrators know that they alone control the final narrative. They know that after their interviews, the editors will carefully edit the transcripts into linear narratives that will be clear and compelling to a general audience. And that after that editorial process is complete, the narrators will be able to approve their final text.

During that first process with the exonerated men and women in the U.S., seeing the narrators read their narratives on paper, knowing that they could make right anything that was incorrect—I can assure you it was a revelatory moment for everyone involved. In general, their previous experiences with the media had not been good. Control over their narratives had never been an option. But now we were giving it to them. It took some getting used to.

I remember visiting one of the exonerees, James Newsome, in Chicago. He had spent fifteen years in prison for a murder he did not commit. Finally released, and given significant compensation from Illinois—only a few exonerees win settlements—James had opened a women's shoe store on the near-south side of Chicago. We had sent him the manuscript of his story, laid out in book form, and that day in Chicago, James and I planned to go over it. We sat down in a restaurant near his store, and he said the narrative looked great, that it was satisfying to have it all there in book form. Then he paused. He hemmed and hawed.

"What is it?" I asked.

"Well, I do have a few changes," he said.

"Good," I said.

"Good?" he said.

We both laughed. This is why I was there, I explained. To make any and all changes that would make the book more truthful. James laughed, and I laughed. Our mutual relief was profound. This was the first time anyone had checked with him before printing a story about his life.

VII. THE END OF THE STORY
IS JUST THE BEGINNING

The Voice of Witness process often continues far past publication of the book. The books themselves have been cited in legal decisions on the local and federal level, and have been taught in universities worldwide, in courses as disparate as constitutional law, comparative literature, Middle East Studies, and restorative justice, and very often the narrators are brought in to help students understand the real-world impacts of policies and laws and systems.

Indeed, narrators are encouraged to speak wherever they choose about the book, the project, their stories. In many cases, the narrators become powerful spokespersons for the issues raised in their narratives. Theresa Martinez, a narrator featured in *Inside this Place, Not of It: Narratives from Women's Prisons*, has become a crucial advocate for the rights of incarcerated women. Lorena, whose story is featured in *Underground America*, has appeared at dozens of events, speaking to community groups, library groups, students in high schools and colleges about her experiences. Beverly Monroe, featured in *Surviving Justice*, has consistently spoken to groups interested in improving our system of justice. "Having my story published led me to my justice work," she says. "It helped kickstart my spirit. And it gave me a framework for talking about my personal experience and about issues of wrongful conviction."

Voice of Witness is now in its tenth year, and the project has made remarkable leaps in its capacity and reach, and overwhelming credit goes to Mimi Lok, our Executive Director, to her board and staff, and to the editors who have conceived and executed an astonishing array of books the last decade.

Mimi Lok herself started as one of *Underground America*'s interviewers. A former public school teacher and journalist from the U.K., she had just finished her MFA in Creative Writing at San Francisco State University and decided to dedicate her last year in the U.S. to volunteering with

Voice of Witness. While working with a team of interviewers, editors, and translators, Mimi was struck by how underfunded and scrappy our operation was—there were, for example, only three working tape recorders between *Underground America*'s dozens of interviewers—and she couldn't help thinking that the organization needed better, well, organization. It needed infrastructure, systems, and financial planning.

Everyone affiliated with Voice of Witness was thinking the same thing, and soon after *Underground America* was published, in 2008, Mimi came on board as Executive Director. She filed the paperwork to make VOW a recognized 501c3 non-profit, and since then, she's grown VOW from a staff of one to six, and that staff has grown the idea conceived in the lobby of Berkeley's Wheeler Hall into a multi-pronged organization with a robust educational outreach program and an ambitious publishing schedule that now brings at least two Voice of Witness books into the world each year.

The books come about in one of two ways. Most often, a proposal is brought to Mimi and her team, and they assess the potential book's viability. They're looking to be sure that the proposal addresses a contemporary, underreported issue, that the editor has expertise in the field they'll be covering, that the editor will have willing participation from a pool of narrators, and that the editor has the editorial sensibility to bring out the level of detail necessary to do the stories justice. It's a tall order, and requires editors of unique skill, sensitivity, and determination. Our newest book, *Palestine Speaks*, took its editors, Mateo Hoke and Cate Malek, four years to complete and involved over 250 hours of interviews and three months of fact-checking. It then required the courage to publish and stand behind the book—a book that strikes to the heart of issues about which there are few neutral feelings.

Courage is necessary for any editor who undertakes one of these projects. Law degrees are not essential, but helpful. Over the years, a striking number of the Voice of Witness editors are dual threats—with both editorial and legal backgrounds. Peter Orner, whose first Voice of Witness book was *Underground America*, was a lawyer who had worked as a volunteer asylum attorney, and who later became a noted novelist. Ayelet Waldman, who co-edited (with Robin Levi) *Inside This Place, Not of It*, was a former public defender who also had become an acclaimed novelist. Alia Malek, who edited *Patriot Acts*, had not only written *A Country Called Amreeka*, a history of Arabs in the U.S., but was also an attorney who spent years in the U.S. Department of Justice. Who better could navigate and explore the Kafkaesque atmosphere for American Muslims after 9/11? None of these are required of course, but passion and an intimate understanding of the socio political context is. Audrey Petty, a creative writing professor at the University of Illinois, had grown up in the shadow of the Robert Taylor Homes, and thus made a perfect listener for *High Rise Stories*. Annie Holmes had grown up in Zimbabwe, and Sibylla Brodzinsky lives in Colombia, so both were able to bring a depth of knowledge and understanding to their work on *Hope Deferred* and *Throwing Stones at the Moon*, respectively.

But it's crucial to note that no matter how much expertise the editors brought to the table, they were repeatedly—reliably—educated by listening to the stories told by their narrators. Again and again the editors have had their own ideas, beliefs, and assumptions reexamined, realigned, or overturned completely by the simple task of sitting with a new person and hearing a new story.

We're grateful to have assembled such an august group of editors, and the quality of the books—their remarkable range and power and attention to the smallest details of a three-dimensional human's life—wouldn't be possible without these exquisitely sensitive listeners.

This book is being published in 2015, at a time when the idea of listening, of empathy growing from storytelling, is having a moment. These words—storytelling, listening, empathy—are newly prominent in a wide array of spheres, from the political to the corporate to the non-profit, but it's nowhere more evident than in the world of education. After a decade or so of zealous devotion to testing students, and punishing teachers and schools that do not measure up to ever-changing standards, recently there has been a national discussion about the importance of shaping students who not only know how to answer multiple choice questions, but who are also three-dimensional human beings capable of critical thought and compassion.

First-person narratives have a unique ability to reach people, and to clarify an issue that might otherwise seem abstract. Studies have shown that when faced with a complicated issue affecting scores of people halfway across the world, we often get confused or become disengaged, faced with the monumental scale of, say, a civil war or a systemic problem hundreds of years in the making. But when we can focus on one person who has lived through that war or was caught in that system, we are able again to see it, to focus and empathize.

This is true for all people, and all readers, but we've found it's especially true for young people, young readers. I've spent twelve years working with high school students through 826 National's network of writing and tutoring centers—in particular by teaching a class called the Best American Nonrequired Reading—and have consistently found that oral histories reach young people more reliably and more powerfully than any other written medium. A few years ago, my Best American Nonrequired class was talking about the War on Terror and the plight of Muslims after 9/11, and I saw the faces of many of these usually engaged students glaze over. They had been hearing those words, War on Terror, since they were in third grade, and it became clear that the words had lost their meaning. They'd heard endless and varied references to the government's post-9/11 policies, but none of these young people had been directly affected by them. The subject, then, remained abstract.

So I brought in an oral history that Alia Malek, editor of *Patriot Acts*, had just conducted with a young woman named Adama Bah. Though Adama was born in the United States, and spoke in a distinctly American vernacular, her father was born in Guinea, West Africa, and in the often clumsy and misguided sweeps made of Muslim-Americans in the interest of rooting out home-grown terrorists, her father and Adama herself became suspects. One night a team of FBI and Homeland Security agents arrived

22

with police officers at their Brooklyn apartment, handcuffed her father and herself, and brought them to a detention center in Manhattan. Adama was held for six and a half weeks without charges, though she eventually came to understand that she was suspected of planning to bomb her school. Because authorities had no evidence whatsoever to support this theory, she was released. Her story was harrowing, but she told it in her own way, peppering her narrative with expressions that any seventeen-year-old would know.

This narrative electrified my class of high schoolers. Suddenly the War on Terror was real. Someone their age, who spoke like them and looked like them, could be pulled from her bed in the middle of the night and held without charges. Thus what had been an unapproachable and distant topic suddenly was very tangible and immediate.

Because these narratives are effective in classrooms, and because we believe that long term, positive change can only be achieved if we foster empathy, awareness and engagement in young people, our education staff, Cliff Mayotte and Claire Kiefer, have been spreading the word and getting Voice of Witness books into classrooms. In 2014, the education program served over 12,000 students and teachers through class visits, workshops, trainings, and through the Common Core-aligned curriculum they create for each book. Sometimes the students are simply reading and discussing the stories. Other times they're asked to interview each other, or members of their community. In these instances, Cliff and Claire offer guidance in creating spaces for sharing stories, often starting with the question, "If you had a meaningful story to share with someone, what would you need to feel safe, to feel brave?"

Our experience shows that through engaging with VOW curricula, students discover their own voices, their capacity for authentic, compassionate listening, and their own relationships to social justice and human rights issues. As they learn from the oral histories of living witnesses, students are also empowered with a participatory vision of history—not as a pre-determined series of events, but as a series of choices made by individuals and groups.

In her Fremont, California, high school class, Praveena Fernes read several VOW narratives and with classmates did her own oral histories, highlighting an "upstander" in her community. "The gift of sharing and hearing someone else's journey changed the way I look at things," she says. "Fifth period English became a source of enjoyment, intrigue, but most importantly, it was a safe haven. The environment took a sharp turn into a whole new universe. I watched jocks talk to nerds. The next day they were laughing together. And later, I saw students interacting with other students. Labels had slowly been peeled off, worn away by a simple English project. Things weren't perfect; a utopia didn't suddenly appear outside of the classroom doors. But the evolution inside that room was out of the world."

Although our education program does most of its work in classrooms, we also serve an increasing number of community cultural organizations, social justice advocates, journalists, non-profits, book clubs, libraries, and more. More and more, we're working with communities impacted by issues portrayed in our book series, sharing tools for facilitating more safe, courageous spaces for storytelling on a community-led level.

Years later Valentino and I went back to South Sudan, this time with the determination to record the stories of women affected by the civil war. Between our 2003 trip and this trip, Voice of Witness, which had been conceived in Valentino's hometown of Marial Bai, had published two books before Valentino and I were finally able to get back to Sudan to begin the interviews that had been planned for what was supposed to be the very first Voice of Witness book.

When we returned to Marial Bai this time, the three women we had met that day in 2003 had all relocated to other parts of South Sudan. But during our time in the village, we came to know a number of men and women who had stories to tell, but none were more important than Achol Mayuol. We heard she had been abducted as a child, had been enslaved and had borne five children by her captor, and that it was only through her own unbreakable spirit that she was able to escape—and more unusually, to return home with her children.

She lived far out of town, in a rural area inaccessible by car. Valentino and I set out on borrowed bicycles, and getting there took us thirty minutes on a humid afternoon, the temperature far over a hundred degrees Fahrenheit. On the way there, on dirt paths, we passed the home-compounds of families small and large, and children ran out from their homes to greet us. Some knew Valentino by name or reputation, and some children had never seen a white person, and yelled *khawaja! khawaja!* as we rode by. We passed a large house that was being built by one of the generals of the former-rebel army, now part of the ruling elite. The home was six or eight times as large as the traditional huts, and was being built in a Western style, with brick walls and a steel roof. We passed goats and stray cattle and dogs, and we heard the crowing of chickens and all around the land was the brightest green from recent rains.

When we arrived at Achol's hut, she was outside, looking far too young to be the woman we had heard about. She was hanging clothes on a line and around her were two young children. We parked our bicycles at the edge of the compound and greeted her. As we were saying hello, another child, a boy of about eleven, came out of the hut, wearing a royal blue soccer jersey. Another child, about six, followed him, then another, perhaps four years old. Soon all five of her children were with us.

Achol invited us to sit outside, on a steel bedframe covered with a thin mattress. It became clear that this was the bed she and her children slept on inside; she brought it outside to serve as a kind of couch. Gently, in Dinka, Valentino asked Achol if she would mind telling us her story. Achol shrugged. She said that the last time she told her story nothing came of it. There had been a television crew, she explained, an international crew speaking English who wanted to know if stories of slavery in southern Sudan were true. One of the regional commanders of the rebel army knew of Achol, and had brought the television crew to her hut. She had been interviewed for an hour, and the television crew left and she never knew what became of them or her story. They had never come back, had given her nothing.

She told all this with little emotion, her eyes either cast downward or looking askance at us. But she told Valentino she wanted to talk, and sitting outside on the bedframe, with her children sitting beside her, she began. We had given the children a new set of crayons, and as she spoke, in an effort to distract the children from the horrific story their mother was telling, I drew pictures of rabbits and birds on paper, and they took the drawings and colored them on the dusty ground.

Over the next three hours, Achol related her experiences with remarkable clarity and linearity. During much of those three hours, Achol's mouth was shaped in a sneer, as if disgusted by having to recount the actions of the man who held her captive. We couldn't finish the story that first day, so returned the next, but even that—the act of returning a second day—seemed to lighten Achol's mood. She greeted us with a somewhat brighter countenance, and we continued on this second day until the story had been told. (Her story appears on page 147.)

When she was finished, the sun was dropping below the treeline and the light was orange, the night cooling. We sat and shared water we had brought in our backpacks, and watched the children coloring on the ground. We asked if she worried about the return of the man who had enslaved her. He had told her that he would follow her, would retake the children he claimed were his. She doesn't worry about that now, she said. She waited fifteen years to be free and she needed to feel free. Her family was here, and they helped her to some extent. But they had a lot to do, she said, they had their own problems. It's hard to help someone like her who has so many children, she said.

"It's a difficult life here," she said. She tried to start a business selling food and tea, but she became ill, a problem with her kidneys, and working that hard was impossible. She was trying to get the medicine she needed, she said. Perhaps if she got that medicine she would feel stronger. If she did, she could resume work.

She said she hoped her children have an easier life than her own. She wants peace for them, and opportunity.

"We will see," she said.

When we finished, we told her that we would publish her testimony exactly as she related it, and that in one year we would bring back the book with her story inside. She shrugged, and the sneer we knew from our first interview reappeared. She didn't believe us. It was getting dark, so we left to ride back into town.

A year later, almost to the day, Valentino and I returned. It was dusk, the sky tinted orange, and we rode our bicycles on the same cracked-earth path we took before. I had a book in my backpack, and in the book was Achol's story.

In the year since we'd last been in Marial Bai, another editor, Craig Walzer, had compiled an extraordinary array of testimonies he'd collected in northern and southern Sudan, and this collection became *Out of Exile: Narratives from the Abducted and Displaced People of Sudan*. The stories Valentino and I had recorded were included in the book, and the book was finished and had been printed. We couldn't quite believe we were doing what we said we would do, which was to return in one year with Achol's story in print precisely as she told it. We had promised her we would do this, but promises are not always easy to keep in a place like Marial Bai.

As we neared her house, we saw her children first. They were outside in the compound, and they saw and recognized us approaching on our bicycles. They ran inside and seconds later Achol emerged. She was smiling. Her smile was wide and bright, a smile we'd never seen before. It was an enormous and shy and astonished smile. We smiled, too. We couldn't help it, everyone was grinning and waving as we flew toward her, because none of us could quite believe that this was happening, that we were back together and this one promise had been kept.

We gave her two copies of the book—more would be kept in town and in schools in Marial Bai—and we all sat together, looking at it, her face and her story there, made permanent and made right.

This *Reader* was conceived of as a way a general reader might be introduced to the work of Voice of Witness. Each of the books in the series is represented here, and choosing only one or two stories from each title was extremely difficult. Our hope, of course, is that this sampling will bring readers to the full texts. If you're moved by the stories in this book, we hope you will become involved, will spread the word, and that you'll continue—in any way and to anyone—to listen.

Dave Eggers
February 2015

EXECUTIVE EDITOR'S NOTE

With every narrative in the Voice of Witness book series, we aim for a novelistic level of detail and a birth-to-now chronologized scope in order to portray narrators as individuals in all their complexity, rather than as case studies. We do not set out to create comprehensive histories of human rights. Rather, our goal is to compile a collection of voices that offers accessible, thought-provoking, and ultimately humanizing perspectives on what can often seem like impenetrable topics.

The stories themselves remain faithful to the speakers' own words (we seek final narrator approval before publishing their narratives), and are edited for clarity, coherence, and length. The narratives are carefully fact-checked, and are supported by various appendices and glossaries included in the back of each book. This supplemental material provides context and some explanation of the issues portrayed. In many cases, names and some details are changed to protect the identities of our narrators and the identities of their family members and acquaintances.

We would like to thank all the men and women who generously and patiently shared their experiences with us through ten years of collecting oral histories, including those whom we were unable to include in our books. We also thank all the frontline human rights defenders working to promote and protect the rights and dignity of all men and women throughout the world. Without the cooperation of these human rights advocates, the Voice of Witness book series would not be possible.

We would also like to thank our community of educators and students who inspire our education program. With each Voice of Witness book, we create a Common Core–aligned curriculum that connects high school students and educators with the stories and issues presented in the book. Our education program provides curriculum support, training, and on-site visits to educators in schools and in invested communities. For more details about our education program, as well as sample education resources, see page 405.

Visit the Voice of Witness website for additional free lesson plans, interview material, and to find out how you can be part of our work: www.voiceofwitness.org.

Mimi Lok
Co-founder, Executive Director
& Executive Editor
Voice of Witness

*Surviving Justice: America's Wrongfully Convicted and
Exonerated* (2005), edited by Dave Eggers and Lola Vollen,
collects the stories of U.S. citizens who were convicted of
crimes they did not commit. At the time of *Surviving Justice*'s
publication, the Innocence Project, a legal non-profit founded
in 1992, had helped exonerate over 175 individuals through
post-conviction DNA testing. Hundreds of other individuals
had seen convictions overturned based on incontrovertible
proof of innocence. Together, these exonerations pointed to
substantive flaws in the U.S. criminal justice system.

CHRIS OCHOA

AGE WHEN INTERVIEWED: *39*
BORN: *El Paso, Texas*
INTERVIEWED IN: *Madison, Wisconsin*

Chris Ochoa's plan out of high school was to work for a few years before applying to colleges. He got a job at a local Pizza Hut, and in his early twenties he moved from his hometown of El Paso to Austin, where he eventually found work at another Pizza Hut location. In October 1988, Nancy DePriest, an Austin-area Pizza Hut manager, was raped and murdered. Chris soon became a suspect. Under intense pressure from police interrogators, he found himself confessing to a crime he did not commit.

MY LIFE IS A BROKEN PUZZLE

Let's say you sit at a bus stop, and an hour earlier somebody just robbed a bank and left a big bag of money there. A bad guy. It's under the bench at the bus stop. Somebody else found it—it's gone.

He goes back to get his money. He says, "Where's my money?"

What is he talking about? You don't know.

He's got a gun, and he puts it to your head, but what you don't know is that this gun has no bullets.

"Tell me where the money is or you're dead."

You tell him, "No, no, no, no. I don't know."

You're just like shaking, because you don't know. If you knew, you would tell him, because you don't want to die. "I don't know. I don't know," you're thinking, "I don't want to die; I got to think of something."

"Where is it at? Where is it at?"

And then you're like, "Okay, somebody took it from here. I saw somebody running away from here. He went that way." Knowing darn well you didn't ever see anything.

Then the guy pulls away his gun and for some reason you see that it doesn't have any bullets, and you feel like such an idiot. But you didn't know. And that's how I felt. They were saying I was going to die.

IF THERE'S ANYBODY YOU CAN TRUST, IT'S A COP

I grew up in El Paso, Texas. From what I remember, I was always a good kid. One time, when I was a kid, a cop scared us. A mean neighbor, she said that we cussed her out and she called the cops. We're like ten years old at that time. The cop came into our house illegally. He had no probable cause—he just went in and scared the living daylights out of us. "You know I can take you to jail for this?" he said.

And then I called my uncle, and my uncle got on the cop: "What the hell are you doing scaring little kids? Isn't your job to try to be friends with them?" And the cop really didn't know what to say. That was the only run-in that I had. I trusted them. You're a kid, the cops give you candy. I was a patrol boy in high school. I always thought, If *there's anybody you can trust, it's a cop.*

When I went to high school, I was playing sports, I was studying. For some reason I became a "C" student, and then I went back to being an honor student. I was the assistant editor of a literary magazine. I took some law class; we did a mock trial. I was the prosecutor and I won the case. And it felt good. Maybe I could do this law thing. Either a lawyer or a major-league baseball player. That's really what I wanted to do. But things happened.

When I graduated high school, I didn't go to college right away, 'cause we had a teacher that said that sometimes when you go to college right after high school, you don't do as well as you would normally. So she advised, "You can go to college, or you can take a year off or two." And I did.

I was optimistic. My future was bright. Really bright. I was a typical twenty-, twenty-one-year-old, having fun, going to rock concerts. Drinking. Working. Primarily working. I used to go to Dallas for big rock festivals—Aerosmith, Van Halen, Boston, all these older bands. I worked at an amusement park during the summer. I was a ride operator at the amusement park, and then I moved on to Pizza Hut in El Paso. After a couple of years in El Paso, I went to Austin, where I worked at different jobs until I settled at Pizza Hut.

I had worked at Pizza Hut with Richard Danziger. We were both cooks, and he left. He quit. And then he came back maybe a couple of months later looking for a job. I was an assistant manager at Pizza Hut by then, and I knew that he was a good worker. He really worked hard so I gave him a job.

I saw him living at the YMCA. I think he told me he had been convicted of something or other, or he was on probation, and so I said, "You can stay with us until you get on your feet. You just have to pay rent." I was living with another roommate, Roger Lewis, before I even met Danziger. I was living with him for a while, then my brother came to Austin.

I had a manager, a boss. I think she and Richard started seeing each other, and he would spend most of the time at her house. So it was like I had a roommate, but I didn't. I was not that tight with Richard. The media portrays us to be really tight, which we weren't. He was a cool person. He was a little bit, I don't know, he was really open, I think, whereas I was not. But other than that, he was just a cool guy. He wanted to be a psychologist. So maybe that was why he was so interested in human behavior and stuff.

But I didn't go out with him and have dinner with him, no. I went out with my roommate, Roger, or my brother, Ralph. And I had other friends that I would hang out with. I guess they were more down to earth, more normal. So it's not like we had this relationship. I just know he was a hard worker and he was a really nice guy. It's kind of impossible for me to sit here and tell you how he really was.

I got the bug to go back to school, to the Austin Community College. I was going to go in the spring of '89. That was my plan.

SUSPICIOUS CHARACTERS

On the morning of October 24, 1988, Nancy DePriest, a twenty-year-old Pizza Hut manager and mother, was raped and murdered at the Reinli Street Pizza Hut in Austin (a different Pizza Hut than the one where Chris worked). After the attacker sexually assaulted the victim, he handcuffed her to the restroom counter and shot her in the back of the head with a .22 caliber pistol. Before leaving, he flooded the restaurant in order to destroy any physical evidence he might have left behind.

October of '88, there was a murder in another Pizza Hut—a robbery, a rape, and a murder. A young woman was opening the store. I had seen her at managers meetings, but I didn't know her personally. The murder was one of those with virtually no leads, and they closed the restaurant for a couple of weeks. Everybody was shocked. All the Pizza Hut employees in the city were shocked about what happened to that young woman.

A couple of weeks later they reopened the restaurant. My roommate Danziger was taking me home from somewhere. He wanted to stop by the Pizza Hut where the murder occurred. And I really didn't. He was curious about the scene, and I found that kind of weird. He was driving, so I had no choice. He drove up to Pizza Hut. I was in the car, and we were outside in the parking lot and I didn't want to go in. We were arguing and arguing, and I said, "Fine, let's just go in."

We go in. He ordered a beer. The whole time I was nervous. I've always been the kind of person that wants to follow the rules. In high school,

I went to the principal's office once. Once. Never went again. Well, there was a Pizza Hut policy you couldn't drink beer at any other restaurant, so we're drinking beer there. He's only eighteen, I'm twenty-one.

And then he wants to look at the scene of the crime. I go, "I don't understand." So he makes a toast, and I toast, but you know, I didn't feel comfortable. I wanted to leave. We left shortly after, but as we were walking out, my roommate stopped to talk to a security guard, and asked him a lot of questions about the crime scene. I don't know what he asked him—I was at the car when he was asking questions.

And we drove off. Apparently, the police officers—the detectives that were investigating this crime—had talked to the Pizza Hut employees. They said, "Whoever did it might come back. And if they come back, if you see anybody suspicious, call us." So that looked suspicious, toasting, and you put it all together, we looked like suspicious characters.

A couple of days later, on Friday morning, I was working and two detectives asked for me. They said they wanted to ask me questions about a burglary. And they asked me if I wanted to go down to the station and answer them, and I said yes. They said I could drive my car or I could go with them—if I went with them they'd bring me back or whatever. Of course, they never brought me back.

THIS IS WHERE THE NEEDLE'S GONNA GO IN IF YOU DON'T COOPERATE

So I go with them. I was naive. I didn't know nothing about the system. I figured they were asking every employee at the Pizza Huts around the city. They take me into some kind of cubicle, what I know now is an inter-rogation room. What I later found out is that I was already a suspect in the murder. It was never about a burglary. They lied.

It was a Hispanic detective that first walked in. When he walked in, he slammed his fist on the table. He starts asking me about why I was inquiring about the murder, rape, and all that kind of stuff. And then he's telling me that if I know something, I should just tell him. Typical inter-rogation, but he's yelling this whole time. He's not being so nice.

He spoke to me in Spanish initially, but I was answering his questions in English, so he laid off Spanish. He was trying to get this Chicano bond thing, and like, you're a cop—how can you ever get that? When it comes to detectives, they want to get their man. They don't care.

He taps his finger on my arm at one point. "This is where the needle's gonna go in if you don't cooperate." He's telling me, "You know, if you know something about it, you can still get charged with capital murder and get the death penalty, 'cause you know something about it." And I told him, "I don't know what you're talking about. If I knew something, I would tell you. I would help you, but I don't know."

So he just kept yelling at me, saying, "If you don't cooperate, I'm just gonna throw the book at you. They're gonna send you to death row; you're gonna get executed." This is going on for hours. At one point a female detective walks in. I was getting tired, and I asked her, "Can I have an attorney?" And she got really upset. She said, "No, you can't have one till you're officially charged."

At some point they give me a polygraph test. I failed it. I failed all three polygraph tests they gave me. Even the ones where I said I didn't pull the trigger, I failed. I mean, there's nothing that I passed.

"If you don't cooperate, this is where you're gonna live the rest of your life, in this cell. Take a good look at it, 'cause that's gonna be your home. You're not gonna be able to hug your mom or your family anymore. You're gonna die in the death chamber. You'll live there until you die."

I don't know what's going on. Everything's spinning.

"Your partner on the other side is gonna testify. He's about to talk. I don't want him to get the deal. The Hispanic always gets the shaft, and the white guy always gets the deal."

I tell him, "I don't know what you're talking about."

He shows me pictures of the autopsy.

"Don't you feel sorry for her?"

"Yeah, I do, but what do you want me to do? I can't help you."

This went on for hours. He said, "I'm just getting tired of this BS. I'm gonna book you. You're young, you're fresh for the prison. You've never been in prison, they're gonna have you." I took that to mean rape.

That was when I gave him the first statement.

The Hispanic cop, Hector Polanco, he was the one writing the statement. He wanted me to say that Danziger was the one that did it, and he came and told me about it, that he did it, all this kind of stuff, and I just went along with what the detective was saying. Signed the statement.

Then I wanted to go home. He said, "You can't go home. We want you to stay at a hotel for your own protection." Then he asked me for some lab samples. Some semen and hair and all that. I gave him the semen and the hair. While at the hotel, I started getting scared, really scared. I called my roommate Roger. "I think I need an attorney."

I was there at the hotel for the weekend. Come Monday, the detectives walked in and they picked me up. And they said, "Okay, now we know you're guilty, 'cause you wanted to call for an attorney, and only guilty people call for attorneys." So now, I don't know what's going on. They take me to another interrogation room. Now they got a tape recorder on. "We think you had something to do with what happened, we think you were the lookout. If you don't cooperate again, the death penalty's there, it hasn't gone away, we're gonna execute you."

So I just say, "Okay, yeah, I was the lookout." I just want to go home. All this time they're saying, "Oh, well, you'll get twenty years." By this time, I know I'm sunk. I'm scared. I didn't know what they could do. You just don't know what can happen. So that confession, alleged confession, was pretty easy, but then all of a sudden they wanted more. They wanted me to be in there, sodomizing her and raping her, and I was like, "No."

But the death penalty's there, so I'm like, "Whatever, okay." By this time I just want to get it over with. This is a long time. I've been there a while. They tell me, "We think you were there," and all this stuff, so I say yeah—I just went along with them. I don't know why, I was just scared.

They start tape-recording it, but the problem was that any time they asked about a detail in the restaurant, my answer was wrong, and then they would get mad. They would say, "Well, was this item there?" And I would say, "Yeah . . ." "Then what color was it?" They had me guessing for the right color. They would start the tape and then would have to stop it 'cause I got the detail wrong. So they would start it, stop it, till they got the details. It took a long time. At one point the sergeant got up and threw the chair he was sitting in at my head. He missed, but he threw it with such force, and I was really scared 'cause those guys were really big.

The interrogation lasted two full days, during which the police repeatedly threatened Chris with the death penalty. His requests for a lawyer were denied. By ten p.m. on the second day, Chris had signed two separate statements, each typed by one of the officers. In the first, he claimed to be the sole murderer of DePriest. In the second, he claimed that while he had participated in her rape and murder, Richard Danziger had pulled the trigger. Chris later retracted this accusation in a third statement, made on March 7, 1989, in which he implicated Danziger in the rape and the robbery, but asserted that he himself was the shooter.

I sign the confession, I get arrested. I went to the magistrate. She was really upset that I didn't have a lawyer on a capital murder case. So she took me to chambers. She yelled at people, said, "I want this guy to have a lawyer. Immediately."

The lawyer they sent me was just out of law school. Young. I didn't know it, but that's bad news on a capital murder. I tell him exactly what happened, and he said, "Okay, fine." He leaves, and then the cops tell him, "No, he's got a confession." And he says, "Okay, you've gotta be guilty." So I told him, "No, I'm not. I'm innocent."

So they get me another attorney—a lead attorney, an older attorney. I tell him the same thing. And he got mad. He wanted me to plead guilty. I said, "No. Isn't it your job to prove me innocent?" He says his job was to save my life, which I guess it was, but he didn't even try to investigate. "There's a detailed confession, you gotta be guilty." I told him no.

But the problem was, the lawyers were calling my mom every day. "He's guilty, he's guilty. You got to get him to plead guilty and to testify. If not, your son is gonna die on death row." So you can imagine what my mom is going through. And she would keep on calling me, telling me, "You got to save your life." No, I don't want to. I don't want to testify. I don't want to plead guilty. I don't want to admit to it.

But she had health problems and had to go to the hospital—had she gone later she would've had a heart attack. People didn't want to tell me. Nobody wanted to tell me till my grandma let it out on the phone when I called from the jail. She told me what had happened with my mom and I got really sad, and it was the hardest choice I ever had to make. I called whoever I had to call: "I'll plead guilty to this."

And I go talk to them, and they want me to plead guilty, but Danziger has to be convicted. They really wanted him. I testified against Danziger. I'm coached before I go into the courtroom and told what to say.

Chris pleaded guilty to murder and sexual assault on May 5, 1989. His sentencing was suspended until after Danziger's trial in late January 1990. At Danziger's trial, Chris testified that he had shot DePriest, but that he and Danziger had planned the crime together, and that they both had raped her. Although Danziger's girlfriend testified on his behalf that she was with him at the time of the murder, she also wavered under the prosecution's threats to bring charges against her, and her statements were ultimately not enough to convince the jury. Danziger's defense, furthermore, could provide no explanation for Chris's testimony. Danziger was found guilty of aggravated sexual assault and sentenced to life in prison. Soon after, on March 6, 1990, Chris also was sentenced to life in prison.

THE LONELIEST FEELING IN THE WORLD

It's like you don't have a choice. Life sentence, death penalty. Life sentence in prison—you're going to die a slow death at an old age—or you're going to die in the death chamber. It was no choice. You're twenty-two years old. What do you do? And if people notice, every confession, every time there's a wrongful convicted guy, most people were in their mid-to-early twenties. The cops are trained. They're going after people that want to live. They know your weakness, and your enemy knows your weakness. That's what he's going to look for.

Danziger's girlfriend, they brought her in. She was saying, "No, he was with me." They interrogate and say, "You know what? We think that you were there. You and Ochoa and Danziger were there—you held her down while she was being sodomized. So what's going to happen—we're going to send you to jail. They're going to take your kids away." A mother's kids. What does she do? She caves in. That's her weakness.

They send me to prison. The first night, they put me in the cell, and then they close the door. When they close the door, and it was the loneliest feeling in the world. I was all alone.

So many things you see in prison. I don't know. I started seeing body bags roll down the hallway. I saw a guy stabbed. A riot broke out in the kitchen where I working. And you just start smelling the pepper spray, and you put a towel on you and it just makes it worse. Tear gas is different. You can put a wet towel on your nose and it's okay. But pepper spray, it just makes it worse.

I had to go through riots. I had to go through lockdown. They would lock the prison down because people were killing each other. And it was pretty bad when they locked down the prison. When we were locked down in the summer it was hot, humid. I remember I sometimes had to put the fan on the toilet so that the fresh air that was bouncing off the water would hit the fan. Or throw water on the floor. You would lay in it.

It smelled bad, and it felt even worse. Tennessee County, Texas. Three days without a shower, three days in the same cell. Fortunately I always had plenty to read. That's all you do, read and listen to the radio. They didn't allow TVs in the rooms in Texas. They do in other prisons, but we didn't have them.

The bars were navy blue, or baby blue. The color would supposedly make you more mellow, instead of the higher, brighter, sharper colors that make you vicious or whatever.

CHRISTMAS EVE

I'd been there almost ten years. I'm thirty years old, I'm looking back on my life. I'm a failure. I have no family, I have no kids, I have no education, no car, no house. I used to get the newspaper from back home. I used to see these people I went to high school with. They had kids, beautiful homes, beautiful wives, and all this stuff, and I had nothing, and I didn't know what I did to deserve it.

Christmas Eve, I was really depressed. No cards came for me. People can tell when you're going to kill yourself in prison—they know. They saw me really sad, and they said, "You'll get a card." Mail call came again. I didn't get anything.

I went up to my cell, I took a razor and I busted it open and I got the razor blade itself and I put it on my arm, and I was going to kill myself on Christmas Eve. I was in so much pain that I didn't want to live anymore. It hurt too much to live. So I just wanted an end.

But somehow, before I did the deed, my morals, everything came flashing back to me—my family, my religious upbringing. I felt I didn't have the right to take anybody's life, not even my own. It really took all I had not to do it. I dropped the razor. I flushed it down the toilet.

I went to sleep, woke up the next morning. I was still in pain. I mean emotional pain, not physical. So I started going to church, not because I wanted God to save me or give me release or whatever. I needed peace.

I found peace. I would go to school, I would work out, weight lift.

43

I would read everything I could find: Bible, love novels, horror novels, everything under the sun. I also pursued my college education, and I got two associate's degrees.

FAVORITE GRANDSON

When I was a little kid, I would go to my grandfather's house, and if I had a hole in my pants or my shirt, he would take the hole and just rip it all to shreds, and I would have no clothes. And I thought that was funny. I would laugh, and my mom would get mad. He would do it to my little brother and my brother would cry. But I was laughing. My grandfather was my best friend. I found out later that I was his favorite grandson.

When I was in prison, he would write me. He would send me money every month. Fifteen dollars to put on my books. It wasn't much, but it was something.

One day, my parents said he was getting sick, he was about to die. The doctor gave him I don't know how many months. Maybe a year. I would tell him, "You can't die, you can't croak." He would say, "I'm not going to kick the bucket, I have to wait for you to get out."

At some point, I just stopped writing. I was like twenty-four. You take people for granted at that age sometimes. He would get mad. Why didn't I write? And I don't know what possessed me, one day I wrote him a letter. A long letter. I thanked him for everything he did, specific instances where he helped me. A heartfelt letter.

My mom said that he died at three in the morning, and my letter got to his house at like seven. And it totally devastated me, that my letter didn't get to him on time. Because I wanted to say that. I mean, I guess something inside of me felt that he was going to die, and I didn't get to say goodbye to him.

But he would always tell us not to cry—never cry for him when he died. He says, "Always cry for people when they're alive, because that's when they want to hear it the most. I'm dead, what the hell are you going to cry for me then?" So I didn't cry.

I HAVEN'T STOPPED BELIEVING IN MYSELF

In 1990, convicted rapist Achim Josef Marino learned from his cellmate that two other men had pleaded guilty to murdering DePriest. Marino had a religious conversion as a result of his participation in a twelve-step program, and in 1996, seeking atonement, he wrote letters to the Austin Police Department and the Austin American-Statesman *in which he confessed that he was the sole perpetrator of the crime against DePriest. The letters described the crime in detail and informed police of the location of the pistol with which he had shot DePriest, as well as handcuffs he had used to bind her, and a bank bag he had stolen. These items were recovered shortly after the crime, but investigators, unsure as to whether the gun was the real murder weapon, took no further action.*

In 1997, Marino again wrote letters, this time to Governor George W. Bush, to the police department, and to the district attorney's office. In response, a homicide detective and a Texas Ranger were sent to interview Chris.

In '98, two cops came to see me, a Texas Ranger and an Austin police officer. They asked me if they could interview me. They said, "There's this guy that's saying that he did this crime with you guys."

I didn't know then, at all, what was going on. I had no idea that this guy who actually did it, who had already wrote them a letter, had wrote Governor Bush a letter, had wrote DAs that we hadn't done the crime, that he had done it. He did a Christian conversion. But I guess they were trying to link us together. Well, I didn't know this guy; he didn't know us.

During that interview I ask one of the detectives, "Hey, what if I call Barry Scheck? What if I get in contact with him?" I had kept up with all the DNA exonerations that Barry Scheck had done. I remember the cop had mentioned DNA initially, and that's the only thing that stuck to my mind when I was first arrested.

He says, "I wouldn't do that if I were you. You're gonna make it worse for yourself." I didn't respond to that. I just looked at him like, wait a minute, they know damn well that if I'm guilty I'm not going to do that.

So this guy's got to be hiding something. I was very afraid that if I gave him any clue whatsoever, or say that I'm going to contact an attorney, they would destroy evidence that might be used to help me.

Distrustful of the officers, Chris repeated what he had said at Danziger's trial—that he and Danziger had raped and murdered DePriest. The officers suspected he was lying to protect Marino. For the next two years, the police searched for a link between Chris and Marino.

So I went and I talked to this prisoner from El Paso that was going home, a pretty good friend of mine. I told him to type Barry Scheck's name in the search engine. And finally somebody from the Innocence Project e-mails him back: "Your friend might have a case, because he has DNA." And he sent me the addresses of the schools with organizations affiliated with the central Innocence Project in New York.

So for some reason I circle the Wisconsin Innocence Project. That's the one I'm going to write. Wrote them an eight-page letter, told them the whole story from the beginning to the time that I wrote them. Just the legal stuff. And I told them, "You know what, I've given up on the system, I've given up on everyone, I don't trust anybody. I've given up on the world, I don't have faith in the system, but I haven't stopped believing in myself."

That was enough for them to take the case. They called me up a couple of months later, and I was really happy.

In 1999 the lawyers and students of the Wisconsin Innocence Project began their search for evidence that would help prove Chris's innocence. In the spring of 2000, John Pray, law professor and co-founder of the project, sent a letter to the police department requesting that DNA evidence be preserved. The DNA laboratory at the Texas Department of Public Safety had saved the evidence, and the police department immediately agreed to testing. At the request of the district attorney's office, the tests were performed in the summer and fall of 2000. The results matched Marino and conclusively excluded Chris and Danziger.

Eventually, in 2000, the cops came to see me again. This time they were friendlier. They gave me another polygraph. I flunked it again. And that's when I told them, "I don't care what your polygraph says, I'm innocent. I don't care what that crap says." So September, October, I don't know when it was, I got the test that exonerated me. The DNA test. They said it matched Marino, and I said, "Who the hell is Marino?" And my attorney said, "You don't know?" I said, "No. What are you talking about?" So then he started telling me Marino is this guy, the actual perpetrator. In a way I was grateful, but in a way I was really angry, 'cause Marino is the one that cost me a lot of years. He took somebody's life. He's caused so much hurt. I don't know him. I don't want to know him.

They tell me I'll have to wait for two months. They'll try to get me out before Thanksgiving, before Christmas. Finally, January 16, they took me to court and they released me.

When I was released, it was celebratory. Every talk show host that I've talked to, they said they admired me, or whatever—because, I guess, I didn't come out angry. I think people like that. The media like that I was forgiving and not this angry convict. I went on *The O'Reilly Factor*. He was angry at what happened. He said, "Why aren't you angry? I would be really angry." I guess he was trying to draw me in to a confrontation. I said, "No, I'm not bitter." And he said, "Okay, Thank you very much, Mr. Ochoa." I didn't last but ten minutes on his show.

THIS IS WHERE I BELONG

I know that my uncle believed in me. My mom says she didn't have her doubts, but she had her doubts. My uncle never did. When I got out, my uncle and his partner had a room ready for me. He had an extra room in his house. So they fixed it up. They had a bed and a TV for me, and they had my Dallas Cowboys helmet-phone—a phone that's a helmet. I would stay with my mom, but I decided that at my uncle's there was more freedom. I had a good relationship with my relatives.

I was really socially awkward. I couldn't look anybody in the eyes. I still don't. When I would go out and I would not be very talkative, friends and family would try to draw me out. Everybody I've seen that just gets out, they're not ready to talk when they get out. So my uncle would take me out dancing to the clubs. He would, like, make the sacrifice.

My uncle, when I got out, he taught me how to dress. He took me to get my prescription glasses. I paid for half, he paid for the other half. I remember picking out my glasses, and I'm looking at the 1980s style, those teardrops. And him and his partner come up and go, "No, no, no! The teardrops are gone. We'll get you some nice, in-fashion little ones."

For a month or two after I got out, I did nothing. I traveled around the country. I started working in about May, April—worked at a concrete company. And then I started school, went to finish my bachelor's degree. I was a business major. Accounting came naturally to me. When I started taking business classes I really took to them well.

And then I took a business law class, and I thought, "This is where I belong." I decided to go to law school, and I decided to apply to Wisconsin, and then eventually I got my settlement.

Barry Scheck, Johnnie Cochran, and all them, their law firm sued the city. Well, I did, I sued the city of Austin and the police department. Eventually we settled. We settled for $5.3 million.

Barry Scheck was the first famous person I ever met. Somebody told me that most lawyers can walk into an airport and not get recognized, but Barry Scheck and Johnnie Cochran go to an airport and they get recognized. They're like rock stars of the law. Barry Scheck is a hero to people in prison. But I met him and he was really, really humble. I guess I expected somebody that was full of himself, but he was so warm and so genuine. He said, "You're going to be in front of the media. Here's some tips for talking to the media." And he told me how politicians speak to media, how you pick three points and stay on them. And when I talk to the press I always remember what he told me, and I carry that through law school.

BRAND-NEW START

Chris was admitted to the University of Wisconsin Law School in 2003, where he became a student of John Pray and Keith Findley, the professors who had worked to free him. He joined the Wisconsin Innocence Project in 2004.

The acceptance letter came, and I realized I was going to law school. I couldn't believe it. A couple of years before, I was at the bottom of the barrel, here now I was going to one of the top law schools in the country. It all seemed surreal. I felt it was like a brand-new start for me. I felt, I finally felt, like there was something that was my own, my very own. It felt like finally my life, it's beginning again, which it actually has.

I was so excited when Wisconsin said yes. When I was in East Texas, in prison, you can tell you're looked down on—you're Hispanic, you're black. They won't say anything, but you can feel it. And here, walking in Madison, the first time I walked to State Street, it was like the people there didn't even, you know, they didn't stare, it was nothing different to them. My biggest thing is that I want to be part of society. I want to be normal, whatever normal is. I just want to walk through a mall, or walk through a street, not be treated different because I was in prison. I did my first year here, and now I'm doing my second year. I do pretty well when I set my mind to it here in school, when I really study. When I read for class, and I go prepared, I really understand it.

But I can't sleep. I wake up in sweats. You know, when you take the law school finals, because those things are like four hours long—I have to get eight hours of sleep. Well I can't—I haven't got eight hours of sleep in forever. When my finals roll around, I have to go to bed at six o'clock at night in order to get the rest. Because I wake up lots of times. That really is affecting my law school work.

My social skills, they're lacking. I'm a thirty-eight-year-old working with twenty-year-olds. I don't fit in. And I'm still shy by nature. People think I'm this conceited guy, but it's not that. People didn't mean to on purpose, but it happens—I say something and it gets dismissed. I would make a suggestion, and they would act like, "What do you know? You've been in prison." A couple months later they would see that I was right.

It's hard for me to be close to people. My family doesn't understand at all. It's kind of hard to trust people. And then, in the prison, you learn not to trust people. You're taught very early on, don't trust anyone. No one. One thing you do learn is, you have to shut off your emotions. You have to have no emotions, 'cause other prisoners, when they see weakness they attack, physically and mentally. So I had no emotion in my heart. Just because you don't have emotions doesn't mean you're not a cool person, doesn't mean you're a mean guy, you're just a jerk. You still treat people with respect, you still help them, but you don't show anything.

I met this wonderful woman. Her name's Robin. I'm kind of happy that now I know, okay, there's nothing wrong with me. Robin shows me how to manage my money. I'm an electronics freak. I used to buy remote control cars, which me and my brother always wanted when we were kids. Remote control cars—it seemed like a good idea. Now, Robin would just kill me. There's a robot I bought at Sharper Image, from the sale rack. It dances and stuff. A hundred dollars. She said, "Why did you get that? You don't use it." I was going to go buy this $300 robot one time, a big one. I mean, he actually serves drinks and stuff. He has a camera, so you send him in to spy on people. But she won't let me. I mean, I could, 'cause it's my money. She would say, "It's your money," but she shows me how to control myself.

My family was pretty poor. When I was growing up, I didn't have much—and I sure as heck didn't have it in prison. I didn't have a TV, I had a little radio, worth eight bucks—that's all I had. And now I come out here and they give me money. It's not so much that I go nuts. Every guy that's middle class, thirty-eight years old, with a wife and kids, they have the ability to go buy a plasma TV. That's all the money did—put me where I was supposed to be.

ONE MILE AT A TIME

I came out of prison with no scratches, nothing.

Sometimes I'll get in my truck and I'm driving alone, and it's such a smooth ride and everything is good. It overwhelms me. I'm just like, "Thank you, God, for everything, for all this I have." I mean, this is a nice house I'm in. I got a forty-two-inch plasma, and people would kill for one of these things.

I'm in law school, and I have met some beautiful people—friends, and Robin. And I've always wanted someone to love me, someone that I could laugh with, and somebody to have intelligent conversations with. She'll give me the good and the bad. There's times when she'll just look at me and I'm like, "I'm falling in love with you."

I just want to be a normal part of society, contribute to society like everybody else does, in a good way. I want people to know that everybody's human whether they're in prison or not—they still live and breathe and they still go to the bathroom like all of us do. They still put their pants up the same way. I think I've learned both sides of the street now.

I plan for the future, but I live my life one day at a time. Kind of like when I'm driving to Chicago—I want to get to Chicago. I have a map, but I know to take it one mile at a time because I may have to catch a detour. But then, I get back on the road.

Chris Ochoa graduated from law school in 2006 and became a defense attorney in the Madison, Wisconsin area. After the economic crash of 2008, Chris also worked with a partner to defend the interests of homeowners forced from homes by burden-some mortgages. Then in 2011, he took a break from his law practice. "I needed time to find out who I was besides just an exoneree and lawyer," he says.

Though he stopped formally practicing law, Chris was connected with the family of a young El Paso man named Daniel Villegas who had been convicted of a double-murder in a drive-by shooting. Up to that point, Chris had avoided wrongful conviction cases, having recognized that it would be too emotionally challenging for him. However, Villegas's conviction reminded Chris of his own—especially the details of Villegas's alleged confession—so Chris took up the case as an informal advisor. In January 2014, a Texas appeals court overturned Villegas's conviction on the basis of ineffective counsel. His former confession was ruled inadmissible in the retrial.

In 2015, Chris is working toward restarting his law career. He also hopes to establish a foundation that will help recent exonerees adapt to life outside of prison.

Surviving Justice: America's Wrongfully Convicted and Exonerated (2005), edited by Dave Eggers and Lola Vollen, collects the stories of U.S. citizens who were convicted of crimes they did not commit. At the time of *Surviving Justice*'s publication, the Innocence Project, a legal non-profit founded in 1992, had helped exonerate over 175 individuals through post-conviction DNA testing. Hundreds of other individuals had seen convictions overturned based on incontrovertible proof of innocence. Together, these exonerations pointed to substantive flaws in the U.S. criminal justice system.

BEVERLY MONROE

AGE WHEN INTERVIEWED: 67
BORN IN: *Marion, North Carolina*
INTERVIEWED IN: *Williamsburg, Virginia*

In 1992, Beverly Monroe was living comfortably near Richmond, Virginia. She had a master's degree in organic chemistry and was working as a patent analyst for Philip Morris. Her companion of thirteen years, Roger Zygmunt de la Burdé, lived on an estate outside the city. He was also a scientist at Philip Morris, at least until a dispute with the company resulted in his quitting and filing a multi-million dollar lawsuit against his former employer. Their families—Beverly's children Katie, Shannon, and Gavin, and de la Burdé's daughter, Corinna—had grown close over the years. Separately from his relationship with Beverly, de la Burdé was carrying on an affair with another woman—an affair that Beverly knew about.

The night of March 4, 1992 was the last time Beverly saw de la Burdé alive.

NOW I QUESTION EVERYTHING

Roger called me, probably—I don't know—nine or ten times that day at work. He was saying, "Mouse, get here as soon as you can." You know, "Get here. Leave." So I ran by my house, threw on some other clothes.

I remember leaving a note for my son, Gavin, on a napkin. Told him I was going to get groceries.

Roger was sixty years old. He was doing a lot of looking back: "What have I done with my life? Everything is a mess."

Financially, everything was a mess. Finances were one of the reasons I wouldn't marry Roger. He was an unstable person, and a difficult person at times. He was both wonderful and difficult, but my finances were stable. His were not. There was no way I would mix my finances in with that. None.

He was wealthy in the sense that he had accumulated a lot of properties and art. But it was all built on things that were shaky. Not that they were wrong. It's like a toothpick castle. You pull one of those things out and the whole thing can go collapsing down on you. It's a lot of juggling. He got overextended.

He was a research scientist at Philip Morris. A very brilliant person, but not an orthodox person. And he was responsible for some of the major inventions for the industry, not just for the company. He had a suit against Philip Morris for $12 million, and they had counter-sued him for $50 million. It was serious. And he was frightened.

That's why he bought the gun. He was afraid—I don't want to say afraid of Philip Morris—but he was. And people close to him knew that. He got a little paranoid about it. It's an area that's not easy to talk about, but it's a fact. It was a huge mess, and it was a tremendous pressure on him.

Roger had all these things going, including this affair with this Polish woman. It wasn't just with her. There were others, too.

I'd been at Roger's that evening. We'd had dinner. While I was there, I was sitting at the piano. Roger had learned a jazz song. I was sitting at the piano and the phone rang. And the message started to come on. He didn't answer it. As somebody started talking, he jumped up and took it off the hook. I had a feeling it was this woman calling him. He took the phone off the hook, and when I left, he hadn't put it back on.

I didn't remember actually driving home. But I remember stopping to get gas because I had rushed to get out there from work. My tank was nearly empty, and it's about a fifteen-mile trip out there to Roger's house. I remember when I was driving into my driveway, the news was on. I keep the station on NPR. I was thinking, it's about ten o'clock. You don't look at your watch when you're doing something, you just have a sense of what time it is. I tried to call Roger. I usually called him, or he called me, just to make sure that I got home safely, or he did. Well, the line was busy.

Then I went to the grocery store. I always get receipts for everything, and I had written a check. I remember pretty much everything about that evening, including waking up in the middle of the night and realizing that Roger hadn't called. I was uneasy. Not worried. Just didn't sleep very well.

I got up kind of early, and I decided to just go out and see him. There was nothing that you could put your finger on, but he had been kind of sad. He'd been talking about his daughters. He was talking about his sense of failure as a parent. He used to always blame his ex-wife, and I would say it's not all her fault.

I didn't know at that point that he'd made a phone call after I left. Roger called Don Beville that night, a friend, but he was also a publisher and he was working on a book that Roger was writing at the time.

Don said the call was so strange that he had written it down on the back of a Texaco bill that he happened to have on his desk. There were three things he remembered Roger saying. One was that tomorrow will be a new day. The weight of the world has been lifted from his shoulders. And everything has been resolved.

But nothing had been resolved. Nothing.

The next morning before work, when Beverly returned to de la Burdé's house to check on him, she bumped into his groundskeeper, Joe Hairfield. She told him she had been trying to call de la Burdé and kept getting a busy signal. Hairfield found a way inside the house and discovered de la Burdé lying on his side on a couch in the library, next to the coffee table where he and Beverly had eaten dinner the night before. Beverly rushed into the room. Hairfield saw de la Burdé's gun and picked it up. Then he replaced it where he thought it had been. Hairfield called the local sheriff's office to report that de la Burdé had shot himself.

THE MEDICAL EXAMINER
CONCLUDED SUICIDE

Gregory Neal, Powhatan County's sheriff, arrived at de la Burdé's house at nine o'clock that morning. Treating the death as a suicide, Neal took photographs of the scene, but did not preserve all of the evidence. The one fingerprint found on de la Burdé's gun was his own. The medical examiner also arrived at the scene and called a report in to the state office in Richmond that concluded that de la Burdé's death was a suicide. Upon learning of the death, Don Beville, the last person known to have spoken to de la Burdé, called the police to inform them that de la Burdé had called on the night of his death and had not sounded like himself.

The local investigator, Greg Neal, concluded that it was a suicide. Neal did whatever he was supposed to do at the scene. Took the photographs.

Roger and I had just had dinner on this coffee table. There was an ashtray there, but it was a more decorative thing. There were two cigarettes in the ashtray. Roger didn't smoke. I don't smoke. I would have known if there had been any cigarettes in there the night before. He would have noticed.

Greg Neal came that next morning, and he photographed that ashtray and some strange ashes in the fireplace. You know how when you burn papers they leave sort of a structural ash? You can see there were papers. He photographed these cigarettes in the ashtray. He noted them as being Marlboro Lights. He made a specific incident report or evidence report. The cigarette butts were obviously something he took notice of.

That morning and afternoon, people gathered at the home. People later had free roam of the house. The point is, if Neal had believed that there was something wrong, he would have sealed off the area. That's so basic. He would have done something. He would not have just left the house.

Neal concluded suicide. And the medical examiner concluded suicide. Roger's ex-wife, who was a doctor, had also called the medical examiner. She said that Roger was supposed to be taking an antidepressant. It was the first I'd ever known of that.

His daughter, Corinna, called the police and said anybody who knew him would believe that this was a suicide. He had a chemical imbalance and this history. He was moody. Unhappy. Ups and downs. Mood swings.

A state police agent, David Riley, hears about all this the day after Roger's death. It's in the newspaper. It's on the front page. Roger, while he wasn't a prominent figure, he's an interesting person and a lot of people knew him. And he had this aura of wealth. Not real wealth necessarily, but the aura. And he promoted it.

So, for whatever reason, Agent Riley gets involved. He was suspicious because—and I'm almost quoting him almost verbatim—suspicious because, "Beverly Monroe was the only person who ever believed or said anything about suicide."

This is just the starting point. All in all, there were maybe six to ten people who told the police and Agent Riley the very opposite of what he claimed was the premise of his suspicion that it was a murder. That's how it starts. That's how easy it is.

IT WAS MENTAL TORTURE

On the morning of March 26, Neal asked Beverly to come to de la Burdé's house for what was described as a routine follow-up to a death. There, Beverly met Agent Riley for the first time.

I go out there and spent from nine a.m. until about eleven-thirty a.m. with Agent Riley. He's very casual, sitting at the kitchen table in Roger's house. Very casual. Not even taking notes that I remember. And it doesn't occur to me that he should, because as far as I know, it was just a conversation. I knew he had a "suicide assessment" form with him, as he called it, and that this was routine. I was the closest one to Roger, and he thought it would be best to start with me.

The entire day was planned and staged, and I don't use those words lightly. Agent Riley started throwing things into the conversation that were contrary to what I remembered. I'm a person who works in technical information, and accuracy is important—it's in my nature. Accuracy. It's the way I am. I'm a detail person. And I tend to have a good memory.

When I was there at Roger's house the night of March 4, we were sitting on the couch and he had this new television. A big television. He was sitting there flipping through the channels and this program came on about Charles de Gaulle. And we watched a little bit of it. But he kind of got edgy and flipped it off.

I remembered that. When you're talking about something like this, you try to think of all of the details because one of the things you think is, *Why didn't I see something? How could I not know?*

Riley told me, "By the way, that Charles de Gaulle program that you were talking about watching wasn't on that evening. It must have been on another evening. But it's normal. You've been through a terrible shock and trauma."

And I'm thinking, from that point on, *How could that be? What's in my mind?* It throws you. So I'm still thinking about that, and then he throws in another one.

He told me, "Some people said you told them you were asleep on the couch that night." And I said, "Now that can't be." I did have a clear memory of that night. But I came to question that memory. It was a kind of mental torture.

The program about Charles de Gaulle did, in fact, air on television the night of de la Burdé's death on March 4, just as Beverly had recalled. After a two-hour interview with Beverly, Agent Riley, continuing to act like he was conducting a routine suicide investigation, suggested that Beverly come to the police station to take a polygraph test. He told her it was routine.

Agent Riley had said, "We just gotta finish this up." He put it as though it was something that was tedious for him to do. As if he's this police officer, and he has to go through all the polygraphs.

Here I am, a Southern lady. The last thing you do is inconvenience somebody. It's so dumb. It's absolutely dumb, but it's the way that I was trained. It's your nature. I remember trying to call my secretary because I thought I'd be back at work in an hour or two.

It was about noon when I left Roger's house. I had had a cup of coffee. I hadn't eaten anything. I got lost on the way to the police station. I was crying the whole way. Sometimes these floodgates would just open.

I had to go through the whole thing with the so-called polygraph examiner at the station that afternoon. I'm crying. I was just sitting there and Agent Riley comes in and he grabs me by the hands. He was somehow trying to impress upon me that there's something wrong, there's something wrong with my memory. He could just see it. He knew it. He had this experience so many times. He is just bombarding me. Over and over and over again. He just can see. He's got to help me. He's right in my face. He had bad breath, and you could just feel his breath.

It's a staged bombardment to try to supplant my real memory with something he's made up so that then he can say that I made some admission or agreed to his theory that I must have been asleep at the house when Roger shot himself.

After one and a half hours with the polygraph examiner, Riley took over and repeatedly insisted that Beverly had been present and asleep in de la Burdé's house when he shot himself. This repetition was a principal strategy of the John Reid interrogation technique, a style employed by many police officers in hope of eliciting confessions. The interview room was wired for recording. The tape recorder was not on when Beverly allegedly agreed to Riley's contention that she was asleep in de la Burdé's house when he committed suicide. Only the last seventeen minutes of the interview were recorded—after, according to Riley, Beverly made her alleged statement.

Beverly was also being observed through a one-way mirror. Two secretaries, the polygraph examiner, and Neal all claimed that they were present in the observation room when Beverly agreed with Riley's scenario.

We have no way of knowing whether those tapes were erased, or whether he intentionally didn't turn it on. His version of it was this—that he told me that morning that this was a potential homicide, and that I might be a suspect. That was very important because their whole case is that I went to the police station, and that I was somehow boxed in by all of this, and I had to adopt his theory in order to get out of something somehow. They claimed all these people were in this little room supposedly all there just when I made this one statement out of that whole four hours that afternoon—that I remembered being there when de la Burdé died.

Later, the police secretaries put it like this: it was like a light flashed. They said they could see it in my facial expression. That's when Riley claims that I adopted his theory. Somehow I saw this as a way out. That suddenly, I latched on—that is what they said—latched on to this theme.

There's no way that that could have been real. You can see it and hear it on that tape that often I can't even talk—I am so exhausted and so sad and crying. There is no way I am suddenly latching on to this like this is a great idea. I am even on the tape saying things like, "I don't understand," "I don't have any memory of that." And here is Agent Riley saying on the tape, clear as a bell, "Oh, you'll remember. You'll see it, you'll see it in your dreams. Eventually you will remember."

Never once did I stop and question Riley. Somebody talking over you for two hours can make you want to get away from them, just in order to let your brain think. It's so forceful. It's so disconcerting. It's intimidating. Even though you don't think there's anything sinister about it.

That afternoon I left the police station about four-thirty, and I could not even walk. Agent Riley had to help me down the stairs and help me with my coat. I was literally a basket case. I really thought something was wrong with my mind. It never occurred to me to say that something's wrong with Agent Riley.

It took us a while even for me to see that one of the techniques he used was talking to me and mixing the events of the evening that I spent with Roger before this happened—the night after I drove home, and the next morning when I went into that room. And particularly mixing my memories of that morning and trying to switch them to some scenario of it actually having happened the evening before. That's how complicated it was. And the way he did this was by talking over me and jumping from one thing to other, from one time-frame to the other, so that if anybody was listening, then they would hear his words and it would sound like it was all that one evening with Roger. But it wasn't.

Memories of my father's death were mixed in there, too. My father had taken his life. It had been years earlier. Some of the memories were the same. Some of the feelings were the same. I kept saying—and this was true of my father's death, too—I should have been there. Maybe I could have prevented it somehow. That one phrase, "I should have been there," this police officer took as, "I must have been there."

IT DOESN'T MATTER WHETHER YOU HAVE A DEGREE IN ORGANIC CHEMISTRY

By May I was really clearer. I'm beginning to get better. I was at work and I got one call from Riley in early May, maybe the first week or so. He said, again, "Have you remembered anything yet?" Well of course I hadn't, and I told him so. And we talked about other things, and it was all kind of casual, and I didn't think any more about it.

He had urged me to see a therapist. I'm really embarrassed about that. When you've been a strong person, an independent person, a can-do person, it's very hard to say something might be wrong with you. There is a stigma about going to see a therapist, not as much now, thank goodness, as there used to be. It was a personal thing as well as a societal thing.

You just feel, that's not me, I'm a problem-solver. But now the problem's with me, and I don't even know what it is. That's how easily someone can dislocate your sense of being in your mind. It does happen to rational, clear, strong people. And it doesn't matter whether you have a degree in organic chemistry.

Then about a month later, I was at my office. There was a big meeting coming up; I'd finally been able to get back in focus. There were a lot of things that I was working on, trying to catch up. It was June 3 and it was also my mother's birthday, and I had planned to call her at lunchtime. I got a call about, I don't know, ten-thirty or so that morning. I was really busy, and again, Riley was very casual. It's like, you know, "I'm just finishing up the suicide report." And he said, "I just want to talk to you. Are you busy?" I said, "Yes, I'm busy, but of course, you know, if you need me, I can meet you."

I'm just a fairly agreeable person, you know. If somebody asks me to help with something, I don't question, I just do it. And especially someone who is an authority figure. I just told my secretary that I would take an early lunch and be back in an hour or so, maybe half an hour. And so he gave me directions to this park. It was a Civil War park not far from my office, you know, two miles down south of there. I had trouble finding the place. I drove up and it was this deserted park, kind of way back behind a commercial area. I pulled up and he was out of his car, no one else around, and he got in my car.

Just immediately, he started talking about how the forensics showed that this was a murder and "everybody knows that you did it," that kind of thing. I was so stunned that I probably don't remember all the things he said at that point. I remember my mind was reeling. Again, you can't imagine—it's truly as though somebody has gotten in your car and pulled a gun on you and said, "I'm going to kill you."

He went from making this accusation, this horrible accusation, to trying to pretend to be a friend and saying things like, "You know, oh, I can understand why you did this." These are not his exact words, but it had that kind of feel to it and that kind of tone to it. And I kept saying to him, "But that's not so, that's not true." Then he said something absolutely horrible that I won't ever forget, which was, "Oh, you should get a medal." As if Roger was some horrible person, some terrible person that would have justified any of that. It was just incomprehensible to me.

Then he changed his tone and started saying things like, "Now listen, I've been a state police agent for twenty-two years and I've never lost a case." He denies saying these things, but I remember them clearly. I don't remember everything he said, but I remember these particular things he said, because, even though I was stunned, every once in a while something would just pierce through my heart and my brain.

He said, "I've got boxes of files and investigation notes on you. I can twist these things any way I want." And I thought, *What, what? How could that be? I'm just me. There can't be any evidence of anything because I didn't do anything.* Of course all that was not true, but he was trying to make me think that. And he said it, just like this: "If you force me to be your enemy, I can make you out to be the black widow spider of all time." He meant, "I can convict you."

He went back to the original theme of trying to get some agreement to his scenario, as he called it, which was that I must have been there asleep and woke up and was traumatized because Roger had taken his own life.

He pulled out one of these yellow legal pads and he had a pencil, not a pen, but a pencil. I said, "You know, I wasn't there." I said, "I remember Roger telling me goodbye. I know that I went home. I probably have the receipt." And he said, "Well this is just a hypothetical." And I remember him using that word, and he wrote it across the top of that page, but of course that disappeared later.

I was still sitting in the driver's seat. The windows were rolled up. I remember that one person had driven up and walked by, and then come back to the car and left. So Riley had told me to roll the windows up. He didn't want anybody to know, I guess, or to hear anything or to see anything. I mean, that's how isolated it was. It was also blazing hot, it was about ninety-five degrees. He had a tweed coat on and he didn't take it off the entire time.

He started writing out this so-called statement to the suicide—what he called a hypothetical. He had about three or four sentences down before I said, "What are you writing?" and he said, "Oh, don't worry about this, this is just a hypothetical." And he said, "I already have this on tape in front of eight witnesses."

He starts writing this down as though I have said it already—that I was there asleep on the couch and that I remember this. And I said, "I don't remember this, I don't think it can possibly be true. I remember leaving, and I remember him telling me goodbye. I wasn't asleep, and he wasn't asleep." But he wouldn't listen to any of it. He just kept writing.

And then he asked me about picking up the gun. He said, "What did you have on?" He never went to a question directly. He just said, "What did you have on?" So I'm thinking, okay, "What did I have on? I had on a long-sleeved sweater." And he said, "Would you have used that to wipe off the gun?" I said, you know, "Joe Hairfield picked up the gun," because I remember Joe saying that he had. I didn't see it.

We'd been in that car a little over two hours, and he says, "You have to sign this." And I said, "But it's not true." That's when he got really ugly. His face turned red and he was very angry. He said that all he had to do was pick up the telephone and by that afternoon it would be all in the papers. I would lose my job, I would be arrested, I would not be able to speak to my family, he would drag my family through the mud. That made me realize if I didn't do what he said that my life was going to be over, my life as I knew it.

This person has the ability to destroy you and they're threatening to destroy your life and your family. I wouldn't have a chance to talk to my boss, explain anything. I'm the person that's responsible for my family. I'm a single mother with three kids in college, and what do you do? It's like someone holding a gun to you and saying you have to do it, you have no other way to go. He basically said that he was either taking me or that piece of paper. What do you do? So I signed it.

I thought I would be able to get away, to get back to my office, to be able to think. He said, "Wait here." We got out of the car and he went to his car and he got his gun, a huge gun, and he stuck it in his belt, and he walked me around through the woods. Almost all of that time he was trying to get me to take some kind of plea. He was just threatening me again. It was not till four-thirty that he brought me back to where the cars were.

I remember I asked him what would he do then? He said he would take this to the prosecutor but that I could go back to my office. He said he would call me. This is how strange it all was. You'd think if you really thought someone was a murderer you would arrest them.

No audio recording of Beverly's park meeting with Agent Riley was ever produced. Riley claimed that Beverly requested that meeting and was quite insistent they meet immediately, not leaving him sufficient time to pick up the recording equipment at police headquarters. On June 10, Beverly was indicted for first-degree murder.

On June 3, 1992, I was accused by Riley. It wasn't something that could happen to me. You know you're innocent. There can't be any evidence against you. What could there be? At that point I didn't realize what the police could do and say in court.

About two weeks before the trial—the trial was October of 1992—my attorney said this name to me: Zelma Smith. He asked if I knew her, if I'd ever heard of her. I said, "No, of course not, I don't have any clue." She was in the Chesterfield jail, which is the adjacent county to Powhatan. I'd never known anybody in jail, and I hadn't been in any jail.

She was testifying to this story, that the year before Roger's death, I called Zelma Smith. This was supposed to be in the spring of 1991. Zelma's story was that I called because I wanted to buy an untraceable gun from her. She said we had met in the cemetery. She brought this gun, and allegedly I gave her a hundred dollars.

These kinds of informants—false informants I should say—are people that see an opportunity to try to buy some leniency or reward, or it comes from police or the prosecutor in setting it up. It's a horrendous tactic. So anyway, here she was in the jail. My attorney sent our investigator there to try to talk to her, and she refused to talk to anybody. My attorney had no way to prepare, because we had no idea what this was even about.

KAFKAESQUE

Beverly's attorney had no idea what Smith was intending to claim at Beverly's trial, which began on October 26. The state's case was built on the theory that Beverly had killed de la Burdé out of jealousy because he was about to abandon her for another woman. The prosecutor presented the jury with the "confession" to Riley's suicide scenario he had Beverly sign in the park. He brought witnesses who claimed that de la Burdé was making plans for his future and was not depressed. He presented forensic evidence that he claimed was consistent with a murder. And he had their star witness, Zelda Smith, testify that Beverly had attempted to buy an "untraceable" gun from her a year before de la Burdé's death. They failed to disclose considerable evidence consistent with Beverly's innocence, including forensic evidence corroborating the suicide; evidence of Smith's actual background and whereabouts during the time she claimed to have met with Beverly; Smith's prior contacts with state police agent Riley in unrelated cases; and the deal Smith expected in exchange for her testimony at Beverly's trial.

In the opening and closing statements, I went back and counted the times that the prosecution used the phrase "Beverly killed," "shot," "murdered." In the space of say a five-minute discourse, it breaks down to almost every thirty seconds. Those are the words the jury is hearing. Kill. Shot. Murder.

The prosecution even had my defense attorneys using these words like "victim," "crime scene," and "murder." There was no crime scene. They were using the term "confession." There was no confession. What there was was Riley's bogus interview to create the impression that I had agreed to a suicide theory that I didn't remember. This is how the murder and conviction comes about. She "must have been there." She agreed to the theory that she must have been there and asleep at the suicide. It wasn't a suicide. It's a murder.

The medical examiner had initially determined that de la Burdé's death was a suicide. After Beverly's indictment, the medical examiner altered the cause of death, labeling it a homicide, and issued a report six months after de la Burdé's death.

As part of his routine investigation, Detective Neal submitted swabs taken from the web of de la Burdé's hands to test for gunshot residue. A handgun releases an invisible chemical deposit, known as primer residue, from the hammer when it is fired. When a suicide is suspected, police routinely swab the web of the deceased's shooting hand. The results came back about three weeks later. The web of de la Burdé's right hand was found to have primer residue, consistent with his firing the fatal shot with his right hand. However, the results from the residue tests were not made available to Beverly's legal defense in their entirety at the trial, leaving her defense unable to use the critical evidence to challenge the prosecution's assertions.

The real issue, if there was to be an issue and it had come down to it, was this: Was this a suicide or was this a homicide? And that's forensics. And of course the evidence was concealed—the evidence of the invisible chemical residue that was on the web of Roger's right hand—that they had since probably before Agent Riley ever tried to talk to me and convince me that I was there at the suicide.

Their theory was that someone—meaning me, Beverly Monroe—had reached down when he was asleep with the gun upside down in the left hand and pulled the trigger. When the so-called expert tried to demonstrate this in court, she couldn't pull the trigger. She tried three times.

The cigarettes found in the ashtray the morning after de la Burdé's death were important because somebody had smoked them and left them there. That meant that most likely, somebody had come after I had left and Roger was still there alive. Obviously the police at the scene thought they were important. So here we are at trial, and the prosecutor's asking Greg

Neal about the cigarettes. And this is where Greg gets extremely uncomfortable. And he says that he somehow didn't think they were significant. How vague can you get? How evasive can you get? What does it mean? It just got left like that.

After Neal was on the stand, the prosecutor stood up and says to the jury, "Look how honest and forthright Officer Neal has been to you folks." They're saying that over and over and over again. It's semantics. It must be Prosecutor 101.

Even if you buy all of this stuff that the prosecution said and forget the evidence, I had a receipt from the store and my canceled check. I was in the checkout line at 10:40. The examiner had estimated Roger's time of death was 10:35 p.m.

I didn't remember at the time that I had talked to somebody in the store, but some guy saw the news of the trial on television. He recognized me from the grocery store that night.

The reason I had talked to him—as soon as I saw him again I recognized him and remembered—was because his little kid was with him. And it was late at night and the child was fussy. I just stooped down and said something to the child. We began a conversation. He said he was a construction worker. He had actually given me his card. I don't remember what happened to it. But if I had been so "cunning," as they said, and set this up, I would have certainly saved the man's card. Come on.

This fellow, Dennis, he called and said, "I talked with this woman." He called the prosecutor's office first, and, in his words, they blew him off. So then he called my attorney. He comes and testifies. He knows exactly why he was in Richmond that night. He lives about thirty miles away, and he'd been to a counselor. They were going through some family problems. He was unshakable because it was true. Duh. It was true.

Zelma Smith testified. You have no way of knowing what the story will be, what she could possibly say, why they would use her, where she came from, nothing. I had never seen this woman or heard of her before. She's very dressed up and obviously very good at this.

So her story is that in the spring of 1991, she supposedly had her business, Zelma Smith's Business Enterprise. She said she'd gotten a message on her answering machine and the person says she's Ms. Nelson. Where she pulled this from, I don't know. In her scenario, I'm Ms. Nelson. It took me a little while to catch on to that, but I'm Ms. Nelson.

So Ms. Nelson calls her back and says she wants to do some business. We meet at Burger King. Now I don't mean to sound pompous, but I've never set foot in a Burger King. I probably never will. I didn't even know the place she was talking about. We meet at the Burger King. And supposedly I'm dressed in a nice suit. I never wore a suit. I am not a fancy person. This is fancy for me—cheap Target slacks, cheap Target shirt, even cheaper Burlington coat on sale. I can dress up, but I've never bought an expensive suit. Never.

That was the first meeting. Supposedly I gave her a hundred dollars and I wanted to buy an untraceable gun. We agreed to meet later. And we met in the cemetery. So I'm there in the cemetery and she brings a .357 Magnum, and I tell her it won't fit in my purse. So I don't take the gun. That was supposedly the end of the story, that she never heard from me again.

If you look at it logically, to make it appear that someone committed suicide, why would you use an untraceable gun when the person has their own gun in the house?

A few times Smith had to look at the prosecutor for clues or cues, I guess you could say. In fact, even the judge said something at one point, for him to stop coaching her on the stand. Looking back, I was in this zone of just being in this surreal existence of the whole trial. It was Kafkaesque.

In order to convict me, the prosecution had to do something in the face of all of the contradicting evidence. This is why they used things like, "She went bonkers." The jury had to buy into that.

It's an easy sell that women go bonkers. They used this against me. The other thing is that it's very easy apparently for jurors and people in the public to believe that a woman cannot be independent. That somehow you're not somebody without this man.

Now, it's true that Roger was a fascinating person, and I really did care about him and I loved him. But I didn't want to be married to him. I had my own life. I was an independent person with a career, a job, raising a family. You wouldn't say that about a man.

It's very easy for prosecutors to sell what I call this biblical story—that women are the root of all evil.

On November 2, 1992, after a seven-day trial and deliberations lasting less than two hours, the jury found Beverly guilty of first-degree murder and use of a firearm in the commission of a felony. On December 22, 1992, she was sentenced to twenty-two years in prison.

I was convicted and then the prosecutor stood up and said, "Well, she's no danger to anybody," and the judge said, "You can go home." I went home, after a first-degree murder conviction. Then three days later, they found out that, well, he was in error; he wasn't supposed to do that. So then I called and said, "Well, what should I do?" He said, "Well, why not come in on Monday?" This was Wednesday. You know, this is how they were. It was strange.

THE CAVALRY IS NOT COMING

I went to the women's prison, where they have two cells for Powhatan County at the end of Cottage Three, which is this antique, dungeon-like place. It was cold. I was hungry. There was only one slot in my cell door. If I looked at just the right angle out of my little slot, down the hall to a door that had another little slot, then at certain times I could see the river. The James River.

It was where we used to go canoeing. Roger and some friends of ours used to go. At times, I could actually see the water. And seeing those trees and that water and that serenity was like looking at a master painting that you knew was real. And I cannot tell you how restoring that was.

What I kept thinking right before Christmas was that the cavalry was coming. And that's a strange way to put it, but it's this thing that somebody's going to come out to that prison, a whole group of my friends and family. Somebody's going to come. You know, it's totally unrealistic. And not an intelligent thought.

I was there from November to mid-February. Then I was put in this basement. It was an absolute firetrap. A basement with chains on the exit doors and in front of that about fifty folding chairs. Filled with cigarette smoke, and I was on the top bunk. I could reach the ceiling from my bunk. All the smoke collects up there.

That room held about thirty-five or forty women. At this end were the black women, and at the other end were all the white women. And I was the only white person at this end. I didn't notice that at first. I was sitting with some of the women that I'd become friends with, and one of the women, I don't remember her name, but her nickname was Red, she had kind of reddish hair. I was sitting on the top bunk, and she said, "Miss Beverly, I have a question for you." And I said, "What?" She said, "How come you're down here with us? And how come you laugh at our jokes?" What could I say? I hadn't noticed. I said, "They're funny." Maybe if it were men, they're more challenging with each other. But women aren't like that. They were more resilient. They had a sense of humor.

I had just been there a few months. In the evenings we had to mop the floor. And you had to take turns mopping the floor. These women would take my turn so I could work on my case. And they would say—it was noisy as all get-out, unbelievable noise—"Be quiet, Miss Beverly is working on her case." This will stick with me for the rest of my life.

UPSIDE-DOWN AND BACKWARDS

Beverly appealed her conviction to Virginia's Court of Appeals. After nearly six months in prison, she was released on a $150,000 bond pending the outcome of her appeal. She returned to her home, which she still owned. For nearly three years, *she and her attorneys fought her conviction in state courts. In addition to getting a $7-an-hour job at a bookstore, she devoted herself, with the help of friends, to investigating the state's star witness, Zelma Smith.*

The bond was set at $150,000, which meant that I had to come up with $15,000 cash for that alone. I still had some liquid assets at that point. The trial cost—just the attorney was a flat $150,000, and then it cost about another $35,000 on top of that. Then the cost of the appeal. I lost track after a while. It's the hemorrhage of cost.

When I'd gotten out the first time, and gone back to my house, my daughters, Katie and Shannon, and my son Gavin and I were on my patio, and the sliding glass doors were open. Katie had put on a piece by Bach. And for the first time, we could sit and hold hands and just cry. The tears just flooded. And nobody could talk. You don't want anything else except to hold on to your children. You really don't care if you never eat again, never sleep again, or anything else.

The appeal process doesn't allow any new evidence, even if it shows there's been fraud or hidden evidence. But I was determined to find out who this Zelma Smith person was, it was so out of the blue. I didn't know the forensics, I couldn't stand to look at that, I couldn't stand to think about that. But I could look into this Zelma Smith thing.

I've got to know how in the dickens this was done to me. Where did this woman come from? And how was this prosecutor able to say, "Beverly Monroe is lying and Zelma Smith is telling the truth"? I'd never heard of this woman until she'd walked in that room. I'd never seen her before. You want to stand up and say, "Stop this farce!" And you can't. You're bolted to that chair. Not by bolts but by fifty-five years of dutifulness and civic responsibility. It's all such a weird farce. That's why it feels like *Alice in Wonderland*. Upside-down and backwards. And you're without any anchor except your family and your friends and your sense of what's right, which has been totally dislocated.

Every tiny thing, every name, everything I found led to something else. I was able to determine that she did not have a business. From the time she was thirteen she was committing crimes and committing frauds and perjury and you name it, and she'd been in prison four or five times already, and it appeared from her record that she had gotten out of prison under unusual circumstances.

They have a sentence-reduction hearing for her after my trial. She did get a huge sentence reduction. She got most of the charges dropped before my trial, I learned. I was able to establish that she had been involved in other cases that Riley had initiated at least three years prior mine, in 1989.

At her sentence reduction the judge at Chesterfield did not buy her whole story. When you get the transcript of that sentence reduction you see that he sees through the whole thing. He doesn't know that she's lying about my case, but he sees that she's a repeat so-called informant.

THIS DECISION CAME,
AND IT'S ALWAYS A BLOW,
A HORRIBLE BLOW

The appeal process has a number of steps. It's a very expensive and a very agonizing process. There's oral argument and there's your petition, and then you have to go through these different briefs and write all of it. After you're convicted, you have to appeal to the state itself. And I know now that had I been selling drugs, I would have had a better chance at appeal than with this case. In a high-profile case, I think the attorney general's office fights much harder and much dirtier. And there's much more reluctance for the courts to overturn that. The last step in the state appeal is the Virginia Supreme Court.

This is right after Christmas of December 1995. That's when everything went down the drain. You're never prepared. The opinion that came down was so—you know, I don't have words for it—again, it's the *Alice in Wonderland* thing. The opinion was that Zelma Smith was absolutely credible. The court stated that Roger's death occurred at 10:30 or 10:35, and that even though I have these receipts saying I was twenty-five miles away at 10:40, that the evidence was sufficient to convict. Nothing wrong here. We see nothing wrong. And this decision came, and it's always a blow, a horrible blow. It means that the rest of your life, whatever you have, is gone. Your house. Your future. Your children's future is scarred forever. Forever.

Beverly's appeal argued that insufficient evidence, Smith's testimony, and numerous other errors rendered her trial unfair and unreliable. The lower courts denied her appeal. She then appealed to the Supreme Court of Virginia. They ruled against her. In January 1996, Beverly was taken back into custody to serve out the remainder of her twenty-two-year sentence at Pocahontas Correctional Center in Chesterfield County, Virginia.

Katie, Beverly's daughter, quit her job as a lawyer and dedicated herself full-time to fighting Beverly's case. Katie began the federal appeals process by filing a habeas corpus petition.

Katie was my attorney, my daughter. Suddenly one day the warden calls me in. She gives me this two-hour lecture about how my daughter can't come visit me on weekends, because she's my attorney. And so this went on for days, and I sat there and I took notes, and I said, "What do you mean?" She's my daughter, but she's also my attorney. And I'd never had any problem before. So this went on and on, and of course nobody outside knew that this was happening.

And so finally the warden calls me in. There's three or four people in the room and she says, "You have to make a choice. She's either your daughter or your attorney." And I said, "You know, I'm sorry, she's my daughter, she's my attorney. I can't say she's not my daughter!" But they weren't going to let her visit me as my daughter if she came on a legal visit.

So this went around and around. So we ended up having to take it to court, sort of tagged onto another case, and force them to admit that it was all something made up. Next day the warden smiles at me and says, "You know, there was never really any problem."

So you have these strange things that happened in prison; they can make up the rules any time they want. They can say if you have a family member, you can only visit one family member. I knew people like that who had sisters, the family could only visit one, not the other twin sister. They'd have to take turns, you know, just crazy stuff.

Beverly was tapped by other inmates as a resource and by prison officials as a teacher. On her own initiative, she set up an informal program teaching English, spelling, and math. Later, she was assigned to teach in the general education program and then in the prison's business program.

There were women who had mental illness. Severe. Lack of education. Women who had—for one reason or another—killed their child. These women were not ostracized because there were always reasons. Everything from postpartum depression to some other circumstance involved. And a lot of physical and emotional abuse. I knew these women. They were not bad people or evil people. It changed my views, because I grew up in a conservative, traditional crime-and-punishment kind of atmosphere.

If people came in from, say, the Department of Corrections, into the classroom where I taught, the first thing I would do, just like I would in any business setting, I would go up and shake their hand. But it had an edge to it because I was determined to do it. I was determined that they would acknowledge me as a person and acknowledge all the women in the room as people at work. You feel like it's a very small way to fight.

One visiting time, Katie was there with her son Asher, who was just four. I could feel him kind of tugging. I stooped down, so I could be right on eye level with him. He said, "Mimi, you've got to come home. We've fixed a room for you, and we painted it green. And there's a really comfortable couch and there's art on the walls." It was a little prepared speech that he had in his mind. "You've got to come home. It's ready for you."

He never lost faith. And it was a different kind of faith. Anytime they were at a wishing well, or he would point to a star, anything, it was always, "Bring my Mimi home." He had that belief that I was coming home.

People working in the prison were not supposed to be personally involved, but sometimes they were. And they were all supportive. They were supportive of Katie. When she came in for a legal visit, they were ecstatic. She was that representation of hope.

There was one officer in particular. When Katie had come on a visit, he kind of whispered over to her and says, "When are you going to get your mother out of here?" That tells you that people understood.

MOST PEOPLE DON'T HAVE A TRUE
APPRECIATION FOR FREEDOM

In 1998, Katie Monroe began to receive assistance, pro bono, from Steve Northup, an attorney at the Troutman Sanders law firm.

Major Hill, who was the assistant warden, came in to the prison dorm and I think it was one of the few times in my life where I felt that my knees were like rubber. That I couldn't walk. She said, "You've got a phone call." She said, "You've got to return the call."

I said, "The phones are right there"—there were three in the dorm— "can I just make it right here?"

She said, "No, you've gotta come to my office."

She was acting funny. So I had to walk, and that thirty yards to the warden's office seemed like forever. 'Course, everybody is just on pins and needles. It was a big topic. Everybody was aware. And so I get down there, and first she talks to my lawyer. She has tears everywhere. She's getting the Kleenex on her desk. I was watching her on the phone talking to him, but still no real clue. Then she hands the phone to me to talk to my lawyer Steve Northup, and Steve doesn't say right away that we've won. He kind of hesitates and says, "Well, the opinion has come in." I'm about to die. It's not on purpose, you know, I think he couldn't get the words out.

And I hear Katie in the background, crying and screaming, hysterical.

I still don't know exactly what the news is. So when my lawyer finally tells me, I can't really be sure. You're just afraid to believe.

On March 28, 2002, U.S. Federal District Court Judge Richard Williams vacated Beverly's conviction on the grounds that prosecutors concealed material evidence at trial. He called Beverly's case a "monument to prosecutorial indiscretions and mishandling," criticized the management of the death scene, described the forensic evidence as "unclear and contradictory," and called the state police's interviews of Beverly "deceitful and manipulative." Williams described the prosecution's case as weak, especially given Beverly's "unrefuted alibi for the time of de la Burdé's death."

I don't even remember the words. It was more about the opinion. That it's in our favor. That we won. After all, all this time. And then I'm hugging Major Hill and she's hugging me, and we're dancing around, and I got a chance to talk to Katie. And we're so emotional we couldn't even talk.

Walking back into the dorms was just amazing. It was pandemonium. I took those steps coming back up the landing and I don't think I even hit a single step. I was flying. I was literally flying. Then it occurred to me that there are all these people there, locked in. Normally, during the day, those bars were unlocked.

I gave the thumbs up sign, and it was just—it was like everybody was being released. It wasn't about me. It was just about that somebody could win, against the system. When your daughter and your family fight and win, there's this other dimension to it. It brings out the best in human spirit, it really brings out the best of what you're capable of doing.

I go down the aisle, and everybody is just reaching out. It's just like this huge victory line.

It takes about a week for me to be released, and every day it's the same kind of bedlam. Every day, people would watch the news and leave a note on my bed: "Have you heard anything yet? Have you heard anything yet?"

By that time, reporters were coming to the prison. And again, the prison was very accommodating. It's a surprising sort of dichotomy going

on. They were joyful, but at the same time, they were doing things to promote the prison. Which was fine.

I was released in April 2002. When I walked out of that gate, the sun
is different and the air feels—it just feels different from inside. Even that
perimeter wire fence. It was a whole different world. A whole different
sun, a whole different feel. You actually feel the touch of the air on my
skin now that I didn't before. And it's a joy. Every nuance of awareness
like that is an absolute joy.

ABSOLUTE DREAD

After Beverly was released, the state appealed Williams's ruling.

*In March 2003, nearly one year after Beverly's release, the state lost its appeal.
The U.S. Court of Appeals for the Fourth Circuit unanimously affirmed Williams's
decision to vacate her conviction. Noting that Beverly was "by all accounts a calm,
gentle, and kind person" with "an impeccable reputation as an honest and law-
abiding citizen," the court went on to list numerous items of potentially exculpatory
evidence that the state had suppressed. The court found that "Smith's testimony
was the Commonwealth's major evidence of premeditation," portraying Beverly as
a calculated killer. The court stated that the case against Beverly "can be fairly
characterized as tenuous."*

*After losing the federal appeal, Virginia's Attorney General decided not to con-
test the decision from the Fourth Circuit Court of Appeals. After the state bowed out,
the Powhatan prosecutor still had the option to retry or reindict Beverly. Under the
threat of reprosecution, Beverly spent thousands more on legal assistance. By that
point she had already lost her home, and had spent hundreds of thousands of dollars on legal fees—even with the pro bono help of attorneys at the Troutman Sanders
law firm and the assistance of investigators and friends.*

We still had to fight this battle for almost two years. We had this sense of
momentary relief at times, and we tried to take advantage of it, but I wasn't
allowed to travel, to visit friends. I wasn't really free. I didn't have my

independence back. I didn't have any real freedom back. I certainly didn't have my life back. The thing wasn't over.

During that year and a half, I stayed with Katie. Asher could come down in the morning and jump in bed with me. So there were wonderful parts, you know. I could read to him, I could hold him.

I tried to give Katie some space by moving around. I did some house-sitting for my ex-husband, and I stayed with my other daughter several times. And so I moved—packed up computer, files, clothes, and everything—I think thirteen times during that year and a half. Then, in June 2003, prosecutors dropped all charges. I have to really give credit to the state here, meaning the state of Virginia, the attorney general's office, for dropping everything. That was a great, great feeling.

After you've been exonerated, after a case has been overturned and vacated, there is no follow-up investigation and nothing to prevent this from happening to someone else. You know, it's wrong. And they know it's wrong. If it were a medical situation, if it had been a car accident, you can demand records. You have some mechanism for getting to what happened. But in cases where somebody has been falsely accused or wrongfully convicted, you have no access to the same kinds of information. Or accountability. As a taxpayer, I find that so horrendously wrong, on top of what happened. There needs to be some way to correct these mistakes. But everyone wants to move on, you know. There's war in Iraq, many, many more horrendous things than what happened to me. It's not about me, it's about accountability in the system. About making things right. Making things work the way we think they're supposed to be.

This is not something that has just happened in the nineties. Or the eighties. Or the seventies. It's been going on since the beginning of time. Power is the problem. And lack of accountability. One person cannot do it. It takes the entire system. To go along with it, or to contribute. And I know this from personal experience. And that doesn't mean these are necessarily evil people. But something happens in the mentality to allow them to think that it's justified. Or to look the other way. And that's what the result is. People's lives are ruined. And it's beyond that. It's our whole system that becomes untrustworthy.

NOTHING FEELS NORMAL ANYMORE

I took off to visit some friends, and I just drove, I drove all the way up, visiting friends all the way up to New Hampshire and back, and probably saw a dozen or so people who'd been particularly supportive, and that was a sense of freedom. These are the feelings and the turning points for me personally, and once I got the apartment I began to do some restructuring.

I had a good education, a super job and career. Somehow it didn't feel like I was sixty-five years old. I didn't feel that age. I didn't think about it being a factor, and I had wonderful contacts, people who were head of human resources with corporations, people who were CEOs, people who I knew through other people, people whom I knew personally.

So I started the job hunt thinking, okay, six months I'll be back in reasonably good shape. It didn't turn out that way. You know what it's like to send out resumés—first you get one together and you update it, you go for interviews. It's an extremely time-consuming process, and you can put a week or more into one application, and then other weeks if you have to follow up and keep that process going, and it ends up being a total waste of time. You don't make any progress. Mostly you just get rejections.

It's been a very, very difficult and discouraging process. I'm not an easily discouraged person and I'm not discouraged now. I know I can get something. But the realization is that I will not be able to earn a half, maybe not even a third, of what I was making fifteen years ago, or have the same sense of responsibility and enjoyment of my job and my career.

Beverly relocated to Williamsburg, Virginia, and bought a home in a community on the James River.

The house is great. I've got a lot of work to do, and I like doing work. The real strain is not having the financial means to do what I would like to do here or to get it in shape. So I spend a lot of my time doing things the hard way, trying to do as much of the work myself as I can. But that's nothing to complain about because again, I'm so fortunate.

It's beginning to feel like my home, but not really—not the home that I had. Nothing feels normal anymore, and when you meet people, they want to know why you moved here. Well, I have the standard thing, that my daughter Shannon lives here. You don't want to just slap them with this whole sad story, and yet you don't want to evade the issue either. So I've talked to my neighbors, because they want to know why I'm looking for a job at sixty-seven. People are just naturally curious. You have to explain to them that you're not a normal person.

Where it's hit me hardest is in losing people. I lost the person that I loved, who took his own life, and I've never really had a chance to grieve, or even be sad. And so those memories have been tainted a lot. Even the things that they said about him, which were untrue, at trial. They had to make him out to be a bad person in order to make it look like I would be somebody who would want to do something to him. They destroyed my relationship with his daughter, his family. Those are things that you can never get back.

My mother, that was hard. Granted, she was in her eighties, but she suffered through this. She went to trial with an oxygen tank. We didn't know she had congestive heart failure. There was never a more gentle, wonderful lady than my mother, and I lost her. She died five months after I was released. And I lost a brother while I was in. He had diabetes, he became blind. He couldn't come to visit. Two months after my mother died, my other brother died. You have these losses that are irrecoverable.

You learn to move on. I've spent a lot of time with the day-to-day things, and doing what I call talking to the river. During prison, to free my mind and to separate myself and to transcend a lot of the pain and dread and anguish, I remember I read poetry. My daughter Shannon had given me some in German and some in English, by Herman Hesse. There was a lot of poetry that other people would send me, even when they didn't know that this was one of my favorite subjects, something that's vital to my existence.

I have a lot of these things and I take them to the river with me and recite and remember and read. That's all so restoring. The other thing is music. I listen to music, particularly to opera and particularly to Domingo, who was always my favorite. For seven years I only heard his voice twice. Those were the most, oh gosh, intense and transcending moments that can take you out of any prison.

In 2015, Beverly continues to advocate for justice reform, working with the Students for Innocence Project at William & Mary Law School and speaking at various conferences and events across the country. She credits her daughter Katie (currently Senior Advocate for National Partnerships with the Innocence Project), family, and friends with encouraging her to speak out about her experience. Also, she and her family are forever grateful to Richard L. Williams, the federal judge who overturned her case in 2002, for restoring her freedom and for voicing strong criticism of the egregious misconduct by police and prosecutors in her case. She met Judge Williams by chance in 2003 at a seminar that Williams gave in Richmond, and the two formed a trusted friendship over the next few years.

Beverly still lives in Williamsburg, Virginia. She remarried in 2009, and describes her husband Dick as "literally the boy next door. Selling my home was wrenching, but I only moved across the street!" She worked as an administrative and legal assistant for a land conservation agency from 2007 until her retirement in April 2014, and she is looking forward to having more time to spend with her family, especially her two grandchildren.

Voices from the Storm: The People of New Orleans on Hurricane Katrina and Its Aftermath (2006), edited by Lola Vollen and Chris Ying, describes the experiences of residents of New Orleans who stayed in the city during Hurricane Katrina's catastrophic landfall on August 29, 2005. The thirteen narrators collected in this book recount the days and weeks that followed, including the fight to rebuild their lives after the waters subsided. Interviews for these narratives took place in the months following the disaster and included narrators that were still in New Orleans and others that had been displaced.

DAN BRIGHT

AGE WHEN INTERVIEWED: *37*
BORN IN: *New Orleans, Louisiana*
INTERVIEWED IN: *New Orleans, Louisiana*

Dan Bright is a New Orleans native who was wrongfully convicted of first-degree murder in 1996 and released in 2004. He is a father of four.

GROWING UP IN NEW ORLEANS

I'm Dan Bright. I grew up in the Florida Housing Project. It's not there no more. They tore it down and they modernized it so the project I grew up in, that's not the projects no more. Right now it's like townhouses. I grew up, I'm sad to say, in the real projects. You'd hear about three, four guys get killed in a day. I had a brother that got killed in the projects.

I have two twin daughters, a son, and my oldest daughter. My oldest daughter is sixteen. My twins are eleven, and my son is ten. And now my twins and my oldest daughter stay with my mother because my twins' mother died. She died of a blood disease called lupus. My oldest daughter's mama is on drugs and my son is with his mother Gloria. I'm kind of like, "I'm screwed all around," but I'm happy to be out and I'm enjoying my freedom and I'm going to look at the bright side of everything. So that's where I stand at.

I was arrested in 1995 for a murder that I didn't commit, and I was wrongfully convicted of first-degree murder in 1996. I went on death row in 1996, December.

The victim had won a Super Bowl pool that gave a thousand dollars. Someone heard that he won a thousand dollars. A woman named Christie Davis got the guy to come out of the barroom, and three guys came out of the alley, and I don't know if the robbery went bad or what, but the witness said no one robbed no one, that somebody came out there and started shooting and ran off.

The police said it was a robbery, but the only witness said it wasn't a robbery. So there is no ground for a first-degree indictment. The Supreme Court failed to do the right thing. Instead of them giving me a new trial or exonerating me, they just downgraded my charge to second-degree murder. They figure, we take him off death row, he'll be happy. But I was innocent. I was going to fight until the end, and I had a legal team willing to fight with me all the way.

I stood on death row five years, a total of ten years in prison. We went through several appeals. They were all denied. Finally, we found the FBI report. In the FBI report, it said they knew who killed the guy and it wasn't me. We took that FBI report and we fought maybe another year. So the Supreme Court finally gave me a new trial. The state, the district attorney, didn't want to go back and have another trial because they knew they had the wrong guy from the start. The truth came out.

When I went to prison, my mother moved to Gretna and she was blessed to get a house. Since getting out, I've been living with my mother. I've been job to job. It's real tough 'cause no one wants to hear that you was innocent. All they know is that you were on death row.

SATURDAY, AUGUST 27

Hurricane Katrina, the eleventh named storm of the 2005 Atlantic Ocean storm season, is gaining speed and intensity over the Gulf of Mexico. The National Hurricane Center (NHC) upgrades Katrina to a Category 3 storm with sustained winds between 111 and 130 miles per hour. After striking southern Florida on Wednesday, Katrina takes an unexpected turn toward Louisiana. President Bush grants Louisiana Governor Kathleen Blanco's request that he declare a federal state of emergency, authorizing the Federal Emergency Management Agency (FEMA) to begin relief efforts.

New Orleans mayor Ray Nagin and Governor Blanco call for a voluntary evacuation of New Orleans. Nagin announces that the Superdome will be made available as a shelter of last resort, but encourages residents to evacuate. Around 80 percent of New Orleans residents evacuate the city.

I thought, as usual, the storm was gon' turn or wasn't gonna be a big thing 'cause we've always been escaping major hurricanes, so I stuck around.

Saturday night they have this club in the Lake Forest Plaza, and I was going there when I was pulled over. The cop—city police—asked me to get out, asked for my license, ran my name in, and said I had a warrant. He's on duty, but I guess he was doing detail work for this nightclub. He's black. I had a warrant because me and my girlfriend, we had a fuss. My neighbors heard the fuss and they called the police, and they said it was domestic violence. It was just a domestic dispute between me and my girlfriend. This was like a week before.

And at this time, the city was asking them not to bring in misdemeanor charges, but the cop was insisting that they bring me in. I don't know if it was the car I was driving. My car was a '97 Jaguar SJ-6, and it was given to me by my aunt. It was in my aunt's name because we never got the titles. Maybe that was the problem. I know what they thought. Either they thought it was stolen or I was a drug dealer. It was one of the two. If a guy is driving a nice car, he better have a Armani suit on, and that's just the way it is. They see you driving a Jag or a Mercedes, they gonna pull you over because it's just New Orleans. They figure if you have the type of car, you have to dress for it.

So when I pull up in the parking lot—you have to remember, this is New Orleans, even the cops is corrupted and envious—his excuse to stop me was to say something about parking in the wrong spot. I wasn't driving, I was parked. He said I was over the line. This guy didn't even want to look at me. I asked him, "What you bring me to jail for?"

He just say, "I have a warrant."

I say, "It's a misdemeanor. You supposed to give me a summons to appear in court or something."

The bottom line is that he brought me to jail for domestic violence, resisting arrest, and drunk in public. I don't drink. He brought me to jail and that's how I wind up in the predicament I was in for the storm.

My exoneration case is well-known down here, and these jailers have a lot of friends. And not only that, when the FBI played their part in the original case—you know, it was in the newspaper like once every week. And when you going against the FBI, man, it's like you labeled. So yeah, I'm always figuring that I'm singled out. Every time I'm around police, I feel like they're watching me, they recognize me. That's just me. But in order for him to insist on bringing me to jail, he had to know who I was.

When the cop brought me to central lockup, the guard asked him why was he still bringin' in misdemeanors, and he didn't say nothing. He just looked at me and pointed at me and told me, "Go on up." So he left us there. So they didn't have a choice but to arrest me and to book me in. I couldn't get out because the bail bondsman had done left.

I was in Templeman III. Central lockup and Templeman III are the same building but different parts of it. You go to central lockup and they will write you in and they will bring you to the back, and that would be Templeman, and I was in the receiving tier. The cell is a two-man cell. When you go in this dormitory, there's an upper level and a bottom level. You got maybe ten cells at the top, ten cells at the bottom. Fortunately, I was able to get at the top level. But now I'm stuck in here, and the storm is coming.

SUNDAY, AUGUST 28

Hurricane Katrina begins the day as a Category 4 storm moving northwest from the Gulf of Mexico. However, at eight a.m., Katrina is upgraded to a Category 5 storm, the highest rating on the Saffir-Simpson scale.

Mayor Nagin orders the first-ever mandatory evacuation of New Orleans at ten a.m. Government agencies begin to evacuate. However, many prison officials evacuate without their prisoners, leaving them in gyms, common areas, or locked in their cells.

So I'm there in central lockup and I'm like, this is a nightmare. I'm seeing death row all over again, like everything is flashing back. I don't want to see this no more.

I used the phone but I couldn't call no one because there wasn't no one to call. I called my family. They was about to leave and they tried to find bail bonds and they couldn't. They couldn't stay here so they had to leave. All of them have left, so now I have to stay here and wait the storm out.

I didn't sleep. I think the lights went out. After breakfast on Sunday we didn't see the guards no more. They gave us grits, boiled eggs, and that's it. This was maybe like six, seven in the morning. So the guards left maybe like nine that morning.

See, every two hours or three hours, they'll come and count us. When they didn't come around to count, I'm thinking, "Where everyone at?" They didn't come. And then lunch came around, they didn't bring food then. I'm really worryin' 'bout "How can I get out this place?" There ain't no bail bondsmen. Living conditions is very bad. And anyone who knows about Orleans Parish Prison know how bad the living conditions is. It's filthy, filthy. You know, it's just rats, roaches, spiders.

I hear guys hollering for the guards to come. They wanna eat. Some guys might want to take a shower. They don't come. It's just total chaos, everybody hollering, banging on things, tryin' to get the guards' attention. No one comes.

MONDAY, AUGUST 29

Heavy rainfall hits the coast of Louisiana in the early morning hours. At approximately six a.m., Hurricane Katrina makes landfall as a strong Category 3 storm in Buras, Louisiana.

At 8:14 a.m., the National Weather Service warns of an impending breach in the Industrial Canal. At nine a.m., the eye of Hurricane Katrina passes over New Orleans. By the time the eye of the storm has passed over the city, the Lower Ninth Ward is already under eight feet of water. At eleven a.m., the first reports begin coming in that the 17th Street Canal has sustained a 200-foot-wide breach.

Late, late—maybe early Monday morning—maybe like four or five. Hard wind, very hard wind. Lights went out in the jail. I was on the top floor. We can look out the window. They had these little portholes that you can look out, and see the rain, the wind blowing, and the water starting to rise.

It was early. You can see that the water is constantly rising. And you gotta remember, we're stuck in these cells. Guys on the first level, on the bottom level, man they hollerin' and screamin'. No one comes. They were hollering for the guards to come. Begging, pleading. You had guys who had broke windows out, burning sheets and blankets, flagging them to try to get some attention. In fact, helicopters was flying over, and guys was holding blankets out the windows, burning blankets to try to get their attention. And no one came and help them.

The water had done got from chest-high to chin-high. So guys was on the top bunk with their head stuck out the ceiling to get air. They couldn't hold their breath that long. So everybody, the whole tier's hollering. You had men that you thought was kids down there hollering, because that's how they sounded.

The lights had done went out, so you can imagine being in this water, in the dark with this water constantly rising. Only thing we had to do now is to break out. We wasn't trying to break out just to be breakin' out of jail, we breakin' out to save our lives.

One guy got out. I think it was the tier rep. I don't think they locked the tier rep's cells. The tier rep is the guy who represents the tier. All the complaints go to him and he takes them to the corrections office. His cell was upstairs. He got a mop wringer, and he went to prying the cells open with the steel rods from the wringer. And those cells, they slide backwards and forwards on hinges, so you can also kick on 'em just enough where they can get off the hinges, and you can squeeze out the bottom of 'em. But you still had to kick on this door maybe like two hours and whoever in your cell, your cell partner, he got to help you kick. You take turns. If your ankles don't break you be all right. But you got to remember you kicking on a steel door. I kick a little while, then he'll kick. You don't want it to come off, you just want it to give way a little bit so you can push it off its hinge and ease up out it.

Then they used this mop wringer that the guy got, and busted a hole in the cell wall. We used the mop wringer 'cause it's made of real thick, thick plastic, and it's got steel rods through it. If you keep banging on something with this thing, it'll crack. Once we'd knocked a chip in the wall, we took the mop wringer loose and chiseled through the concrete. The rods are about the size of a dime or a quarter around. It wasn't like chiseling out of the walls. It was chiseling to the next cell.

It was like a moment of panic. I can't really explain it. The mind is very constructive if your life is in danger. You can basically use anything that's strong to get out. And you gotta remember it wasn't no five or ten minutes. It was over a period of hours. When we did it, we saw it working and we just kept doing it. You bust a hole in that wall, the guy would come out. Now, you got to go in that cell and get the other guy out. All the cells is next to each other, so you got to knock holes in those cells to get all those guys out, and some guy was breaking out through the door, kicking on the door like we was kicking.

You got old guys in these cells, too. They couldn't kick on those doors and we couldn't help everybody. In fact, they had an old guy—well, to be perfectly honest with you, I don't think this guy ever made it. He had a heart attack in there, and he was just laying on the bed, not moving. There were a bunch of guys who didn't get out, that we couldn't help.

The guys at the bottom were just hollerin' and screamin'. The police had left. No one was in Central Lockup, no one. We had to go down to help most of 'em. When you go down, the water is maybe up to my chest. So we had to go under there and try to help them out, then come up for air. These guys are on that first level. They're scared to death. They think this water gon' continue to rise, but the water stopped maybe to your chest but they had no knowledge of that water gonna stop.

The police ain't gonna tell you that. They will lie and say that they got everybody out, but they're lying. Now if you would go in that jail, if they haven't patched those holes up that we made, you would see what I'm talking about. They got holes all through the wall. They hurry up, they tryin' to cover their tracks. Lotta guys drowned in there.

But most of us got out Monday night. We didn't see a guard until we got out. When we finally got out, that's where the guards were at, outside. They were sitting there on boats. Just sitting there waiting. They know we were gettin' out. If you got out and you made it, they will put you on a boat and bring you to Broad Street.

They have the Broad Bridge right there, and that is how all of us got onto Broad Bridge.

I say about a thousand guys escaped, but they couldn't go nowhere. There was just too much water, so they was just giving up. They might swim two blocks and come back. The police weren't even really much going after those guys. Whenever they come back, they'd just put 'em on a wall, tell them stand on the wall right there, and when they get room on a boat, they'll put us on the boat and bring us to the bridge. "Put your back to that wall right there and don't move till the boat come back."

The water is chest high. You walk to the boat. You gotta get in there yourself. They're taking three to a boat. The guards didn't say anything. They didn't want to be there. They was quitting, like, "I'm gonna check on my family." They were tryin' to find boats for theyself to go, to leave.

And they bring us to the bridge, the Broad overpass. That's the name of it, the Broad overpass on Broad Street. That was Monday night.

TUESDAY, AUGUST 30

There are between 50,000 and 100,000 people remaining in New Orleans, and 80 percent of the city is underwater. The Army Corps of Engineers assigns army Chinook helicopters to drop three-thousand-pound sandbags to repair the breach in the 17th Street Canal. These attempts fail.

I was on the Broad Street Bridge from Monday night up until Thursday with nothing to eat, no water to drink.

But the guards from the prison, they was drinking water. They had cases of water and they wouldn't give us a cup of water. They wouldn't give us nothing. They was taunting us with the water. They was givin' their dog water. They would take a bottle of water and pour it in their dog's mouth before they give it to us. They were right there with us, they didn't care, they didn't care at all. Majority of 'em were white, and some of 'em were black. I'm not a racist person. I don't look at color, I look at financial status. If you poor, it don't matter if you white or black, you gon' get mistreated in Louisiana. You might get some favoritism if you're white, from another white guard or somethin', but if you don't have nothin' we in the same boat.

Wherever you sit at, you couldn't move. They tell you you can't get up. So you sittin' on this hot concrete. For four days you can't move. And there were guys defecating on theyselves, urinating on theyselves. You couldn't move. They thought you were gon' try to jump in the water and swim off. But the bridge is surrounded by water, so even if you trying to go somewhere, it's all water. There's nowhere to go. And if I'm not mistaken you can go on the Internet and see this bridge, with the prisoners on the bridge. It was on CNN. So now you're just stuck in that one position. You got guys faintin', catchin' diabetic comas and seizures and heat strokes. Then you had guys, on the first day, Tuesday, they couldn't urinate. They might feel obligated to let you stand up and urinate over the side of the bridge, but most of the time they said, "Nah, sit down, don't move," so guys gotta urinate on themselves, defecate on themselves. It was a nightmare.

Guys were just fed up, tired, aggravated. Guys were like ready to say, "Just shoot me, get it over with. It's too much suffering."

You couldn't do nothing. You just got to take it all in. You had guys drinking that filthy water. You had guys actually drinking that water on the streets. The guys would like take their boots or their shoes, and tie a string on it and throw it over the side of the bridge and get some water and reel it back in. I just had to tough it out. I wasn't gonna drink that water.

They're making us all sit in these lines along a path. There's maybe a hundred guys on this line, a hundred guys on that line, and they're walking through this path with their guns and their dogs so the dogs can just snap at you at any time. It wasn't like they was lookin' for drugs or anything. They were just bored, so they did what they did. Put fear in guys. And they were big dogs, German shepherds or somethin'.

You had inmates gettin' fed up, so one guy might stand up and say, "Man, we want some water." They'll shoot him with a rubber bullet or a Taser gun. Rubber bullets, beanbags. The next day, maybe like a day after, you got the Department of Corrections officers from Angola and Hunt prisons coming out here to help out. Now, they're comin' down here with an attitude 'cause they don't like people from New Orleans no-way. They shootin', they sprayin' mace on everybody. It's random.

I seen two guys get Tasered. Then after they Taser you, they hog-tie you. They consider you anywhere from three to four hours, and if you keep protesting, they figure you gonna start a riot or you gonna get everybody to help, to stand up against 'em, to rise up. So they gonna try to deny you that.

I'm thinkin', "Just stay calm and stay out of their way," because if you shoot me with a Taser gun for no apparent reason, I have to defend myself, and I don't want that because I know what's gon' happen. If you shoot me with a rubber bullet or hit me with a billy club, I'm gonna have to defend myself. So what I do, I just stay to myself and hope this would hurry up and get over with.

I'm thinkin' we gonna die on this bridge, either from starvation or dehydration. No one care. These people is gonna go on a killing spree and kill everybody on this bridge. They was looking for a reason to shoot someone, especially the guards. You have to remember these guards, the ones comin' from Angola and these other parish jails, these guys are like, excuse my language, backwoods hillbillies. All they do is hunt. I knew 'em because I know how they operate from me being around them in Angola. And all I'm saying is all it gon' take is one person for these people to go shooting us. They had some guns. They had assault rifles. They had handguns, they had shotguns. They had the right equipment if they want to slaughter us. They had the right equipment.

WEDNESDAY, AUGUST 31 &
THURSDAY, SEPTEMBER 1

Mayor Nagin orders the 1,500 members of the New Orleans police force to abandon any search-and-rescue operations in order to focus on stopping widespread looting. Lt. General Steven Blum, chief of the National Guard, orders the first deployment of 3,000 troops over the next twenty-four hours.

The state of Louisiana's Homeland Security Department denies the Red Cross permission to enter New Orleans, fearing that the Red Cross's presence in the city would pose a safety hazard and also encourage residents to stay.

A majority of the 7,000 prisoners being held in Orleans and Jefferson Parish jails are relocated to Hunt Correctional Facility—a male-only, maximum-security prison in St. Gabriel, Louisiana.

We prisoners don't leave off this bridge till Thursday morning. We went on this bridge Tuesday night.

They had buses on I-10 lined up, but we couldn't get there, so they built a scaffold, and they forced all of us down this scaffold. Now you got to remember, you got handicapped guys out there, you got guys afraid of heights. From the Broad overpass, it is like an eighty-foot drop, and we're not experienced in climbing up and down scaffolding. But they forced us to go down. They didn't care if you didn't want to do it.

On the bridge, there was a lot of hatred, like towards the inmates. You had to walk down, and the guys who couldn't do it, they set them on that side, and after everybody who was healthy enough to climb down the scaffold, they'll take the old guys and put 'em on boats, and bring 'em around.

They put us all on buses Thursday and bused us to Hunt Correctional Center. I was just ready to go lay down. We think we gon' get some food, some cold water. And it only gets worse. The nightmare continues.

It was a prison football field. Each correctional center has their own football team, and they have their own field. And we were sleeping on their football field. They didn't even have restrooms out there. If you had to defecate, urinate, you had to do it right where you at. So you imagine defecatin' in front of maybe like twelve hundred people on a football field.

They didn't have pillows. All they gave us was one blanket to sleep out in the open. You have to remember Louisiana's made out of swampland, so at night everything get marshy. This blanket's soaking wet, you soaking wet sleeping on this ground. Morning time, it's burning-up hot. And you got the gnats, got mosquitoes.

They didn't give us showers. They set up these big ol' spotlights they put over around the field. And they have this pipe, they got a pipe that comes out the ground, a faucet. That's the only water we had. We didn't have any cold water, just faucet water that come outta the ground. There were two of them. You gotta wait in line. You drank out your hand. Drink out your hand or put your head under the faucet, let it run in your mouth.

You got the guards that's outside the gates, with the assault rifles, the hunting guns, waitin' on you to try to escape. They got this field, they're patrolling it. It's like you're a wild animal in a cage. They didn't come in there, they didn't step foot inside that gate. They didn't wanna do anything. They didn't care. In fact, they was like, laughing. It was all a game to them because, you have to remember, in this state, no one likes New Orleans. New Orleans is like a outcast to other places. That's how they look at it. They figure everybody in New Orleans is troublemakers. And I'm'a tell you, anywhere in the prison system, the guards do not like any inmate from New Orleans. They don't like 'em.

They would get in this crane and lift theyself up over the fence and just throw sandwiches. If you get one, you get one. If you don't, you don't. That's too bad. That's how we eat. And if you don't jump, you don't get your sandwich, you ain't gonna eat. They was treating us just like wild animals or something.

Everybody was on that field. They had federal prisoners mixed in together with state prisoners. You got guys with all different types of charges: murder charges, armed robberies, rapes. Then you got guys like us with misdemeanors like obstruction of sidewalk, trespassing, tickets. Everybody's equal; put everybody in this one yard and lock us in there.

You got Len Davis in there, the crooked cop who was on death row. Anybody who follows the news know who this guy is. When they found out who he was, they took him out. Maybe like twenty guards came all like fully armored. Hurry up, came and snatched him, and got him out of there. He was gon' get killed 'cause they had guys plottin' on him, they was gon' get him. Homemade knives, shanks and everything.

I saw stabbings. Guys would go around jacking guys' blankets from them, stabbing them, beating 'em up. You had gangs out there. Gangs was formed like, "We going to stick together. This ward going to stick together, this ward going to stick together."

All in all, everybody was basically fending for themselves. You got federal prisoners on one side of the field, and most of those guys in federal prison is under the protective custody. So either they snitched on somebody, or they don't want somebody to know they there. So now they all form in one group. It's like a gang now. So you have all kind of people out there.

You had guys like this going around, jigging guys for their tennis shoes. You gotta remember, all our shoes was wet, so if somebody got some good tennies, yeah, right. And then you got some sick guys out there, man. You have a female guard who's in the watch tower, and these guys masturbating on the tower, where the women can see 'em at. So you're being disrespected from all angles now. And in prison, doing that would get you hurt. It'd definitely get you hurt if you masturbating in front of another man. That's called disrespect. So you being disrespected from all angles, man. The inmates is disrespecting you. It's horrible, man.

And when some of the inmates broke out of Central Lockup, they also got into the property room, and so they had guns. I saw two guns on the field, on the football field. I seen this. It was, if I'm not mistaken, it was Glocks 'cause I know they was plastic. They was real guns.

This is facts also: in Central Lockup, the guards broke in the property room and took all our money and jewelry. My daughter called my phone and one of them answered it. Answered my cell phone. That's how I knew that they were stealing. And when he ask, he tried to get my daughter to give him the number so he could know the number of my phone. That's how I know they was breaking into the property room.

So this was worser than being on the bridge. We went from worse to worser. The guys is calling the guards for help—the weaker guys—and the guards is laughing, like, "Get it how you live." That's what they say.

FRIDAY, SEPTEMBER 2– SUNDAY, SEPTEMBER 4

President Bush signs an aid package of more than $10 billion for immediate use in relief efforts. After touring the New Orleans area, Bush addresses the Katrina crisis from the Rose Garden, pledging an additional 7,000 troops to aid the cause. Governor Blanco declines a federal takeover of the Louisiana National Guard, thus also prohibiting active-duty troops from entering New Orleans to help. FEMA announces that the Superdome and Convention Center are completely evacuated.

They anticipate more evacuees will arrive, but they will be bused out as they come. All told, approximately 42,000 residents have been evacuated from New Orleans.

New Orleans police kill at least five New Orleans residents on the Danziger Bridge after those residents opened fire on government contractors hired to repair the 17th Street Canal.

I was on the Hunt Correctional Facility field for four days, from Thursday until Sunday. The buses was coming in and out every day, gettin' guys, bringing them to other facilities, places. That's how I wound up at Rapides Parish Prison in Alexandria, Louisiana.

They're taking so many of us off the field, bringin' us to other prisons around the state. Wherever, however you got in the line, that's where the buses was going. Everybody would line up and just get on those buses. No one knew.

They put us in a dormitory, maybe like fifty guys. They did feed us better, much better, but it's very small portions so you're still hungry. We didn't eat solid food in, what, eight to ten days, so the little food they're feeding us we appreciate it, but it's not enough. And you have to remember, these prisons already have inmates in there, guys who live in this parish, so they still have to take care of the regular inmates. So now they're not gon' take food out their mouths and give it to us. So we gotta get the scraps.

I was in Alexandria a month. A month, month and a half. You know, this is all confusing to me. I'm still in a daze. You have to remember, I'm confused, I'm angry. I had not been convicted of anything. I was exonerated from death row. It's like a nightmare.

As soon as I got to Alexandria, when they find out who I was I was singled out. They were trying to put me in isolation 'cause they didn't want me around nobody else. I had been on death row so I'm being picked on, and beat, and cursed out. They right here in my face screaming and hollering. They called me nigger, city slicker, killer, death-row killer, all kind of stuff, man. I was sent to the hole.

In fact, some of them thought I was still on death row. Now how can I be on death row and I'm in here? So man, it was all kind of stuff going on.

MONDAY, SEPTEMBER 5 – SUNDAY, SEPTEMBER 11

On Monday, the breach in the 17th Street Canal levee is repaired.

Mayor Nagin orders that all people remaining in the city should be evacuated, by force if necessary. FEMA begins distributing $2,000 to each family affected by the storm, but questions surface about the credibility of FEMA director Michael Brown's resumé. On Friday, Secretary of Homeland Security Michael Chertoff removes Michael Brown as manager of Katrina relief efforts. A week later, Brown resigns as head of FEMA.

Water levels begin to recede in many areas.

After I was transferred from Hunt, they were just holding us in Rapides Parish Prison in Alexandria. They didn't know what none of us was in jail for, they was just holdin' us. The only thing they had was a record of whoever been in jail before. They didn't have any current charges, so now the lawyers had to come in. We had to tell 'em our charges. What they did with the misdemeanors, they was kinda letting us go, but they had to find out if we were really charged with misdemeanors, so now they have to go through this process. And this took maybe like two weeks, just sittin' there. I read. Anything I get my hand on I try to read. The numbers I'm calling wasn't going through because all the phones was shut down.

This attorney, Phyllis Mann, she came with a human rights group, and that kinda like backed the guards off us. Phyllis never looked at me, but she was reading my file and she saw my name, and not too many lawyers in this state don't know my name. They don't know me but they know my name. When she looked up she say, "You don't remember me."

And then I looked in her face and I remember I had met her before and that she was a human rights lawyer. I'm telling her to get word to my lawyers Ben Cohen or Clive Smith or Barry Gerharz, let them know where I'm at. She called Ben, and Ben went to work from there.

Once again I'm put out front. I'm the leader of the inmates now, in fact, because they had to go through me to talk to Phyllis, or Ben, or one of those guys. So the corrections officer found that out, and they really didn't like me then. And you talkin' about some big old country boys: six-five, three hundred pounds. And every time the lawyers would come to see us, the officers would say I was on the yard, or I had a clinic appointment. They was lying, I was right there on the tier. And I would be the last one to go in. I was painted the bad guy.

When we finally went to court, this little hick court, kangaroo court, they had shotguns, pistols in the courtroom. Ain't nowhere in this country you going to go to a courtroom and see twenty guards in the courtroom. Not the hallway. In the room with guns, shotguns. And I'm like, "What the hell is going on here, man?"

I'm just ready to get outta here. I'm ready for this nightmare to be over with, and I'm ready to go. This is what happened. I was blessed to have these lawyers who move faster and gave them this ultimatum. What Ben did, he filed a writ of habeas corpus to produce our bodies in court 'cause you know, misdemeanors don't carry no more than thirty days for the charges I had. So now you holdin' me over these thirty days. Either give me a bond or cut me loose. So they cut all the misdemeanors loose and brought us to these shelters.

I stayed at the shelter for a few hours. When we finally went to the Red Cross, that's when I really was eatin'. I spent a few hours there. Then my pops came got me. They got me a room in a hotel, and that's the first time I could get comfortable, take me a nice hot shower, and relax in the hotel room. We stayed there maybe like two weeks and we came back. FEMA paid for it. Very good two weeks.

My family was in Dallas, and after we left the hotel, they rented a house on Tulane and Mississippi in New Orleans. But I couldn't go there because it's already overcrowded. And I wouldn't feel right living with my mother. I'm a grown man.

I don't know where I'm'a be. I might be in a shelter again. I might be on the streets because I don't have the finances to even rent me a place. And FEMA is givin' me all kinds of runaround.

I don't know if they mad at me because I got off death row. I don't know but it's like they tellin' me they can't give me nothing more because I wasn't head of the household. So I'm in all kinds of bad situations. But I'm not going do nothing where I'm gonna wind up back in prison, that's for sure. I have to find a way to make money, and I'm not going to go through any illegal channels to make any money. Right now I'm gutting houses out with a friend.

Basically, at first, we talked to our family members. We both have big families, so we clean their houses out. We have masks, we have all the proper tools and equipment, but you don't get used to that smell. The smell by itself will make you sick. And not only the bodies, but these houses being locked up, and the mold and the water eatin' all that stuff up. And then you got the iceboxes and the deep freezers. And the icebox smells worse than a body.

But in New Orleans, insurance people just don't want to pay people for their houses. So I'm on hold. I have the houses but people can't pay me because the insurance people don't want to pay them. So that's why, when I ask about money, I must really need it. And the work is out here, but I say this again, the corrupt officials, they playing on a larger scale with the contractors. They're getting kickbacks and giving the contracts to who they want to give to. And I'm not one of those big fishes where I can get a big contract. I have to wait and get the scraps, the crumbs, gutting houses out. It's just New Orleans.

Anyway, most of our work is being done in New Orleans East. That's basically the Ninth Ward. My mom, my mother's house, it was a brick room, so it can be rebuilt. It's still on its foundations. It's just the inside. I seen it, it just needs cleanin' out. It's a big brick home. It did survive. The only damage they had was the roof where my pop had to break out the roof to get out. He stood on a roof three days.

He's a stubborn old man. He's not gon' leave and he's like the rest of 'em. He thought this wasn't really gon' happen. And my pop said the levee didn't break accidentally. My pop said he heard a blast and when he first looked out the window, out the door, it was just a little wind and rain. My pops, he's an electrician, so at first he thought that that bang was one of those electricity buckets on the poles. When he heard the bang, he didn't pay no attention, he thought that the electricity bucket go out. And he was sitting in his lawn chair, and he looked on the ground and saw the water risin' up.

So my pop, he gets up and he sees water, but it ain't but ankle high, so he go looks out the door and there the water is coverin' the entire house and he hear the door rattlin' like the water trying to push in there, so he turns around and runs.

As he runnin' to the attic the water busted in. He took a two-by-four that he had up there already and busted the roof open and stood up there. It was up to where he was at. His feet was in the water while he was on the roof. And my pops, he's like an asthmatic. He needs this pump. And he didn't have no pump, he didn't have nothing. He left all that. My pops, he had all his stuff was sittin' on the table.

They blew a levee so the majority of the water won't come uptown. It's the Florida levee. You gotta remember, the Ninth Ward's like the lowest income, the poor. So that's what pops said happened, and he stood on that roof for three days.

He can't swim, so he stuck there. He gotta wait for them people to come and get him. He saw guys in boats, but the boats were full, so they couldn't get him. He had to sit right there on the ledge, by the chimney port, the chimney of the house. A guy in a boat came and got them after like three days.

LOOKING BACK

New Orleans is where my history lies. It's like, you can't go nowhere and see another Bourbon Street. And that's why I'm so tied to New Orleans. And I figure, if I'm not doing anything illegal, why would I keep havin' to run and hide? I've stayed in San Francisco. I've stayed in Richmond. I've stayed in Houston and Dallas. New Orleans has its own flavor. This is where I'm born and raised. It's just the officials, man, the corruption. It's not everybody. It's just a few corrupt officials.

I'm surprised that this guy didn't evacuate this prison, the sheriff. He was supposed to evacuate. The mayor gave a mandatory evacuation. That includes the sheriff too. He was supposed to evacuate the prisoners. He didn't do it. Sheriff Gussman, this guy didn't come. He didn't come to Central Lockup and say, "We're going to get you all out, and everything will be all right." He didn't give no motivational speech. He didn't do anything. You know what he said when they asked him about it? "They belongs in there."

I'm surprised that it wasn't handled more professional. I'm surprised that y'all would let this happen on a larger scale. What you figure? If you keep us in there, that you's gon' still make money? If we go to another correctional facility, that facility get the money from the federal government. That what you worryin' about?

Now, now you have to worry about the lawsuits, the repercussions, because what you did was wrong. Now you have all these lawsuits comin' at you. This sheriff, I seen this guy with my own eyes, on CNN, and he stood right there and lied and said he went in there personally, him and his officers went in there and got everybody out. We never seen this guy. This guy ain't never step foot on that bridge. He never step foot in the parish jail, and he damn sure never step foot on Hunt field and told us what was going on. This guy just looked at us like we was cattle. So he's lying, and I would love to see him and talk to him, debate with him.

For several years after Katrina, Dan Bright lived with his parents in the Ninth Ward and helped them to rebuild their home. He also won a modest settlement from the state of Louisiana for his wrongful conviction. Aside from helping to rebuild his community, Bright worked with the Innocence Project New Orleans to help address other wrongful convictions in the area.

The Ninth Ward was one of the areas of New Orleans hardest hit by flooding, and in 2015 it continues to recover slowly. Almost ten years after the storm, the area is a patchwork of new development and abandoned blocks. It is estimated that only 25 percent of the residents in the Ninth Ward have returned since the storm.

Underground America: Narratives of Undocumented Lives (2008), edited by Peter Orner, collects the stories of people living in the United States without legal status. The twenty-four narrators in this collection make up an integral part of the American work-force, as well as social and cultural life. They are often the parents and children of U.S. citizens, and yet have faced, among other hardships, exploitation at the hands of human smugglers, employers, and law enforcement, along with the ever-present threat of deportation.

Pictured at right: the U.S.-Mexico border

LORENA

AGE WHEN INTERVIEWED: *22*

BORN IN: *Puebla, Mexicoi*

INTERVIEWED IN: *Fresno, California*

Lorena is a twenty-two-year-old college student who hopes to study medicine one day. She left her home in Puebla, Mexico at the age of six, walking across the desert with her mother, stepfather, and two brothers. The family now lives in Fresno, California. In addition to being a student, she works full-time in a real estate office. The interview for this story took place on a weekday afternoon, while Lorena was working. The first part was conducted in her car, as she drove from her office to a warehouse. At the warehouse, Lorena continued to tell her story in English as she sifted through boxes, trying to locate an old file her boss had requested.

MY MOM DECIDED THAT
SHE HAD TO LEAVE THE COUNTRY

I have a very young mom. I'm twenty-two and she's thirty-eight. She had just turned sixteen when she had me. She had my brother that very next year, a few days before I turned one. Then two years later, she had my youngest brother. She's really like my sister. I've never missed having a sister. I always hear everybody else saying that they wish they had a sister that they could talk to, and I never really had that need.

My biological dad was, or is, an alcoholic. He used to beat my mom and us, so my mom took us to stay with my grandparents, who were in Puebla, Mexico. They had a very poor house, very basic, just cement walls. It was a two-story house, but it was open. You went into the house, and the first floor was the patio area. You walked directly to the stairs, which went up to the kitchen and a bedroom. But downstairs was another bedroom. That's where my great-grandpa and my mom and the kids, us, slept.

One time, my father kidnapped me to get back at my mom. My mom had gone to a party or a dance, and she left our door open slightly, because we didn't like it completely closed. If she had left it closed, we would have woken up and flipped out. I remember my little brothers were asleep. The youngest was two, and my other brother was four. So we were very little. And my father came in in the middle of the night. I remember I was in shorts and a little tank top or something. No shoes, no sweater. I don't remember where he took me that night, but I do remember the next day he took me to a bar. Before that, we went to somebody's house, and he asked for a pair of shoes for me. The shoes were gargantuan, like clown shoes. That next day, we went to his sister's house, and we just happened to get there when my grandma was there, too. So that was the end of that. But I remember that when we got home, everyone kept making fun of me because I had big, huge clown shoes.

I remember my little brother, the one that's just one year younger, telling me, "You know the reason why he took you? It's because you don't sleep with your head covered." That's a four-year-old's explanation for it. My brother always slept with his whole body covered.

To get away from my father, and to try to do something for us, my mom decided that she needed to come to this country. She came here by herself the first time, when she was twenty-one. She crossed the border, just went through the desert, like so many do.

I remember that period when she had gone away. And I specifically remember this one time that my grandmother was walking me to school. I heard an airplane go by, and my grandma told me, "Oh look, there goes your mom." I was six years old at that time.

There was a lot of blackmailing from my dad while she was gone, with him trying to take us all from my grandmother. So when my mom met my stepdad while she was here in the U.S., she married him right away. Not married legally, but married like the Mexican way—just move in together. My stepdad fell in love with my mom very quickly, and when he found out that she might lose her kids, he said, "Well, we can go to Mexico and pick them up. Then we can just come back and live here."

I remember when my mom came to get us. It was in the middle of the night. That was the first car I had ever seen. I don't even remember what kind of car it was, but I remember the color exactly. It was brown, like a chocolate brown, and it was really shiny. I was just enamored with the car. I was thinking, *Wow, that's a real car, and it's here. We're really cool.*

My stepdad very rapidly took me in, more than my little brothers. He had me on his lap in no time, and we were just talking and talking. I don't remember if my grandma or grandpa had told us anything about us leaving. I remember that by leaving, that meant that we got our mom back, but we would be losing our second mom. We called our grandma "mom" for a long time, too.

I vividly remember how heartbroken my grandma was, knowing that we were leaving. We were like her children. And it was just like in the movies, when the little kids are waving bye from the back of the seat. I think about it still, and it just breaks my heart. I knew I wasn't going to see them for a long time, but I didn't think it would be sixteen years.

THE BOTTOM OF THE FOOD CHAIN

I remember walking through the desert. It was my mom, my stepdad, my two younger brothers, and me. I was six, so my brothers were five and three. I was so hungry. That is something I don't ever wish on anybody, that kind of hunger. And the only thing I could think of was, *If I'm hungry, then my brothers must be hungry.* I started getting worried. We were literally in the middle of the desert.

That night, we fell asleep in between some bushes. It was early in the morning, like six or seven o'clock, when I woke up. We were in the middle of bushes on top of other bushes, so we were completely covered. It was all dry, so it was really noisy. And so nobody could move. I remember waking up, and I kind of jerked my foot to the side a little bit, so the bushes made a loud rustling noise. And there were actually INS agents on the other side of the bush. When they heard that rustle, they looked in the bush, and we got caught. There were other people with us. I think it was seven, eight of us. But they weren't family, so I don't remember who they were.

I felt horrible. This was totally my fault, and I knew it, and I just could not live with myself. I remember my mother and stepfather getting their hands tied with those plastic handcuffs. I wanted to kick the INS agents, because I was thinking, *We are good people. People that get tied up are bad people.*

They walked us to the van and they took us to a cement holding cell. It was a big room, and they were holding a lot of other people already. There was this lady with a baby, a brand-new baby, like less than three months old, on her back. And my mom was begging her for a little bit of Gerber that she had for her baby, because we hadn't eaten or drank anything in I don't know how many days. At first, the lady didn't want to give us any because that's all she had for her baby. But then she did give us some. And I remember my mom feeding us that Gerber with her finger.

That night they let us go, they dropped us back across the border. Not even a day went by and we tried it again. Fortunately, the second time we were successful. I remember walking through a canal, but there was no water. One of the coyotes was holding my hand, and he asked me if I was tired, if I wanted him to carry me. And I said, "Oh no, I can do this. This is easy." I said, "This is as easy as the three-times tables. Three times one, three times two, three times three." I remember they were making fun of me because I said that.

We got to somebody's house, and they let us take a shower. My mom bathed us all. From there, we got to a little tiny trailer. A one-bedroom trailer. It was for the three kids and my stepdad and my mom. It was in Lamont, which is about twenty minutes from Bakersfield.

My youngest brother was crying. He didn't like my mom. When we got to Lamont, I forget what my little brother called my mom, but she said, "No, I'm your mom." And my brother said, "No, you are not my mom, my mom is Juana." That's my grandma's name. And that broke my mom's heart, of course.

The first weeks, all we could afford to eat was soup and some beans. I understood that we were poor, and I understood that we were kind of at the bottom of the food chain, so I never demanded stuff from my parents. My little brother, though, the one that was five, like the third time that we ate beans back to back, he was frustrated. He said, "Beans again?" But he said it in Spanish, and he said it like a little kid. We still make fun of him for that. He was just frustrated with beans.

I started school that very next day after we arrived at Lamont. And I remember being very scared, because as soon as I walked into the little school office, everyone there was speaking English. Even though Lamont is more of a Hispanic-populated town now, back then it wasn't as much. Everyone was speaking English, and we didn't know English. So I really felt lost. But I got a wonderful teacher, who was the perfect American girl-next-door. Blonde, blue-eyed, everything. She tried so hard to speak Spanish and to try to make me understand. She really comforted me.

A lot of the kids were mean. Especially the girls were really mean, about me not knowing English and not being able to understand what the teacher was saying. We used to sit in groups. I think we were taking a spelling test, or maybe a cursive test. I was writing something down, and I happened to look up to think, and one of the girls, I still remember her name—Laurie Greiger—she grabbed her paper, and she said, "Don't copy off of my paper." She said it really loud so everybody could hear. Little things like that. And little things like, "Oh, you're not good enough to talk to me because you don't know English."

The very first years my mom and stepdad worked in the fields. They picked everything that was in season, from lettuce to grapes to cotton to carrots. Everything. Soon after that, they got a job at the local packing house. That's a step up from farm labor, so that was a really good thing. They were there for a long time.

Then my stepdad got a job doing construction stuff. And my mom started working at a clothing factory. She was working in that factory with a fake Social Security number. Her supervisor knew about it, but she was a really good worker, so the supervisor just said, "I'm not INS. It's not my job to be verifying those, so as long as you don't give me any problems."

She was there for about five years, until one of the workers that was in the same situation got herself documented and decided to make problems for everybody else. She kept telling the boss that if she didn't do something about all the people that were working there without documentation, she would go to the police. So they had to let all of those people go, and my mom lost her job.

That's when she started sewing for a lady who sells clothes at the local swap meet. She would start work at five o'clock in the morning, and sometimes she wouldn't finish until eight, nine o'clock at night. They made sweatpants and sweaters from really cheap cotton. Some of the clothes they made were knockoffs. Not really name-brand clothes like Louis Vuitton or anything, but Levi's, Ecko, Tommy Hilfiger. My mom got paid about ten cents per pair of pants, or ten cents per sweater, so she had to make hundreds and hundreds of pieces of clothing for it to even be worth it for the day. After that stopped working out, she got a job at a bakery, where she rings people up and cleans the bakery and stuff like that. That's where she's been ever since.

MY JOB AS A HUMAN BEING

My first job was working at that same bakery. I started when I was about sixteen. I did the exact same thing as my mom, just cleaned, swept and mopped, rang up people. I was only there for a few months. They really liked me, but the owner of a Mexican meat market would go there to buy bread to sell at her store. She watched me ringing up people and could see I was quick. She asked me if I would like to work for her on the weekends, and I said, "Sure." And for a while when I was in high school I was working the two jobs.

I was using my cousin Sabrina's name and Social.[1] Sabrina has good papers. She's my stepdad's niece, so she's really not related to me, just by marriage. She was in Mexico, so she didn't mind, since she wasn't using it. And she could use the tax return, because she has like three kids or something. She was helping me get work, and I was helping her out, too. I worked, she filed the taxes, and she got the tax return.

I was still working at the meat market when I started college at Fresno State in 2002 as a biology/premed major. I was lucky that I started college before Governor Gray Davis got booted out. He was the one who signed the law that allowed undocumented immigrants to pay in-state tuition. So, actually, it's doable to go to school if you work. Otherwise it would have been extremely difficult. But if I wasn't undocumented, I would be getting financial aid. I probably wouldn't have had the need to work so much, and I would have finished school by now.

I had to sign an affidavit stating that I graduated from a California high school, that I'd been here a certain number of years, and that I would get legal residency as soon as I was able to. I think that last one is for those conservatives who think we're just educating terrorists. It's pretty ludicrous. I mean, who wouldn't want to get legal residency?

During my freshman year, my advisor—who is really the reason why I'm still in school—told me about this awesome internship in North Carolina, helping farmworkers. And I said, "I have to do this."

I've always reminded myself that the only reason why I'm in school

---

1. The Internal Revenue Service requires employers to report wages using a Social Security number. Therefore, in order to be legitimately employed in the U.S., you must have or be in the process of applying for a Social Security number. While being a U.S. citizen is not necessary to obtain a number, foreign workers must have appropriate immigration documentation from the Department of Homeland Security.

and I have a good job is because my parents did backbreaking labor so that I could go to school. I've always felt like I need to give back to those people, because those laborers out there in the fields are like my parents.

I didn't get accepted the first year, but the second year I did. I almost backed out, though, because I was afraid I'd get detained at LAX, and possibly even sent back to Mexico. I kept telling my advisor, "Okay, what if they ask me for this? They'll ask me for an ID." He said, "No, you'll be fine. You deserve this. You need to go."

My parents didn't want me to go. My bosses at the time, the owners of the meat store, didn't want me to go, either. They told me that I was putting myself at risk for something that wasn't necessarily valuable. They told me they couldn't promise me my job when I came back, even though I had been there for three years, and I'd been a really good employee. I probably would still be there if it wasn't for the internship. But I was trying to make something better, trying to broaden my horizons, and I had people telling me not to do it. So, I think that's why I did it, because people kept telling me not to do it.

I told my mom, "You know what, Mom? God's going to take care of me. I'll be fine." And LAX had absolutely no problems with me. In North Carolina I was picked up at the airport with another intern. We went to somebody's house and ate there. That was the first time I ever tasted tofu, and vegetarian something. It was horrible. I couldn't eat it. That first day was really difficult for me. It was all too hippie-ish.

But later, we went to the headquarters, and I met the other interns. We left for our training, which was up in the mountains, and it was beautiful. I loved it. They started training us on the causes we were going to fight for, like the Taco Bell boycott. We were fighting for a penny raise per pound for the tomato pickers in Immokalee, Florida. They told us we would be marching, and we would be picketing in front of Taco Bells,[2]

---

2. The Coalition of Immokalee Workers backed a four-year boycott of Yum! Brands—the parent company of Taco Bell, KFC, Pizza Hut, and other chains—that resulted in Taco Bell agreeing to pay an extra $100,000 per year to its tomato growers in Florida.

and in front of stores to protest Mount Olive Pickles, too.[3] And right away, I thought, I don't know if I want to do this. It was a little too much exposure for me, and I didn't know if I'd get into any trouble. I was nervous.

After that, we all left to go to our respective places. I was placed with another intern, and we stayed with a wonderful family. The wife's name was Rosa, and the husband's name was Francisco. They had a little girl and a little boy. The boy was about two or three. He was adorable. And the little girl was so smart. She reminded me of me when I was little. I loved listening to everything she said. While we were there, she started school, and it was wonderful for me to be able to see that. That's like planting a seed to me.

So the organization that I worked with helps farmworkers. They knew where to send you if you had legal trouble, if your boss was being bad to you, or if you needed food. We did food drives, too, distributing food baskets to farmworking families.

I was also placed with a medical school. The school was just starting a research project about pesticides and the effect they have on children, even though the children are not the ones that are in the fields. The researchers wanted to see how much of those pesticides that the parents ingest and breathe in and get on their clothing and on their skin actually ends up on the kids. They also wanted to know how educated the families were with respect to pesticides. It was really eye-opening, because a lot of these families, they didn't even know what pesticides were. And they didn't even know that they were bad. One lady actually said, "Are they bad?" You just think that's common sense. But they don't know. They don't have access to the Internet. They don't even have TVs to watch the news.

Part of my job was to educate people. I'd tell the women things like, "Make sure that when your husband comes home that he changes outside, that he doesn't come in and sit down on the couch with the kids or play

---

3. The Farm Labor Organizing Committee, a union representing 8,500 Mexican guest workers, sponsored a five-year boycott of the Mount Olive Pickle Company—the nation's second largest pickle company—which resulted in an agreement to raise workers' wages.

with the kids in his work clothes." Or, "Make sure that you wash your husband's clothes separate from the baby clothes and your clothes. Make sure that the kids don't play with those clothes."

A lot of these people lived either in the middle of fields or in very close proximity to fields, so that when the airplanes sprayed, the people would get all the drift, even if they were inside. So I'd also say, "If you hear an airplane, close your doors. Don't let your kids go outside. Don't open your windows." A lot of common sense stuff.

And we were able to help in other ways. We were helping the people from the medical school get their data by collecting urine samples from the kids. It was really surprising how many of the families were willing to help us out. They had to get the first urine of the day from the kid, then put it in a little bag that we gave them. And if we didn't come to pick it up, it had to be kept refrigerated. At first I thought, *Oh, these people won't want to do all this,* but they did. They were as interested as we were to find out how bad these pesticides really are, and how much they're affecting their families, even though the kids aren't directly exposed to it.

My experience at the internship opened my eyes to a lot of injustice that I didn't want to know about before. The way that farm labor is in North Carolina is very different from how it is here in California. In North Carolina, the men in the camps still live in barracks-style homes. When we visited families, those were people who lived there year-round, that rented either a trailer or a house in the middle of the field and made a life there. But the people in the camps are all men that have been brought over to North Carolina to work.

There's H-2A camps, where the workers who are here legally live, and there's undocumented camps.[4] The undocumented part of it all is so dark and kept in the back. It's almost like a "don't ask, don't tell" type of thing. And undocumented people are very scared in North Carolina to let anybody

---

4. The H-2A program allows farmers to hire non-immigrant foreign workers for seasonal work. The employer is required by law to provide appropriate housing, reimbursement for transportation, tools, and other necessities.

in. There were undocumented camps that were literally in the middle of tons of trees. Unless you knew that there was a little path through there, you wouldn't even know the camp was there.

We went to several of these camps, and it broke my heart the way that they lived. At the undocumented camps, we weren't able to go inside any of the dwellings. We were only able to go inside the H-2A camp dwellings. And they were horrible enough. Prisoners probably live in better conditions and more comfortably than these people do. If you put any kind of animal in that type of dwelling, there would be riots. And just to see what legally is required for the grower to have for them . . . They're only required to have one toilet per fifteen people, and one showerhead per ten people. There are all these men, living in barracks-style homes with no privacy, just a bed. The mattresses are years and years old. They have bloodstains from other farmworkers that have been injured or even died. I heard horror stories of farmworkers that had died from heat exhaustion and tobacco illness.

When I saw all this, I told my supervisor that my mission is to change one person's life. Educate one person, so if their boss tries to be bad to them, they'll say, "No, I know you can't do that, that's against the law." If I can do that, then I've done my job as a human being. I at least wanted to give them knowledge to defend themselves with.

These people don't have transportation. The nearest store is literally miles away. The grower picks them up in a bus at whatever o'clock in the morning, before the sun is up, and takes them directly to where they're working. Then he drops them off when they're done. Once a week, on Sundays, they'd get picked up at a specific time to go into town and wash their clothes, buy groceries, buy whatever they need. So my supervisor and I would go to the camps to see if people needed anything. There were a lot of times we took people to the doctor because they didn't feel good. And there were a lot of times we took people to the store, so they could buy a calling card to call their family, who they hadn't seen in a year.

I still keep in contact with the family that hosted us. The husband,

Francisco, was a farm laborer for a long time, so he knows all the farm-workers. All those farmworkers are pretty regular. They get called back every year, if they don't get blacklisted for causing problems. Francisco knows most of them, and they still ask about me. That's flattering.

GOD LETS US DRIVE

When I came back to California, I had to start looking for another job. I'd heard about a job as a runner at Benson-Thomas Real Estate, so I walked in and asked for an application. I'd never had an office job, and I was pet-rified. I didn't even know what a runner was.

They called me in for an interview that very next day. Both of the bosses were there, Grant Thomas and his partner Fred Benson, the quintessential Republican white male. And the office manager Geri was there too. It was a really intense interview. I expected them to call me the next day, whether yes or no, and they didn't. After a few days I didn't hear from them, and I thought, *Oh great, I didn't get it.* And it made me feel like people who are like me, in my situation, Hispanic people, we don't get office jobs. I was sure I needed to go get a job at another meat market, or maybe helping somebody clean houses, or babysitting.

Then Geri called me, on the last Friday of August 2004, and offered me the job. I came in that Sunday, and Geri started training me and told me what I needed to wear.

Image was everything for Benson-Thomas. I had to wear heels. I had to wear slacks. And I just threw myself into the job. I would deliver flyers to all the listings, all the houses that we had for sale. Pick up closing pack-ages. Pick up gifts. Pick up documents. Take documents to escrow. Take deposits to the bank. Anything that needs to leave the office or come to the office, the runner would do it.

I really didn't think I could be office material. I thought, *I'm not refined enough, and I'm not the quality of person that they're looking for.* The company was predominantly targeted toward white, upper-class real estate buyers, so I kept thinking they'd eventually realize that I'm just this Mexican girl that doesn't know how to speak to people and conduct herself appropriately. I didn't think I would last. But I did. I ended up staying.

When I started working there, I was still pretending to be legal by using Sabrina's identity. At first, if they'd say "Sabrina," I would just keep working. I wouldn't pay attention until I realized, *Oh shit, that's me.* I was working there for about four or five months, but then Sabrina decided to come back to the United States. My aunt, who was the middle person between the real Sabrina and me, called me and said, "You need to quit. Sabrina needs her identity back." I was crushed. I loved my job. Sabrina's from New York. If she lived in California, we could both use her Social and pretend she was working two jobs or something. But she couldn't be working in New York and California at the same time.

So finally, one day, I came in with tears in my eyes. I couldn't even talk. I told Geri, "I need to talk to you." I felt guilty that I'd lied to them, and I was really scared of how they would take it. Everyone had been so helpful in training me. I didn't even know how to use a fax machine before I started there. They literally shaped me to be someone productive at an office. They treated me like family.

Geri and I went next door to a Mexican restaurant, where we used to hold meetings and interviews. I showed her my Fresno State ID and told her, "This is truly who I am. I'm really sorry that I lied to you. But I just want you to know that I didn't do it out of malice, or to hurt people. I did it because I had to, because I need to pay for school."

She asked me, "Did this girl know that you were using her identity?" I told her yes, and I explained it to her.

I was amazed when she said, "Well, we'll see what we can do, but you're not going to have to quit." She said, "Grant won't have a problem. The only one we have to talk to is Fred." Because, like I said, he's the conservative one.

It was two days before Fred came into the office again. I was so petrified. I couldn't eat, I couldn't sleep. He came in for literally ten minutes, just to pick up some stuff. Geri said to him, "We need to talk to you."

We went over to the Mexican restaurant again. I just knew he was going to say, "Well, I'm sorry for your situation, but we can't keep you." Geri told him. She was like my lawyer. It's like she was making the case for a saint, or an angel, or a virgin or something.

And Fred said to me, "Why don't we just pay you in cash?" Like he was saying, "Why don't we go down the street and get a smoothie since it's hot?"

My tears were just flowing down. I looked at him and said, "Fred, that's a big deal. You can get in a lot of trouble for that, and I don't want to put you in that position."

He said, "You've been too good to us. We can't let you go." I think it was that day or the next day that Grant came in. I was up at the front doing something with flyers. He said, "Sabrina, come here." I grabbed my notepad and pen, and I went up to his desk. I was about ten feet away from his desk. I didn't want to get any closer. He said, "Come closer." I came right up front to his desk, and he said, "Come over here, come around."

I thought, *Is he going to hit me?* He was sitting, and I was standing right next to him. He reached over and hugged me. He said, "Don't worry, we're going to take care of you. You're going to be okay."

I couldn't even explain how grateful I was. Pretty much everybody has left the company now that there have been money problems, including Geri. But I won't leave him, because he literally risked his life for me. He still could go to jail for a long time. Because of me.

Not a lot of people at work know that I'm undocumented. Fred and Grant know. And Geri knew. As far as the other employees know, I'm on payroll. They pay me eleven dollars an hour. And I work about twelve hours a day, every day, seven days a week. There's no overtime pay, though, no time and a half or anything like that. I can't be on the company health plan, because I'm not a legal employee there. So I use the clinic at the university for my doctor's visits. I usually only go see them for a yearly check up. The only thing that I do have to do is visit an eye doctor every six months, because I use contacts. I pay for it out of pocket, which is pricey, so I ended up shopping around for the cheapest place. Now I go to Sam's Club, which I know I shouldn't go to because they're a monopoly, but that's all I can afford without any health insurance.

I've never been sick enough not to go to work. In my family, you go to work, no matter what, unless you've to be hospitalized. I haven't even taken a vacation since I started working there. I do get holidays off, though, like Christmas or July Fourth.

My boss, Grant, is the most unselfish person I know. The car that I drive is actually a gift from him. It's a Volkswagen Beetle. He leased that car for me for two years, so that I wouldn't have to worry about a car payment or an insurance payment. And I use it to drive all over town for my job. I learned how to drive in North Carolina. One of my supervisors there taught me. I don't have a license, of course, so I'm always looking out my mirrors to make sure there's not a cop behind me. The way that my mom says it is that we have Jesus's license. God lets us drive.

I've been at this job for three years. Now, I do everything from being a runner to being office manager to being chief operations manager. I don't have a job title. If you ask anybody at that office what my job title is, I swear they will say, "Everything."

A lot of people at the office, like Geri and Fred, would always tell me, "You have to assimilate, you have to become American." And I'm all for that. I'm all for speaking English. I'm all for respecting this country, because I love it. It has given me opportunities that I couldn't have otherwise. In Mexico, I probably would have been a mom of three or four by now. I wouldn't have an education. I know that.

But it's really hard for me to keep my identity of being Mexican. I'm very proud of being Mexican, but being Mexican now is almost taboo. And I don't describe myself as Hispanic, or Latina, either. Because Latina is like, *Latina with an attitude*. The fighter Latina, but not the good fighter. The troublemaker. Chicana, the same way. Chicana is, "Oh, you're always protesting for something, you're always angry at something or somebody."

I really don't know what to call myself now. I'm Mexican. That's what

I fill out on applications. That's where I was born, and that's legally my citizenship. Or, I guess I'm a Mexican-American. I love both countries. I love my heritage. It's beautiful, and it's old. Its traditions have lasted for centuries. A lot of Americans wish that they had that. I get that a lot from my office, that they wish they had that much tradition, that much heritage and history. But I also love this country and the opportunities that I've been able to have from here.

WALKING TO THEIR DEATHS

A few weeks after I got the job at the real estate company, in September of 2004, I started an organization on campus to help local farmworkers. I glow a little when I talk about it because it's something that I created.

I had come back from North Carolina full of fire and a revolutionary spirit. We'd had students selected for this internship every year before I made the trip, but no one had come back and done anything. I couldn't understand, after seeing all that—what was going on in the fields—for ten weeks, that no one would want to come back and continue the fight. I said to myself, *I have to do it.* We have to keep educating people about the issues.

So I got some students together at school and talked to them about what I wanted to do. The Taco Bell boycott was still going on at that time, so we did a lot of demonstrations on campus, especially about the treatment of farmworkers by a particular tomato grower. We visited classrooms and spoke at different local events. And then, finally, Yum! Brands, which owns Taco Bell, agreed not to buy tomatoes from that grower anymore.

We also helped with passing the Emergency Heat bill[5] into law in California, to reduce the number of farmworker deaths from heat stress. So many farmworkers were dying from heat exhaustion. We helped organize a press conference with one of our state senators, and we were the

---

5. The Heat Illness Prevention section of the General Industry Safety Orders adopted in California on June 15, 2006.

only student organization there. It was in the middle of a field, at noon, right when the sun is strongest. All these reporters had to walk through the dirt and sit on buckets and listen to a state senator talk about why it was so important to get this law passed.

Another student and I dressed up in all black. We were supposed to be grim reapers. We had crosses and flowers and candles for three men who had just passed away of heat exhaustion, one right after the other. We were basically saying that if the law didn't pass, then when the workers walked toward the field, they were walking to their deaths. We almost passed out from heat exhaustion ourselves, but it all went great.

As a result of the law, farmers had to provide a shaded area. And a shaded area is not a tree. They had to provide a canopy or something like that. And they had to provide drinking water for farmworkers. The law also said that farmworkers could not be penalized for taking breaks if they felt sick. Before that, farmworkers wouldn't take breaks for water or to rest for fear of being sent home or not being called to work the next day.

After that, we started getting up to thirty people or sometimes more at our meetings. But now the membership has dwindled. I was president for two years, but this past year somebody else has been president. I guess nobody runs something as well as the person who created it. A lot of the passion dies.

IT'S ABOUT HELPING PEOPLE

I'm hoping and praying to be done with school next year, in 2008. That would be my seventh year. It's just getting more and more difficult to keep going through this. I still love being in the classroom. I still love learning about biology. But I'm only taking one class right now. First, because that's all I could afford at the time when tuition was due. Second, with my job, there's no way I could take more than one class. That's an ongoing struggle, between work and school. I have to work a lot of hours so I can pay for school. But working so many hours takes tons of time away from schoolwork.

I used to be a straight-A student. But now, the time I have allotted for school after working twelve hours a day, seven days a week, is very minimal. No matter how much I want to read that chapter or how much I want to do extra research for that paper, my body just won't let me.

Last quarter, I did horribly. My job was being so demanding, and so was school, that I got really sick. I started developing ulcer symptoms. I became anemic. I was having anxiety attacks. I started thinking that I need to choose, either work or school, but my fiancé insisted that I can't quit school. And I know I can't. I have to do it for myself. Because I know I can.

After college, I'll hopefully go to medical school. I know I have what it takes to be a doctor. I have two legs and two hands. I have eyes, and I can read. So, what's stopping me? My mom raised me to never think money is going to stop us.

A lot of people ask me how I'll pay for medical school. I can't apply for loans or scholarships. I'll just deal with that when it comes. I have never once thought about what kind of house I'll buy when I'm a doctor, or what kind of car I'm going to drive. It's not about money for me. It's about helping people, especially the farmworkers.

After medical school, I'll probably pursue either neurology or emergency room surgery—because I love fast-paced stuff—until I can open my own clinic. When I went to North Carolina, I decided that I want to have a mobile clinic, so I can go to those camps, and just help them. It was so painful being there. Everyone misses their kids and their wives. And then to be sick, too. Some of these people are diabetic, and so they need insulin. They need all kinds of stuff.

We risked our lives to come to this country, and I have the opportunity to go to school. Why not go all the way? I always thought I was pretty smart. Because I don't have very many tools to defend myself with, I know that knowledge is the only thing I can arm myself with. When you have an MD after your name, very few people are going to tell you no, for anything.

Through high school and college, Lorena worked in support of the DREAM Act, a piece of bipartisan legislation first introduced by the U.S. Senate in 2001. The act would provide permanent legal residency to undocumented individuals who had come to the U.S. as children more than five years prior to the act's passage. Though the act didn't receive enough support to pass, in June of 2012, the Obama administration established the Deferred Action for Childhood Arrivals (DACA) program under the auspices of the Department of Homeland Security. DACA provided temporary legal status for some applicants who entered the U.S. as children. Lorena applied and was accepted, granting her legal status for two years with the possibility of renewal. She renewed her status in 2014.

Lorena continues to work at the real estate company, and she is pursuing a real estate broker's license and teaching credentials. She tells us, "I've been able to contribute to my local economy, and I've donated thousands of dollars to local charities and non-profit organizations. It feels great to be able to say, 'Yes I'll support your son's football team or your daughter's band fundraiser.' That's what being an American is about—leaving this land better than it was when you received it."

Underground America: Narratives of Undocumented Lives (2008),
edited by Peter Orner, collects the stories of people living in the
United States without legal status. The twenty-four narrators
in this collection make up an integral part of the American
work-force, as well as social and cultural life. They are often the
parents and children of U.S. citizens, and yet have faced, among
other hardships, exploitation at the hands of human smugglers,
employers, and law enforcement, along with the ever-present threat
of deportation.

Pictured at right: Chinatown, New York City

MR. LAI

AGE WHEN INTERVIEWED: *40*
BORN IN: *Fujian, China*
INTERVIEWED IN: *New York, New York*

Born in the southeastern Chinese province of Fujian, Mr. Lai ran into problems when his family violated the one-child policy.[1] He paid smugglers to provide passage out of China and arrived in the U.S. as an EWI[2] after a year-long journey, which took him through Thailand, Cuba, and Mexico. Mr. Lai has since traveled around much of the U.S. working as a cook to pay off the huge debt he owes his smugglers. He also sends money when he can to his wife and two sons back in Fujian. We first met in the Chinatown offices of a non-profit serving the local New York Fujianese community. It was there that the polite, reserved Mr. Lai showed us the extent of a recent injury, unwrapping his bandages to reveal a reddened, swollen hand with a deep v-shaped scar. Over several more meetings held in a nearby Korean restaurant, Mr. Lai, now forty, speaks slowly in Mandarin, explaining more about his life and the events that brought him here.

---

1. China's one-child family policy, first announced in 1979, generally restricts couples from having more than one child. The policy emerged from the belief that economic and social development would be compromised by rapid population growth.

2. Entry without inspection. Refers to immigrants who enter the U.S. without official scrutiny.

I WAS A SIMPLE KID

The place I grew up was called *Cheung Lok*—Long Happiness. It was a very small farming village. People grew rice and sweet potatoes. There were only about three hundred families, a population of about a thousand. My whole family were rice farmers. I have five siblings—two older sisters, two older brothers, a younger sister. I'm the fifth child.

I was a simple kid. Nothing really bothered me. As long as I had food to eat I was fine. I didn't think about whether I was happy or not, whether my parents were rich or poor, if I had good clothes or not. Those things didn't concern me. I went to school until third grade, and then I had to quit. My parents said, "Don't study anymore. We don't have the money." So I left school and started looking for work. There were too many people, and not enough food and work to go around. Everyone was a farmer, but nobody had more than a small piece of land to work. It wasn't enough. My siblings weren't going to school, either. My older sister went to school for five years but had to quit for the same reason.

So I went in search of work—herding cattle, making bricks. I was about ten years old when I started looking after cattle. I'd take them up to the mountains, herd them so they could graze on the mountainside. Thinking back to it now, it was kind of fun, always being up in the mountains, running around with the cattle. As I got older I found work making bricks. I was seventeen years old then. After that I worked various jobs in construction, which I continued to do until I came here.

Of all my siblings, I'm the only one who came over to the U.S. By this time, I was married, with my own family. We were still very poor. There still wasn't enough money coming in to the family, and I wanted to find a way to make more. Also, I thought that America would be more free. You can say whatever you want in this country, but China is very strict in so many ways.

The one-child policy, for example. When I was a kid, there wasn't such a thing. People could have as many children as they wanted. But later, population control became very strictly enforced. Officials would go to homes and check up on people, put them under surveillance if they suspected them of "illegal pregnancies."[3] They came to the house one day and warned me about having more than one child. Luckily my wife wasn't at home, as she was heavily pregnant with our second son at the time. We wondered if they already knew, if someone had told them. We'd heard a lot of stories about bribery, forced abortions, forced sterilizations. This seemed to happen more in rural places—I don't know if it was because more people in these areas broke the law, or if it was easier to get away with those kinds of methods there.

People found ways around it, like not registering the birth of their first child, quickly having a second one, and then registering them as twins, which are allowed. We couldn't do that, as we'd left it too long—our first son was already five when my wife became pregnant. We were scared they would come back. There weren't too many roads open to us. We decided we had to run. My older sister took us in. She has an old house with an upstairs. My wife and I just hid up there all day, too scared to go outside. If her neighbors found out, they would have reported us and officials would have come for us. We were in hiding for a little over two months. My wife had the baby at my sister's house. Later I found that officials knew about our second pregnancy and had come looking for us. When they couldn't find us, they went to our house and tore it down.

I was really angry about this, but I couldn't do anything, couldn't say anything. The whole family would have been in trouble. You had to be careful. You couldn't offend the party. You just can't criticize the government there. If you do, you'll get thrown in jail. There was also the six thousand RMB fine for having a second child.[4] We were poor—we couldn't

---

3. Varying provincial laws determine what constitutes a legal pregnancy. Generally, population authorities determine legality based on family history—if the family's first child was a girl or disabled, the family is allowed to have a second child—and whether or not the area's yearly child quota has been reached.

4. RMB (short for renminbi) is the official currency of China. Six thousand RMB was approximately $725 U.S. in 2000.

pay it. It was during this time that I first started having ideas about going to America. I'd been hearing people talk about how democratic America was, that there was freedom of speech. At the time I thought I could go over, and then send for my wife and my sons, and then we could have two or three more children! I love kids, I really do. But after I left, the government forced her to have a hysterectomy. If you refuse to do what they say, they'll throw you in jail, or demote you at work. Or if they can't find you they'll destroy your house.[5] That's what they do. That's what they did to us.

The feeling that I had to find a way out for myself and my family grew stronger and stronger over the next few years. We just couldn't go on like this. This was no way to live. And I had so much anger toward the government that I really got to thinking that if I didn't get out, then I'd probably just end up in jail. I just had no faith in China. I didn't know how I was going to do it, but I knew I had to go to America.

I'D JUST EAT, SLEEP, EAT, SLEEP

I can't remember much about the journey. I started in Fujian. I was given a Thai passport. The person in the photo is me, but the name is not mine. This was all arranged by the snakeheads.[6] I was introduced to them by some people from my town. I didn't really know who these people were, the ones who introduced me. Just people you come into contact with, when you go out, to a bar or something, they'll say, "You have this problem? Why don't you contact so-and-so?" They were just people who were like me, in a similar position. We'd get to talking and they'd say, "I know someone."

The snakehead I met said he would take care of everything, but that it would cost me $30,000. The deal was payment upon delivery—I would

---

5. In May 2007, riots broke out in Bobai, Guangxi, in the wake of a new crackdown by the provincial government on families that break birth-control regulations. Financial penalties increased and parents who failed to pay were punished by having their property confiscated or destroyed.

6. Snakeheads are human smugglers, generally from China. The term has also been used to describe anyone involved in any aspect of a human smuggling operation, either locally or overseas.

arrange to borrow this amount from loan sharks in China, then pay off the big snakehead when I got to the States. The money would go to collectors back in China, who would then give the money to the big snakehead.

It didn't matter if I trusted these people or not. I just had to try it. I agreed to everything. I got my Thai passport, and went to the airport with this guy. We stood in line together at the border control and I was supposed to follow him. I was nervous, but nobody stopped us, they just let us through.[7] We got on the plane to Thailand. I traveled with this guy, just the two of us. The whole flight I was very excited, very happy to be making the journey. Somebody came to fetch me from the airport in Thailand. I was a little scared at that point—what was I going to do if I got caught and put in jail? But the guy said I wasn't going to get caught, that everything would be fine. I was happy to believe him—my mind was set on getting to the States, the sooner the better.

I spent about three months in Thailand. I was locked in someone's house, I don't know where. I was told it was Bangkok. Everything was provided for. I'd just eat, sleep, eat, sleep. There were about twenty of us. There were about two, three people who kept order—the enforcers. They were all men, Chinese. They spoke Putonghua. They were average-sized, young, about twenty-seven, twenty-eight. Very fierce. They told us we couldn't go out, it was too dangerous, we might get discovered. They kept saying, "You'd better stay in line, or you'll be beaten."

They treated us fine, as long as we kept quiet, as long as we didn't say anything. If you started saying the wrong things or started getting jumpy, they might come and beat you. I saw this happen to guys who said the wrong thing. They beat them right in front of you. If you fought or argued, they beat you. They treated the women the same as the men.

We slept on the bare floor. Just two blankets, one underneath on the ground, and one on top. There were about two bedrooms and one lounge,

---

7. Law enforcement authorities in China and many transit countries are often paid to aid illegal immigrants entering and exiting their countries.

about ten people sleeping in each room. We could go anywhere within the house, but not outside. It wasn't that big, about twenty square feet. There was no furniture, nothing in the house. There was a kitchen. There were two people in there who cooked. We weren't allowed to make our own meals. Whenever it was time to eat, they'd shout, "Food's ready!" We ate quietly. The food was Chinese style—rice congee. It was okay. As long as we had something, we didn't complain.

The others in the house were all from the same province as me, Fujian. Many from Fuzhou.[8] We would talk about what we used to do back home, what we were going to do when we got to the States. It was mostly men. Some of the others grew up in cities, some were from farms like me. Some were older, and some were younger. But mostly men. They were all single people there. Nobody was with their family. There were a few women, but I didn't really get to know them. The women were all by themselves, too. They didn't come with their families. The women were grouped together, the men were grouped together. The men would spend the days playing Chinese chess, poker, chatting with each other. We were really bored, but there was nothing we could do.

I didn't know I was going to be there for such a long time. I didn't know it was going to be like this. I was thinking, *I wanted to go to America to be free, but here I am, locked up like a prisoner.* It didn't make any sense to me. Whenever I asked the enforcers how much longer we'd have to stay, they always said, "In a few days. We'll let you go in a few days." I got tired of asking. I felt helpless. Eventually I became numb.

It was difficult to think clearly about anything. I wondered how my wife and children were. Once or twice I was able to call them, but I didn't get to talk with them for very long—the enforcers didn't let us make long phone calls. And I didn't have money to make too many calls. When I spoke to my wife I just told her to take care of herself, the kids. That I was in Thailand, everything was fine. Even if things were bad I would always tell

8. The capital city of Fujian.

her I was fine. I didn't want her to worry. I didn't want her to think this was a mistake. I knew she was very worried about me, but I kept telling her, "Everything's fine, everything's good. I'm doing well. I have food to eat, I have a roof over my head, so don't worry about me."

When I spoke to my sons, I told them, "Your dad really misses you."

They asked me, "When are you coming back?"

And I said, "Dad isn't coming back. He's going to America, and in the future you'll come too."

BE QUIET AND WAIT

One morning in September, the enforcers woke us up and told us we had to go. They didn't even give us time to get our things together, just told us to leave with the clothes on our backs. But I was quick, and I managed to take a small bag with me. Five of us were flown to Cuba on fake visas. The other people, some had already left here and there. You could say I made some friends there, but I haven't seen them or stayed in touch with any of them since I got to America.

It was bad in Cuba because there was still more waiting. Just as in Thailand, we couldn't leave the house. The Cuban enforcers said it was even more risky here, because it was more obvious that we were foreign. They weren't as fierce as the enforcers in Thailand, though. They didn't beat us, they just told us to be quiet.

Including the five from the Thailand house, there were a couple more Chinese people, so in total there were six or seven people in the house. We stayed on the second story of the house and slept on the floor. It was a bit better than in Thailand because there was carpeting. In general the place was okay, reasonably clean. At least here we could make our own meals, since none of the enforcers could cook. We ate chicken, rice, things like that. We requested the enforcers buy groceries for us. We told them what we wanted, gave them some money, and they went out and bought the food. But since they were Cuban, we couldn't really communicate all that well. A lot of hand gestures and miming, "We're hungry, we want to eat," and they'd say "okay" by nodding their heads.

We were told to be quiet and wait, that there was another snakehead in Cuba who was arranging the next step of our journey. We were there for three months, until one day we were told to pack our things—we were being taken to the airport to go to Mexico.

So this was already around six months of traveling, stopping, traveling. I really had no idea it would take so long, and still I hadn't reached America. Back in Fujian, the snakehead told me it would take about ten days to get to America. Maybe I would have reconsidered if they'd told me the truth about how long it was going to take. Maybe I still would have done it. I don't know.

AS SOON AS I GET TO AMERICA, I'LL BE AMERICAN

We got to Mexico by plane. All of us were really happy. I kept telling myself, "I just have to keep going. It's my last hurdle. And as soon I get to America, I'll be American." We spent four months in Mexico. The same kind of thing, locked in a house. But this place was really big. Outside there were pigs, chickens, sort of like a farm. There was corn growing in the middle of the land. There was so much that you could just go in there and pick it. The whole place was fenced in. We could wander around, but not beyond the fence.

So it was a bit better than before—at least you could walk outside in the fresh air—but it was very quiet. Very dull. There wasn't much to do. The same as before—sitting around, chatting, playing chess. We were prisoners still. By this time, though, I had become used to this kind of situation. I had become used to all the waiting. I wasn't frustrated in the same way.

Sometimes I was quite happy; other times I felt that my heart was far from being at peace. I felt that I was getting closer to America, but until I actually got there, I couldn't be at peace. Sometimes I thought, I can't believe I've been gone for so long. But I had a lot of faith in myself. I had no regrets. I knew I would get there in the end.

One morning we were told to get into this big truck with about a hundred other people. There were only about ten or so Chinese. The rest were Mexican, Guatemalan, Salvadoran. As soon as we got on, we were moving. We spent sixteen or more hours in the truck. It was very difficult, very uncomfortable. We were standing or leaning the whole time. There were no windows except for a small one above us in the roof. It was very, very hot. Very crowded. We didn't make any stops, not once during the sixteen-hour journey. We were given plastic bags to go to the bathroom with. The smell was really bad. I thought, *This is just too much. This is too harsh. This is not how you treat human beings.* But I also thought, *If this is the only way to get to the States in one piece, I have no choice but to tolerate it. At some point it will be over.*

Eventually, we arrived somewhere that had a lot of cornfields. It was about one in the morning, very dark. We were told, "At the other end of the cornfield is America." Then we were told to get out and go into the corn and follow some people. The corn was very tall, taller than me. All I could see was a railroad track running alongside us one hundred meters away, so whenever a train came by we would squat down. Next to the railroad track was a road. Police cars drove back and forth, patrolling the border, so you didn't dare make yourself seen. We were just walking and hiding the whole time, following the leaders. We spent about five hours walking. I didn't get tired, though. All I was thinking of was, *America, America.* I could see it at the other end. Eventually we got to a wire fence. One of the leaders cut a hole in it. He pointed to the cornfields and said, "This is Mexico." Then he pointed to the other side of the hole in the fence and said, "This is America."

I crawled through that fence and got to the other side. I can't tell you how happy I felt at that moment. The first thing I saw on the other side was a railroad, and a police post. So we had to hurry up and stay down, especially since the sun was starting to come up. Further along the railroad there were three cars—before we went through, we Chinese were told the cars would be waiting there for us. We ran to the cars, got in, and were driven away.

We were traveling for maybe five, six hours with two Chinese guys—the driver and another guy. They didn't tell us where they were taking us. They just said, "This is America. But we're still going to go further." Somebody said New Mexico, but I didn't know for sure. We stopped at a motel on the way. It was good to have a break—get showered, brush our teeth, change our clothes. The second night, I was driven to Los Angeles. When we got there the guy with the driver said, "You're really in America now. Give me the money."

What the snakehead told me back in Fujian—he was a liar. He lied about the time it would take. He also lied about the fee. He told me it was going to cost $30,000. But when I finally got here I was told that I owed $60,000. He said it was more because it took a lot longer than it was supposed to. I thought this was really unfair. But they wouldn't let me go until I gave them what they wanted.

I had only been prepared to borrow $30,000 from the loan sharks in China, so there was no way I could come up with the extra money just like that. Those snakeheads, they never tell the truth. But one thing is true—if you don't pay up, you're not going to live.

At the time, I was staying with three others in an apartment near a Hawaiian supermarket. One woman and two men. They hadn't paid the snakeheads yet, either. The people guarding us were young men. One of them was younger than me by five or six years. They were Chinese. If these enforcers went out, sometimes they would take us out with them. If they didn't go out, we didn't go out. We were never allowed to leave the apartment by ourselves. It was better than being locked up before, because they took me out a few times. I didn't see much though, as I was only allowed short trips to the supermarket to buy fruit, vegetables, that kind of thing. Most of the time we were indoors, watching TV and videos all day.

It was the three of us men in one room, and the woman in her own room. The enforcers stayed in another room downstairs. We slept on the floor. We couldn't really talk. If you spoke loudly, the enforcers would hit you. They kept saying, "Hurry up and get the money. If you don't get the money, we'll beat you to death."

I was constantly phoning home to try and raise more money. I called family, friends, whoever, to get them to help me. I was desperate to pay off the snakeheads and start my life in the U.S. After a month or so I managed to borrow $40,000, but it still wasn't enough. By that time the others had all left. They'd found the money and paid up. Eventually my older sister was able to get hold of some different loan sharks who lent me the extra money. After two months in Los Angeles, I had the $60,000 to pay off the snakeheads. When the Los Angeles snakeheads had received confirmation from the China snakeheads that the fee had been paid, I was free to go.

I DIDN'T KNOW WHERE
SOUTH CAROLINA WAS

I was given a plane ticket for New York City under someone else's name. It didn't even match the fake Thai passport I was carrying, but nobody checked when I came in. I knew nobody when I arrived in New York, nobody. Nobody came to pick me up when I arrived. I was all by myself. I just got in a cab. I'd been told to just say, "Chinatown." And so I did. The driver said, "Okay." When I started seeing Chinese letters on shop fronts and street signs, I told the driver, "Stop here."

I had no idea where I was going to find a place to live. I asked some people in Chinatown where I could find a hotel. The people there said there were several hotels nearby. That's how I found the Wu Shing Hotel, which had rooms for $15 a night. I stayed in my own room, but it was tiny. You pretty much just walked in, took your shoes off, and lay down.

At the hotel there were a lot of people staying there who had also come from Fujian. I got to talking to one guy who said he was from Wang Tau. I told him, "I've only just got here. I want to look for work tomorrow.

Where should I go, what should I do?" He told me not to worry, there were recruitment agencies nearby. He'd take me to one in the morning.

So that's what happened. The agent there said I could start working right away in a Chinese restaurant. I didn't have to sign anything, but I had to pay them thirty dollars for finding the job for me. I was given a phone number for the job, area code 803. They said it wasn't in New York, that I had to take a bus there. They told me how to get to the bus station on 42nd Street. When you get there, they said, buy a ticket on a Greyhound bus to South Carolina.

I didn't know where South Carolina was, but after buying the ticket I had only two dollars left in my wallet, so I thought, *Okay, it must be pretty far.* Still, I didn't expect to be traveling for hours and hours and hours. In the end it took about seventeen hours, almost a day, to get there. But I didn't mind. I was excited about getting my first job in the States, excited about getting my first wage and being able to send money back to my family. I wanted them to see I was doing all right, and that it was the right decision to come here.

PEOPLE IN MY SITUATION

It didn't work out very well in South Carolina. Straightaway the restaurant boss said, "You don't know how to cook!" And it was true. At the time I didn't know anything, I had no experience. I thought I would be given the chance to learn. Instead he got me to do basic kitchen work like cutting meat, vegetables, that kind of thing. He just kept me on for three days and then told me to go back to New York. I was really upset. I'd gone all the way down there and only managed to earn $180. I had to spend half of that to get back to New York. I felt unhappy, really defeated.

Then the recruitment agency found me another job, at another restaurant. This one had a 914 area code: Westchester, New York. Thirteen days at this place, doing more menial kitchen jobs. Philadelphia after that. The longest job I had was in Florida. I spent two years there. I'd been fired five or six times before I ended up in Florida. I also worked in Virginia, Queens, North Carolina. A few days here and there, generally menial kitchen work. Also a few days in Ohio. Texas. Alabama. Massachusetts. New Hampshire. Indiana. A lot of places! Seattle was the farthest. I don't know why the bosses fired me after such a short time. I worked hard, did my best. But maybe they got impatient with my lack of experience. Maybe they thought there were plenty more people like me.

Some places were okay, in terms of living standards. The owner of the restaurant would say, "Sleep in the basement," or "Sleep in the lounge." I don't remember a lot about the places. It was all pretty much the same to me. I spent all my time working—a kitchen is a kitchen, that's what you see, what you do. Queens had a lot of black people. North Carolina was very clean, not a lot going on. I felt very comfortable in Houston—it had a Chinatown, with Hong Kong supermarkets, Vietnamese restaurants, a lot of Asians. I was there a little over a month. In Kentucky, I lived up on a mountain with the other restaurant workers. Every morning we would get picked up and be driven down the hill to go to work. We lived in a very old house, about one hundred years old. The wood was rotting, the whole place was unhygienic; it wasn't comfortable at all.

When I worked longer at jobs I would make about $1,600 a month. The recruitment agency would tell us beforehand how much we would be earning. So, $1,600 sounds good, but you're working very long hours. I'd work about twelve to thirteen hours a day, six days a week. You're on your feet the whole time and have to work really fast, otherwise the bosses yell at you. The money I sent home would go to my family. I'd send the money in U.S. dollars. My wife would change the money into RMB and put most of that toward paying off the loan sharks.

There wasn't a definite time that I would send money home, because I wasn't always working regularly. When I had a job, when I had money, I'd send money back. If I didn't have a job, I wouldn't send money back. I'd usually send about a thousand, two thousand dollars home each time. The loan sharks charge very high interest. For the $60,000 I borrowed, every month I have to pay over a thousand in interest. So even though I've been in the U.S. for a long time, I still have no money. I hear the interest has been getting lower as people get wealthier in China. So if I borrowed $60,000 now instead of five years ago, the interest would only be about $600 a month. A lot of people in my situation have killed themselves because they couldn't pay back the money. They couldn't even pay the interest. I've always thought I just have to keep going. I have to keep working and pay off this debt.

In between the jobs I always came back to New York. Whenever I got fired I'd come back, because it's easy to find work from here. Sure, I got tired of working in so many places, but I had no choice, with so much debt to the loan sharks in China. I had to borrow from them to pay off the people who got me here—the snakeheads. So I was tired, really tired. But as I say, I had no choice.

Most every boss I had was bad. Out of every ten bosses, eight were bad. They were horrible to everybody who worked for them, but especially to people without documentation. They would keep saying, "If you want to keep this job, do your work properly. Otherwise, leave!" Or, even if you were dead on your feet from exhaustion they said, "Work faster! Don't laze about!" Last year, in Indiana, there was an incident. There were two cooks. One of the cooks accidentally sprayed the other one's face with oil while he was cooking. So the manager told the cook who sprayed the oil that he had to compensate the other. He had to pay. But the manager took the money and kept it for himself. It was $3,500. He took it out of the cook's salary. Two months' salary. And he told him, "Get out. We don't want you here." Both the cooks were undocumented. The manager said, "I'll go and get Immigration. I have documents, you don't." So the cook had to leave. He didn't dare try and stay or fight for his pay.

MAYBE THIS IS JUST THE WAY IT IS

I'd been working at this Chinese restaurant in Kentucky for about two months. I was one of five, six kitchen staff. I worked as a cook, a wok handler. It was a typical job—long days, twelve to thirteen hours in front of a hot stove. I kept to myself most of the time. I didn't really socialize with the other kitchen staff. I'm pretty quiet with people I don't know well. I don't know how to drink or tell jokes. The boss was Cantonese-speaking, so we didn't communicate well. Sometimes he got impatient when I didn't understand what he was saying, then another worker would translate and I would get it. But apart from that, things were fine.

It was a typical morning. There were several workers going in and out of the kitchen to the alley. The kitchen was small and cramped, so we'd use the alley for things like peeling vegetables, washing dishes and pots, that kind of thing. I went out there a few times to throw out some hot water. There was another worker nearby, a woman, who was washing dishes. I didn't really take much notice of her at the time, but I remember that at one point she left the tub of dishes. I wasn't paying attention. She must have gone inside the kitchen or restaurant to get something. After throwing some water out, I went back inside the kitchen to my stove. Suddenly everyone heard screaming—the woman came inside the kitchen, holding her hands up and screaming that her hands were burning with pain.

Then she ran inside the restaurant and came back with the manager. He had a really angry look on his face. He started talking to the workers. I could understand "Bleach . . . water." So I guessed he was saying that somebody had put bleach in the woman's bucket of dish water, and he wanted to know who'd done it. Nobody said anything. Several times he pointed to me, saying "Was it you?" Of course I just kept saying, "No, it wasn't me" and "I don't know anything." But he kept pointing and asking and I knew then he'd decided it was me. I didn't understand why, I hadn't done anything—but I noticed the woman had her eyes to the floor. The manager saw me looking at her and he waved his hands about and said what I thought was, "No, she wasn't the one who accused you."

Still, he kept pointing at me and asking, "Was it you, was it you?" Maybe he thought if he kept on at me, I'd eventually admit it. But I kept saying no, which made him angrier and angrier. He starting pushing me around, but I didn't fight back. I just turned away and went back to my stove. I just wanted to get back to work.

The next thing I knew I was getting struck from behind—at first I didn't know what was happening, but then I turned around and it was the manager hitting my back, my arms. I tried to defend myself, push him away, but it was difficult—the kitchen was so cramped, I had no space to move. I couldn't get out. I was scared. It seemed like a long time that he was hitting me. There were five or six other workers in the kitchen—some of them stood and watched. Others were carrying on with their work as if nothing was happening. I think they wanted to help me, but were too afraid. Even when you see something bad happening, you have to think of yourself. These are just people you work with—you get along just so you can work. All you really care about is keeping your job.

Then the manager grabbed a cleaver and started attacking me with it. I couldn't believe what was happening. It seemed like he really wanted to hurt me, but when he actually cut my hand open and saw all the blood, he just looked really scared and ran away.

Maybe I passed out, because I can't remember exactly what happened next, except that the police arrived, and then an ambulance, and then I was in a hospital bed. Everything after that is pretty vague, even now, months later. I just know that the whole time I was in the hospital I was afraid that I'd lose the use of my hand. At the same time, I was hopeful that the law would help me. I thought, *The police, they'll do something*.

The people at the Kentucky hospital were all very kind. They didn't ask me to pay any medical bills. They said it was a terrible thing that happened. The doctor there cut my hand open and then he reconnected something, maybe the bone. He warned me, "If you're not careful, you could lose the use of your hand. And when it gets better, it's still not going to be 100 percent normal."

While I was in the hospital, someone, maybe the police, arranged for a Putonghua-speaking lawyer to come and see me. This lawyer said that the police had gone back to the restaurant and couldn't find the manager. He also said the manager had a previous record, for assault, and that the police were still looking for him. I wondered if I wasn't the first worker he had attacked. The lawyer said that for now, there was nothing else that could be done.

After about two weeks my hand was stabilized, but I still couldn't move any of my fingers. I was in a bad situation. I had no job, and the police still couldn't find the manager. This made me feel hopeless about getting any kind of compensation. It also made me feel unsafe. I didn't know what the manager was thinking, if he wanted to get come after me for revenge or something. So I had no choice but to get my things together and buy a bus ticket for New York.

Back in Chinatown, the first thing I did was go and see a man called Mr. Chen. He works for a foundation that's known for helping Fujianese people. I told him about my problem, and he said he'd try and do what he could. Hopefully he can help me. Since the attack happened, three months ago, I've been out of work. I can't handle a wok. I can't do anything.

I can't move my thumb. My whole hand is reddened and very swollen, very stiff. The scar goes down the wrist like a V. Two big cuts. That's where the tendons are severed. I can't tighten my fist. I use this brown stuff on the skin—Chinese ointment. I've been seeing a local Chinese doctor for this. He says I'll only regain 50 percent of the use of my hand.

We're all upset about the situation. My wife wants to be here. My sons are already eleven and fifteen years old, and they don't know when they'll see their dad again. I still want to get them over here, but how can I afford it, how can I arrange it? All I wanted was to make a better life for my family, but instead I've missed my sons growing up, and I've been apart from my wife for five, six years already. But even with my hand like this, even if I have to do the worst kind of work for the worst pay, my chances of paying off my debts are still better from here than in China. And even if I did want to go back, it would be impossible—I have no money to get out of the States. So you see, I have to stay.

I've heard no news about the manager in Kentucky. I have no idea what's happened. My lawyer, the one in Kentucky, has told me nothing new. I don't even know if he's helping me anymore. When he found out the restaurant wasn't covered for liability, he said, "We'll just talk about this later." I don't know what's going on in his mind. Maybe he thinks he's not going to get paid because the restaurant doesn't have money, doesn't have insurance. I don't have any news about it. I don't know if the manager was ever found, or if he was charged or not. I admit I still have some anger toward him. I don't understand how you can treat another human being like this. I have thought about finding my own lawyer here in New York. So maybe I'll ask Mr. Chen. Or maybe this is just the way it is. Maybe you just have to accept things and get on with your life.

DESPITE EVERYTHING THAT'S HAPPENED

My life now is very hard. Now that I'm not working, I stay at home, in a hotel. I share the room with five others. They're also workers, immigrants, people in similar situations. Sure, you're friendly, you all come into contact, get to know each other, but then you leave. Nobody really stays anywhere for long, so it's hard to make real friends. I can't think of the future right now. My head's full of troubles, full of worries. I can't sleep. I owe the loan sharks a lot of money. I'm separated from my family. But despite everything that's happened, I still don't regret coming over. I really don't. I still think it's better being here, trying to sort out my problems from here, than going back to life in China.

My wife and I don't talk very often. I don't have a lot of money to call her. She knows what happened, but she doesn't have all the details, how bad things have gotten. I don't want her to see the state I'm in. It'll only make her worried and feel helpless. Sometimes we'll call each other if something's happened, here or back home with the kids or someone in the family, if something's going on. If nothing's going on we won't call each other. But when we do talk, no matter what the situation is, we always end up saying the same thing to each other anyway, even if it's not true. "Don't worry, everything's all right. I'm doing well. I have food to eat, I have a roof over my head, so don't worry about me."

In 2015, New York City continues to be a major center of Fujianese immigration to the United States. Neighborhoods in Brooklyn such as Sunset Park, Bensonhurst, and Borough Park have booming Fujianese communities. Many Fujianese have fled persecution back home, though many have also emigrated for purely economic reasons. Claims for asylum by Chinese immigrants in the U.S. vastly outnumber claims by immigrants from any other country.

Out of Exile: Narratives from the Abducted and Displaced People of Sudan (2008), edited by Craig Walzer, tells the stories of sixteen narrators who were displaced from their homes in Sudan as a result of decades of conflict. Most interviews for *Out of Exile* took place in the summer of 2007, two years after open war ended between Sudan and South Sudan, but four years before South Sudan became an independent country.

ACHOL MAYUOL

AGE WHEN INTERVIEWED: *28*
BORN IN: *Marial Bai, South Sudan*
INTERVIEWED IN: *Marial Bai, South Sudan*

Achol told her story while sitting on a bedframe outside her home in Marial Bai. Her five children sat with her, and sometimes went in and out of the hut behind her. She spoke very quietly, and with visible disgust toward the man who had kept her for many years as a slave-concubine.

I WAITED FIFTEEN YEARS TO BE FREE

I was born in Marial Bai around 1980, and I'm the second of nine children. My father was a farmer with many cows; he was relatively wealthy. As a girl I was just like the other children. I would build toy houses with sticks and mud. We would play house. We girls all wanted to grow up and be mothers someday.

When I was about three years old, I saw the *murahaleen* attack Marial Bai and burn it to the ground. My parents didn't think it was safe to keep me there, so they sent me to live with my grandmother. My grandmother lived near a Government of Sudan military post, so we thought we would be protected. I was about six years old when I went to live with her.

I had spent about two months there when the war came to us there, too. One day I heard gunfire and cannons, and we ran into the bush. I was hiding with some other children when we saw horses—people on horseback—all around us. They shouted at us, and they reached down trying to grab us. They grabbed many children and threw them onto their horses. When a child ran too much, the men jumped off their horses and beat those children badly.

I was running through the grass, away from a man on a horse, when I felt a large hand under me. I was lifted up so quickly I lost my breath. And then I was taken away. We were all taken away. They gathered us in a nearby field and they divided us up that day. The different horsemen would take the people they wanted, and we would go in groups to different parts of the North.

My group walked for many days. The slave masters were on horses while we walked. I was barefoot and the paths were so hot. My group was about thirty boys, girls, and women. Some of the women didn't make it. They would get tired and the *murahaleen* would simply kill them. This would get rid of the dead weight and would motivate the rest of us to walk faster.

We walked for many days until we reached a clearing under a tree. They had set up a fence around a tree, the same kind of fence used to keep cattle. This is where they put our group. We were combined with many other groups until there were a hundred or so of us. There were many adults, but mostly children and teenage girls. The men who had captured us left, and the men who remained to watch over us were older, and were armed with knives and guns.

On that first day we were given orientation. The men were speaking Arabic while another man who spoke Dinka translated. We were told, "Your homes have been destroyed. Your people are gone—your fathers, mothers, parents have been killed. The village is gone, there is no life back there where you're from. Now the only choice is to accept the person to whom you've been given. Accept them as your father and mother. Do what they ask you to do. Anyone who does not follow this order will be killed, just as you've seen many of your fellow Dinka killed."

We stayed there for six days, sleeping on the ground and being fed meager things. Some of the captives did not survive the six days in the fence. A few women complained about our situation, and they were killed. They were shot. They shot one pregnant woman who had not complained. I think they thought they had made a mistake by abducting a pregnant woman, so they fixed that error by killing her. They killed an older woman for the same reason. It was the young boys and girls they really wanted. We were worth something.

Eventually, the buyers came to see us. Older men, farmers mostly, came in their robes. A man would arrive and say, "I need some boys to take care of my cows and my goats." Some would come and say, "I need girls, young girls, to help me take care of my housekeeping." Some buyers would take a teenage girl for other reasons.

For six days people came to buy us, divide us. They were buying and selling cattle at the same location. We were the same as the cattle.

BOUGHT BY A TEACHER

The person who purchased me was an elderly man named Abdul Karin Mohammed. He took me to his farm, and along the way he avoided big towns. They did not want the interference of the government or any other slave owners.

We arrived at his farm. It was a big farm, a plantation, where he kept cattle and other livestock. The man had two wives. With one wife, he had ten children. With the other, he had nine children. It was a huge compound—nineteen children of various ages, much activity.

There were other Dinka children, abductees, who were already there. There were three girls and five boys were kept by the same man. The boy slaves were mostly older, so they were always used to take cattle to the pasture far away. The girls would take care of the goats and sheep closer to the compound. When we grew older we girls were made to clean the home and take care of the children. We were shouted at every day, always called *abeeda*—slave. We were always reminded of who we were. "You are here to work," they told us, "Do whatever job you are asked to perform. You are a slave."

We ate leftovers from whatever the owner and his family had eaten the day before. It was never enough. We slept on the ground every night, while the slave master's children slept on new beds. When the slave master bought new clothes for his own children, the old clothes were given to us.

If one of the master's children wanted you to do something, you had to do it. The kids were worse than the master. You had to do whatever they pleased. If you didn't, these children would beat you, tie you with ropes, and leave you lying there for hours.

We were all given Arabic names, and were taught Arabic and the Koran. I was forced to do away with anything that was of my culture. I was forced to study Islam and Islamic ways. I was forced to undergo different rites of passage than the Dinka ways, including genital mutilation. I was forced to abandon all my beliefs and customs. I grew up there, from age six to sixteen.

ADUT SHOWS THE WAY

There was one older Dinka girl who lived at the compound. Her name was Adut and she was my close friend and hero. She was tall and dark and strong. Every day she talked about escape and made plans to leave that place.

One day she tried to leave, and was caught and beaten. She had scars all over her body from disobedience and trying to escape. They had beaten her with a cane and with other instruments. But Adut was still determined to leave.

She came up with a plan. She planned to take the goats out to pasture and lead them far enough away from the houses that she could then run. When the day came to try this method of escape, I was not part of Adut's plan. I was too young. But she did escape that day. She walked the goats far away from the compound, and then she ran. She ran for three days, and we thought that she had successfully escaped.

But on the fourth day, she returned on the back of a horse. Our owner had hired horsemen to track Adut, and they found her soon enough. She was brought back and she was tied up and beaten. She was tied up for many days, outside, so we could all see her. The owner wanted to make an example of her.

After that, Adut did not try to escape again, but she left soon just the same. She was sold off as a wife to another farmer nearby. She became one of the wives of this man.

Adut would come back to visit us every few months. But she had changed. She now advised us not to try to escape, that it was impossible and that we would just be bringing punishment upon ourselves, that we could be killed. She told us that the only way out of this slavery was to wait. To wait until a day came when the war was over and the armies of South Sudan triumphed. The day would come, she said, when we would be redeemed. Someone someday would find us, she said. Someone would recognize us.

SOLD AGAIN

I stayed with this slave master and his family for ten years. I was six years old when I was brought to him, and sixteen when I was sold again. Usually a slave kills himself or herself, being enslaved as long as I was. But I did not. Then he sold me.

One day I was told by my slave master that I would now go to another person, that I was to be wife to a new man. I was told that I would have to obey him, and stay with him, and not attempt escape. I was told to remember that whenever I tried to escape, there would be nothing to go to, that there was nothing left of Dinkaland. He said that because Dinkaland had been destroyed, I must accept this new man as my husband. I had watched Marial Bai burn, so I did believe some of this.

He told me about this new man over many weeks, and I waited for the day the man would come. When all the details were agreed upon, a car arrived. There was a man and a woman in the car. I was put in the backseat and was driven away. The man was one of the brothers of the man whose wife I was to become. The woman in the car was the brother's wife.

We drove for two days. The man who bought me lived close to a city. They had a farm, and they kept cattle. The home was a compound of several houses, with each of the man's brothers occupying one home. Each brother and his wife had their own house, and each had many children. The man's mother and grandmother each had their own house, too. It was a large complex, all kept by this one large, wealthy family. They were well-educated. All of the man's nieces had gone to school.

After I saw the property, I met the man who had just bought me. He was a very old man, perhaps sixty years old, and named Akil.[1] He was a well-educated man, a teacher in the secondary school. He had no other wives and no children. I'm not sure why. He told me that he had paid money for me, so he had the right to keep me. He told me that I was his property, and that he could do anything he wanted with me.

My duties were to fetch water from the reservoir, wash clothes, and cook breakfast, lunch, and dinner. I had to keep the house clean and cook for guests when they came to visit. I wasn't treated well, but I wasn't treated like a slave. There was a lot of work, but the other brothers' wives did similar work. We all worked for the men. If I was productive and worked hard, I was treated decently.

And though life settled into a routine, I never felt any love for the man who bought me. I never accepted my situation. Always I dreamt of escape.

I had been living at this man's home for two years when I became pregnant by Akil. I gave birth in the hospital to my first child, a baby girl. She did not live long, only two days, and then she died. I don't understand why she didn't live.

I had another child the next year. The second one, a boy, he survived. Eventually I had three more children by Akil. They were treated well. They were treated as the legitimate children of Akil. They slept in beds and were fed well. I was always treated as something less than a real person.

---

1. Achol never referred to her second captor directly, being unwilling to utter his name. For the ease of reading this narrative, we will call him Akil.

I was still a slave, but the children were considered the proud offspring of this man. They were sent to Arabic school and were being groomed to take over the farm when he died.

Even with the children under my care, I was not allowed to go into town. The family had big homes in town, but I was kept away from that. At this time in Sudan, keeping slaves was not accepted by all people. Someone who wanted to keep slaves had to do so out of the public eye. If I needed something, I had to ask one of the other wives, and she got it for me. I spent all my time on the farm, caring for the children and cleaning the house.

ESCAPE AND REDEMPTION

One day Akil told me to get dressed in the best clothes I had, and to get the children dressed in their best clothes. He planned to bring us into town to have our picture taken. This was the first time he ever wanted to bring us all into town.

We arrived in town, all of us dressed up. We walked to the photo studio, and just outside the studio, I saw three Dinka men. They were tall, and they looked familiar. I caught the eye of one of the men, and he asked me if I was a Dinka. Akil looked at me; he was afraid. I was not afraid. I spoke to the Dinka man and said I was a Dinka, from Marial Bai. I told him that this man had purchased me and was keeping me against my will. I said this in a mixture of Dinka and Arabic, because I could not remember much Dinka.

One of the Dinka men said, "Aren't you the daughter of Achokuth?" He recognized me! This man was related to me, an uncle of mine, named Ny Nyang. And among the men there was also another distant relative of mine, named Deng Mul.

Immediately Akil was aware there was trouble. He said that it didn't matter that I was taken when I was young, that he had bought me legitimately, that I was his wife. The Dinka men did not accept this. They told the man we were all going to the police station immediately. And we did. Along the way Akil realized that he would not win this battle. He began to protest, telling the Dinka men that he would release me if they would allow him to take his children. But my uncle and the other Dinka men were not satisfied with this, either. They insisted that we all go to the police station, and said that I had suffered enough and that I was entitled to keep the children I had birthed and cared for.

My case became a big court case in the town. It took about twenty days and involved many of the powerful people of the town. There was also an agency working in the area called Christian Solidarity International; they were working in Sudan, redeeming abducted people. They helped to free me—because there were Westerners there, attending the court hearings, nothing corrupt could happen.

All along, Akil tried to trick everyone. At one point he said he wanted to take the children home for a moment to get some clothes. But the court and my relatives saw through this ruse. Akil planned to take the children away and never come back. But the police kept me and the children together in the courthouse. All along my relatives, the Dinka men, fought for me. They said that they had lost Achol once, and would not lose her again.

When the judge finally ruled in my favor, Akil was not even around. He was working that day, but one of his brothers came to court that day in order to hear the verdict. I never saw Akil again. But he sent word through his brothers that he was not finished with me. He made threats, sent through his brothers, that someday he would find me and kill me. But I don't worry about that now. I waited fifteen years to be free and I need to feel free.

BACK IN MARIAL BAI

I came back here to Marial Bai in 2004. I had forgotten Dinka, all of it, but I began to learn it again. It took me about two years, but now I speak the language again.

My family is here, and they help me. But they have a lot to do, and they have their own problems. It's difficult to help someone like me who has so many children. They help me with my emotional strength. They support me when necessary.

It's a difficult life here. I tried to start a business selling Sudanese food and tea, but I became ill, a problem with my kidneys, and now working that hard is impossible. I'm trying to get the medicine I need. Perhaps if I get that medicine I'll feel stronger. If I do, I will resume work.

I hope my children have an easier life than mine. I want peace for them, and opportunity. We will see.

———————————————

Achol Mayuol's family continues to live near Marial Bai, and the village has grown into an important economic center in the Bahr al-Ghazal region of South Sudan. Shortly after the publication of Out of Exile, *the Valentino Achak Deng Foundation completed construction of a secondary school for young men and women in Marial Bai. Secondary education is still unavailable in much of South Sudan, especially for girls (only 1 percent of girls complete high school in the country). Today, the school has over 400 students enrolled.*

South Sudan won independence in 2011, but the young country continues to face many challenges, including inadequate access to food and water, a worsening refugee crisis, and conflict between the state's military and rebel groups.

Out of Exile: Narratives from the Abducted and Displaced People of Sudan (2008), edited by Craig Walzer, tells the stories of sixteen narrators who were displaced from their homes in Sudan as a result of decades of conflict. Most interviews for *Out of Exile* took place in the summer of 2007, two years after open war ended between Sudan and South Sudan, but four years before South Sudan became an independent country.

ALWEEL KOL

AGE WHEN INTERVIEWED: *33*
BORN IN: *Mulmul, South Sudan*
INTERVIEWED IN: *Cairo, Egypt*

Alweel's smile shone and her voice chirped in Arabic as she told her story deliberately and in deep detail. We took breaks for chocolate and tea after difficult episodes. It took two days for her to unfurl all of her experiences, reaching back to the village in South Sudan where she was born, to the Nile in Khartoum and then, years later, following the river north to Cairo. Listening to her speak, it was difficult to comprehend how this beautiful, gracious, intelligent woman had undertaken such a journey. But Alweel remains luminous.

I WANTED TO LEARN WHAT
THE TRUTH REALLY WAS

I can close my eyes and paint a picture of Mulmul, the village where I was born. I can see houses made of straw and children playing on the way home from school. I remember how much I loved school—I was an excellent student and my teachers loved me. I loved math and English the most, and I can picture the English books. I would read the English words out loud, even if I didn't understand their meanings.

I remember playing with my dolls. I put a cloth on a brick to make a bed for the doll. Some of my cousins were lazy, but I was always helping in the house, washing and carrying things for my mother when she would take her cooked foods to the market. I can hear myself singing all day long, dreaming of being a famous artist and celebrity.

I remember my large family, my parents, my two brothers and five sisters, my aunts and uncles. My two parents were Muslims, but the town was Christian. When we were growing up, my friends would go to church and I would go with them. I would go every day, and they would tell us stories about Jesus and the crucifixion. I used to have my cross to wear, and we used to pray before meals. My father was a very democratic man. He used to say it's a choice, and you choose your belief, and everyone should go with what his heart believes. I believe that God exists and he loves me. I like the story of the crucifixion. Everyone was standing around Jesus waiting for something to happen, and he said, "Please, Father, forgive them, because they don't know what they're doing."

My father was big and tall, but he was a kind man who would laugh and play with us so much. He would solve people's problems. He was a leader of our tribe, and a worker on the bridges and roads. I don't remember much else about him. My mother was always a very sweet person who took good care of her children.

I remember that there was a cat in the village named Endewah, and I used to get upset when the children would tell me that my eyes looked like a cat's eyes and call me Endewah. I used to cry every time! But I would go to my mother and she would help me. She would remind me, "No, you are not Endewah, you are Alweel."

SOMEWHERE ELSE

I lost my parents in 1985, on the day when people came to our village and burned it. My father and uncle died that day, and I lost my mother.

I was only ten years old, so I didn't know anything about a war. One evening, armed men came to our village to catch certain people. They attacked our home, tied up my father, and threw him to the ground. I saw him get killed. My uncle was killed after my father, and then my aunt threw herself on my uncle's body and they killed her, too. There was so much blood everywhere, and I was so scared. My mother used to tell me to become a doctor, and I hated the thought because I couldn't deal with blood like a doctor should. But when I saw my father get killed and I saw all his blood, I couldn't think about anything else except blood.

My mother was far away from home, at the market in Abyei. They took me and my two brothers, Farid and Deng. They put us in a Land Rover car and inside were other children I had never seen before. They told us that the one who runs away will be shot. They drove for an hour or so. They took us to a faraway place with tents and houses made out of hay and with lots of other kids. It was a camp where they kept many cattle and many children. There were policemen in charge of the place. They wore uniforms and called themselves officer and sergeant.

They made us herd sheep and small cows. When they took me to the cattle, I asked, "Where are those other children running?"

The man said, "They are running to go to school." I did not believe him. Of course not. These men had killed my father. I knew at that time that I was not safe.

At night they put us in a big tent so full of children. They served us very bad food and gave us blankets like the ones from relief workers. They separated me from my brothers. I had no idea where my mother or my sisters were.

I stayed like that for maybe ten days. Then a cow stepped on my foot, and it started swelling; then I wasn't walking, I was limping. We had to walk early in the morning and come back at night with the cattle. There was no medication for me, and I showed them my swollen foot and they didn't do anything. They pushed me to the floor. I found a couple of stones, a small pile of hay, and salt, and a small pot of water. I heated the water and the salt, and I started putting the water and the salt on my foot. In a couple of days it became better. I had learned this from my mom. I saw her doing this.

When my foot healed, I ran away. There was a family traveling with their camels; I saw them, and I walked up behind them. They were riding their camels and I was walking on foot, but when I came close, they knew there was a child behind them. The man saw me, and I told him my story and he was kind to me. He took me to his children, and they gave me milk and food and my stomach felt good. I remember the son's name was Almer, because he was so nice to me and so cute, and didn't make me feel like a stranger. They took me to the city of Abyei.

The sultans in town—the local leaders—told me that they knew my story and they knew about the people who died in my area and about my father. They knew stories about people being taken, like me. I told them I wanted to go somewhere else. They put me in a truck and gave me money in case of trouble, and they gave me a letter to give to the church in El Obeid to the North. El Obeid was the biggest place I knew, so I went there. I was trying to find my mom.

The truck drove for many hours. I wasn't afraid of those I was traveling with in the truck. I was afraid of the people who attacked me before. I was afraid they would come and take me again.

I went to the church and there was a missionary and a priest; I talked to the priest and I talked to the missionary and told them my story. They listened to me. They gave me two choices—either they would send me to Khartoum or take me to school here. At the time, I did not know what a "Khartoum" is. We had it in the books, but I didn't know what it is, so I asked. They said it's a big, big city. They have many churches and organizations, and there are many priests there and it's a bigger city than here. I chose Khartoum.

OH, THAT'S A GOOD GIRL

There were many people on the bus to Khartoum, but I was traveling alone. The road wasn't good and it took two days to go two hundred miles. It was a nice trip, but I was a bit tired so I would sleep sometimes. When people would take a break to pray or to eat or anything I would just go down with them for air.

I didn't know anything about my destination, but when I arrived I felt a bit safer. It seemed like a clean city with nice buildings, not those huts we had in Abyei. Khartoum is bigger and nicer than the South. Once I got off the bus, I asked where to find the Roman Catholic church of St. Peter and Paul. It was in Amarat, close to the airport. I went to the church and gave them the letter. They didn't say anything. To this day I don't know what was written in that letter. They just kept asking about me and my family and what happened. They said they were very sorry, and they would take me to school and take care of me. The church had a school in it, so I went to school there. They got me money to buy some food and clothes for myself.

I met a girl from the Shilluk tribe named Angelina, and we became very good friends. She was the same age as me. I showed her where I lived, and she showed me where she lived, and then I moved and lived with her, east of the airport. They lived in a hut covered with plastic sheets and a big room built with mud and a big space outside.

Angelina was living with her family. Her father was dead and her mom was married to another man. She had younger siblings and older ones—a younger sister called Regina and four boys. I was very happy at school and with this family of nice people. I became another member of the family. They spoke a different language than me so I didn't understand them. But Angelina knew Arabic so I could speak to her.

School was good; I was happy; the teachers loved me; it was excellent. The other students were a mix of Arabs and people from the South, but I don't remember them. Angelina was my only friend and the only one I talked to. We wouldn't say much. She didn't want to sit and talk about boys, and I was very shy as well. The kids would make fun of Angelina. She would get upset and angry. Angelina is a bit tough, and sometimes she would beat other children. Sometimes when many of them would come and beat her back, I would defend her.

After school, we would work with her mom and try to make some money, and help ourselves. We would go to houses and clean and get paid a few pounds. We would brew alcohol and sell it in the home. You get a big plastic container, cut the top off, and you fill it with dates, water, yeast, and sugar. You heat it with fire, punch little holes, and let the water go into a pot underneath. You leave it for three days and it's ready. Everyone would come drink it—Southerners, Arabs, people from Darfur. When Muslims would come, they would take it and drink it at their home. I never tried it myself, even to taste for cooking. If I wanted to know if it was strong, I would put it on a plate and light a match. If it flamed, it was good. If not, it was bad.

I was happy then. I used to talk a lot about my family, but I couldn't find anyone to guide me to them. Part of me wanted to go back to the South and just find my brothers again or just run into my mom. I was almost eleven years old then.

I went to a government school for middle school, and to church for Christian education and to pray. I lived with Angelina's family still. People would see me living without my family, and they wouldn't say, "Oh, that's a good girl." They would look at me badly.

GOOD FOR MARRIAGE

When I was sixteen, I was in love with a guy name David. He was very good-looking, and went to university, and was smart, but his life was very complicated. And he drank. His two parents were dead and he was raised by his paternal aunt. His financial situation was very bad. Sometimes I think I should have waited for him. One of the reasons I lost hope was because his family wouldn't agree for me to marry him since I had no family.

I was seventeen in Khartoum when I met my man, Akaich. He was

Dinka like me. After I finished middle school, I went to high school. I went to a special school called Agrazella for refugees from the South, because our Arabic is different from the other students' Arabic. I met another girlfriend in the new school named Nimera. Nimera's family is well off, and her father had his own workshop where they did metalwork and artwork; they had a big house with many rooms. The man I'm married to is Nimera's uncle. Through Nimera, he married me.

I was in Nimera's kitchen and I was helping her cook. It was a big household. Nimera's father had five wives; each of his women had many children, and I was helping to cook for all of them. Akaich saw me and was pleased by me. Dinka men like women who are hard workers, and he saw me as a hard worker and he liked me. He told Nimera, "I like this woman and I want to marry her." He said that to Nimera the day after he first saw me. He said she is good-looking and hardworking, and I like her. And that was it.

For the Dinka, the most important thing is that the woman is hardworking. If she is hardworking, knows her responsibilities, and can keep the family under control and keep things going according to the norms and the traditions, she is good for marriage. Beauty and height are good as well, but they are extras.

When Nimera told me the proposal, I thought she wasn't serious. I said, "No, because he looks old." He was about forty at the time and I was seventeen. I said, "I don't want him." But something happened that made me marry this man: I wasn't able to pay the expenses for my schooling. Akaich started giving me money, with no relationship actually happening, just as Nimera's friend. He bought me a uniform for the high school and gave me money to buy things. After two years, he asked me again to marry him. And I told him, "Well, I cannot say anything. I will ask Angelina's mom." She acted as my mom and invited Akaich to talk to her. Akaich went to Angelina's mom and he asked for my hand in marriage, and they agreed and I married him.

I was not very happy. I did not love this man. He was a liar. I had my conditions for marriage. I wanted to finish my high school education and go to university. He promised me he would support me. But after I got married, he said no more going to school and no more education. He used to beat me up and fight me over it. He used to hurt me, but he didn't break any bones. When we grind garlic, we use something with an iron handle to smash it, and he hit me with it in the leg and caused problems with my knee. Sometimes when I would walk, my knee would pop out, but now I'm better.

IT WAS ALL LIES

Akaich was very jealous when a friend would come to visit me. He said, "No, they're only coming to see you and take you to another man." At the very beginning, Akaich said he was not married, but it turns out he was married to another woman. She was Dinka as well. In the house where we married there was a woman with her two children. He told me it was his brother's cousin, but it turned out that it was Akaich's wife, and those children were his children.

Nimera never told me about the other wife. She didn't tell me about the other children. After I married, she got married herself and left for Nairobi. She was not a good friend.

I worked at home. I was the one cleaning and washing and doing everything. I would go to the supermarket to buy flour. The same month I married I got pregnant. I had to leave school. I thought about running away, but where would I go?

After I had my son, Deng, I became pregnant again less than a year later. It was 1995. I stopped breastfeeding Deng, because they say that it's bad to breastfeed a child while you're pregnant. One day, I came home from the market and saw the other wife with her breasts out feeding my child. The wife was pregnant and she said my baby was crying. I thought that because she was pregnant and breastfeeding it might harm my child. At that moment, I decided I didn't want to stay in that house anymore.

When my Akaich noticed I stopped breastfeeding, he asked why and started beating me up. I told him I was pregnant. He said if I was pregnant, the child was not his. It was not true. My husband was jealous. Even when I would speak to his cousins, he would get jealous and say I was sleeping with other people.

When I argued with Akaich, he went to the court and filed a complaint against me. He got an arresting order, and I was arrested by the police for being pregnant with a man other than my husband. The punishment for something like this is prison.

I was detained for three days. My husband kept my son, Deng, for those days. They took my statement and there was an investigation. I said my husband was a jealous man. I said I'd had a relationship with a boy before I married, and my husband thinks I still have a relationship with him. It was all lies. Nothing had happened. After they finished the investigation, they appointed a guardian to speak for me to officials, because I was not important enough to defend myself. Nimera's father spoke for me. He wrote a letter to local sultan leaders telling my story. One of the leaders came and took me out of the prison. Everyone in the neighborhood was talking about me. I was given a very bad name.

After that, I had to go to the court. The judge spoke to my husband first, because he was the one complaining. My husband said this is my wife, and she is pregnant from another man. The judge asked me for my say. I told him, "Your honor, it's a lie. Akaich is my man, I am living with him, and I have been pregnant for several months with his child." The court asked my husband to bring witnesses to show I was pregnant with another man.

When we left the court my husband started beating me in the street. My back was hurt badly, and my whole body was traumatized. When I got home, I lost my babies. A midwife came to take my babies out. They were twin girls; one of them was dead already and the other lived for five days.

After this, the house was so full. People came from the neighborhood to give me the evil eye and feel happy about my loss. When someone would come, they would say, "Oh yes, she deserves it." Everyone was surrounding the house demanding to know the name of the other man. It is a tradition that when a woman goes with another man, she should say who the other man is. When the twins were born, people were saying the man should come and sacrifice two sheep or else I would never have children again. I told them I don't have a man. I was bleeding badly, a whole tub-full of blood. All day I was so tired, and I'd lost my babies, and there was lots of blood, and I was so thirsty and so weak. I asked for water and they said, "No water for you unless you tell us the name." I was so thirsty that even talking was hard. My tongue would stick to the top of my mouth. They said, "No water unless you talk."

They brought local Dinka sultans to the house. I told them the father of the children was a northern Arab from across town, but it was a lie. It was not true. My husband became so happy, and everyone was so happy because now they could go to this man and take cows or property from him as compensation. The neighborhood would get to share this compensation to right the wrong. This is the tradition in all of Sudan. Those uneducated people had ancient traditions, but I was just so thirsty and I wanted to live. I said it to save my neck. They gave me water.

It was evening, and I told them I would give details about the man in the morning. That day my husband came with a sultan and two witnesses and asked me about what I had said yesterday. I started lying to them. I told them the man was a trader from another neighborhood. I wanted to keep them happy. They took me to court with the witnesses. I told the judge I had lost my babies. They gave me twenty-one days in prison. The judge asked me, "Is this all true?" I said that I had only said what I said because I was thirsty. The judge asked my husband if it was true that they had kept water from me. My husband said yes. The judge said the session was over. He said he was finished until there was real evidence, and I would not go to jail. He said he would call us back to court in two weeks.

My husband had a lawyer, but I didn't have one. When we were in the court that time, a lawyer came up to me and said he wanted to support me if I paid him. I told him, "I have no money and that's why I have no lawyer." He gave me some free advice: He said in court I should ask my husband if he's ever seen me with another man. He said that was the most important question to ask so the judge could see my husband was lying.

When we came back two weeks later, the judge asked for my husband's witnesses. My husband said he could not find them. The judge asked if I had anything to say. I asked my husband if he had ever seen me with another man. My husband said no. The judge decided I was innocent of adultery. I went back with Nimera's father. Even though my husband was his cousin, Nimera's father was very supportive of me.

I wanted a divorce. Akaich only wanted to separate, but he did not want divorce. I went to the special family court for non-Muslims and asked for a divorce. Then my husband converted to Islam, because in Christianity I could get a divorce for what he had done, but not in Islam. They took my case from the non-Muslim court to the sharia court. The sharia judge said this man was my husband, and he doesn't want to divorce you so you must stay with him.

I had lost all my defenses now. I couldn't do anything. He was a criminal. He was evil. I just gave up. Now I was not really married, but not divorced. The elders of the neighborhood decided we should stay together. I asked for a home of my own. My husband agreed. He said he would slaughter two goats in memory of my lost children. He said he wanted to sleep with me again to make new children. I said no.

He left for Singa, the village of his childhood, and took his other wife and my child, Deng. I followed him to Singa to get my child. When I went to his house, he beat me up. I went to the police station to file a report, and I was taken to the judge. My husband came to the court; he said he was a Muslim, and I was his wife and I belonged to him and the child belonged to him. He told the judge that I just wanted to roam around and not stay at home. I knew nothing about sharia law, and I just lost. The judge said I was married to this man and I must stay with him.

I returned to Khartoum and lived with Angelina again. My husband stayed with his other wife. My husband came back six months later with my son and some money. He stayed for a week. This was when I became pregnant with my second son, Bol.

Akaich did not give me my own house. He took me to Nimera's father's home and put me there. He gave me about five Sudanese pounds every day.[1] I used to go out and work to support myself. I would wash clothes and iron them. I would get paid by the dozen, about two pounds for a dozen pieces of clothes.[2] For about six months, I was happy there. My fun would be to sit and chat with the many wives of Nimera's father, maybe have some Sudanese coffee and eat. Soon I moved in with Akaich again.

Eight months later I had my second son, Bol. I was imprisoned for fifteen days for making alcohol. They came in and arrested the women for brewing. We always hid the alcohol in the ground, but the soldiers found it by poking with their rifles. I was in the shower. They made me get dressed and take my son because he was breastfeeding. I went with them. The prison was really dirty and smelly, and people slept on the floor.

After fifteen days in jail an officer came to me. He asked who had brought me to jail and I said I don't know. He said he would talk to a judge to set me free, because people looking like me should not spend any time in jail. This officer was nice, and very cute really. The nice officer took me out of jail and put me in his office with my son. I wasn't sure if he was trying to have a relationship with me, but he just gave us tea and milk and desserts for my child. I was able to sleep in a bed that's usually for officers. After three days I was allowed to leave.

Akaich was an army soldier, and I knew that the war in the South was becoming very severe. People were evacuating and coming to Khartoum. They would all talk about how they lost their families, like me. Sudanese television would never say anything about that. There was a TV show called *Sacrifice and Battlefield*. They would show the brave northern soldiers as heroes—coming and conquering, and being brave and noble. They were

---

1. US$2.50.

2. US$1.

not showing the truth about the fires they set or the kidnapping. They only showed brave heroes.

The southerners in Khartoum were treated so badly. In the past, the graveyards would be mixed with Muslims and Christians. Now they didn't let the Christians get buried in the same places. They burned small huts in the city, the places where people like us would live. They would start burning it down, not caring what's inside. Shortly after I left Angelina's hut the second time, it was burned down. They besieged the area, and every small house they saw they burned. Angelina's family was moved in trucks to a faraway place called Jabrona.

Akaich was upset about this because he was southern, too. In March 2000 he decided to leave work. When he tried to leave, they detained him, imprisoned him, and said he was working with the rebels. We were at home when they took him. The people who came weren't even from the army, they were from security. They don't wear uniforms, and you can't report on them, because they don't even exist. They are secret.

They came to the house at three a.m., tied my husband up, and started beating him. They told me that if I reported them, then my husband and I would just disappear. My husband was a big, tall guy, but they were bigger and awful. They took him away.

After five days, the same men came back again, also at night. One of them threatened me with his gun and said, "If you file a report you will die in the same way we killed your husband." Then I knew that they had killed him. While they told me to keep quiet, they raped me. I only saw three of them, but I am not sure how many it was. My children were asleep in the small room next to mine, but they were asleep and did not come out. When the men finished, I ran outside after them to see their car. I saw a big Land Cruiser like the state security uses. After they drove away, I took my children and I left.

My feelings about Akaich did not change when he died. He was a liar. But I never wished him to die. If he had died naturally, it would have been fate. But he was killed by men, and they hurt me in his name after he died.

OUT OF SUDAN

As a result of the rape, I had become pregnant. I brought my children and went to live with a woman I knew. She was living in a building that was still under construction, and she was getting paid to keep strangers out. One day on the street I met a German man named Andreas. He worked as an engineer. I started cooking and cleaning for him. I told him my story, and he helped me and was very supportive and gave me lots of money. While I was working for Andreas I had the baby, a son named Ashweel.

Andreas gave me the idea to come to Egypt. He told me that if I come to Egypt and tell the United Nations my story, I might get to go somewhere else. I wanted to do it. He helped me get official papers and documents. I had to pay lots of money for passports and documents and it took months, but Andreas helped me. Even after the first agent just stole my money, Andreas gave me more money to try getting papers a second time. That time it worked. I remember I got the passport on September 11, 2001.

Once I had my passport, I went to the airport to buy my exit visa. It was the last step before I could leave. Ashweel was seven months old, so he was old enough to travel. When I came back, I couldn't find my oldest son, Deng. At that time, Deng was only seven, so he would not have gone away himself. My son Bol said his grandmother had come to take him to the market and then they would come back.

They did not come back. I was so afraid and I was confused. I didn't know what to do. I thought maybe to stop my traveling plans and look for my child but then I didn't know where to look, and I was so afraid to complain to the police. I called my mother-in-law. She said she didn't want Deng going to Egypt. She had taken the child away to her home village in Singa.

The next day I went on a seven-hour journey to Singa. I don't know what they told Deng while he was there, but when I saw him he didn't want to talk to me. Maybe they told him they would hurt him if he talked to me, but Deng is my son, my son, and I couldn't understand. The family said they didn't want me to take the child. My husband's cousin tried beating me up, and I just ran away because I was afraid they would kill me. I left. I was emotionally destroyed.

I could not stay in Khartoum. If I stayed longer, my visa would expire, and getting another visa is an issue in itself. I was thinking that I would come to Egypt and then come back to take my son. Then I found out that when you talk to the UN, you are cut off from Sudan. I could not go to the Sudanese embassy, and I could not go back to Sudan. I had to find another way to get my son to Egypt.

I left Khartoum with two of my sons. I took a train to Halfa, on the border. It was a tiring trip. I was carrying two babies. The trains broke on the way. Everything was very cold and dusty. I had to squeeze onto seats, and there was no place to move. I spoke to the other people, and everyone was talking about Egypt and Sudan and about their own tragedies, so I found out that other people had bad things happen, and not only me.

INTO EGYPT

I dreamed that I would go to Cairo and find my family and live with them again like when I was a child. I arrived in the city on a bus. We arrived at night. I was feverish. One woman traveling with me told me to go to a doctor and get some medication. Another said no, if I went to the doctor, they would see my passport and put me in quarantine and send me back to Sudan, because they were afraid of malaria. I didn't go to the doctor.

I went to the church at Abbassia because they receive refugees there. The bus stopped near the church, and many were there to pick up other passengers. I had nobody to pick me up. I had no blanket and it was very cold that night. It was November 16, 2001. I slept with my children in the church and slept near a woman called Abuk. I don't remember where she was from. Abuk had a big blanket with her from Sudan. It was really big. I shared with her and my children.

In the morning there were people selling tea and sandwiches, so I ate.

The church people brought more food and juice and milk for the children. Abuk had a family in the Ardeliwa neighborhood, and I went with her to that house. I stayed there for a week, and then Abuk and I got our own flat. Her family helped me get a job in the Zamalek neighborhood cleaning. I worked for Egyptians. It was a tiresome job for many hours every day. I would leave at eight-thirty and come home at ten at night. The food they gave me in the day was not good, and they were not very nice to me. The mistress was merciless; every day I had to polish the wood and metals in her very big house. I worked for her for four months. Abuk would watch my children at home, because she had family in America so she did not have to work.

I was not making much progress. I made seven hundred pounds a month, and I paid over five hundred just for rent. I was safe, but I was very tired all the time from long work and my babies.

Andreas had told me to go to the UNHCR as soon as I came to Cairo, but I couldn't.[3] At the Abbassia church I had met a woman named Flora who said she would give me fifty pounds if I let her borrow my passport so that she could use it to buy alcohol and cigarettes from the duty-free shop. She kept my passport for a week. When I got it back, I went to the interior ministry building, the Mugammah, first. People said I had to go there first for an entry visa or else I would be kicked out of the country. I got a stamp there, and then I went to the UNHCR.

In 2001, the UNHCR was different than it is now. They gave me a piece of paper that proved I had visited them, and they made an appointment for me two years in the future, in 2003. In two years they would interview me, they said.

3. The United Nations High Commission for Refugees was established after World War II to help peoples displaced by warfare. Today, the UNHCR administers to over 10 million refugees around the world.

A DREAM

When I got to Cairo I contacted my sister-in-law, Lena. She lived back in Singa, where my son Deng was being held. She was sympathetic about my lost son. I sent her money and put her in contact with the same guy who helped me get my passport. She was afraid and was telling me maybe there would be a problem, and I said, "No, it's okay, I just want my child." She took Deng from Singa, and he went to Khartoum with Lena to get his photo taken to finish the documents. He stayed with her in Khartoum for about a month. At the border, Lena pretended Deng was her son and brought him to me in Cairo at the close of 2001.

It was like a dream. I never imagined I'd find him again. He told me lots of bad things happened to him in Singa. He used to shepherd the sheep, and after school he had to polish people's shoes on the street. His stepmom would beat him, treat him badly, wake him up early, and he would work all day. He told me he had wanted to come to me when I saw him in Singa, but my husband's other wife was beating him up and treating him badly and he was so scared.

I WAS NOT BROUGHT THERE
FOR A GOOD JOB

In 2002, I got a new cleaning job with a German man named Michael. He was so sweet and tall with black eyes. I started out working for him, but it became a romantic relationship. We dated for two years, but no marriage happened, because Michael was already married. His wife was in Germany, and they were sort of separated. His job ended after two years, and he went back to Germany. He paid me very well, though, and took care of my children. He still calls me to this day to check on me.

Michael was good to me, but in the first Cairo year I had so much trouble. A friend of mine named Ragah was walking with me in the Agouza neighborhood at eight p.m. We were crossing the street, and a Saudi guy in a car stopped near us. He asked me if I wanted a good job and I said yes. He was dressed like a Saudi in long robes. It was just after I had left my cleaning job in Zamalek so I wanted a job. He said his house was across town, and he needed me to start today. I told him I had to go tell my family, and he took Ragah and me to see Abuk so I could tell her I had found a job. Ragah didn't want to come with me, but I told her, "Ragah, you have to come with me so I can show you the house because I don't want to go alone." It was a BMW and the glass was tinted; two men sat in the front and we sat in the back. I didn't know they were criminals because they looked like wealthy Saudis and they talked like Saudis, so I thought they were Saudis.

Inside the car, everything was dark from the dark windows. Every once in a while, a driver would get out of the car and make a call on a pay phone. I began to get nervous when he stopped driving. They took us into an empty apartment. They sat us in a room on a couch. The Saudi guy was beside me, and then me and Ragah and then the other guy. They closed the door and locked it. I felt my heart beating and something wrong was happening. The apartment was not even as good as my own.

I was not brought there for a good job.

One guy told me he wanted me to sleep with him. I said, "Me sleep with you? Did you bring us here so you could use us?" He slapped me and he had a knife. He said if I opened my mouth, he would cut me into pieces. He took me to the next room. There were other men in there standing in a line. It was on the third floor of the building, and all the doors and windows were closed. The man who slapped me said, "Take off your clothes." I tried to pull away, but he took out his knife and then he raped me.

The other man originally with us was still in the other room with Ragah, beating her up very hard. After I was raped, I went in there and saw an open window. It was the third floor. I thought that if I threw myself off I could die. The same guy who raped me raped Ragah.

A man from the other room came for Ragah. He told Ragah to go sleep with him. The man beat her up and dragged her away. Then I saw the men in the other room run out of the house quickly.

I ran to the other room and saw Ragah hanging out the window and screaming. She was only holding onto the wall of the balcony. The neighbors turned on the lights and they saw. People came onto the street in their underwear. Some brought mattresses so Ragah could jump. Ragah let go and fell onto the mattresses.

When the first Saudi ran out, the neighbors grabbed him by the robes. Ragah was screaming. She was naked like the day she was born. Everyone came around with wooden sticks. I didn't know if people wanted to hit me or hit the man. I grabbed Ragah and we ran to the Saudis' BMW car, because I was afraid to stay in that neighborhood—it looked bad and strange. We got to a bridge, and the driver opened our door and said to get out. We told him to take us to the police. He said he would not and tried to give us money. I said, "I don't want money, just take me back to my home."

A car stopped close to us. An Egyptian man got out and asked if something was wrong. I said yes and told him what was happening. He went to speak with the Saudi and then got back in his own car. The Saudi driver started grabbing me to get me out. I said, "I will not get out until you take me to the men of law."

He drove me and Ragah toward our neighborhood. I saw the Egyptian private car driving behind us, so I felt a bit more trusting. He stopped once and said he was going to get money. He came back with a folder. When he drove again, we went to a construction site. He stopped the car and pulled Ragah and me out. Ragah was still not wearing anything. The Egyptian came. He took the money. The Saudi and the Egyptian beat up the two of us so badly that Ragah and I were lying on the ground and couldn't move. The cars left. It was very dark, and I wasn't able to see the license plates. There was no point in complaining to the police. They left us lying on the ground by the street.

The men had dropped two hundred pounds next to us.[4] I took off my

---

4. US$35.

shirt and gave it to Ragah for a cover. We took a taxi home. I never went to the police. I had no evidence and I was new to Cairo.

THEY DID NOT GIVE ME A REASON

In November 2002, I got a telephone call to go to UNHCR for my refugee status interview. A man named Ahab interviewed me and a woman was there. They asked me questions. It was a bit weird, because they would ask me a question and then go out of the room. When they came into the room again, they would ask me how I felt after being raped. The entire interview lasted half an hour.

I really didn't get to tell them anything. They were not compassionate. When I would cry in my story, they would not comfort me. They stopped and asked if I wanted to move the appointment to another day. I said I just wanted to get it done. They got bored, and the woman would leave and come back again. It ended. I went back in two weeks to get my results. I found I was rejected for refugee status. They did not give me a reason. They gave me a month to appeal.

I was upset. I wondered why I came to Egypt. Now I was very upset. I think that the laws of UNHCR are good, but the people there do not care about refugees. We come from Sudan, and we only know about the UN for help. We go to their office and the security guards outside treat us like shit.

I wrote an appeal in December 2002 and gave it to the UNHCR office. I received an answer in October 2003 telling me I had an interview appointment for an appeal on May 5, 2004. When May 2004 came, I was working in Alexandria, because the family I cleaned for had moved there. I told them I had to be back in Cairo by the fourth of May at the latest. The madam told me she didn't want me to go, and if I wanted to go, I should leave and never come back. I told her to give me my money and that I would go, that the only reason I worked was to support myself while I waited for that interview so I could get away from Egypt. She said no, because she didn't want me to leave. I did not have enough money to travel back to Cairo and I knew nobody else in Alexandria, so I missed my interview. I made it to Cairo two days later. The UNHCR gave me another appointment for June 6, so I was lucky.

When I returned on June 6, I found out that there was a decision from Geneva. They had stopped giving interviews to all Sudanese. I asked why. They said it was because Sudan now has peace as a result of the Naivasha negotiations.[5] They said to wait until December and then we would have more news. They gave everyone there a yellow card, which means your case is undecided. Yellow only keeps them from deporting you. When December came, there was no news.

At All Saints' Cathedral, they had a meeting and said there would be financial aid for yellow-card people. I had my three kids, and I needed the money. To get the money, I had to register with Caritas, the Catholic Relief Services. The security outside the building was absolutely awful. None of the clerks inside would come and talk to us. They treated us like wild animals. They said come back another time. I needed to make money. I gave up.

A SMALL FAMILY

I go to the church in Abbassia, and the sultans sometimes meet there. Anyone who doesn't have a family goes to them for news of their family. In 2003, I was invited to Sakakini Church, and there in the office, they told me they had found my brothers. My brothers didn't look the same as when they were children. Their faces hadn't changed, except Farid became fat and huge, his face chubby and big. Deng is still thin, so his face did not change. When I met them, it was a beautiful moment. I cried a lot. I kept them with me at my home. It was a very good time. My brothers would sell hair creams in the market and help out in photo studios. That is how we got money and supported ourselves. Me and my children and my brothers were like a small family.

---

5. Discussions in Machakos and Naivasha, Kenya led to the signing of the Comprehensive Peace Agreement between the government of Sudan and South Sudan independence groups in 2005.

Deng and Farid told me about their time in the cattle camp when we were separated. They told me they ran away as well. They went to another city, not Abyei. Then they walked to Abyei, and then to Khartoum. Deng told me that Farid was very young at the time and got sick on the way. They were both under ten years old. They reached Khartoum. From Khartoum they came to Egypt.

They told me my youngest sister is in Dallas, Texas, and married with twin girls. She's very happy there, and I would love to meet my nieces.

They told me my mom was in Australia. She had taken a different route to Khartoum, then to Cairo, and now she was resettled. My brothers had signed papers to meet our mother, and Australia had accepted. They were ready to see her soon. My mom sent me a form, so I filled in the form, enclosed my case, and sent it in a letter. A lawyer went to my mom and delivered the news that I was rejected. Maybe it is because of my failures with UNHCR.

The foreign lawyer helping my mom is a very nice person and used to call me every day from Australia. My mom went to the refugee affairs office and complained and said, "This is my daughter, and I want the right to have her here." The lawyer was a very good person, and they sent me another form. Australia didn't reply to the second form. There is nothing to do now. My brothers were resettled in 2005. They are with my mother, and everything is good in Australia.

I found another person here in 2004—my friend Angelina from Khartoum. She heard of me, got my phone number, and called me, and now we see each other all the time. Her mother is dead now, but she's here with her four kids and she has another in her belly. She was married, and she had a dispute with her husband who got married to another woman. He took the money, the car, the house, and everything, so she came here. I am lucky to have my friend Angelina again.

There is a man named Abdel Monid who I met in Cairo in 2005. I had met him in Sudan years ago. He is a Muslim from Darfur. When I saw him in Cairo again we recognized each other. We started to see each other in a relationship. He is a short guy and I'm taller than him. I couldn't find a man tall enough for me! He is a nice man. He was nice to my kids and would come visit us. He manages a cybercafé. I helped him start it by lending him a little money. It was a good job for him. We got married on September 1, 2005. When he asked me to marry, I thought having a man in the family would make our life better in Cairo. Eventually I came to love him, but only eventually. Then it turned out he is not so great. He stopped treating my kids well, and they hate him now. One day last year he disappeared, and now I hardly see him. I have not heard from him in months.

THE LAW

This year, 2007, on January 11 at four a.m., I was on my way back home in a taxi from a friend's birthday party. A police car stopped us. There was an officer inside and two younger police also. The officer got out of the car and asked the taxi driver for his license. The officer found the driver's license had expired. He came to the back and asked me for my ID. I showed it to him. He asked for my residency permit. I told him it is attached to my husband's ID. He told me I had to get out and go to the police station to answer questions, and then I could go home. He put me in the police truck. Only the officer would talk to me. The other two looked nervous. I wasn't nervous.

I sat in the middle seat and one man was on either side. The officer said to me, "Listen, I got you in this car because I like you."

I did not expect him to say that. I respected him because, when he was asking for my identification, he was very professional. I said, "What do you mean that you like me?"

He said, "It means we can be friends, and I can help you with problems, and you will never regret knowing me."

I told him, "I am sorry, but I am a married woman, so I cannot sleep with you. We can be friends, but we cannot have a relationship."

He told me we could be friends and talk on the phone, but he would take me to the police station first. I hoped he would just take me to prison for ten minutes and then let me go.

They did not take me to the police station. The officer took my hand and put it on his penis. I started shaking. I told him I wanted to go home, but he said, "No, just five minutes, and then we'll go to the police station." The officer pulled me to the back of the car, and the other young policemen went up to the front so it was just the officer and me in the back. They drove to a dark area by a bridge. All three left the car and they smoked. Then the officer came back and sat beside me. He said, "I want to sleep with you, and then I can take you home."

I told him, "No, take me to the police station or leave me here; kill me before you sleep with me."

He said, "There is no way out. You must sleep with me."

I said, "I cannot sleep with you because I am on my period."

He said, "Okay, if you can't have sex with me, then you can give me oral until I come and that's it." He took out his gun and said, "If you don't do this on your own, you will do it against your will." He pulled my hair and made me do it.

Then he opened the window to talk to the other guys. There was a box of tissues in the front of the car, so I got some tissues and I wanted to keep some of the officer's sperm. Then he put on his clothes and he left. He ordered the other two men to do the same to me.

Then came the big, fat, lower-ranking policeman. He told me to do the same to him as I had done to the first. He took off his trousers and his underwear. He held me by my neck and he made me do it to him. After the fat one was done, I cleaned the sperm with a tissue and this time I hid it in my shoe.

The fat one left. The third guy was a nice guy. He came in and sat beside me and found me crying in the car. He said, "Don't cry, I wouldn't hurt you," and he didn't do anything. He sat beside me for about fifteen minutes to make the others think we were doing something, but he didn't do anything.

The morning was coming. When I saw the place in the light of day, I took note of where I was. The two that abused me went in the front, and the kind one joined me in the back. I had a small black bag with my phone and passport and 440 pounds.[6] The men in the front took my bag; they took 400 pounds and left me 40. The officer told the man beside me to hail a taxi and pay the driver ten pounds. I told them I wanted my money back, but the officer pulled me out of the car. I shouted and shouted and screamed for my money back. The officers were nervous because the taxi driver was watching. The kind officer went and got my money back and asked me if I was still upset. I told him no. When they drove away, I memorized the five numbers on the license plate of the police car. I thought of their faces again and again so I would not forget them.

I told the taxi driver to take me to the police station in my neighborhood. The driver asked why and I told him. The driver said it would be safer to wait and go with a lawyer. He took me home.

IN THE MORNING

At home in the morning, I called my friend and told her everything that had happened. I asked her if she had the phone number of the protection office at the UN. There was no answer when I called.

I sent him a message to please call about something urgent. Ashraf at the protection office called me at ten a.m. from his office. I told him everything, and I told him about my evidence. He said it was good that I acted bravely. He gave me an address for a women's rights organization. I went there and told them my entire story. They referred me to a lawyer named Mohammed Bayoumi.

It took a week for me to find my husband to get our residency document from him. When I told my husband what happened, he was very upset. Then he went to the district attorney's office with a report. One attorney read the report for an hour and then said he could not do anything, and we would have to take our case to a higher level. We went to the chief of the district attorneys, and we worked with their office. I described the men,

6. US$80.

gave them the tissues, and gave them the car number. The lawyers asked me questions, and I answered until they were done.

I can trust the district attorney. When I went to file the report, the office was serious about it. He asked questions and summoned people and confronted them in front of me. He was very harsh and upset with the police. I trust the attorneys, because they took the tissues with the sperm and analyzed them and they have taken blood from the officers to analyze it. They showed me a lineup to identify the officers, and I was able to point them out. The three police have been suspended from their jobs since January of this year, 2007.

The day after the attorneys confronted the police, there were police cars all over my neighborhood. They were asking for me. They wanted to take me to meet the head of the station and settle the matter now. I was not in the neighborhood when they came. A neighbor called my phone and asked if I had seen the police outside. I told her I was away and did not know. Another friend called and said the police were going through the buildings looking for me.

The soldiers found my son Deng. They asked him about his mother. Deng's friend whispered in the Dinka language that he should not answer. Deng does not really speak Dinka, but he understood and he shut up.

My friend Asunta called and came to where I was, outside the neighborhood. She told me I had to hide, and I became very scared. I called my lawyer Mohammed Bayoumi. Mohammed Bayoumi told me to hide anywhere I could, that police wanted to erase my case. I hid in Asunta's home and thank God they did not find me. They knocked on the door, but Asunta opened the door wide and smiled so they trusted her when she said she was alone. If they had done a good search, they would have found me.

FAST TRACK

Mohammed Bayoumi took me to the UN. I had an interview and the UN said they would get me a blue card for full refugee protection. About a month later I got the blue card. Mohammed Bayoumi gave my case to the American Embassy, the Canadian Embassy, and also the Australian Embassy. The Americans and Australians said they would only consider me for resettlement if my file was referred by the UN. So far the UN has done nothing. But the Canadians are considering me for resettlement. The process is called fast-track resettlement, because I am in danger here. They could take me any time, but I have no news yet.

If I traveled to another country, I might have protection from another government. Right now, nobody protects me. The United Nations does not protect me, Egypt does not protect me, my husband does not protect me. My husband told me that according to Islam, what happened to me means that I am no longer his lawful wife. I know he is just a coward and irresponsible and doesn't want to support me in my ordeal, and so he is finding excuses for himself. Without protection, my life is in the hands of God.

Now I am trying to get residency stamps, so I will be allowed to get copies of my police report and give them to the UN so they can help me get resettled. But the residency stamps are controlled by state security, and I think the officer's family has a hand in stopping me, because I still have no residency stamp after nine months of this.

PLEASE FORGIVE HIM

One day the officer went to Mohammed Bayoumi's office and said I should go to the district attorney's office and say I was lying about everything. Bayoumi took him close and said, "Between you and me, man to man, did you do this?" The officer said, "Yeah, I did it."

Bayoumi said, "You're telling me you did this, and you want me to go tell my client to lie? If she denied everything now, I wouldn't allow her! I would let her go and pursue the case myself!"

We found out that the officer's father is a lawyer in the Court of Appeals, and his uncle was once head of national security. He seems to be a guy from a very big family. But I don't care. I just want to get my rights, and I just want to see it go through. I don't care if I get killed.

Somehow the officer got my phone number. The first call came from the officer's mother. She called and said whatever I want, if I want all the money of the Queen of Sheba, she would give it to me if I end this now. She admitted yes, her son had made a mistake, but it was just a simple one and that now he could lose his career, so please, please forgive him. I said your son should pay for this. If it was my brother and your daughter, I'm sure you would find justice for your child. She cried over the phone to forgive him for the mistake. She said Allah would never forgive me if I did not forgive him. I said that if it was only her son that did this to me I would have forgiven, but he also ordered other men to do this to me. He thinks he is the master of the world. He thinks everything belongs to him. But it is not so. The mother cried and I hung up.

The officer called. His other relatives called. I met the officer and his family two months ago. The officer's father comes to my lawyer's office all the time to bother him.

His mom came and met me in Bayoumi's office, begging for me to deny the charges. She told me her son's wife wants to divorce him now, and he can't see his baby—please forgive him.

I said, "Madam, I'm a grown woman with children. If you think about what your son did to me, and if I had fought back, and they had killed me, what would have happened to my children?"

She said it was a mistake but promised Allah would take care of everything. She said I should forgive because Allah will take care of me.

I HAVE TO BALANCE

My children are beautiful. They go to a good school. They have become afraid of the police. Every time my youngest son Ashweel sees the police, he runs to me. Every time I go out, he says, "Mom, don't go away; the police will take you." My boys are now thirteen, eight, and six. They are not so tall yet, but my whole family is tall and soon they will be tall. They don't mind about Sudan so much. They want to meet my mother in Australia.

Sometimes they speak to my sister's children in Texas, and they want to visit there. For my boys, it is more about family than land.

These days I work as a hairdresser. For a short time I worked as a hairdresser in a Kenyan woman's shop, but now I work at my home and go to people's houses when they ask for appointments. I enjoy the work. I have loved hair since I was a child in Sudan. I am good at the job.

I am grateful to God that I am here and I am alive. When my mind needs peace, I go to my friends and we chat and we have a coffee. We use a special mix of ginger and cardamom. We boil it several times. We sit and drink and chat. Sometimes I listen to music with my children. I listen to Bob Marley, and I share it with my children. "No Woman No Cry." My children like 50 Cent and R. Kelly, and I sort of like them, too. I am a single mother, so sometimes I am a mom, sometimes a dad, sometimes I am a sister, sometimes I am just a friend. I have to balance.

I have no idea what will happen in the future. I don't even have an idea of what is happening now. I do not know if Canada will take me for resettlement. Even if they do, maybe I should not leave Egypt yet. I do not want to end my case against the officers. Maybe I will get justice. People should be strong in such situations and never weaken or give up. They should stay strong.

In 2015, the refugee crisis within Sudan continues unabated. Of the hundreds of thousands displaced by war every year, many head north into Egypt. For decades, Egypt has been a common destination for many fleeing Sudan due to its proximity and relative stability. It is estimated that more than 2 million Sudanese have settled in Egypt after being driven from their homes by civil conflict. However, Sudanese in Egypt face many difficulties. Rampant discrimination and exploitation of Sudanese refugees is common, and difficulties of life include minimal legal protections, few employment opportunities, little access to public services such as education, and the threats of physical violence, kidnapping, and human trafficking.

Hope Deferred: Narratives of Zimbabwean Lives (2010), edited by Peter Orner and Annie Holmes, tells the stories of Zimbabwean citizens who lived through the country's long slide from triumphant independence from white rule into chronic instability marked by politically motivated violence and hyper-inflation. The interviews centered around the 2008 general elections, which were marked by a resurgence of political repression not seen since President Robert Mugabe came to power in 1980. Zimbabweans from all walks of life, including a number who were forced into exile, expand upon their broken dreams and stubborn hopes in this wide-ranging collection.

Pictured at right: Harare, Zimbabwe

PAMELA AND THEMBA

AGES WHEN INTERVIEWED: *27 and 28*
BORN IN: *Harare, Zimbabwe*
INTERVIEWED IN: *Harare, Zimbabwe*

When they first met, Pamela and her husband Themba were both employed in middle-class jobs in Harare. As the Zimbabwean economy started to falter and inflation skyrocketed in the early 2000s, the parallel (illegal) market took over. In 2002, seeing an opportunity to leave his office job, Themba began to import foreign cars illegally from across the border and sell them in Zimbabwe. To supplement her regular income after the birth of a new son, Pamela too entered the "informal" economy, selling clothes and food. Eventually, Pamela and Themba decided to form a small company that provides horticultural products to farmers. While so many Zimbabweans, and a number of people in this book, chose to leave the country, either for economic or political reasons (or a complex combination of both), many like Pamela and her husband have chosen to remain in the country, for better or for worse. Today, they own and run a small business in Harare, where they live with their two children.

HERE IN HARARE,
WE ARE SO REMOVED FROM IT ALL

PAMELA: I grew up in a nice house. And we had a modest life. Every day, you know, we had bread, tea with milk, sugar, a good sandwich, cold milk, eggs, everything. The whole works. Yes, we went to good schools—but then, everybody could do that. Because the money had value. Zimbabwe had one of the best education systems in this region. And now, we are trying to send our kids to South Africa for them to get a good education.

It's totally the other way around. And Zimbabwe was also regarded as the breadbasket of Africa. We used to export our produce to Botswana, South Africa, Mozambique, all those places.

I'm not saying there didn't have to be changes. Take land, for instance. Black people, communal farmers, had all the poor land. And then in the fertile areas, the land was all reserved for the white commercial farmers. So of course the land had to be redistributed.

But the horror stories that we heard, some of them were so terrible. I mean, here in Harare we are so removed from it all. But you would see it on the telly. Say, for example, a white commercial farmer owns a farm. He employs many workers. He provides food for these workers. Then the veterans come and take the farm. The white farmer is not given time to even pack his things. They say, "Right now, leave this place, we're taking over all of it." You know? And he had to leave everything that he's worked for his whole life. He's been in Zimbabwe since I don't know when. Just like that. And he has to go. If he refuses, then repercussions.

CHICKEN AT THE DRY CLEANERS

THEMBA: There was no transition. It was just, "Look, we're taking it right now, we're moving in." So the method of acquiring these farms was harsh. And the result was a significant change in the environment, especially in the business environment throughout the country.

Economically, things became unstable. Costs went way up. Then things started going bad. Not only the cost of transport, of fuel. Prices across the board were changing, and inflation started to rise. There was so much happening. Everything was just going too fast. There were shortages. Food shortages. There was no production on the farms. There was no production in industry. Different sectors were suffering. Inflation started rising more.

We called this new era of high inflation and all the problems that went along with it "the black market." In the beginning, I was very ambitious. At that time, if you wanted to survive, you had to be experimental. Things—groceries, commodities that weren't obtainable in the formal markets—you'd find them outside. You had to go out hustling.

You had to go to the person dealing sugar. Sugar was a good business because, in fact, almost no one could find sugar. People couldn't find fuel either. So there were people dealing in fuel. You could deal in almost anything. I remember once I was at a soccer match and my friend said to me, "Hey, if you want chicken, go to Second Street. The dry cleaners, they have chicken." The dry cleaners are selling chickens! It was true, they were getting chickens from the farmer who was afraid of taking it to the supermarket because he was forced to sell it for the price that was below his production price. So he was selling it from the back door of the dry cleaners.

Because, you see, prices were being controlled by the government. Now, when this happens, the value of something increases. The control on certain commodities reduces the supply, so the people are forced into using the black market.

Now, if you got caught you could get penalized. If you're caught with the maize or rice, you know, it would be confiscated by the police. Same of course with sugar.

PAMELA: I remember even Orange Crush got on the market. A lot of the time, you could never find anything anywhere but on the black market.

THEMBA: Amid all this, the corrupt environment thrived. There were only a few powerful people who had access to commodities. For example, those in the marketing control boards. These top officials would channel certain things—grain, sugar, and fuel—to the black market. And that's how the black market thrived and the powerful became richer and richer.

But with corrupt activities going on from top to bottom, the economy itself started falling. Production suffered. The government started losing lots of money. The currency started falling as well. Then, within a few a years, we got to a point when the unemployment rate was over 90 percent or something. Industry wasn't functioning at all.

No products and no imports. It was very difficult to manufacture. So, when that year started, I think we're talking late 2003, people would start bringing in things. There were a lot of cross-border traders going to the regional countries—South Africa, Botswana, Mozambique—and bringing back commodities to sell. And then inflation just shot up, kept on going, higher and higher.

Yeah, it was hard. And I was involved in it, buying and selling on the black market. There was a lot of risk. You could be raided, your product could be taken away. In time, it became more and more dangerous. There were police raids. I knew I had to get out of it and into a more legitimate business, something more formal.

A BANANA FOR 10 TRILLION

THEMBA: The Zim dollar first crashed in 1997, and ever since it has just been dropping. This is a situation that we couldn't imagine, that we didn't think of. Right now, we are taking zeros away from our currency.[1] We're into the trillions now.

---

1. Along with frequent devaluations of the national currency, the Reserve Bank of Zimbabwe redenominated the Zimbabwe dollar in August 2006 (one revalued dollar equalling one thousand old dollars) and again in 2008, when ZW$10 billion became equal to ZW$1. Overall, ten zeros were cut from the currency in this way, but the numbers soon climbed back into the trillions.

Zim dollars now? I give you 10 trillion Zimbabwean dollars, and you can't even buy a banana with 10 trillion. No one wants that money. It's painful, but, hey, I'm a Zimbabwean. We should be using our own money. At one time, it was quite a strong currency. We've sort of adjusted. We know our money is useless. We are not looking to the Zim dollar for anything. We have money in the bank, but it's just Zimbabwean money. It's not doing anything, and it's pointless for me to go and wait in line for two, three hours to get 10 trillion dollars, which can't even buy a banana. It's all about foreign currency today.

But then, some people really have no way of getting hold of any foreign currencies. So they go to the bank every day to get their 10 trillion dollars and you always wonder how they do it. But the money, it's not making sense.

PAMELA: People out there are hungry, people are very hungry. And then you're thinking, How are these families surviving? How difficult it must be—especially for the men, the breadwinners—they can't buy a loaf of bread at work, to eat at work, and then their families are starving at home. In Zimbabwe, it's almost as though you are either poor or you're very rich. The poor, they can only afford just one meal a day. That's in the evening. I suppose in my family we are lucky, because we are able to eat every day. We are really not that hungry—yet. And the very rich? It's like they are not living in Zimbabwe.

When I think about it now, I think back to the liberation war. It is sort of history repeating itself, you know? We are in another war. I will say this is a sort of war too. It's a war because every day you are struggling to survive. When you wake up, there's no electricity, there's no water, and there's no food.

For the first four years of the recession, my husband and I were on our own. We didn't have so many responsibilities. Who knew it would go on for over ten years? We used to think, *Oh, maybe next year it will be over.* And then of course, we got married, had kids, and you're not thinking about leaving when you've got young kids. We stay here because we have young kids.

Sometimes you really do think about it though. You think, *Okay, so what am I supposed to do? Stay with the kids and watch them die of hunger? Or leave them so I can go and work in maybe South Africa, and every month send back money for food?*

A few months back we almost left for South Africa. Because, yes, that's what you're thinking. You wake up in the morning and there's nothing to eat. There's no cornmeal, there's no sugar, there's no cooking oil, there's just nothing in the house. And you're thinking, *Why shouldn't I go to South Africa and work? My kids would be living a better life because I'd be able to provide food, clothes.* But I never did leave, because we thought we could actually make it.

THEMBA: And look, there are things you have to believe in. I'm a very patriotic person. I love Zimbabwe. I've been to other countries in the region, and they don't compare to what I have here. Someone has to stay behind and protect it. So yes, I still do have hope.

PAMELA: We are not working for ourselves anymore. We are working for our kids, because we want the future to be brighter. Now, if we give up, or if something was to happen to us and we leave our kids where they are, they would have a really difficult task in front of them. They'd have to start from the bottom.

After six years, two presidential elections, and a currency switch from Zim to U.S. dollars, Pamela and Themba continue to run a number of what Themba calls "opportunistic ventures." As the ongoing political tug of war stretches on, the national economy shrinks. Themba tells us that since 2011, 711 companies have closed down in Harare. Key industrial sites have turned into ghost towns. A rubber factory in Bulawayo is now a warehouse for Chinese imports. In a former engineering works, people cook and sell cornmeal porridge and barbecued meat (sadza and braai). Themba blames the elite for the rampant corruption and abuse of power, "a draconian rule of mass distraction," with officials using public providers as their private businesses. However, he sees himself as a beneficiary of the chaos due to his entrepreneurial mindset. "I believe I can survive anywhere," he says. "I can put together an idea, get my hands dirty to safeguard the welfare of my kids." What his generation has experienced, he says, must end with them. He says a new group of leaders—not rulers—must emerge. "We've been living in a stormy hot environment and we are still waiting for the rain to come down."

Though Zimbabwe was featured on the 2015 New York Times *list of top tourist destinations, the country must now buy much of the food that it used to produce. Tough profits flow once more for international corporations and the wealthy, political speech remains constrained and aspirations hamstrung, while poverty continues to deepen.*

Nowhere to Be Home: Narratives from Survivors of Burma's Military Regime (2011), edited by Maggie Lemere and Zoë West, includes twenty-two narratives of men and women who lived under Burma's oppressive fifty-year military rule. The book was published just after the country held the first national elections in twenty years, which were viewed by many as an attempt to enshrine and legitimate military rule under a thin veil of democracy. The major opposition party, the National League for Democracy, refused to participate over questions of fairness under the widely criticized new constitution. Later that year, opposition leader Aung San Suu Kyi was released after fifteen years of house arrest.

Picture at right: Mae Sot, Thailand

KYAW ZWAR

AGE WHEN INTERVIEWED: *40*
BORN IN: *Rangoon, Burma*
INTERVIEWED IN: *Mae Sot, Thailand*

We met with Kyaw Zwar in a compound where he works with youth activists. The walls of the compound are covered in graffiti sporting the group's logo, a thumbs-up symbol. Activists strategize for revolution and practice beat-boxing and guitar around the compound (the group also releases music videos and albums). Kyaw Zwar had been released from his second internment as a political prisoner in Burma just weeks before we interviewed him. According to the Assistance Association for Political Prisoners (Burma), as of November 3, 2010, there were 2,203 political prisoners detained in Burma. They include monks, students, musicians, comedians, elected members of parliament, and lawyers.

I WANTED TO LEARN WHAT
THE TRUTH REALLY WAS

If I explained how I became a political organizer, I would have to tell you my whole life story. Ever since 1988, I feel like the military regime took me, put me in a pot, and has been shaking me around. I'd say it's getting worse.

I was born in Rangoon in 1970. I am the youngest person in my family—I have three brothers and four sisters. When I was young, I didn't know about politics, and I was not interested. I felt that I had freedom.

Rangoon is not developed but it is crowded. I would say the place where I lived is beautiful. There are different kinds and classes of people in Rangoon. There are those who are struggling for basic needs, and those working as government personnel in different government departments. My family was middle class. My father sold car parts, my brother sold building supplies for homes, and my sisters sold betel nut.

I went to school in Rangoon. I went from noon to four in the afternoon, and the teachers would take turns instructing us. But sometimes I would run away from school. On those days when my friends and I had some money, we would go to Inya Lake to swim and spend our time there.[1] At the time when school was supposed to end, we would go back home.

My favorite subject in school was history. I didn't like world history when I was young, but I liked learning about Burma's history. We had to learn about Burmese dynasties in the past as well as the English and Japanese eras in Burma. I learned a little bit about the different ethnic groups of Burma in school, but if I wanted to learn more about different ethnicities, I had to read books from outside the country. I wanted to learn what the truth really was.

OUR SOCIALISM WAS NOT LIKE REAL SOCIALISM

When I was eighteen years old, the uprising happened. I still wasn't that interested in politics, but my enthusiasm grew from the anger I felt when I saw the military kill university students.

In 1988, Ne Win was the head of state and he was using the Burmese

---

1. Inya Lake is in Rangoon. On its banks are the elite neighborhoods that contain Daw Aung San Suu Kyi's compound and the late general General Ne Win's residence.

Way to Socialism to control the country.[2] There was only one party in the whole country and he was the head of it. He ruled the country as a dictatorship—our socialism was not like real socialism.

There are many reasons that the protests happened in 1988. One of these is that the Ne Win government put everything under state ownership, and they abolished the currency notes used in the country at the time. The reason they gave was inflation, but they didn't offer most people new currency to replace the old. People were angry. If you had that money, you could just boil it in water—it had no use any longer. Some families and university students just burned it.

My family had quite a lot of money at the time, but after the government declared that we couldn't use it any more, we just gave it to children to play with. To survive, my family could sell off our materials, like car parts and building supplies, but we could not sell a lot. For six months, we struggled. Like everyone, my parents said the government was really bad.

Discontent grew among many of the university students, because they no longer had enough money for tuition, transportation, or food. At the end of every month, their parents would send them money for tuition and daily expenses, but the students could no longer use it. Their discontent became the spark for the '88 uprising.

THEY COULD CHALLENGE HIS POWER

I didn't see the demonstrations in March, but I heard about what was happening because I was near Rangoon. The demonstrations started on March 13. The fighting actually started the day before, when students from the RIT—Rangoon Institute of Technology—got into a big fight with one of the sons of a BSPP official.[3] The students were angry because one

---

2. The Burmese Way to Socialism was Ne Win's plan to build up the Burmese nation after independence.

3. The Burma Socialist Programme Party was the only legal political party in Burma from 1962 to 1988. The party congress met periodically and repeatedly "elected" Ne Win as its chairman.

of them got injured in the fight, but the son of the party official was only detained for a moment by the police and then released. Because of this, the students went to protest on March 13. A clash broke out that night, and a student named Maung Phone Maw was killed.

After those incidents, the students were very angry. On March 16, students from both the RIT and Rangoon University marched together. The students were protesting government oppression, demanding that they investigate the death of Maung Phone Maw and take action against the people who killed him.

Ne Win knew that if he didn't oppress the students, they would be able to challenge his power. That day, the students started marching through Rangoon. When the students were at the bank of Inya Lake, riot police came and aggressively started cracking down on the protest. A lot of students started running into the lake to escape the brutal crackdown, and some of them drowned. The riot police also beat and killed some of the students.

Both male and female students were put inside extremely crowded trucks and transported away. I was in Insein Township and I heard one of the trucks as they went through the city to Insein Prison. The people inside were shouting, "We're all dying inside the truck! We are students— we were unjustly arrested!" I heard they overcrowded that prison truck so much that some people could not breathe and they died of suffocation.[4]

After the March 16 protest, the government closed all of the universities and made all of the students return to their homes. The government didn't want the students to assemble and form organizations.

Although it happened so long ago, we can still feel what happened that day, especially when we are standing at the banks of Inya Lake.

---

4. Forty-one students suffocated to death in the van. This incident became a lightning rod for the student democracy movement.

THE '88 UPRISING

The protests continued throughout March, but everyone stayed quiet in April and May.

The university students left Rangoon and went back to their hometowns to spread news about what had happened. They talked to high school students about the ways the government had oppressed them. The students' feelings were growing even stronger.

When the schools opened again in June, the students formed a demonstration camp at Rangoon University. Young people, including high school students and workers, joined the university students at the demonstration camp and went out on the streets together to protest. They were really angry at the police and wanted action to be taken against those who'd killed the students.

Some students didn't go back to their hometowns and instead stayed in Rangoon so that they could organize protests to bring down the Burma Socialist Programme Party. This was the start of the '88 uprising.

Groups of students were marching, and people joined them. On June 18, 19, and 20 they were marching in the streets, but they were shot at on June 21 in Myaynigone. Some students were killed. More and more groups joined the uprising until everyone was involved. With the force of so many people, combined with their dissatisfaction, the '88 demonstrations became a fight to bring down Ne Win's government.

THE MILITARY SHOT DIRECTLY AT US

In August of 1988, the government started to really crack down.

I marched in Rangoon on August 9 and 10. At the front of the crowd there were monks and students giving speeches. The army and riot police were cracking down on the protesters. The army used guns and the riot police used batons and shields. The police marched and hit the students with the batons at close distance. When using the batons didn't seem to be successful anymore—because some students were able to resist police by throwing stones—the government switched the soldiers who were on duty. Then the army soldiers came close and shot at the students. The soldiers marched forward step by step, firing their guns.

Even though people were really angry, they became very afraid of the consequences for marching, because Ne Win had told the military not to shoot in the air, but to shoot directly at the people.

At the time of the demonstrations, I just helped in general with everything. For example, I took responsibility for providing water and food to demonstrators, and I looked for medicine if it was necessary.

We marched to the sections of the township that were not actively involved in politics yet. We marched in big crowds so that we could encourage the young people to be brave and come join the protests. If the number of people who were marching was small, I'd go around and organize other people to join with us. We also persuaded the women, and eventually they went on to form the women's union and other organizations. Our forces became stronger.

In a lot of places around Rangoon, the soldiers shot and cracked down on the demonstrators. There was also shooting in other states, but it was the worst in Rangoon, because that's where the government was located. Students were shot in front of everyone.

The military coup happened early on September 18, 1988. On that morning, the students marched in the streets. The government cracked down and there were more casualties. The army was deployed everywhere, and martial law and a curfew were declared. During the crackdown, General Saw Maung from the State Law and Order Restoration Council announced that the government would prepare for a multi-party democratic system, and that it would allow parties to register. Eventually we saw political parties come out to register. But while organizing the parties, some of the party leaders were arrested.

I don't know how other people felt at the time, but I was very angry. I felt like I was one of the students. My own discontent began there.

I DID NOT FEAR ANYTHING

You could say that the first time I started to have real political views and knowledge was during the uprising in 1988, when I started to listen to speeches by Min Ko Naing, the leader of student groups in Burma—the All Burma Federation of Student Unions.[5] In the '88 demonstrations, Min Ko Niang persuasion, organization, and the firm path he took made him a really worthy leader.

The ABFSU has a long history. It was originally formed by General Aung San, and was involved in the struggle against colonialism.[6] Under Ne Win's regime, the ABFSU became active again. Then Ne Win abolished the ABFSU and bombed their office. He targeted the student groups because they produced all of the educated people and politicians who resisted him.

After the military coup, there was no more marching, and I had to become involved in the democracy movement in different ways. After high school, I could not continue my education and go on to university because all of the schools and universities were closed by the government in response to the uprising. I thought about what to do next. Many of the people who were involved in the protests were National League for Democracy members, so I contacted the party.[7] Older party members gave me books to read, so I began to have more ideas about politics.

I decided that I wanted to work with the NLD youth. I submitted an application to the NLD and I was accepted as a member and an organizer. After the coup, we needed to be part of organizations in order to increase our political power.

I started going to Daw Aung San Suu Kyi's compound on January 1,

---

5. The All Burma Federation of Student Unions traces its roots back to the 1930s, but reemerged during the 1988 uprising under the leadership of Min Ko Naing.

6. General Aung San is Burma's independence hero who led the fight against British rule. He is the father of Nobel Peace Prize winner Daw Aung San Suu Kyi.

7. The National League for Democracy is the party of Nobel Prize winner Daw Aung San Suu Kyi and former Tatmadaw Commander-in-Chief U Tin Oo. The NLD won Burma's 1990 elections.

1989. We met at her compound every week and discussed young people's issues and the political situation in Burma. When she had free time, she would tell the students to choose a discussion topic. At the time, there were about twenty or thirty students going there. Sometimes she told the young students about international and Burmese politics.

Sometimes I went to her compound once or twice in a week, and sometimes I slept there for two or three nights. I visited the compound for a few months and then I left in July. What I cannot forget is how Daw Aung San Suu Kyi gave encouragement to the young people when we felt unhappy. She always steered us the right way.

Daw Aung San Suu Kyi has influenced me more than anyone else. She does what she believes in, and she never gives up. She always told us that the young people must take leadership roles and that other people must open a door for young people to bring changes in the country. That is my best memory.

At the time, my family was worried for me, because if you are involved in politics in Burma, if you work with the ABSFU or if you meet with Daw Aung San Suu Kyi, you will very likely be imprisoned. The more active you are, the more you're at risk. They didn't want me to be involved in politics. When I returned home in the evenings, my mother would say, "Come and stay with the family. Stop your political work." She cried and explained her feelings to me, but I didn't want to listen to her. I continued participating because I had hope and enthusiasm.

I did not fear anything at the time. Everyone has their own personal problems, right? I didn't care about mine. I just wanted to be involved in politics because I wanted there to be change.

I THOUGHT THEY WOULD
DESTROY MY FUTURE

Daw Aung San Suu Kyi was put under house arrest on July 20, 1989. At the time I was working at the NLD office in Insein Township, and I was responsible for youth and information. In August, I was arrested because I'd organized people to ask for Daw Aung San Suu Kyi's and her deputy U Tin Oo's release. When they arrested me, I felt like the government destroyed my enthusiasm.

On that day, there were seventy young people in the office. We heard that the army would come to arrest us and we didn't want everyone to get arrested, so we asked many of them to leave. But when the army surrounded our office, there were eight leaders still inside.

Four trucks full of soldiers came to the office. There were about thirty or forty soldiers. They came in the office and destroyed our signboards that asked for Daw Aung San Suu Kyi and U Tin Oo's release. They also broke the NLD flagpole, they broke the windows, and they threw our papers on the floor. They insulted us and called us names like "motherfuckers." They said, "Who are you? What are you doing? Even if I kill you, I won't lose my position—I'll get promoted."

We replied, "We have an agreement with the government that we can have this office, so you cannot come in here violently and destroy it. If you want to arrest people, you must have the order to arrest, and then you can come in and make the arrests." They closed the office and arrested all eight of us and put us in a truck.

At nineteen years old, I was the youngest activist. The other arrested NLD members were in their twenties, up to about forty years old. When they put me in the truck I wondered, *What will happen to me? Maybe they will take me to interrogation, and then they will beat me or kill me.* I was very worried—I was sweating, you know. I thought they would torture me until I became handicapped and destroy my future. I was also very worried about my mother, because I thought she would feel bad about my arrest and that the condition of her heart would deteriorate.

It was only forty-five minutes in the truck to the interrogation center at Insein Prison. The rest of the NLD members encouraged me, saying, "Don't worry, they will not kill us. They cannot kill us." They tried to make me feel better. I felt encouraged when they said those words.

When we first arrived at the interrogation camp at Insein Prison, we were separated. Each person was handcuffed and taken to a separate room. My body and my head were tied to a post with a rubber rope. I had to squat down with my knees apart and my bottom in the air. Then they put a water container over my head. It had very little holes in it that water dripped through. The water dripped and dripped and dripped, hitting my head. After five minutes it felt like bricks were falling into my head—it was very painful, and hard to endure.

Under my feet there were two needles, so I had to squat down and put my feet out a little bit. If I put my feet down under my body, the needles could pierce my feet and go into my muscle. My thighs became very rigid and very hot because I had to squat down for so long. Sometimes I fell down to the floor and they kicked me.

They would ask me things like, "Did someone tell you to call for Daw Aung San Suu Kyi and U Tin Oo's release, or was this your own idea?" I responded that our eight leaders decided by ourselves and that we implemented it. I didn't mention the other seventy people involved so they wouldn't be beaten. The eight of us took full responsibility. Other people may think that we were very courageous for answering their questions in this way, but we had to do it. We had to accept the difficulties we would experience. If we answered in any other way, other people would also have gotten in trouble.

I had to stay in the squatting position while they interrogated me. If I responded that I didn't know or if I lied to them, they would ask me the questions over and over again until I gave them an answer.

I was in the interrogation camp for eight days.

SIX YEARS WITH HARD LABOR

After they finished with us at the interrogation camp, we were sent to the military court. I saw the other leaders there, and we were so happy to see that nobody had died.

When we arrived at the military courtroom, all the jury members were in military uniform. I was not able to speak at my trial, and we weren't allowed to hire lawyers. I knew I had no hope of escape, no hope of being released.

The trial took only around half an hour. After fifteen minutes, the judge stopped the trial for another fifteen minutes and then came out and opened the envelopes. He read everyone's names. Then the judge said, "Under emergency law, you are charged with destroying the state." Everyone was sentenced to six years with hard labor.

My mother came to the trial. As I was being taken away she came out to see me on the street. I was in the military truck and my mother was only a few feet away. She mouthed to me, "How many years?" I raised six fingers. She seemed fine, and she asked, "Is that six months?" But when I said, "It's six years," she was so shocked she fell down. That is my most unforgettable memory of that day.

IT WAS LIKE MY MOUTH WAS SEWN SHUT

When I was put in Insein prison, the officers said to us, "If you are in prison, you become a prisoner. No one is a *political* prisoner here. Every prisoner has to work. You have to do the work that we order you to do." We replied, "We are here for our country. We didn't commit any crimes or steal anything. We have our dignity and we cannot do this kind of work."

When they tried to force us to work, we went on a hunger strike. There were forty-nine political prisoners. At first they told us that if we didn't do the work, they would take us somewhere to meet with higher prison officials. But instead they put us in an isolated room that was dark and dirty, and they beat us.

One and a half months after our isolation started, we were allowed to see our families. When my family came, I went out of the room to see them. But there were two sets of iron bars separating me from my family. I had fifteen minutes to meet with them. I was allowed to talk about family, but not politics—if I talked about prison conditions then I would be put into the dark room again, or my family visits would be canceled. A prison worker accompanied my family during the visit and recorded what we were saying on a piece of paper. They do that for every political prisoner, but not for the other prisoners. I really wanted to say more to my family, but it was like my mouth was sewn shut.

When prison staff or officers got drunk, they would verbally abuse prisoners like me. We asked the other prison staff to take action against these abusive officers. We did another hunger strike, refusing to accept our meals if they didn't take action against them. The hunger strike lasted four days. They put us in the dark room and kept telling us, "We will take action against those people who are not cooperating!" We talked to each other and decided not to oppose them any longer because people would die. The prison staff didn't care what happened to us, so it would have been useless if one of us died in prison.

After twenty days in the dark room, we were taken to Tharrawaddy Prison in Pegu Division. We had spent over a month in Insein Prison.

WE HAVE TO RESIST THE TORTURE TOGETHER

Tharrawaddy Prison was strange to me. When I arrived, they asked us to do hard labor in the prison compound. They made the prisoners smash stones, dig the earth, or carry waste from their toilets. There were two hundred political prisoners there, including older people who couldn't do hard labor. The prison officers said they would punish us if we did not do it, so all the younger political prisoners got together, and ninety-seven of us decided to resist their orders. We knew that we could be beaten to death.

I didn't think about my family or my country at the time. Instead, I just kept thinking, *We have to work together. We have to resist the torture together.*

When the prison worker came and told us to do the hard labor, we said we wouldn't do it. We told him we wanted to meet the prison officer. Then the prison officer came to us and said, "Whoever is not willing to do hard labor, leave the room." Ninety-seven of us left the room, and the prison officer said he would send a senior prison officer to meet with us.

We were separated into groups of five, and then they put each group in a different cell. They asked us to sit with our hands on top of our heads. After more than an hour, around seventy prison staff came into the compound and poured water into our cells. It was December and it was very cold. They didn't give us blankets—we would have to sleep on the cold, wet floor.

About half an hour after they poured the water into the cells, they took us outside and told us to sit on the ground with our hands on our heads again. The five of us sat in a line and three prison staff stood behind us and started beating and kicking us. They used canes and rubber sticks, and they beat our waists, our backs, and the back of our necks. Tharrawaddy Prison is in a field, so no one can hear when you scream or shout.

They beat us so much, and then they made us walk on our knees and elbows back to our rooms. When we got back to the room, ten of the prison staff came into our room and beat us again, for two or three hours. They said it was because we refused their orders. The prison officer told us, "It doesn't matter if we beat you to death."

They would come and pour water into our rooms three times a day, morning, noon, and night. They beat us a lot—I had bruises on my body, and my waist was in pain as the weather got colder. People had other kinds of injuries, and some people were vomiting blood. One of my friends was disabled and used a cane to walk, but they tortured him just as badly as the rest of us. Another friend of mine was paralyzed from the waist down because of the beatings. Two months after they beat me, my lungs became swollen.

After beating us for the first two weeks, they lessened the punishment and forced us to stay in squatting positions for the rest of the month. They made us squat with our bottoms in the air and our hands on our heads for a long time. It was very hard—our legs got tired, and we had to keep our hands very straight on our heads so that our arms were straight over our shoulders. If we got tired and moved at all, they would say, "Which hand or leg is tired? Give me your hand or leg." Then they would beat that hand or leg. Sometimes we would move around if we didn't hear the guards' footsteps outside, but sometimes we got caught. We had to sit in that position from seven a.m. until we ate lunch at eleven a.m., then from one p.m. until four p.m., then again after dinner from six p.m. until nine p.m. We weren't allowed to talk to anyone. The senior-level government people are responsible for this torture, because the prison staff has to follow their orders.

WE WROTE POEMS

While we were in the prison, we were not allowed to read or to write. All we could do every day was sit in the positions they told us to, eat, and sleep. We became so tired of our lives.

Sometimes we would talk about politics with our friends, and sometimes we would debate why we weren't successful in '88, but we were really tired every day. We wanted to read, and we wanted to know about what was happening in the country. Whenever my family or other families came to visit, they brought us cheroots, a kind of Burmese cigarette. The cigarettes were rolled into pieces of newspaper, so we would unroll the cigarettes and take out the newspaper pieces. Then we'd soak them in water to be able to see the letters and the words in the news. We'd read the clippings and discuss them with our friends. But we could never know exactly what the real news was because the pieces were very small.

Sometimes we wanted to write poems, but we didn't have any pens or paper, so we tried to make clay boards. During the day we were allowed to go out at bathing time for two hours. We'd take clay from next to the bathing area and make it flat. The walls inside the prison were painted with limestone, so we soaked the powder off the limestone with water and then we applied it to the clay. After that, we used nails to write on it.

My friends and I made a patrol for the security staff. If the security staff was coming, the patrol person would raise the alarm so we would all know, and we'd hide the clay boards.

We wrote poems, but if they saw that we were writing, they'd put us in the dark room and punish us. I wrote about my life experience. For example, I wrote about the moment when I had to depart from my mother. Or sometimes if I remembered my girlfriends, I would write songs. After we wrote something, we'd share with our friends. We'd read our poems and songs to each other, but then we had to erase them.

When I was in prison I heard my mother had been hospitalized. I felt very bad when I heard that, like I wanted to do something to myself. I thought that my mother's health condition was because of me, and I felt I didn't deserve to live any more. At that time, we were given blankets—I had plans to use mine to hang myself.

I told one of my friends about my feelings and asked him to do some things for me if I died. My friend felt very bad about what I wanted to do. I asked him not to tell other people, but he did. My friends started to watch me, to make sure I was okay. Even when I was sleeping, some of them would stay awake to watch me. They told me that I had to think about how I was working for our country, how it was not bad to do political work. One of my friends came and encouraged me, "You didn't do anything bad to your mother, so calm down. Killing yourself is against our religion. You are doing a good thing for the country." All those things encouraged me.

Then my mother got better. We all had a common problem while we were in prison. We suffered mental problems. We had to think a lot. Sometimes we felt happy, smiling and joking around with our friends or while remembering our past. But sometimes we would remember our mothers, and then we would cry. We thought a lot about our families and friends. We thought about the times when we were in school. So it created mental problems for us, you know?

THE WARMEST PLACE

I was released from prison in 1994. In Burmese we have a saying: "The day you are released from prison and the day you get married are the happiest times in your life." But I was not happy when I was released from prison because I knew that a lot of my friends would still be in there.

When I was released from prison I could not sleep alone any more. At night, I would go and sleep with my mother, because being with her feels like the warmest and safest place in my life.

When I slept, I'd dream about my experience in the prison. Sometimes I would wake up suddenly and I would shout a lot. My family would come and say, "What happened to you?"

I also had problems when people shut doors loudly, because the prison staff usually slammed the doors of the cells when they locked them. When I was in my house and my nephew slammed the door very loudly, it would upset something in my mind. I would go and beat my nephew, even though he was very small. I can see how my mind was affected.

When I came out from prison, sometimes I didn't want to talk to my friends. I would go and sit in a quiet place and I would think about my time in school, my friends, and my family. If we compare ourselves to ordinary people it's not obvious, but we former prisoners suffer from mental problems. Some of us become addicted to drugs and alcohol.

Sometimes I thought about changing my enthusiasm for politics and just relaxing. I saw my friends who were fairly successful in business, and I thought about becoming like them. But it was only thoughts; I still had the passion to fight for change in my country.

I FELT FURTHER AND FURTHER
OUTSIDE OF SOCIETY

In Burma, people discriminate against those who have been in prison. They talk about "the kind of people" who have been in there. When I walked around, my neighbors and anybody who wasn't involved in politics would not talk to me. I thought, *Why do they treat me this way? I went to prison for these people.* It was very, very painful.

I had one friend I'd been close with since we were kids. We went to school together and I would visit his home. His mother was very friendly, and his home felt like my home—I have very good memories of that. But when I got out of prison and went to visit him, his mother told me that even though I used to be friends with her son, I couldn't visit her house because I had done something against the government. The military intelligence was following me and keeping track of what I did, so if I talked to her son, her son might get in trouble and could be arrested.

Sometimes I would think about my place in life. I was working for these people, but as time passed by I felt further and further outside of society. The main reason people act like this is fear. Fear is also the main reason we can't get democracy—that's why Daw Aung San Suu Kyi tells people to be free from fear. The young people in Burma are afraid of the government, and they dare not oppose it. But the government should be afraid of the young people, because throughout history young people have been a very powerful force. Young people should not be afraid. All real thinking has been taken out from the youths' brains. They only think, *We have to struggle, we have to get money, we have to eat.* If you go to Burma, you will see that a lot of children are illiterate. Children work as waiters, young boys sell lottery tickets and work as agents in soccer gambling. In Thailand, I've witnessed children from Burma working on construction sites; I've seen small girls sewing. I think these children should be going to school. But they don't have opportunities to learn.

If the young people become educated, I believe that the new generation has the power to change the government—but it will take time. I've been working with young activists, and I know they have power and they care.

I RAN AWAY TO ANOTHER PLACE

I began to talk to my other friends who had been released from prison. We discussed doing something about politics, because the political situation at the time was very quiet, very calm. We wanted to hold a literature discussion so that people would read about politics.

As we were working to organize the literature discussion in December that year, two new activists that worked with us got arrested. Because of this, some of my friends also got arrested and the police went to my house and asked my mother about me. My mother told me not to come back home because I could be arrested too. My family gave me money to run away.

I ran away to Kawthaung, which is a town in the Tenasserim Division in southern Burma. I had no money left so I had to do some manual labor there. I wasn't able to work as hard as the owner wanted, so he forced me to quit after the first day. This place was new for me and not like Rangoon; I felt very depressed. Then I went to Thailand to try and survive. It felt like a different world to me. In the beginning I got trafficked in Chumphon. I was sold to a manager of a pig farm, but I escaped after three weeks.

I spent about thirteen years there, staying in many different places— Ranong, Chumphon, Phuket, Nakhon, Phang Nga, and then Bangkok. I took jobs as they came because I had to survive.

I did some work in restaurants, hotels, fishing boats, and construction. I even started a business with a friend, making steel buckles, but we didn't always make a profit. I did all those things just to be able to survive, but they didn't give me any satisfaction.

I was drinking a lot throughout my time in Thailand. At the time I was very depressed. I missed home and I thought my life was useless.

Sometimes when I drank, I would remember my family or maybe my colleagues in prison. In 2005, my father passed away. My auntie told me

KYAW ZWAR

on the phone when I was in Bangkok, but it wasn't possible for me to see my family. I had my family, my community, my country—but I wasn't allowed to stay there. Living in Thailand, I felt like I was outside society. The whole time I was in Thailand, I was very depressed by the situation in Burma. Even though I had done a lot of political work, it hadn't been successful. And I wasn't in contact with any of my former political colleagues from Burma who were staying in Thailand. I didn't believe that change could come to Burma unless it was done by people who were inside the country, in direct contact with the government. But in 2007, the Saffron Revolution was a big push. It revived my urge to join politics.[8]

I was at a restaurant in Bangkok when I ran into one of my close friends from prison. The UNHCR had resettled him to the U.S. after he'd lived in the refugee camps, and he was visiting on his U.S. passport.[9] I had tried to avoid seeing him in Bangkok, because I didn't want him to ask me, "What are you doing now? Are you working for your country?" But we started talking and he encouraged me to do political work again. We discussed politics over three days, and we talked about the politics inside and outside Burma. He said, "The young people are working for politics in Burma. They are trying their best, so we shouldn't avoid this—we should cooperate."

My friend had an office in Mae Sot, on the Thailand–Burma border, and he told me to go there and start working in politics again. When I arrived in Mae Sot I saw some of my other activist friends and I felt very encouraged. Even though it was very dangerous for me to go to Burma, I wanted change in my country. I had hope that the Saffron Revolution marches would bring change, so I decided to go back and join the protest.

8. The Saffron Revolution was a large, monk-led uprising that took place in August and September of 2007.

9. The Office of the UN High Commissioner for Refugees is a United Nations organization with headquarters in Geneva, Switzerland. The primary mandate of UNHCR is the protection of refugees and finding durable solutions for refugees, including assisting in the voluntary repatriation of refugees to their home country, integration into the country of asylum, or resettling refugees to a third country.

WE WOULD TRY AGAIN

When I was at the border checkpoint between Mae Sot and Myawaddy, I tore my passport apart and then I crossed the water into Burma.[10] It was my first time returning to Burma in thirteen years. Although I expected the worst, I decided I would just face whatever happened to me.

I left Thailand on September 24 and I arrived in Rangoon two days later on September 26. I didn't go and see my family because my name was on the government blacklist. The blacklist has all the names of people the government considers to be destroyers of the state, guilty of causing riots and unrest. I could have been arrested if I went back to my home.

I had contacted my friends to get involved in the uprising, but the military was already cracking down heavily and arresting people. People couldn't go out in the street. I was sad that people were not in the streets any more, but I was not disappointed. I thought if we could not do it this time, then we would try again. I couldn't join in the protest movement above ground then, because I knew some of my friends had been arrested, and information threatening my security would probably leak from them. So I retreated. Some of my friends were in hiding too. We discussed how to reorganize the scattered democracy groups.

I helped organize with the people I knew from before. I helped people avoid arrest and suggested places for people to hide. I was also trying to connect the people I knew with other activist networks, to make sure they all worked together. Then I set up my own network with our young people.

When I went back to Rangoon, it took me one month to look for and join my friends who had gone into hiding. I rented an apartment there because I wanted to see if the situation would change, but nothing did, so I spent three months figuring out how to travel around Rangoon safely.

---

10. Myawaddy is a town on the Burma side of the Moei River, which divides Thailand and Burma. It is one of several official border-crossing points between the two countries.

I also rented three or four apartments that my friends and I could stay in to avoid arrest. I stayed in Rangoon from September until December.

I returned to Thailand in December for a training about leadership and nonviolence. I saw some of my old friends again and we discussed some of the next activities that we would launch inside Burma.

A NEW WAVE

I went back to Burma in the first week of January 2008 to plan some special events for Independence Day and to do campaigns on Union Day with Generation Wave.[11] Generation Wave is an organization of young activists that had been set up after the Saffron Revolution. I wasn't involved with them when the organization first formed, but one of my old activist friends told me I should work with them because I was young. The name is Generation Wave because we already had the '88 generation, and we wanted to create a new movement, a new generation with powerful force. We decided to organize a protest that would take place in March, so we contacted our friends in Rangoon to organize with them.

But when we were ready for the protest, some of our friends were arrested, so we had to go into hiding in Rangoon Division. Zayar Thaw, a hip-hop singer in Burma, was arrested, and a lot of the Generation Wave members were arrested too. So I had to avoid arrest and went into hiding. When my friends got arrested, our force was brought down.

My friend whom I lived with got arrested when he went to meet with the ABFSU. He wasn't known as a Generation Wave member, but when he was tortured at the detention camp, he leaked some information. My friend couldn't resist the torture and revealed information about the protest and where we were living.

When we got the news about this, we had to leave our apartments.

11. Union Day is celebrated on the anniversary of the signing of the Panglong Agreement, an agreement between General Aung San and a number of Burma's ethnic groups that they would work together in an independent, federated Burma.

The plan for a protest in March was canceled. We called all our friends and sent them to stay in places very far from Rangoon; we couldn't tell anyone where we sent them. I ran away to Pegu Division for a month.

During that time, I had to move around. In the morning, I might be in one place, but that night I would sleep in another place. I contacted some friends I had worked with before. The Saffron Revolution anniversary was approaching, so my friends and I discussed what we should do to prepare. I couldn't go to see my friends, so I contacted them on the phone. I also talked to groups like the ABFSU so that we could cooperate with each other. I was very careful not to be arrested, because I knew that if I ended up in prison I would face the worst possible situation.

Then I returned to Rangoon in April, and the members of Generation Wave came together. In May, Cyclone Nargis happened, and we went to help the Nargis victims with things like food, water, and accommodations. We continued helping until July, and then we started to plan a demonstration for September 2008. In July, I went back to Thailand for a training with some other Generation Wave members. After it finished, we returned to Burma, held trainings locally, and increased our membership.

I work with Generation Wave because I want young people to have new ways of thinking and taking action. I came into politics when I was young; sometimes young people want to do something, but adults become a barrier for them. Our country's situation has become worse; it is not like other countries. Everything is very restricted, even if you just want to go from here to there. I was nineteen when I went to prison and twenty-four when I got out, but I still had to promise my mother that I would be home by seven p.m.

"ARE YOU KYAW ZWAR FROM GENERATION WAVE?"

We discussed our plans for a September demonstration with monks and with the ABFSU. One evening in early September, I got a phone call from a man whom I had already met about the demonstration. His group had a lot of members, and we needed their help in launching the event. He wanted to meet the next day. Even though I was feeling uncomfortable, the next morning I went to meet him at a tea shop.

Before I left, I told three Generation Wave members to come and watch our meeting from a distance. The man was already there when I arrived. When I ordered a coffee, three people came up to me from behind, and four people approached from the front. They asked, "Are you Kyaw Zwar from Generation Wave?" They already knew who I was. They were plain-clothes police who had been pretending to sell newspapers and pretending to be waiters. The man who called me to arrange the meeting must have been tortured a lot in prison—the police made him do it.

I was sent to an interrogation center for a month. When I was in the interrogation center, the prison staff tortured me to get information on Generation Wave, and on who was involved in the protest. I didn't tell them anything important. I was beaten, and I endured the pain. They didn't give me any food or water. I had to drink water from the toilets.

I was taken to court for my trial. I was charged with crossing the border illegally, having contact with illegal organizations, and forming a group, through establishing Generation Wave. It wasn't a military courtroom and I was allowed to have a lawyer and witnesses, but the prosecution also had a lawyer and witnesses, and I lost.

In October, I was sent to Insein Prison again. On the day when I was brought to the prison, my family came to meet me. "We don't know what you are doing," said my mother. "Son, I am only able to see you when you're in prison."

I got sick during my second time in prison. I had a very high fever.

If I asked for medicine in the prison, they only gave paracetamol, so I had to ask my family to send medicine. There were some political prisoners who were doctors, so they told me what medicine I needed. My second time in prison, I wasn't asked to do forced labor and I was allowed to go out of isolation for an hour every day. The political prisoners were still very united. We read books and discussed Burma's current political situation.

SOMETIMES WE THINK WE'RE CRAZY

I was released in September 2009. I saw that my friends all had happy families. I felt really discouraged, and I thought, *I don't have a family. I have nothing now.* But I tried to calm myself by remembering that I was doing this work for my country. If I want to do this kind of work, I need to forget other things. Even if there is someone I love, I have to stay far away. I need to make sacrifices.

If Burma gained democracy, I would not stay away from my family and live in another country. I would establish my life, do things for myself personally. But it is difficult to think about how I would do this. Ever since I got involved in politics, I haven't been able to think about anything else—it has changed me. I can't think about the future any more.

Sometimes we think we're crazy. But we have hope, and we continue working toward our goal. I've met other politicians, our brothers, who have forgotten their goals and are living a relaxing life. But I cannot leave this work because I want my friends to be free. My friends are in the prisons. Now I sit here, in Thailand—I am free, and I want my friends to be free as well. That's why I cannot leave this work. I want to fight for my friends.

Since I am forty years old, I cannot be a member of Generation Wave any more—the age limit is actually thirty-five years old. But I have plans to continue working as an activist. We don't accept the constitution, so we will continue to fight against it. The government will do what it wants in the 2010 elections, so we need to fight against it all the time.

I haven't had a chance to see my family, and when my father died I could not go to his funeral. I have been away from my family for so long that I am not sure what my mother is like any more. People like me, who are more active and want change, we suffer the most—the government shakes our lives the most.

_____

Since 2011, reforms have slowly been implemented in Burma, including the release of some political prisoners, the relaxation of media censorship, and the further opening of the country to international investment. Burmese can exercise significantly more freedom of expression regarding political views, though activists and media workers are still threatened and arrested unjustly. Moreover, Burma's military remains in open conflict with some of the country's armed ethnic opposition groups, and has targeted ethnic minority civilians. The government also continues to deny citizenship to, and to systemically oppress, the Rohingya, a Muslim ethnic minority group.

Patriot Acts: Narratives of Post-9/11 Injustice (2011), edited by Alia Malek, collects narratives of individuals in the U.S. who, after September 11, 2001, were needlessly swept up in the War on Terror and found themselves subjected to a wide range of human and civil rights abuses, from arbitrary arrests and torture to workplace discrimination, bullying, FBI surveillance, and harassment. The interviews for this book were conducted leading up to the tenth anniversary of 9/11.

ADAMA BAH

AGE WHEN INTERVIEWED: *23*

BORN IN: *Koubia, Guinea*

INTERVIEWED IN: *East Harlem, New York City*

On March 24, 2005, Adama Bah, a sixteen-year-old Muslim girl, awoke at dawn to discover nearly a dozen armed FBI agents inside her family's apartment in East Harlem. They arrested her and her father, Mamadou Bah, and transported them to separate detention facilities. A government document leaked to the press claimed that Adama was a potential suicide bomber but failed to provide any evidence to support this claim. Released after six weeks in detention, Adama was forced to live under partial house arrest with an ankle bracelet, a government-enforced curfew, and a court-issued gag order that prohibited her from speaking about her case. In August of 2006, Adama's father was deported back to Guinea, Africa. Adama, who had traveled to the United States with her parents from Guinea as a child, also found herself facing deportation. She would spend the next few years fighting for asylum and struggling to support her family in the United States and Guinea.

WE ALL DID IT?

I didn't know I wasn't an American until I was sixteen and in handcuffs.

I came to the United States with my mother in 1990, the year I turned two. We originally came from Koubia in Guinea, West Africa. My dad was here already, living in Brooklyn and working as a cab driver. He went on to open his own business later.

Then came my brother, who is now nineteen, my sister, who is seventeen, and two more brothers who are thirteen and five. I'm twenty-three. We moved to this apartment in Manhattan, and we've been living here for thirteen years.

I think a lot of people in Africa and third-world countries hear about the riches in America. It's the land of opportunity. So my dad came here for that. From the stories that my mom tells me, their lives back in Koubia were farming and that's it.

Growing up in New York, I remember having many "cousins" around. They're all Guinean. They weren't real family, but whatever community members we had here, I considered them family. I remember having them come over, I remember us running around and messing up things.

My friends were Latino and African-American. At that time, I fit in with them. I was going through the same issues as them, like boys, going through puberty, he said/she said kinds of things. Those were the kinds of problems that I wish I had now.

I went to public school until seventh grade. My dad wanted me to learn about my religion, so he sent me to an Islamic boarding school in Buffalo, New York. What's weird now that I look back is that my parents aren't really religious, we didn't really go to mosque. But my dad heard about the school from somebody who recommended it.

I was thirteen when 9/11 happened. Every teacher came in late, and they sat us in a humongous circle. My teacher said, "I have to talk to you guys. For those of you who are from New York, I want you to brace yourselves. I have some bad news. Sometimes things happen in life that we don't understand." She started telling us about God and how to be patient and steadfast. And then she said, "The Twin Towers were hit today."

I remember freaking out, panicking, trying to reach my family.

And then she called us back for a second meeting, that's when she announced that a Muslim might have done it, and that there might be hatred against Muslims. When I heard that, I was like, "Wait, what do you mean? We all did it? We didn't plot it. I don't have nothing to do with it. Why are we all getting the blame for it?" So many thoughts went through my head that time: *Who is this Osama bin Laden guy? What is he up to? Why would he do this? This is against Islam.* None of us knew who bin Laden was. We were making jokes about the guy. My friends said, "Your name is very close to his name: Adama, Osama."

When I finally reached my family the next day, they told me they were fine, and my dad said, "*Shh*, don't even talk about it. Be quiet, bye." He would not talk about anything over the phone.

THE WAY I LEFT NEW YORK CITY WAS NOT THE WAY IT WAS WHEN I CAME BACK

I felt 9/11 when I came back to New York for Ramadan break.[1] There were six of us classmates who had to get on a plane to come back to New York. At that time, we covered our faces. I remember coming to the airport dressed all in pitch black with our faces covered. We were even wearing gloves; all you could see were our eyes, that's it.

I couldn't believe the looks on the everyone's faces. Everybody was scared, pointing. You saw people turn red. We were whispering to each other, "What's going on?" Honestly, I was scared. I thought those people were going to beat me.

We didn't know what was going on around the country. We didn't

---

1. A holy month of the Islamic calendar that Muslims observe by fasting between sunrise and sunset.

know about the hate crimes—we didn't know anything, though the day after 9/11 someone threw a rock through the window of the school.

That day at the airport, we were given extra screenings, our bags were checked, we got pulled to the side. The guards were so nasty to us, the people were so nasty to us, the airline was so nasty to us. I remember us boarding the plane and the captain looked at us and shook his head.

It made me feel like crap because I was being singled out. I'm thirteen, I've never been through something like this. I've never had racism directed toward me before. I've been sheltered from things like that. So, that was my first time. People cursed at us, yelled at us, and sucked their teeth, saying, "Go back to your country, you Talibani, go back to Osama bin Laden."

This whole time, I thought I was American. I thought, *You can't touch me, I'm American.*

My parents didn't know I wore any garb until I came home. My mom opened the door, she saw me, and she closed it back. She told my father, "You have to tell her to take this off. I told you not to send her to Buffalo!"

They disapproved of my *niqab*.[2] They said to me, "Take that off, take that off."

When I originally left New York City for school, it was peaceful and happy and everybody was cheery and saying hello. When I came back after 9/11, everyone was like, "What do you want, where are you from?" There was more fear. The fear was toward me, and I felt the same way. People didn't take the time to talk to me, or ask me why I was wearing a niqab. Walking down the street, people would curse at me, they would even throw things. It was just nasty. It actually made me want to wear it more.

---

2. A type of face veil.

OH, YOU'RE NOT UGLY

I came back to New York public school for ninth grade. I left the Islamic school because I didn't like it much. I remember telling my dad, "I'm too controlled there." I wore my niqab for a few months with colored contacts to make the niqab look pretty. Might as well make something look pretty.If you can't see my face, look at my nice eyes! But it was actually fun. I didn't have any problems in high school. The other kids always asked me to see my face, though. Like, "I wonder how you look under there? You're probably ugly." We would make jokes about it. I'd say, "Yeah, I look hideous. That's why I always wear it, of course!" Then, after a while, I thought, *This is not a mosque.* So in the middle of ninth grade, I took it off, because you know what? This niqab is not a must. It's really not.

So one day I walked into school, I was still wearing an *abaya*, but I had my face uncovered.[3] My teacher just looked at me and said, "Adama?" And I remember all the students just coming in to look at me, in the middle of English class, to see what I looked like.

They said things like, "Oh, you're not ugly! You have nice teeth."

I replied, "Thank you." I was just smiling.

WHAT DID I DO?

The morning of March 24, 2005, my family and I were in the house, sleeping. Someone knocked on the door, and my mom woke up and went and opened it. These men barged in, waking us up. I always sleep with the blanket over my head. They pull the blanket off my head, I look up, I see a man. He said, "You've got to get out!" I'm like, *What the hell, what's going on?*

I saw about ten to fifteen people in our apartment and right outside our door in the hallway. They were mostly men, but there were also two women. Some had FBI jackets, and others were from the police department

---

3. A loose robe, usually worn with a *hijab* (head scarf).

and the DHS.[4] We were all forced out of the bed and told to sit in the living room. They were going through papers, throwing stuff around, yelling and talking to each other, then whispering. I heard them yelling at my mother in the background, and my mom can't speak much English, and they were pulling her into the kitchen, yelling at her, "We're going to deport you and your whole family!"

This whole time, I was thinking, *What's going on? What are they talking about?* I knew my dad had an issue with his papers, but I didn't think that my mom did. They kept saying, "We're going to send all of you back to your country."

Then I saw my dad walking in, in handcuffs. They had gone to the mosque to get him. It was the scariest thing you could ever see; I had just never seen my father so powerless. He was always this guy whom you didn't mess with. If he said do it, you did it. He was just someone you didn't cross paths with.

They took him to the kitchen, whispered something to him.

He sat down, looked at us. He said, "Everything's going to be fine, don't worry."

And then I knew nothing was fine, I knew something was wrong. They told him to tell us what was going on. He told us that they were going to arrest him and they were going to take him away.

The FBI agents told me to get up and get my sneakers. I was thinking they wanted to see my sneaker collection. I have all types of colors of sneakers. I went and grabbed them. I said, "I have this one, I have this one, I have this one."

One of the agents said, "Choose one."

My favorite color is blue, so I picked up a blue pair and told the agent, "This one."

He said, "Put them on."

I said, "Okay, but I know they fit me."

---

4. The Department of Homeland Security.

He said, "Put them on!" He was very nasty. Then he said, "All those earrings have to go out." I have eight piercings on each side, a nose ring, and also a tongue ring. I went to the kitchen to take them off, and they followed me in there.

My breath was stinking. So I asked, "Can I at least brush my teeth? My breath stinks really bad. Can I use the bathroom?"

They said, "No. We have to go. You're coming with us."

I said, "Where am I going to go? Am I going with my dad?" I put on my jacket. They let me put my head scarf and abaya on. Then one of the women took out handcuffs. I panicked so badly, I was stuttering, "What did I do? Where are we going?"

First time in my life, I'm sixteen years old, in handcuffs. I looked at my dad, and he said, "Just do what they say."

My mom didn't know I was going. When we got out the door, she said, "Where she go? Where she go?" The agents said, "We're taking her," and they held my mom back. The man who seemed to be in charge put his hands on my mother to stop her.

They took me and my dad and put us in the same car. I was scared. I said to him, "What's going on? What's going to happen?" My dad said, "Don't say anything, we're going to get a lawyer. It's okay, everything is going to be fine."

There were two Escalades driving with us. I was looking around, paying attention. I recognized the Brooklyn Bridge, I recognized a lot of landmarks, but I didn't recognize the building where my father and I were taken. We got out of the car and we walked past a security booth where the cars drive up to, before taking a ramp beneath the building to the parking lot. Once we were inside the building, they put me in my own cell. It was white, with a bench. No bars. No windows. There was a door that had a tiny glass pane, and I could see who was out there. I just saw a bunch of computers and tables, and people walking back and forth and talking. I kept seeing them talk to my dad.

I don't know how long I was in there. I was nervous, I was panicking,

I was crying, I was trying to figure out what was going on. And I was constantly using the bathroom.

The toilet was an open toilet, though. There was a camera on the ceiling in the middle of the room. I was wondering, *Can they see me peeing?* I just wrapped blankets around me as I was peeing.

I'M NOT THIS PERSON

I was taken out of my cell to be interrogated. Nobody told me who they were. It was just me and a man, sitting where all the computers were. Nobody else was around me. There was a guy all the way down at the other end with my dad, but that's about it.

He asked me questions like, "What's your name? What's your age? What's your date of birth? Where were you born?" They knew I was born in Guinea. Then he asked, "What is your citizenship status?" I said, "American." He asked me all these questions about my citizenship status. Then after a while, he said, "You know you're not here legally, right? You know why you're here today, right? You weren't born in this country. You know you're not American?"

For a second, I was just so mad at my parents. It was as if one of the biggest secrets in the world had just been revealed to me. I don't know if it was to protect them or if it was to protect me, but that was the biggest secret someone could ever hold.

The guy's attitude didn't change when he realized I didn't know what was going on. He was nasty the whole time. He just sat there explaining the process to me. He asked me if I wanted to see a consular officer.

I asked, "What is a consular officer?"

He said, "You don't know what a consular officer is? Those are people from your country. From Guinea."

I said, "What about them? What do I have to see them for?"

Finally, they called my dad. They gave us a document about how we could see a consular officer. My dad knows how to read English, but he said to me in Pular,[5] "Pretend you're translating to me in my language." Then he said, "Whatever you do, do not say you can go back to your country. They will circumcise you there."[6]

My dad wasn't just coming up with a way to stay. There was a real fear of female genital mutilation in Guinea. It happened to my mom. In order to get married in Guinea, a female would have to be circumcised. My dad's brothers would do it, they would make sure I got circumcised. My parents made a decision when they had girls that they would never do it. That's the main reason why our parents never took us back to Guinea, not even to visit.

The guy told my dad, "Hey, you've got to get up, you've got to leave."

To me they said, "We have to fingerprint you." When we were done with the fingerprints, they took a picture of me. I was then sitting on a bench in the main entrance when this young lady walked in. Her name was Tashnuba. I had seen her at the mosque before, but I didn't know her personally. I just recognized her face and knew her name. I said "Hi," but in my heart, I started panicking, thinking, *What the hell is she doing here? Who am I gonna see next?*

Finally I was brought to another room. This room had a table, a chair on one side, and two chairs on the other side. A federal agent walked in. She said, "I need to talk to you about something." The questions she was asking had nothing to do with immigration. They were terrorism questions. She asked me about people from London, about people from all over the world. I thought, *What's going on?*

The male interrogator told me that the religious study group Tashnuba was part of had been started by a guy who was wanted by the FBI. I had no idea if that was true or not.

---

5. A language widely spoken in Guinea.

6. Female genital mutilation is a cultural rather than legal issue in Guinea. In June of 2001, the State Department issued a report that cited 98 percent of women in Guinea between fifteen and fifty as having been victims of female genital mutilation. Since then, campaigns to eradicate or alter the process have resulted in a significant decrease in recent years.

The study group at the mosque was all women. So it was women learning about religion, women's empowerment, why we cover, how we do the prayer, when to pray, things like that. It was more for converts and new people who had just come into Islam. There was nothing about jihad or anything like that.

I wasn't part of the group, but Tashnuba was. We were the same age, sixteen. So, they asked me about this group and they told me they'd taken my computer and my diary. My diary was a black-and-white notebook. I had phone numbers, I had notes, I had stories in it, I had everything. Basically, they asked me about every contact in there. They asked me about every little thing. But, there's nothing in there about jihad, there's nothing in there about anything that's suspicious. There was nothing in there at all. So I wasn't worried. They said, "We have your computer, we can find whatever you're hiding." I said, "Go ahead, look in my computer. I have nothing to hide."

They kept making a scene, like there was something big there. They said, "Don't lie to us. If you lie to us, we'll have proof, we'll catch you in your lie."

I knew there was nothing in my computer, but at the end of the day, I started to doubt myself. I thought, *Okay, what's going on now? Is there something there?* Their technique is to make you start to doubt yourself. But then I thought, *Wait a minute, I'm not this person they say. What are they talking about?*

The interrogation lasted a long time. This Secret Service guy came in. He asked me how I felt about Bush. I said, "I don't like him." I was being very honest with them. There was nothing to hide.

The Secret Service guy was aggressive. He said, "I don't understand—why do you choose to cover when women choose to wear less and less every day?"

I said, "It's freedom of choice. Some people want to show some stuff, some people want to hide some things. Some people want to preserve their bodies, and some people don't want to. Some people want to show it to the whole world."

He said, "I don't understand. You're young, why are you doing this?"

Then they asked me about Tashnuba. They asked me about her name, they asked me about her family, but I told them, "I don't know her."

They said, "Tashnuba wrote you on this list."

I said, "What list?"

They said, "She signed you up to be a suicide bomber."

I said, "Are you serious? Why would she do that? She doesn't seem like that type of person."

They were trying to make me seem like I was wrong about who I knew and who I didn't know.

They took me out of the interrogation room briefly, because my dad wanted to talk to me. They had him sign papers consenting to let them talk to me because I was underage. We didn't know that we were supposed to have lawyers. The FBI never told us that.

My dad said, "Everything is going to be fine. I want you to be brave. I'll see you later."

YOU PUT ME ON A LIST?

Back in the interrogation room, they told me Tashnuba and I were going to leave. I said, "Where's my dad, can I say bye to him?"

They said, "He left already."

I started to cry because I'd had my dad there the whole time. I said, "Where is he going to go? What are you guys going to do?" They said that he was going to see an immigration judge before the day ended.

I asked, "When am I going to see him? Where am I going?"

They told me to stop with the questions. They brought Tashnuba and handcuffed us both, hands behind the back. The cuffs were very tight, and I remember they left marks.

We got back in the Escalade. I'm very traumatized when I see Escalades now. This time, I didn't know where they took me, but it was on Varick Street in Manhattan. When we arrived at our destination, the agent told us to walk in casually because all these people were walking past us on the street. He said, "Act casual and people won't say anything."

Tashnuba and I, all by ourselves, got in this elevator. We went up, and we went into this large room that was divided into smaller holding cells. The cells didn't have bars but were enclosed with glass. They put us into our own cell. From there, we saw a bunch of men in one of the other cells, all yelling and screaming and talking, all in orange jumpsuits. Tashnuba and I just looked at each other.

She said to me, "You put me on a list?"

I said, "No! They said you put *me* on a list."

We both realized they had been trying to set us up. So they didn't have anything on us. They'd come for her early in the morning, too. They didn't detain her parents, they just detained her. Later I found out why they'd taken my dad. After I'd been reported as a suicide bomber, the FBI started investigating my whole family. That's how they found out about my dad being here without papers.

Tashnuba and I were then trying to figure out what was going on, what they were going to do, if they were going to release us.

That's when a lady walked in. She said, "What are you guys in for?"

We said, "We don't know."

"I hear you guys did something."

"What did we do?" We were asking *her* for information.

She said, "We're going to take you to Pennsylvania."

Tashnuba and I looked at each other, like, *Pennsylvania?* I said, "What are we going to do in Pennsylvania?"

She answered, "They didn't tell you? There's a detention center there."

YOU NO LONGER HAVE RIGHTS

The FBI drove us to Pennsylvania, across state lines, without my parent's permission. We got to the juvenile detention center late at night. When the FBI agents dropped us off, I wanted to scream, "Please don't leave us!"

I didn't want to be left there. I didn't know where I was. There were too many faces for one night for me.

The female guard told me and Tashnuba we had to get strip-searched. We said that was against our religion.

The guard said, "It's either that or we hold you down."

I said, "Hold me down and do what? I'm not doing a strip-search." I'm stubborn like that, but I was in a situation where I had no choice.

So, she said, "Who wants to go first?"

Tashnuba went first. They searched her hair, checked her body parts; they checked everything. She then had to take a shower and change into a uniform they gave her, and then she had to go. When they took her downstairs, the guard said, "Okay, your turn."

The guard stood there and said, "You're going to have to take off everything. Take off whatever you feel comfortable with first."

I said, "I can't do this. I can't." I was in tears. My own mother doesn't look at me naked. It's my privacy. I said, "It must be against some law for you to do this to me."

She said, "No, it's not. You no longer have rights."

"Why not? What did I do?"

"You're just going to have to take your clothes off."

I was crying, but she just looked at me and said, "Kids here sneak in things and I have to search you."

I had on my abaya, and that was the first thing I took off. Second thing I took off was my head scarf. Third thing I took off was my top. Fourth was my bra. I stopped there for the longest minutes. I put my hands across my chest, just to get that little dignity for myself.

She said, "Come on, I don't have all day."

I said, "I can't do this, I can't, I can't."

"Drop your pants."

So, I took off my pants, I took off my underwear, and I kept my legs closed against each other, trying to cover myself. I was just holding myself with the little bit I could.

She said, "You cannot do that. You have to let loose, or else I'll call another guard and we'll hold you down and search you. This is your last warning. If you want me to call someone in, I'll call them in right now, but it's not gonna be nice. We're going to hold you down and search you."

I said, "Okay." I let go of my arms.

She said, "Lift your breasts."

I lifted my breasts.

She said, "Open your legs more."

I opened my legs.

She said, "Put your hands in there, to see there's nothing."

I said, "There's nothing there!"

She said, "Just do it."

I did it.

She said, "Turn around, put your hands up."

I did that.

Then she said, "All right, now put your fingers to your hair, pull at your ears. Show me your ears, open your mouth."

I showed my mouth.

"Show me your nose."

I put my finger up my nose, put it up so she could see.

Then she gave me a blue uniform: sweat pants, socks, underwear, a bra, and a hair tie, and a little towel and washcloth. She told me to take a shower in five minutes, and then she left.

I knew I only had five minutes, but I just sat at the corner of the shower and held myself and cried. I was thinking, *I cannot believe what I just went through.* I was just crying and crying and crying. I don't know how long, but then I just told myself that I had to get up. I washed myself really quickly. I've never felt like I needed God more than I did on this day. So, I did *ghusul*, which is like a special shower for prayer. I prayed, "God, you've got to hear me for this one. I've never asked for anything that I desperately needed beforee." I dried myself and put my clothes on. There was a little mirror there. I looked into it. My eyes were red from crying.

The guard returned and told me I had to take off my head scarf. I said, "It's part of my religion." And I was having a bad hair day, I was not ready to show my hair. She let me keep the scarf, but later the supervisor took it from me once she saw me.

I was then taken to my cell. As we walked, the guard said, "You must keep your hands to your sides at all times." You had to look straight, you couldn't look anywhere else. There were cameras everywhere, but I wasn't listening, I was looking around.

I still didn't know why I was there. I didn't know if it was immigration or if it was for the stuff they were interrogating me about. When I got to the cell, all the lights were out. I could see Tashnuba in the corner, praying. There was one blanket, and it was freezing cold in there.

We stayed up the whole night talking about everything. I found out her mom had just had a baby; my mom had just had a baby too. Tashnuba was the oldest, I was the oldest. I asked her age, she asked my age. I asked what school she went to, what she was studying, what she wanted to do with her life.

We were laughing, like, "Pinch me. This is a prank."

She said, "Maybe it will be all be straightened out by tomorrow."

I don't know how we fell asleep, but I remember at one point we were both crying.

THERE GOES A TERRORIST

I was just so angry, and I was trying to contain all this anger. I was so mad at America as a country. I remember the first morning in detention, we went for breakfast and we were supposed to salute the American flag. I'm like, "Fuck the American flag. I'm not saluting it." I said it. During the pledge I put my hands to my side, and I just looked out the window.

Each morning I did that. I remember one of the guards asking me, "How come you don't pledge allegiance?"

I said, "You guys said it yourself. I am not American."

Nobody told me what was going on. I wasn't brought before a judge until probably my fourth week there, and it was via video conference.

An article came out in the *New York Times* about why Tashnuba and I were there, that we were suspected of being suicide bombers. I never saw the article while in prison. I saw it when I came out. After the guards read what happened, things changed. They would whisper, "There goes a terrorist," or "There go those girls."

After the article came out we got extra strip-searches, about three times a day, and the searches got stricter. They would tell us to spread our butt cheeks, and they made nasty, racist comments. I remember the guards laughing and going, "Look at those assholes. Look at them. These are the ones that want to take our country down." Things like that.

If I talked back, they would tackle me down and I would be put into solitary confinement. All I wanted to do was get out. I knew that I was going to have to take shit from everyone, because I did not want to be in solitary.

We also lost a lot of privileges because of the head scarf. We weren't allowed to use the bathroom privately. So when I had to go, I was like, "I hope I stink this place up, I pray that my shit would make this place close down or something. I hope my poop brings toxins."

I remember even having tissue stuck up my butt when somebody did a strip-search once, and I did it on purpose. I was like, "I hope after this, they'll think, *I will never want to strip-search her again.* It didn't work. I still got strip-searched. I even tried leaving caca there. I tried everything.

THERE'S A RUMOR GOING AROUND

Those first three weeks I was there, my family didn't have any idea where I was. They had to do research to find out, and hire a lawyer. The lawyer, Natasha, came to see me at the detention center. She asked me, "Do you know why you're here?" I said no.

"There's a rumor going around about you being a suicide bomber."

I laughed so hard.

She said, "That's not funny."

I said, "Are you serious or are you joking? If you knew me, you would laugh and say, 'Hell no.'" I have a family, I am somebody. I wanted to live. I said, "I'm not ready to meet God yet."

She said, "But they're not charging you with anything except overstaying your visa."

My mom came to visit me after my lawyer left. She was so skinny. You could tell she wasn't eating. It was the worst visit ever because she didn't want to say anything at all. When I asked about my dad, she just said, "He's fine." She knew that he was being held in New Jersey at the time. I just knew that she was upset. She was so drained.

A WAY TO GET ME OUT

After a while, my lawyer called. She said she had good news. "I have a way to get you out of jail. You're going to have to wear an ankle bracelet."

I said, "I'll wear anything."

The day that I was supposed to be released from the detention center, I said goodbye to Tashnuba in the cafeteria. I wanted to hold her and let her know it was going to be okay. But I couldn't hug her, or it would've been solitary confinement for her. So I looked at her and I said, "May Allah be with you, and be patient." And I walked away.

I haven't spoken to Tashnuba at all since then. She'd told me that her mother made an agreement with the federal government: if they released her daughter, they would go back to their country. I think their country was Bangladesh. So as soon as she was released, it was right to the airport.

I stayed there six and a half weeks. By the time I came out, I was seventeen. Federal agents picked me up. This guard walked past, and he said, "Arrest that fucking nigger terrorist." But I didn't give a damn, I was so excited I was leaving. The whole world could burn down, but as long as I was leaving, I didn't care.

HOME AGAIN

As soon as we got to New York, I was just so excited and happy to be home again that I forgot I had to wear an ankle bracelet. I thought everything was going to go back to normal, but in a way, I knew deep down inside things would never be normal again, because I was so traumatized.

We came back to my house. My mom had to sign papers, and they released me. They put the ankle bracelet on the same day.

Once a week I had to report to Federal Plaza so they could check the bracelet. When I got there, I recognized it was the building where my father and I had been taken to a few months ago. I just looked at it and my heart started beating so fast. It triggered the memory, and I started to cry so badly I just could not control it. It was one of the most traumatizing moments of my life.

I wore the ankle bracket for three years. You can still see my bruises from it. My heel always hurts. This is all black from the ankle bracelet. I had to wear the bracelet and check in every week. I also had to be under curfew, which was 10:00 p.m. and then 11:00 p.m.

Every night our phone would ring, and I would have to press this button and they would have to hear it. I couldn't get any sleep. The man who put the bracelet on me told me, "If you take it off, we're going to put you in jail. If your phone is off, you're going to jail." That was the best threat you could ever make to me. They never said how long I would have to wear it. It was pending my immigration case. I was only ever charged with overstaying my visa, that's it. They wanted to deport me.

For days, my mom didn't want to talk because she thought they were recording us with the ankle bracelet. She was always like, "*Shh, shh.*"

I'd say, "They're not listening."

I didn't know if they weren't listening, and I didn't care. I'd get on the phone with Demaris, my friend from high school, and we would say things on purpose, like "Fuck the government!"

I MISS HIM BEING THE ONE
WHO TOOK CARE OF EVERYTHING

My dad got deported around 2006. That was the hardest. I didn't see him for a long time after I got released from juvie. He was in New Jersey. I wasn't allowed to go, because it was outside the distance I could travel with my ankle bracelet. My mom and my siblings were able to visit, but they couldn't go a lot because it was a lot of money to get out there.

They made an exception to let me travel to New Jersey just before he was deported. I couldn't look at him. I was just crying the whole time.

He said, "I hope you take care of the family. It's your job." It's always about, "It's your job, it's your responsibility, you're the next person in line."

I miss a lot about my dad. I miss his company. I even miss him yelling at me. My brothers and sister, we used to walk around saying our dad was a dictator. But we needed him. I just miss him being the one who took care of everything. I didn't have to worry about everything; no bills, no nothing.

WE WERE STARVING

I thought I was going to be able to come back to school, that the government was going to apologize and write me a check, and I would be set for life. But it was the opposite way around. When I came back, I had to drop school to work to support my family. No way my dad can work in Guinea; there are no jobs there. So I support my father, his family, my mom's family, and I support my family here too.

I would work three or four jobs, whatever kind of job I could find— babysitting jobs, cleaning houses. I worked at an interpretive service for a while, until I found out that could get me back in jail, because I had no documentation.

Sometimes we were starving. For days there would be no food in the house. Finally we met a social worker who told us we could get public assistance. Nobody tells you about this stuff.

I started feeling distant from my friends because I was going through something that none of my friends had gone through. I was growing up really quickly, maturing so fast.

Everything that I do in life is to take care of my family. Everything revolves around them. My family here wouldn't be able to stand on their own feet, not without me. I didn't want my brother and my sister to work at all. I didn't want them to miss out on what I missed out on.

But I was drained. When I came back, I was emotional. I would come home angry, like, "Leave me alone, don't touch me."

Now that I look back, I wish there was something that could have been done. I wish I would have told my story to a newspaper, but I was always afraid to say something, because they always threatened me with going to jail.

That's why I kept so silent and cried about everything. I feel like it's too late for me now.

I AM NOT AMERICAN NOW.
I AM A REFUGEE.

In 2007, Adama was granted asylum on the grounds that she would face forcible circumcision if deported to Guinea. In court, her mother gave testimony on her own harrowing experience of being circumcised.

I had the ankle bracelet up until I got asylum. The day I got it taken off, I had the cheesiest smile. I went to the guy I had to report to every week, and when he took off the ankle bracelet, I said, "My legs! That's what my legs look like!"

But for at least a year, I still had a feeling I had the ankle bracelet on. I felt like it was still there. And sometimes I would be out, and I would think, "Oh my God, my curfew," and I would just start panicking. I had to calm myself down again.

I am not American now. I have asylum. That means I am a refugee.

I AM NOT GOING TO GO THROUGH THIS

In 2009, to celebrate winning her asylum case, Adama arranged to take a vacation in Texas with friends. When she tried to board her flight at LaGuardia Airport, a ticket agent told her she was on the No-Fly List. Federal agents came and handcuffed her and took her to the airport security station, where she was held for almost thirteen hours before being released.

In 2009 I started working for a family as a nanny. I met them through an old friend who was also working for them. They are a very nice family, they spoil me too much, beyond spoil. They pay me on time, they take care of me, they give me Christmas bonuses, they give me vacations, they take me everywhere.

We were supposed to fly to Chicago on March 31, 2010. I went to the airport before them because I just wanted to know if there would be any problems or anything. I was there with my luggage, and I had brought a friend because I was afraid of repeating what had happened before. I don't know why, but I just had a fear that something was going to happen. I even called my lawyers, but they said nothing should happen, that I should be fine. But I got to LaGuardia Airport and a problem did happen.

The same thing happened as before. The airline supervisor called Port Authority police and other government officials. I called my lawyer and he came. They kept asking me questions, like, "What did you do to be on the No-Fly List?"

I wasn't able to get on the plane. I could tell the family were disappointed. They ended up taking the other babysitter. I lost money that day. They were going to pay me for going, and I was counting on that money.

As soon as I got out of that room, something in me just triggered. I told myself, "I'm done. I'm tired. I am not going to go through this again." I told my lawyers, "I want to sue these motherfuckers," and so we filed a lawsuit against Attorney General Eric Holder, FBI Director Robert Mueller, and Director of the Terrorist Screening Center Timothy Healy.

About a month later, we received a letter from James Kennedy of the DHS[7] Traveler Redress Inquiry Program, but it didn't tell me anything. It didn't tell me why I wasn't allowed to board my flight at LaGuardia or what would happen if I tried to fly again.

Some months later, my friend gave me a ticket to go to Chicago, on November 12, 2010, as a gift. I didn't know if I could fly, but I didn't know how to find out if I could without trying again. It was LaGuardia again. This time, I walked up to the ticket machine, punched in my name, and it said, "Go see a ticket agent." I said to myself, "I'm not going to be able to fly." I gave the ticket agent my name and my state ID, and he printed the ticket. I looked at him and said, "You printed it?"

He said, "Yeah."

"And it went through?"

"Yeah."

When he gave me my ticket, I started to cry. He was just looking at me, like, is this girl nuts?

I WANT TO LIVE MY LIFE NOW

I grew up too fast. I experienced some things that a lot of people around me haven't, so it's hard to talk to my peers. I've never gotten to escape. All my friends went to college, and now, four years later, they've all graduated, and I'm just like, "Wow, they're graduating college and I haven't even gotten there yet."

I have a bigger picture of life. But I feel like things are not changing as quickly as I want them to. I want to be done with school already, I want to have my own car, I want to be in my own space. I want to live my life now. I don't mind taking care of my family, but for once, I want to do something for myself: I want to go and do something overseas. I want to be a traveling nurse. I want to help people, I want to educate.

---

7. The Department of Homeland Security.

Even though everything is said and done, I still live in constant fear of federal agents taking me or any of my family members. They did it when I was innocent, and they could do it again. I have so much to lose, including my family. I remember the look of helplessness on their faces the day they took me and my father away.

Still, the United States is my home. It's the only place I really know. I am hopeful for this country, because of people like me and my siblings. We know how it feels to suffer, so we can change things. Now I study Islam on my own. At the end of the day, I still believe in God, because I feel like things could have been worse; I could have been in Guantánamo Bay. I still have my family, I still have my health. So, in a way, I know there is still God. There has to be something you can believe in at the end of the day.

The same year that Patriot Acts *was published, Adama Bah was the focus of a short documentary called* Adama. *As part of the release of the film, she began speaking in front of audiences about her arrest and other experiences with the justice system. In 2010, Adama married a man she'd been seeing for over a year. The same year, her father was able to return to the United States on a new visa. Adama gave birth to her first son, Mohammed, in 2014, and is expecting another child in 2015.*

Inside This Place, Not of It: Narratives from Women's Prisons (2011), edited by Robin Levi and Ayelet Waldman, tells the stories of people who have suffered human rights abuses within the U.S. women's prison system, including sexual assault and harassment from prison guards, invasive medical procedures, and dangerous neglect. The interviews for this collection took place over ten months between 2009 and 2010. The two narrators included in this collection used the pseudonyms of Olivia Hamilton and Irma Rodriguez in the book, but have since used their real names as ambassadors for the book and in their advocacy work.

ASHLEY JACOBS

AGE WHEN INTERVIEWED: *25*

BORN IN: *New Orleans, Louisiana*

INTERVIEWED IN: *New Orleans, Louisiana*

Ashley lives with her husband and three sons in an apartment that FEMA (Federal Emergency Management Agency) provided for her family because they evacuated New Orleans after Hurricane Katrina.[1] We sit at a table in her breakfast nook as she shares her story: abandonment by her mother, teenage pregnancy, forced evacuation from her city, and imprisonment. Ashley gave birth to her youngest son while she was in prison serving a six-month sentence for embezzling money to pay her bills. During the birth, she was chained to an operating table and given a forced and medically unnecessary cesarean section. Ashley gave birth to another child in July 2011, but because of Ashley's C-section in prison, her local hospital was unwilling to allow her to try for a vaginal birth and she was forced to have another C-section. When we meet, the son she birthed while imprisoned (now three years old) bounds around the apartment wearing only a diaper. He occasionally interrupts our interview to squeeze his mother's leg. During the interview, Ashley describes her distrust of both the prison and the healthcare system, and she also describes her precarious journey toward reestablishing her life post-incarceration.

---

1. Ashley's narrative was originally published under the pseudonym Olivia Hamilton.

AND THEN THE HURRICANE HIT

My grandma tells a story about when I was a little girl, that one day I got a broom and started beating my doll with it, saying, "That's what my mom does." After that, my mom sent me to live with my grandma in Louisiana, St. Charles Parish. My relationship with my grandma was really good, but she was strict with me.

My brother and sisters stayed in Georgia with my mom. I still talked with my mom some, not a lot. I had a lot of resentment, I guess, for her sending me to live with my grandma when I was so young. I think the problems began when I was around twelve. It was never my grades, it was just that I was in trouble with the juvenile detention people all the time for fighting and running away. I was trying everything to get my mom's attention. I think I realized I was doing it the day I got sent to juvenile hall. Usually I'd just go to the ADAPT Center[2] when I was in trouble, but the last time I ran away, when I was about twelve, I was sent to the St. James Parish Juvenile Detention Center in New Orleans for ten days. I was hurt and mad the day my mama came to see me in juvenile hall. But then I finally realized I shouldn't be doing all this, and when I went home to my grandmother's I just got myself back together.

I got pregnant at seventeen, and my boyfriend and I got an apartment together. I had my first son, Emmanuel, when I was a junior in high school, but I still graduated with a 3.8 GPA. I got help. For instance, there was this lady from Africa who'd opened a school for teen moms. She got government funding to open it, and she'd look after the students' babies, all the way till they were able to go to Head Start.[3] I didn't have to bring diapers, food, nothing. All I did was drop him off every day, and that was a blessing.

---

2. A social work and child resources organization.

3. A federal program promoting school readiness for young children (ages three to five) in low-income families by offering educational, nutritional, health, and social services.

I graduated high school in 2004, and my then-boyfriend and I headed to Augusta, Georgia, in a raggedy car to live with my mom. But my mom let me down, and six months later I moved back to Louisiana to start all over again. I started Bryman College at the beginning of 2005 and I met my new boyfriend, who is now my husband. And then, that August, Hurricane Katrina hit. Before the storm reached us, I got in a car with my boyfriend and baby, and we started heading toward Georgia. We stayed with a friend of my brother's, which was a hectic situation every day. It was only a two-bedroom apartment, but at least it wasn't a shelter. During that time, I wrote a lot of bad checks because it was hard for me to get a job. I didn't have money for food, and you know, it was just a lot that we were dealing with. It was the only way really at the time that we could get anything.

Eventually I got a job at McDonald's. My brother was working, and my dad was coming up with some money to send us so we could maybe rent a trailer or something. But then three or four weeks after we got out here, I spoke with my mom, and eventually she let us stay with her.

I'D MADE THIS HUGE MISTAKE, AND I REGRETTED IT

By the end of 2007, I had two kids and was four months pregnant with another. I was living in Marietta, Georgia, and working two jobs—I was at Kmart and Pep Boys.

Well, one day I got an idea. I had a friend at Kmart who used to do fake refunds. She'd say a customer was coming in and she was refunding stuff that wasn't really being refunded. So I did it the first time and I didn't get caught, but of course I was scared. I said to my friend, "We didn't get caught. Let's not do it again." But we really needed the money. I was behind on a lot of bills, and I was trying to catch it up.

One night, my friend came through my line to check out little items like diapers and different things—some of the things that I needed—and

I didn't charge her for everything. Diapers and stuff like that I would never ring up. We would do that a lot.

That night the Kmart loss prevention officer was outside smoking a cigarette, but I didn't see him at the time. When I got ready to close up, he called me and my friend to the back, and of course they'd caught it on tape. He asked us how long we'd been doing it, and I lied, "This is my first time." And then he basically told me, "Write what I tell you to write, and then I'll let you go home."

I think the total he had us taking was $1,200 worth of stuff, and I said, "I didn't take that much," because we'd only taken $300 worth. But he said, "But we have other stuff that's been taken," even though I told him I hadn't taken any of that.

Then he said, "Well, we're gonna press charges." I think he was trying to save his job at the time, 'cause they've got to catch people, and I don't think he'd been doing too good in that department. I got arrested and taken to jail that night, but I bonded out.

About two months later, I got a letter in the mail saying there was an arraignment. I honestly thought it was for Kmart, but when I got to court, I found out it was for Pep Boys—I'd been doing the same thing there. The judge was sending everybody to jail that day, and I was totally scared. So I got up there, and the Pep Boys loss prevention officer said he'd called his manager because he really felt bad for me. He said I was a good worker, and that he knew the situation I was in. He said, "Well, I asked my manager if there's a way that you can make payments, but he's not budging. He says it's too much." It came to something like $700. The judge put me on a bond on my own recognizance. She basically let me go home that day without my needing to post bail, and told me that I needed to turn myself in the following night. It was like her trusting me that I was going to come back. She said, "I think you made a very bad mistake. I want you to go home, pick your kids up from daycare and make sure they're stable. Tomorrow at nine o'clock, you need to turn yourself in."

In my mind, I was thinking, *Okay, well, I've never been in trouble before, so the only thing they can do is put me on probation.* And that's all I kept saying to myself. But when I finally got to court, I got a court-appointed lawyer, and he said, "Well, the judge is saying eighteen months." And I was like, "Huh? I've never been in trouble before! I can pay the money back!" At the time I had $1,500 on me, which I'd saved from my taxes. My lawyer talked to the prosecutor, who said, "No. She's got to serve time."

Then my lawyer told me, "Go home for the weekend and get yourself together with your kids." He said, "The only thing I can say is that I'll try and talk the prosecutor down. Any other judge, and I think you would've been okay. But I don't think she's gonna budge."

So I went home and finally I called my grandmother, my dad, and everybody, and let them know what was going on. Of course they were all shocked, because I had never said anything about it before. That weekend was real, real hard. I was scared, because I didn't want to leave my kids. I guess it just hurt me because I'd never been in trouble, and I was doing all I could to stay out of trouble. But I'd made this huge mistake and I regretted it. I think that was the most that I felt—regret. Leaving my kids—I didn't know how to handle that part.

And so that Monday came, February 18, 2008. I had to be in court at nine. I told my oldest son, "Mommy might have to go away for a while to help some people. But once I've helped them, I'll be home." My husband kept saying, "You're not going. You're not going." When I got to court, every part of me just knew what would happen.

So I got in front of the judge and I said to her, "I'm truly sorry. But you know, I have never been in trouble before this. I just graduated from college and I'm pregnant. This is not what I thought I would be doing right now." The judge had her head down the whole time. She looked real, real sad. And then she said, "The only thing I can say is that I have to send you to jail, because your co-defendant has already gone. But I'm sorry. I think you're on the right track. I think you just made a mistake that you've got to serve the consequences for." I was sentenced to a year, and the judge said, "Hopefully, you'll do six months on good behavior, with nine years' probation." And I thought, *Okay, so you're going to send me to jail. And then I have to pay all this money back—one hundred a month until it's paid back—and then probation for nine years. Nine years.*

THEY SHACKLED MY STOMACH
AND MY FEET

When the court bailiff took me from the court to a holding cell in Georgia, a guard put the cuffs around my belly and on my wrists, like a chain. When I sat down, the cuffs were real, real tight, so I was basically standing up the whole time. For a while, I was complaining about how tight it was, and other inmates were complaining too. Finally the guard came back and loosened the chain around my belly, and then I was able to sit down. The whole process was just long, and I was hungry and tired.

I think the thing that upset me the most was that they wouldn't give me water in a cup. I was not about to drink out of this faucet where you wash your hands; it was right over the toilet bowl. So I just stayed thirsty. By the time I did finally go through the holding cell, the guards gave me a sandwich to eat. Then they took us all on upstairs to the jail, and once I got upstairs, one of the female guards told me, "I won't be able to put you in a bottom bunk until you go see the doctor and he says you're pregnant." I was six months pregnant! I said, "No, for real?! You want me to climb this bunk bed?" She said, "Well, I can't give you a bottom bunk." I just said, "Ma'am, I can't climb this." And then she just walked out. Another inmate told me, "You can have my bed." So she put her stuff on the top bunk, and I took the bottom. And finally I went to sleep.

I was there about a month before I actually saw a doctor. I didn't have vitamins there, and I had no prenatal care. I didn't really complain if I was in pain or anything, because the infirmary was real nasty. There was poo on the walls. It was just nasty. Then one day, when I was seven months pregnant, the guards called me down. They shackled my stomach and my feet and took me to see an OB-GYN. I mean, you walk like this through the front door looking as if you've murdered someone, and I just thought it was really degrading. I know I made a mistake, but I don't think I deserved to be ashamed or embarrassed in this way. And even once I'd got in the back where the actual doctors' offices were, the shackles didn't come off. They took them off my feet, but the shackles stayed on my stomach.

The doctor complained that I wasn't getting enough water, vitamins, or fresh fruits, and that it could affect my baby's brain. The county doesn't give you fruits, and it's not like I could buy them. So I just tried to drink as much water as I possibly could.

My kids came to visit me sometimes with my boyfriend. My boys were five and three then. The first time they came was really hard. They were beating on the glass, trying to come through it. I was so mad at myself for putting them through this.

It felt like my pregnancy was the only thing that was keeping me going. I was eight months pregnant when I finally left the county jail and went to prison.

NOBODY CARES IF YOU'RE PREGNANT

When I was moved to the prison, I couldn't take my books that had been sent to me in jail, or anything like that. I had one picture and I had my Bible, but all the rest I had to send home.

I was taken to prison with other inmates in a cramped, hot van. Some of them were also pregnant. When we got there and were getting off the van, the guards started yelling at us, "Nobody cares if you're pregnant! You shouldn't have got in trouble. You're a sad excuse for a mother. You don't care about your kids!" It was a mess. It was real hard. There was another girl there who was pregnant, and she'd been there before. She said to me, "Don't let them get to you, girl." But they had already gotten to me. I just felt like this wasn't the place I was supposed to be.

The guards wanted me to stand up straight, but I couldn't. I was totally drained because I hadn't slept since three that morning. I was eight months along at this point, and I was huge. Eventually, one of the male guards said, "Okay, go get her a wheelchair." The female guards were actually harder on me. So I got in a wheelchair, and they rolled me on inside. When I got inside, the guards made me strip, bend over, all that. Then they made me take a shower, and afterward they gave me a sandwich and a juice. You would think that they'd give you more food, being pregnant, but they don't. You just eat what everybody else eats.

It was a whole process. I had to learn how to talk to the guards, and that I had to address them with "Ma'am" or "Sir" and "Good morning." Or when they walked by, I had to stop. I had to ask permission to speak. Finally they gave me all my stuff in a bag to put on the bed.

I couldn't carry the bag like they wanted me to. There's a certain way you had to hold it, a certain way to walk, and I just kept dropping it. It was about ten pounds—it's your clothes, it's everything in there—and I wasn't even supposed to be lifting that. But the guards kept yelling, "You'd better not drop it again!" And I was like, "Uh, ma'am, this bag is heavy. I'm trying my best."

When I got in the dorm, the inmates were pretty cool and they helped me make my bed. I think, with most of the women in there being mothers, they could imagine how it felt to go through this while pregnant. Most of them were pretty understanding, and they didn't mind helping me out as much as they could.

My family was very supportive. My grandmother made sure that I had money in my account, my dad and uncles too. My mama did most of the writing as far as letters went, and she sent a lot of pictures and just different things to help me get through. I could call my grandma any time, but it was hard for me to call my boyfriend, because you couldn't call cell phones from prison, only landlines. Also, you couldn't get a visitation until about two months of being there. It didn't make any sense for me to even start that process, because my lawyer told me that, nine chances out of ten, I would be getting out in six months. By the time

I got to the prison, I'd already been in county jail for two months. I had to wait another two months before I would be allowed visitation at the prison, so it would have been four months by then. And by the time they'd gone through processing everybody, it probably would have been time for me to go home.

I SAID I DIDN'T WANT TO BE INDUCED, AND THE CAPTAIN SAID, "THESE ARE ORDERS"

My due date was May 24, 2008, just before Memorial Day weekend. A female doctor from the Atlanta Medical Center came to visit me on May 22. At that time, I wasn't showing any signs of labor. We did an ultrasound, and the baby hadn't moved one bit. I wasn't dilated at all, wasn't even close, and I wasn't having any pains. She said I should be fine through the weekend, and that everything was normal about my pregnancy.

Then, on the evening of May 23—this was a Friday evening—the guards called me, and they told me to pack my stuff. But I hadn't even had one contraction, so I asked a guard, "Where am I going?" And the guard said, "I don't know. They just called and said for you to pack your stuff." I thought, *Okay, maybe I'm going home!*

I got over to the infirmary, and the captain said, "Well, the doctor from the prison says he's going to send you in to be induced." When I asked why, she said, "Because your due date is May 24, and that's going to be a holiday weekend." I said, "But I'm not even in pain or anything! I don't want to be induced, I'm not even late. Nothing's wrong with me!" And she said, "Well, these are orders."

They put me in a room and shackled me. I was more upset than anything that the baby just wasn't ready, and I didn't want to be forced. They gave me Pitocin, but it wasn't working.[4] Later, in the middle of

---

4. Pitocin is an intravenous medication commonly used to induce labor.

the night, the doctor came in to check on me. He came in and he started poking inside me with an instrument—I'm not sure exactly what it was, it looked like a little stick. He put it inside me and started poking the bag of water, where the amniotic fluid was, so he could bust it. It was a lot of pain, and I said, "You're hurting me." He stopped, but by then he had swollen up my insides.

Then he said, "Well, if you don't move any more by tomorrow, we're going to have to do a C-section." I said, "So you come in here, and you poke me to death, and now I'm swollen! I have never had a C-section in my life. My oldest son was nine pounds—no cuts, no slits, no nothing. And you're going to make me have a C-section?"

The next day, the doctor came back, and he took me in to have the C-section done. A sergeant came in and said, "She needs to be shackled. She's no different from anybody else." I was hurting and tired. I said to the sergeant, "Ma'am, there is no way I need these shackles. I'm not going anywhere, I'm in too much pain. You've got a guard in my room. And I don't know if you have kids, but this ain't something fun to have your hands shackled for." But she made them keep the shackles on me when I went in for the C-section.

The doctor gave me an epidural. I went through with the C-section, and finally, the baby came on out. It was a boy. The guard held him up to show him to me. Even then, they never took the shackles off me.

This C-section I was forced to have—I doubt that it's legal. I don't remember signing any paperwork. But I never looked into talking to a lawyer. I was hoping there was something I could do, but I was told that I had no rights. The guard said to me, "You lost your rights the day you walked in here."

I named the baby Joshua. I wonder about him—does he remember all that we went through? The guards made me put the prison address on the birth certificate. That's something you have to deal with for the rest of your life.

I was fortunate, you know. One of the guards there gave me her cell phone because she didn't agree with a lot of what was going on. She said, "Call your boyfriend. Let him know you had the baby." She let me talk to him until the phone died. It was a blessing.

IT FELT LIKE MY BABY WAS DYING

After I left the hospital, my boyfriend picked up the baby and took him home. I guess for me, walking out of that hospital, knowing I was leaving my son—it killed me inside. I felt like I was being punished for the one mistake that I'd made in my life. I just remember looking at my baby, and kissing him, and crying, and not wanting to go. The nurse who was holding him was really hurt too. She asked me, "Do you want to kiss him again?" And I kissed him one last time, and they took me out the door.[5]

It felt like my baby was dying, that I was abandoning him. I felt like I owed it to him to be there, and I wasn't. I felt like maybe he would hate me, or resent me, or when I got home, he wouldn't know who I was. It hurt. It just hurt.

I got back to the prison with staples in because of the C-section. But I couldn't go back to the dorm until the staples came out, and so, on top of me being hurt and stressed, they put me in this infirmary with nothing but four walls. There was no TV, nothing.

I was supposed to stay there through the weekend. During that time, I had nobody to talk to, and all I could really do was cry. I didn't want to

---

5. Most prisons separate parents and their newborn infants after forty-eight hours. As well as causing emotional distress, the separation of mothers and their children also threatens the health of infants by posing serious barriers to breastfeeding. The Fifth Circuit of Appeals ruled in the 1981 case *Dike v. School Board of Orange County, Florida*, that the right to nurse is protected under the Fourteenth Amendment. However, the same court determined in *Southerland v. Thigpen* that the state could overlook this guarantee in prison. Some states, like New York, have taken steps to recognize the universality of this right, guaranteeing women in prison the ability to breastfeed their children for a year after birth, though in other states the reality of prison life has rendered breastfeeding impossible.

In at least thirteen states, babies can be placed in prison nurseries, though access is often limited to women with short sentences for non-violent offenses, and some parents prefer for their children to be raised outside prison walls.

eat, I didn't want to do anything. And then one of the guards told me, "Well, if you don't eat, we're going to make you stay here longer." So I made myself eat because I didn't want to stay in there that long. All that was going to do was drive me more crazy than I already was.

By then I was mad at everything. I was mad at myself. I was mad at my mom. I was mad at everybody. I had only been back there but about five weeks from the hospital, and I got in a fight. It was with a girl who was looking for trouble, and she picked a fight with me one night. She hit me and hit me, and I fought her back. So of course, they took us to lockdown. That's the worst place to be. I mean, you can't look out the windows because they're all blacked out, and you can only bathe on certain days. I was down there for three weeks. My birthday was July 18, and I was in lockdown for that. But my mom sent me a whole bunch of cards and pictures, and I would call my grandma, and she'd be like, "You still down there?" And I'd say, "Yes."

The day I got out of lockdown was the day I got the news that I was going home on August 14. I had two weeks left! I thought, *Thank God! Finally!* I stayed up the whole night before the I was released—I was so excited, and I just wanted to leave. I was just so ready to get out of there.

ALL STORMS END

When I got out of prison, my boyfriend came to get me. At that time, his mom had the two younger kids and my grandmother had my oldest son. It took me a while to get the kids back. I missed them terribly, but things were bad. The gas in the house had been turned off, the phone was off, the cable was off. The truck I had was gone, and my credit was totally messed up. Everything was in a total wreck. I couldn't be bringing the kids back into that type of situation. I wanted to be able to have food stamps first, and I wanted to try to get the house together. It was nasty, it was dirty. I was just in a depressed situation, and I was upset with my boyfriend, who wasn't working at that time. I was mad because I'd left him with $1,500, and he got money every month from my dad and my grandmother, so I couldn't understand the house being in a total wreck when I got out of prison. I was totally mad about my money, and why everything was gone. I also felt a lot of resentment toward society.

Eventually, I was able to get a job at the mall food court. I saved up, and I got a car. Once I got the car, I could get back and forth to work. And finally, when we were more financially stable, we got the kids back.

Once I got out, I got in the church. I was always in the church, but I strayed for a while when I first moved out here to Georgia. But once I got out of prison, I joined a choir and I also went to Bible study and Sunday school. And, you know, I got myself back together for me and God. For me and school. For me and work.

Eventually I got laid off from the food court because they didn't have enough work for me, and it's been totally hard for me to find a job since. Whenever I'm filling out a job application, I get scared when I get to that question where I have to put down that I have this conviction. I feel like I'll never have the opportunity to explain what happened. So it's like, do you lie, or do you tell the truth? And, you know, every time I get to that question, I stumble.

I think my medical treatment in prison was cruel, degrading, and shameful. Being shackled, being forced to have that C-section—it was the worst feeling, mentally and emotionally, that I have ever been through. And I feel like it would be so unfair for me to have been through all this and not say anything about it to somebody. I always felt like everything I went through was definitely for a reason, and that it made me a stronger person. So my goal now is to help prevent somebody else from making the same mistakes, with the stealing, the whole scenario. Right now I'm working with young women through my church. I want to work with these young women because when you get to a certain age, there are things you go through, there's pressure to do things that you may not want to do. I've also been without a mom, and I know how it feels to want that. There's a gap in your heart where you need it. A grandmother's love is awesome, but a mom's love is something totally different.

Through God, all things are possible. Even though I was mad at my boyfriend and my mom, God has built those relationships again. Now my mom and I share a beautiful relationship, and my boyfriend is now my husband. This shows that all storms end and the sun will shine again.

———————————————————

After sharing her story with Voice of Witness for Inside This Place, Not of It, *Ashley began speaking about her experiences at public events, and she has helped teach classes about oral history interviews. She also worked with the organization SPARK to push state legislation to end the practice of shackling pregnant women in Georgia prisons. Today, Ashley is living with her family in Tampa, Florida, where she works as a medical assistant at a walk-in clinic and helps facilitate classes about oral history methodology.*

Inside This Place, Not of It: Narratives from Women's Prisons (2011), edited by Robin Levi and Ayelet Waldman, tells the stories of people who have suffered human rights abuses within the U.S. women's prison system, including sexual assault and harassment from prison guards, invasive medical procedures, and dangerous neglect. The interviews for this collection took place over ten months between 2009 and 2010. The two narrators included in this collection used the pseudonyms of Olivia Hamilton and Irma Rodriguez in the book, but have since used their real names as ambassadors for the book and in their advocacy work.

THERESA MARTINEZ

AGE WHEN INTERVIEWED: 45
BORN IN: *Los Angeles, California*
INTERVIEWED IN: *California*

Theresa Martinez spoke with us while still in prison.[1] A woman who looks much younger than her age, Theresa had her dark brown hair pulled back in a braid, and she wore a prison-issue white baseball jersey and blue denim pants. The prison garb did not hide all of Theresa's tattoos, which mark significant experiences in her life: her past loves, her gang affiliation, the daughter she had at fifteen. Theresa has spent much of her life in and out of prison, mostly on drug-related offenses. During that time, she went through several rounds of rehab for her drug abuse, and has now been clean for over three years. In 1990, while in prison, Theresa was misdiagnosed with HIV, and for the next seventeen years was treated with extremely toxic drugs that were contraindicated for her other illnesses. She spoke to us of the discrimination she experienced as an HIV patient, the effects of the HIV medication on her health, and the prison's refusal to accept responsibility for her misdiagnosis.

---

1. Theresa's narrative was originally published under the pseudonym Irma Rodriguez.

USING DRUGS SEEMED NORMAL TO ME

One of the first things I remember was when I was five years old. This big blue car pulled up to the trailer where I lived with my mom in LA, and a lady with a big old hat came and put me in the car. She was from Child Protective Services, and she took me away with her. Later I found out that someone had called Child Protective Services because of my stepfather, Luis. He never molested me, he never touched me. But he was a heroin addict. I remember smelling burnt matches all the time as a kid. I still hate that smell.

That day, Luis had gone out to cop some dope and left me alone in the trailer with the outside of the trailer door tied shut. A lady in another trailer saw that and called the police. Luis was just getting home when the police arrived, and I'll never forget that feeling. I was so scared that they were going to arrest him, and that they were going to take me away. And of course they did. Child Protective Services took me to court, and the judge didn't let any of my immediate family members have me. I remember screaming, but it didn't matter. I went back and forth between my grandparents and my godparents for a while, but finally the court agreed to let me live permanently with my grandparents.

My mom would try to get me back, but she was an active heroin addict—Luis had turned her on to the drug—and the court wouldn't give her custody. She tried hard, even getting herself on a methadone program. And she was doing good, she always kept jobs. I remember her going in for her methadone treatments. They'd give her a lockbox for her take-home medication, and it looked just like a lunch box to me; I remember I wanted one like that for school. But all her efforts made no difference to the court, and they wouldn't give me back to her. In the end, my mom got hooked on pharmaceutical medications—Valium, codeine, anything that was a downer.

My grandparents tried their best with me. My grandma was a cafeteria dietician and my grandfather was a janitor. He did floors, she cooked, and they supported me to the best of their abilities. But even so, I didn't have too much of an affectionate childhood. I wasn't hugged a lot, I wasn't nurtured I think the way I should have been. My family just didn't know how to do that.

My grandfather couldn't read or write, but still he expected respect. When the social workers came to visit, he thought that it was the most disrespectful thing for the government to come knock on his door and expect to just come in. I remember after the social workers left he would be so angry and offended. But he was scared, too, of the courts and of Child Protective Services. His guard was up, and he treated me like a princess because he was afraid they'd take me away. He'd say to my grandma, "Don't touch her, don't yell at her. Just give her what she wants." In the end, though, I think I would have been better off disciplined instead of enabled with toys and candy and ice cream.

My grandmother tried to teach me that to be the best person you can be in society, you just have to do what's right. But my grandfather had no education. He just rolled with the punches, ditching and dodging. So I had two different kinds of nurturing, good and bad. In my case it just happened that the bad nurturing outweighed the good nurturing. Soon enough, I started learning how to manipulate. If I didn't get what I wanted, I knew that all I had to do was scream, and I got it.

In second grade I started having visitations with my mom on the weekend. At the beginning I never really wanted to go with her. I didn't trust her. But in sixth grade, when I started developing, things began happening. I started wanting to smoke, I wanted to pluck my eyebrows, I wanted to do all sorts of stuff my grandparents wouldn't allow. And at my mom's house I could do anything I wanted because she was hardly there. I'd have boys over, I could leave and not come back until the next day, and she wouldn't question it. She'd yell, but all it took was a pill and a glass of Kool-Aid to keep her quiet.

In seventh grade I ran away for four days. My grandparents finally gave up on me. They couldn't control me any more, so they gave me to my mom for good. By that time, the courts were already out of our lives, and the only person we had to worry about was the welfare social worker. That was nothing; we just had to go in, dress nice, and show that I was in school. That was it, and we got our checks.

Once I was back with my mother, it all started: the cigarettes, the drinking, the hanging out with gangs and going out with boys. I even became a prostitute, and I started using drugs. With my mother already living the life of an addict, it seemed normal to me. My mother did it and my stepfather did it and everyone else out here was doing it. I'd walk outside my mom's apartment and there were gang members drinking and smoking and whatever.

IT'S LIKE THE CYCLE WAS NEVER BROKEN

I was locked up at the age of twelve for truancy, being a runaway and a delinquent, and for using PCP.[2] My grandparents were devastated when they found out. They just couldn't understand how it had gone wrong. But they were loyal, and when I was in juvenile hall my grandmother would not miss a visit. That lady was the first one there and the last one to leave. I remember the counselors there would give her lists of things I was allowed to have, half of which I didn't even need, and she would bring every single thing on the list. My grandma even started bringing things for the other girls, too. It was like she was the grandma of the whole unit. All the girls knew that when she was coming, everybody was getting something.

I was in for three months, and then they let me out. But I was only out for a couple months and then it began all over again. It was like a cycle. I would be out for a little while, and the probation would come and pick me up again, out of nowhere.

---

2. Phencyclidine, a synthetic drug also known as angel dust. Users experience distorted perceptions of sight and sound, as well as symptoms resembling those of schizophrenia, including hallucinations and extreme anxiety.

I wrecked my teenage life. To me, life was hanging out and going to parties and going to the drive-in with the guys.

Once, when I was fifteen, I was sent to a juvenile probation camp instead of juvenile hall. When they began letting me go out on passes to go home for the weekend, I just left. That's when I got pregnant. By then I was drinking alcohol and smoking PCP on a daily basis. When my baby daughter was born she was taken into custody and I was sent back to juvenile hall. My grandparents were too old to take care of the baby. By that time, though, my mom had gotten off the methadone and was able to get custody of her.

I was so glad my little daughter didn't end up in foster care. I hear a lot of stories about sexual abuse here in prison. I've seen women crying on the phone because they've just heard that somebody had touched their little girl in the wrong areas; I don't think I could endure hearing that about my baby. And it breaks my heart to hear these girls talking about having sex with their fathers, of being abused. I might have had a harsh childhood, but not like the stories that I've heard from the women in here. There are some really hurt individuals in here, and I'm not talking just mentally, but physically—scarred and damaged so they can't have kids. So it makes me so grateful that my mom was able to rebound and care for my daughter. At least she avoided being abused in foster care. But of course, in the end, she had a baby at fifteen too. It's like the cycle was never broken. My mom wasn't married and had me young. I wasn't married, and I had my daughter young. I only hope my granddaughter will be able to break the cycle.

YOU CAN GET ACCUSTOMED
TO THE LOSS OF DIGNITY

The first time I was sent to prison, I was eighteen. I was convicted of possession, transportation, and sale of PCP. I had large quantities, apple juice bottles of that stuff. My first trip to prison was for six years, and I've pretty much been in and out since then. Now I'm in my mid-forties. In the first institution I was taken under the wing of lifers who knew I was a baby and couldn't take care of myself. A lot of them played mom and a lot of them played sister, and they taught me the morals and principles of how to carry yourself, and the dos and the don'ts of surviving in prison. I learned that you have to carry yourself right, carry yourself with respect.

It's hard to explain how degrading prison is to someone who's never experienced it. You are told when to wake up, when you can bathe, when you can brush your teeth. You stand for twenty minutes waiting for a door to open just so you can walk in a line and go eat. You're given three minutes to shovel down your food and then you're right back in that line, waiting for the door to open up again so you can go put your stuff away. Through all this you have constant yelling over an intercom.

There's a lot of heartache, a lot of crime, and a lot of violence and chaos. Crammed into a building with 200 women you've got 200 different kinds of cultural backgrounds, ethics, beliefs, attitudes, and emotions. You've got 200 different ways of processing emotions. There are some women who can't read, some who weren't even taught how to shower. They come in here and they are stripped of their dignity. They can't even go to the bathroom without male staff watching. You can get so accustomed to the loss of dignity that your standards just disappear.

But some women come in who have never even taken off their clothes in front of their own husbands. They get so upset and so embarrassed, they cry. What makes me the saddest is that I find myself hardening up, saying things to them like, "What are you crying about?" I have to remind myself to have compassion. Just because I'm used to it doesn't mean someone else is. It's so sad to see women coming here who really don't know how to deal with prison. They've never been out of their homes. They're in here for ridiculous stuff: making bad decisions, helping someone out. They were just so naïve and gullible that another person was able to reel them in. And they're incarcerated with people who've committed murder. It's like one pit. Everyone's thrown in one pit.

YOU'RE CONSTANTLY LIVING
ON THE EDGE

It's two o'clock in the morning, how did this door get open? Even now, when things are supposed to be better, COs routinely come into our rooms and take our things. A lot of us have arts and crafts supplies to make cards with, like cardstock and markers. We might also have books or other small things. Routinely the COs will come with their gloves and bags, and they take everything. You've got three blankets? Trust me, they will take them away. You have a homemade pillow sewn up, they'll take that. You're constantly living on edge. Sometimes I feel like they set some women up. They know who's going to blow her stack about having her things taken, and they purposely target her, just so that she will lose it and they can bust her.

I WENT IN FOR ANGEL DUST
BUT I CAME OUT USING HEROIN

There is an abundance of drugs in prison, more so than on the streets. It's the currency of the place. You buy it, get it for free, do whatever. Maybe you become a runner, do a favor for an inmate, she'll give you half of the drugs. Even your tray of food—hamburger night, pork chop night—you take the pork chop back, you get dope in return. I went in for angel dust, but I came out actively using heroin. I had tried heroin in the free world, but I wasn't an active heroin addict because of my mother. I knew I didn't want to follow her example, so instead I'd used PCP. But when I got to prison I started using heroin, and by the time I got out I was hooked.

After that I was just in and out of jail and prison. Out for sixty days, back in again. In for four years, out again, violate parole, back in again. It was the same thing over and over again, for years. The only thing that changed was that in the early 1990s I switched from heroin to crack cocaine. Every time I went into prison, I came out with a worse addiction. Crack cocaine is just overpowering, I can't even express what it's like. I'm clean and sober now, and I look back and say to myself, "God! What the hell was I thinking?" I look at my arms, at the scars and tattoos, and I see how girls without them can wear pretty shirts and stuff, and it just makes me so sad. I just had no sense of worth. It just didn't matter.

It took me a long time to get clean. I've been in and out of programs. I've worked with sponsors, I've gotten therapy, I've done outpatient, I've had intensive family therapy counseling. It seems that when I did the intensive family therapy, that's what caused me to reuse drugs even more. A lot of the help I got was court ordered; it was nothing that I ever chose to get. I wasn't ready for it, and I was scared. Fear turns into anger and anger turns into resentment and resentment causes you to use, because if you don't know how to deal with the resentment in a healthy way, you have to numb it. So I'd use more. It was only when I was really ready to face all that stuff, when I came to it on my own, that I got clean.

The first time I got clean was for nine months. It was in 2004, and I had just been paroled. Rehab worked that time because I was ready, and because I had extensive care and a structured program. Through the program, I got a maintenance job, and so I went from rehab straight into work. They helped me get financial aid, I picked a college, got into it. They helped me all the way through. But I relapsed and ended up back in prison. I went back in in 2006, and I'm due to be released very soon. This last time I went in, I got clean again, and I've stayed clean for two and a half years.

But I used for a long time, and my body is a mess. I bruise easily; I just tap myself and I end up with a raised, painful lump. I've wrecked my body so much that even just having a menstrual period, I'm doubled over in pain. I haven't been able to get pregnant since I had my daughter. My periods are so bad that the prison doctors are monitoring them now. But that doesn't mean anything. They're not trying to fix the problem, or even diagnose it.

IN PRISON, YOU HAVE NO INFORMATION.
YOU DON'T KNOW THE TRUTH.

In the middle of 1990 I was diagnosed with HIV. While I was in jail, I was seen by officers from the public health department, interviewed and counseled, and given a blood test. It came back positive, and I have to say I wasn't surprised. With my history of drug use and the prostitution, it made sense. But you can imagine this diagnosis was devastating to me. I even tried to commit suicide.

I was sent to the prison's Chronic Care Program (CCP), where they kept people with chronic illnesses. In the CCP I had restrictions galore. I couldn't go to any other prison, I wasn't eligible for transfer to less restrictive institutions, and I was medicated. For almost ten years I was on three combinations of HIV therapy. They'd test my white blood cell count and it would come back really low. They'd screen my blood for my viral load, and the results would be terrible.

The side effects of the medication were awful: vomiting, diarrhea. Every day I had to stand in the med line, sometimes for hours in the heat. I was also regularly sent for chest X-rays with the other HIV women. And of course, because of the open treatment and the marked bags of medication, everyone knew I was HIV positive. People would harass me, the COs would discriminate against me. The whole system discriminated against HIV patients. For example, in 1999, I wanted to transfer to Valley State Prison for Women. They had just opened a dry cleaning vocational training program, and I was a perfect candidate for it. The prison agreed that I fit all the criteria and should be sent to the program. Then they decided they weren't going to house HIV inmates at VSPW. They were going to keep them in one place so they could be treated together.

Then, in 2007, after more than a decade and a half of aggressive treatment, the prison finally decide to retest me. The test came back negative. Negative! It turned out that I was not HIV positive, that I never had been.

This negative result was confirmed in 2008. The first HIV test they did back in 1990 was wrong.

I'll never know what happened to the original lab reports, whether they were falsified or whether it was just due to incompetence. They've retested me a few times, as recently as last year, and I'm still testing negative. But at the same time, I worry that maybe I have a special strain of HIV that's just not showing now. Am I gonna pop up with full blown AIDS a few years from now? I can't stop thinking, *How could I have had so many lab tests that showed high viral loads in my blood?* I'm scared. As it is there are so many diseases, like with the hepatitis they've got the whole alphabet now. How do they know for sure that I don't have a silent strain of HIV that's just hiding? I have no access in prison to medical information beyond what they tell me. That's what it's like to have a disease in prison. You have no information, you don't know the truth. In fact, I don't even know if I can trust this last test. Am I really negative? I don't know what to believe right now. I don't know what to do. I wish I could go see a doctor out in the free world who could screen my blood and see once and for all if I'm really HIV negative.

After all this testing happened, I petitioned for a hearing with the chief medical officer. Before prisoners can bring a law suit against the Department of Corrections, they first have to file an in-house grievance. It took me exactly nine months from the time I filed the grievance for the Chief Medical Officer to hear it and interview me. When I walked into the hearing room, there was a whole panel of people— medical officers, public health officials, nurses. They were ready for me. The public health nurse who initially sent me to be tested claimed that she'd never interviewed me. But how else would I have been referred for treatment? She insisted that she had no record of that, that she didn't recall it. It was ridiculous. We all knew that I'd been treated for HIV, but she kept insisting that she'd never given me the diagnosis.

The people on the panel claimed that it wasn't their fault, that they simply treated me for a disease they were told I had. They refused to acknowledge that they were the ones who told me that I had the disease.

IT'S LIKE YOU'VE BEEN PUT
IN A LITTLE BOX

Out in the world, when you get a diagnosis of a serious disease like this, you would go get a second opinion, just to be sure. But in prison, that isn't an option, so you have to rely on their diagnosis. You have to trust them. That's what I did, and look what happened. My advice, even to people in the free world, is to be your own best advocate. Do your research, get on the computer if you have access to one. Try to find out as much as you can, and make sure you get a second opinion.

My liver has gone through the stress of processing HIV medications, which can cause damage. But I don't even know if there has been any damage, because they won't test me. So I'm trying to monitor my own body to see what the effects of the drugs have been. I've had a series of problems which may be related to the HIV treatment, and may be related to my many years of drug abuse. For example, I've had my gall bladder out. I also have neuropathy in my legs, which causes terrible pain. I don't know the cause, but many other HIV-positive patients I know experience the same kind of pins and needles in the bottom of your foot where you can't even step on your foot. I wake up at night sometimes because my whole leg feels like it's going to crack off.

It took around nine months for the decision from the hearing to come through, and during that waiting period they kept sending my forms back to me, telling me that the wording was incorrect or that the filing dates were incorrect. Because I had to go through this process before even considering a lawsuit, I resubmitted three times, but each time they'd send it back, claiming there were these sorts of clerical errors. But during the process I had a public interest attorney from the prisoners' rights group Justice Now with me, so I was sure that the forms had been in perfect order.

In the end, the prison refused to accept responsibility. They blamed the mistaken diagnosis on the lab, and told me to go ahead and take it up with them. I tried to do that, but the lab had been shut down by the government because it was falsifying tests.

I also have, for years, been testing positive for tuberculosis. Each time they say it's a false positive. When I had the HIV diagnosis they would say that a false positive was a side effect of the disease. But now, I don't know why I keep testing positive.

I also have these ongoing gynecological problems that won't clear up on their own. I keep testing positive for vaginal bacterial infections. I've had Pap smears that showed abnormal cells, which they diagnosed as a bacterial or fungal infection. They've given me a variety of medications for these vaginal problems, including medications for herpes, despite the fact that I did not test positive for the disease. I've also tested positive for hepatitis C, and I wonder whether the hep C diagnosis is accurate.

More than anything I've gone through in my life and in prison, this medical stuff has messed me up. If you live in the free world, I don't think you can really understand. When you're in prison, it's like you've been put in this little box, and little slips of paper are put in the box with you, with pieces of information. You can't verify it, you don't know if it's true, you don't know what to do or how to act. And worst of all, there's no way of you getting out of this box. You just have to keep breathing.

Theresa Martinez was released in 2010 after serving a total of twenty-three years in prison. She served on the board of Justice Now, an organization dedicated to addressing injustices that incarcerated women face. In 2014, she spoke at a UN convention in Geneva on racial discrimination. In 2015, Theresa lives in Los Angeles, where she speaks at schools and conferences as an advocate for women's rights in prisons.

Throwing Stones at the Moon: Narratives From Colombians Displaced by Violence (2012), edited by Sibylla Brodzinsky and Max Schoening, tracks nearly five decades of violence against civilians at the hands of Colombian guerrilla groups, the national military, and paramilitary forces. The interviews for this book mostly took place during a two-year period starting in 2010. Though a period of calm followed a peak of violence at the turn of the twenty-first century, the conflict, fueled in part by the drug trade, continued.

Picture at right: El Jobo, Colombia

SERGIO DÍAZ

AGE WHEN INTERVIEWED: *21*
BORN IN: *El Jobo, Bolívar, Colombia*
INTERVIEWED IN: *Bogotá, Colombia*

From the time he was a small child, Sergio Díaz dreamed of playing soccer professionally. But his dream ended at the age of thirteen, when he stepped on a land mine and lost his left leg. The Colombian government has reported 9,755 civilian and military land mine victims between 1990 and March 2012. Most mines— often homemade contraptions made of plastic syringes and beer bottles—are planted by leftist rebels to block the advance of government troops, but more than one third of all mine victims, like Sergio, are civilians. We met Sergio at a rehabilitation center in Bogotá, where he was waiting for a new prosthesis.

WHEN I HEARD THE FIRST BOMB

When I was little, what I loved most was to play soccer. I was good. I was on the school team, and every afternoon after school I'd kick a ball around with my two little brothers. My dad promised me that he'd support me in becoming a professional player, or at least a coach. That was my goal.

I first realized that there was conflict in Colombia when I was eight years old. It was 1999, and my family and I were at the farm where my dad worked, near El Jobo, in Bolívar province. At about one in the afternoon we heard an explosion in the surrounding hills, and then immediately after, we heard shots being fired, bombs going off, and then a plane came and opened fire. I was excited when I heard the first bomb, when the combat started. I don't know why—maybe it was because I liked action movies. But then the combat went on and on, and I realized that it was serious. I got so scared that my face changed from this color to that, and I was given sugar water to drink to calm me down.

At first my dad told the family to gather in the living room. Then he decided it was too dangerous there, so he took us to hide under a concrete ledge at the back of the house. He wanted to get our minds off what was going on, so he tried to distract us by telling us jokes and stories about his childhood.

Things calmed down about three hours later, and my dad took us back to the house but told us not to speak loudly or run around. Then, at about eight in the evening, a group of guerrillas came to the property. That made me more nervous. I recognized them as guerrillas because they had a yellow flag on their armbands. They said that they'd clashed with the marines and that there hadn't been any casualties among the guerrillas. They told us we had no reason to worry because nothing had happened, and then they went on their way.

The next morning, the marines came to the property. They crossed the farm on the same trail that the guerrillas had used, but they didn't stop. We didn't have any problems with the marines because by then a light rain had fallen and erased any trace of the guerrillas' footsteps. If the marines had known that the guerrillas had come by, my dad would've been mistreated. At that time, the marines said that all farmers snitched to the guerrillas when the troops went by.

Generally, the marines always treated my dad like a guerrilla. When they passed through the farm, they'd cut the barbed wire and my dad's cattle would wander onto other properties. He had to stop doing whatever he was doing to go and fix the fences again. One time, in September 2003, he asked the marine commander not to damage the wire fence there, and to make a single gate where the troops could cross. So the commander called him a guerrilla, and said that all farmers in that region were guerrillas. My dad just stood back and didn't answer him. Whenever they called him aside I would try to sneak up and listen to how they treated him badly just for living in the countryside, just for being a peasant.

My dad always told me and my two younger brothers, "If one day you catch the fever of going off with an illegal group or serving in the military, keep me as a father in your heart, but do not visit me." He'd tell us, "I don't want to have a child in any group, anywhere. Neither to one side nor to the other."

Every time my dad left the farm, I'd get scared. I was afraid he'd get caught out there and get mistreated, or that he could be hurt or killed. I'd stand at the gate and look constantly to see if he was coming. When I'd see him coming, I'd get so happy that I'd run up and hug him. He would hug me back and tell me, "You're a fool. Nothing's going to happen to me." I would say, "No, it's not that I'm worried, I was just watching." But he knew.

I GOT AN IDEA THAT I SHOULD GO BACK

In January 2004, I was thirteen years old. I was on school vacation, so I was helping my dad on the farm. Early on January 9, my dad sent me to get some mules from the pasture to carry milk into town. I went with my two younger brothers. We had to walk one kilometer up a hill to the pasture where the mules were. While we were walking, I had a premonition. I got an idea in my head that I should go back, that I needed to go back. I was going to turn around but it was my duty to go to the pasture, so I didn't. I kept going, and chatted with my brothers to keep my mind off that feeling.

We arrived at the pasture where the mules were grazing. My youngest brother Michael, who was ten years old, grabbed the first mule. My other brother Tito, who was twelve, went after another mule, and I went for the other. When I went up behind the mule to grab it, he ran off to the right. I tried to cut him off and I stepped on his rope. Suddenly, I heard an explosion on the ground. I'd fallen to the ground, my ears were ringing, and I felt this heat wash over me. I didn't feel pain, really. I was so disoriented that I wasn't sure whether it was a dream or reality. I even managed to stand up but I fell down again. I tried again and fell. I didn't understand why I kept falling. That's when I looked down and realized I'd lost my left leg. It was destroyed.

My brothers had jumped up on a big rock and were crying. It was very hard for me when I saw my leg, but I told them calmly to come get me and take me home. They were afraid to come close. They yelled for my dad, and in a matter of minutes he came running with a cousin of mine. I remember seeing him coming and that's when I started crying. But I was relieved to see him. He picked me up, and then I passed out. He says that when I was in his arms, I said, "Don't let me die." I don't remember that.

MY LEG TOOK WITH IT
ALL THE HAPPINESS

I woke up two weeks later in a hospital in the city of Cartagena, about two and a half hours away. I couldn't move anything in my body. My head was bandaged, my hands were bandaged, the leg that was still half good was bandaged. I had shrapnel in my head. My dad told me that when he found me, he'd taken me to the village, and from there I was taken to the municipal hospital in El Carmen de Bolívar. There, they amputated my leg. I was in a coma at the time, and since there was no improvement they took me to Cartagena.

While I was in a coma the nurses had tied me up. It was the hospital director's idea. I didn't understand why I was tied up, since I couldn't move anyway. She told me that it was in case I got overwhelmed by what had happened when I woke up. But I knew I'd lost my left leg. I told her, "No, untie me. What has already happened has happened."

When I woke up I actually felt my two legs. I could wiggle my toes and everything. But I looked down and saw the space where my leg should have been. My mom cried when I did that, but I didn't cry.

I felt that my leg had taken with it all the happiness that I'd had. I spent forty-five days at the hospital, and during that time they made me see psychologists. But they said the same stupid things all psychologists say. The best psychologist I had was my dad. He's my role model, and he knows how to cheer me up. He would make me laugh and try to get me out of my depression.

IN THE BLINK OF AN EYE

My father left the farm, afraid that there were other mines on the property. I was the first mine victim in that region, but two days after my accident a man also stepped on a mine nearby. I think it was the guerrillas who'd laid the mines, because even though the military commit the worst abuses, they don't lay mines.[1] My family moved to the main town of El Carmen de Bolívar, and my dad sent a nephew to the farm to collect what he had there—all the chickens and cows. He went back himself once, to hand over the land to the new owner. After that, he worked on other farms, but he never recovered the prosperity he once had. It was all so hard for him. He couldn't get over my accident, or that everything he'd achieved over so many years of hard work was gone in the blink of an eye.

My dad once said, with all the pain in his soul, that it was best that it had been me who stepped on the mine. I asked him, "Why do you hate me so much?" And he said, "Had it been a member of the marines that stepped on it, maybe I wouldn't be alive—maybe none of us would be alive." The truth is that there would have been so much anger that the marines would have taken it out on him. They would have immediately

---

1. The FARC utilizes land mines more than any other armed group in Colombia, according to the Colombian Campaign Against Land Mines, the preeminent NGO monitoring the issue.

said that he knew the mine was there and hadn't warned them. So it was better that it wasn't a member of the marines who'd stepped on the mine.

While I was recovering in El Carmen, my little brothers would play soccer, and when they saw I was watching, they would change games and do other things, so they wouldn't see me sad. Sometimes they played soccer far from where I was so I couldn't see them.

In July 2004, I went to a Red Cross rehabilitation center in Bogotá, where I got my first prosthesis. I'd promised my mom that the next time she saw me I would be walking. I learned to use the prosthesis very quickly— I'm very agile with it—and when I went back to El Carmen in December, I was walking.

Soccer is what I miss the most. I've tried to play soccer with the prosthesis, but it's too hard to move my body the way I need to. It's really heavy, and my back hurts. I did work as assistant coach for a neighborhood team though, and in 2009 we were the league champions. Then I said I didn't want to be assistant anymore, that I wanted my own team. The coach who I was working with said, "Let's change roles. You'll be the coach and I'm the assistant." And we were champions again! That motivated me.

I really enjoyed coaching until I had a problem with one of the players. He yelled at me a lot, because I'd tell him how to play. He said things like, "You don't even play soccer, and now you come and teach *me* how to play." So I decided not to continue with the neighborhood league. I heard my team was champions again, twice.

I'm finishing high school now. I'd stopped studying because of the rehabilitation, but I'm now in eleventh grade.[2] I've thought of maybe studying medicine, but chemistry is my worst subject, and chemistry is important for medicine, I think. So I don't know. I don't know what comes next.

---

2. The Colombian high school system goes up to the eleventh grade.

Since Throwing Stones at the Moon *was published in 2012, more than 300,000 Colombians have abandoned their homes due to ongoing violence and conflict, raising the country's internally displaced population to around 5.7 million people, the second highest in the world. Through the start of 2015, the Colombian government and the country's largest guerrilla group remain engaged in peace talks. Meanwhile, civilians throughout the country continue to suffer killings, disappearances, and serious abuses by guerrillas and neo-paramilitaries.*

Refugee Hotel (2012), edited by Juliet Linderman and Gabriele Stabile, is a book of oral history and photography that documents the experiences of refugees first arriving in the United States, and then their adaptation to life in the States in the years after. Many of the initial photographs (by Stabile) were taken starting in 2007. Interviews conducted by Linderman took place three and four years later, in 2010 and 2011.

Pictured at right: Dena Dawoodi

FARAH IBRAHIM AND
MAHMMOUD DAWOODI

AGES WHEN INTERVIEWED: *35 and 40*
BORN IN: *Baghdad, Iraq*
INTERVIEWED IN: *Charlottesville, Virginia*

Farah Ibrahim and her husband Mahmmoud Dawoodi were both born in Baghdad, and raised in different middle-class neighborhoods. They grew up during the Iran–Iraq War, which ushered in a long period of fear, instability, and uncertainty that continued to worsen throughout the 1990 Gulf War.

FARAH: In a way, my life was similar to what every American child has. I had a good education, and many friends. The only difference was that we lived under a dictatorship. When I was a child, fear and anticipation began to grow because of the first Persian Gulf War between Iraq and Iran. There were secret police everywhere, and you couldn't trust anyone. If you said the wrong thing in front of the wrong person, you could get taken away in a second.

MAHMMOUD: War was reflected in every kid's personality growing up at that time. Kids would take a piece of wood and make it into a machine gun. Air fighters were coming and hitting the targets inside the city, and sometimes the sirens sounded when I was in school. The sirens were so loud, kids would fall over from the sound. One day, a missile hit a school in the town next to Baghdad. More than 200 kids died or were injured.

FARAH: When the first George Bush came in 1991, after Iraq invaded Kuwait in the Second Gulf War, it was intense and terrifying, because we heard the bombs and we felt them shaking our houses.

MAHMMOUD: One day my family was sitting around the table for breakfast and we heard a very loud sound. It was horrible,and everything—the tea, the cheese, the egg—flew off the table. We knew a missile had fallen down and exploded.

FARAH: Under United Nations sanctions, the economy collapsed. There was no money, no food. It was like living in a big prison. People started selling whatever they had just to survive. It sounds silly, but I remember as a child missing chocolate. Because of rations, for years we were banned from using sugar for anything other than basic cooking—so there were no cakes, no baking. Also, we didn't have electricity except for one hour a day. In 115-degree heat, we had nothing but a small fan. Whenever my family got together, my parents would compare our life to the golden days of Baghdad in the '60s and '70s, how they were able to travel, the culture, the before and after. It was clear to me that my life wasn't the life normal people in other countries lived.

After graduating from university, Mahmmoud found it impossible to find a job as an engineer. All he could do was watch his country crumble around him. In 1995, he signed up for military service,with the sole purpose of obtaining a passport upon completion of training. Because there was no official war in Iraq at the time, he was released after eighteen months. In 1997, passport in hand, Mahmmoud fled to Jordan, where he tried to register as a refugee with the United

Nations and worked as a high-school science and math teacher until his contract expired four years later. In 2001, Mahmmoud returned to Iraq, with the promise of an engineering job at Al-Mustansiriya University. Two years later, U.S. troops invaded Iraq for the second time, marking the beginning of the Iraq War, and giving rise to unprecedented sectarian violence between ethnic groups. At that time, Farah's family home was located on an arterial road in Baghdad that U.S. troops patrolled with tanks and heavy artillery. As the war raged on, the Iraqi government disintegrated, and the nation descended into lawlessness and militia violence.

FARAH: In March 2003, the U.S. military entered Iraq. My family saw clouds of dark smoke surrounding the neighborhood. We watched the U.S. troops on Al Jazeera. At first, we thought they were coming to free us. We knew that if Saddam was the bad guy, the United States couldn't be the bad guy. We thought the U.S. was fighting for other people's freedom, and we had such respect for the way Americans are. This is why we were hopeful. But as time went on, that changed, and eventually we thought, *Are they just neglecting us because our lives are worthless?* I met Mahmmoud in 2003. At that time, we were both working at Al-Mustansiriya University, where we had both gone to school. We got married in November 2004 and moved into a one-bedroom apartment upstairs from his family house. In April 2005, militia police wearing army suits came to my husband's house and took his younger brothers and his father.

MAHMMOUD: It was April 16, 2005. I had gone to visit my brother in Kirkuk, in Northern Iraq. I had also bought some real estate there. The next day my sister called and said there was a big group of militia who came into my house and took my father and two younger brothers. I knew they were looking for me. They wanted everyone who worked at the university. I am a nuclear engineer, and there aren't many of us, so everyone knows who we are. They killed many people like me—educated people and engineers.

FARAH: We don't know why. But different militia groups would target groups of people, starting with the military officers,then doctors, pharmacists, and engineers.

MAHMMOUD: I reached Baghdad the next morning and I contacted the police, who were communicating with the captors. They told me the captors would release my father and brothers. They released them that same day, but before they reached our house, another militia stopped their taxi at an intersection and took my father away at gunpoint. Later, my friends told me to go to the morgue. But my heart told me that my father was there even before I saw him. His side and his face were blue because they'd beaten him, and he was an old man.

FARAH: His father was originally from Kirkuk, so the whole family traveled to northern Iraq. Mahmmoud got a job there. I couldn't go with him at first because I was still working at the university and there was only enough housing for the workers. Also, we were hoping the situation in Baghdad would improve, and that he'd be able to come home. But things only got worse, and being away from each other became something we had to manage. Mahmmoud would drive down to Baghdad almost every weekend, and in 2006 I became pregnant with Dena.

After giving birth to her daughter Dena in 2007, Farah moved to Jordan permanently, where she registered as a refugee with the United Nations. She arrived in Charlottesville in January 2008. Farah now works as a full-time caseworker at the International Rescue Committee, the agency that resettled her. She shuttles Dena to and from Arabic classes, dance lessons, and after-school activities.

FARAH: I wouldn't want my daughter to live her life in Iraq, but I will always want her to know she is from there. I want her to be proud of who she is, and where she came from. The language, the culture, and the love of community is important to maintain, because life is so individualized for

Americans. Here, I am me, I'm a person, I decide how to live my life—not my family, my husband, or my neighbor can tell me what to do. For me, it's a controversy. I can understand it as being liberated, but being part of a community is important for Iraqis. I'd like Dena to be an American, in a way that she will be confident and educated and have faith in herself as a woman. But it's not easy; you must accept the mistakes you make, and you're responsible for what happens to you. One thing I found strange is that in American culture, people say, "I'm sorry." When I first arrived, I interpreted this as an apology for the actions of American troops and the government towards the people in Iraq. But I quickly realized that what they really meant is, "I'm sorry to hear it, I'm sorry you experienced that." Some Iraqis refuse to come to America, the country they hold responsible for everything that's happened in Iraq. For me, maybe I was living with my head in the clouds—America, the land of opportunity—but when you're desperate, you think of nothing but survival. You want assurance that you're going to be safe to start a new life. I feel safe here. I can think about my future and my family's future—I can plan for tomorrow, next week, next month. In Iraq, all we cared about was surviving one more day. I'm learning to dream again. I hardly speak to my neighbors in Charlottesville. In Iraq, you have to know your neighbors. It's part of your character. I have been absorbed into the culture of life here, though my mother sometimes doesn't like that I am more inclined to adapt to the American way of life. It's nice to have a community supporting me, but it's also nice to be who I am and what I feel. But it's hard, because I have to put one identity in the shadow when I act on another. For example, in my work, I have to treat all clients the same. I cannot be more helpful to Iraqis, or try to take a shortcut for them. From an Iraqi perspective, that makes me a bad person. It means that I'm a selfish and self-centered person, because I think about myself, my work, and my family more than my community.

Mahmmoud was selected for the United States resettlement program in July of 2010, and he was eventually reunited with his wife and daughter. When we first

met him in the spring of 2011, he expressed disappointment and unhappiness with
his employment opportunities in Charlottesville, and Farah worried that he felt
undervalued and resentful. But on our most recent visit, one year later, Mahmmoud
excitedly spoke about his life in the United States, how he's negotiated his past in
Iraq, and the future he imagines for himself and his family in Charlottesville as
new Americans.

MAHMMOUD: Charlottesville is different from other cities, and I like it that way—it's quiet, it's peaceful. Living here versus living in Iraq is like living in the sky versus living on the ground. Here, things are arranged. You've got your job, and you can do whatever you want to do. It took me only nine days to get a job as a mechanic. I got work at Allied Auto Repair, as an assistant. I don't depend on my degree. I know it's difficult for other educated refugees, but I'm not shy for the work I've done. If there is anything they want me to do I'll do it,because I want to start my life over again. At first, I worked as a mechanic, but there was no business, so, I left and found a job as a cashier at Kroger. I applied to be a bus driver, and a housekeeper at a school, where I work maintenance part-time. I'm now taking classes at Piedmont Virginia Community College in English and math, and I will take the test for GRE. And then, I'll try to get my Master's degree in engineering. For me, it's difficult because I have family in Iraq, so it will always be my home. But at the same time, home is where you feel safe, and where you find all that you love: family and friends. Dena, the next generation, sees her parents in America; she is an American, that's where her life and family is. I will have to travel to Iraq one more time, to decide where I really belong. But getting my U.S. citizenship is especially important to me. I was a citizen in Iraq, but I didn't feel the way I feel here. In Iraq it felt like jail, like the jungle. Here, I own my car, and I will own a house someday. Millions of people are dead. Five million children are orphaned. From a civilization that began 6,000 years ago, from the Babylonian era, we are now at zero. Whatever the United States did not destroy, thieves, burglars, and militia murderers did.

FARAH: A refugee is something I never thought I would be. I came from a wealthy country where a lot of people used to immigrate. It was a refuge for people who encountered hardship, not the other way around. But when I became a refugee in the U.S., I gave up the citizenship of the country from which I fled. We are not Iraqis anymore. We are not citizens of anywhere. Of course if it were up to me, I would live in my house in Baghdad forever, but that life is impossible now. I do want to be an American citizen, because this is the country that took me in and is helping me raise my child, even though this is the country I didn't choose. I don't have any dignity being known as an Iraqi.

MAHMMOUD: Before the war, I would say, "I am Iraqi." Now, I feel I'm Kurdish—the Kurdish people live in the north, and think they are different than Iraqis. I hate being Iraqi, I feel ashamed of being Iraqi, and of everything the government did. But, in Charlottesville, my identity is still Iraqi, for better or worse.

FARAH: I know that not everybody understands us, but in Charlottesville we've finally found a safe and secure home. "Home" means future plans, looking forward to tomorrow, and feeling safe about today. It means having the rhythm of my life restored.

By the end of 2014, Farah and Mahmmoud had settled into a house they bought that year, and which Mahmmoud renovated himself. At that time, Mahmmoud was working as a maintenance engineer at a nearby hotel and Farah had been promoted to full case worker, receiving Afghan and Iraqi refugees, and anticipating Syrian refugees as well. Many of the Iraqi refugees that Farah works with have fled encroachment by the Islamic State. "Baghdad is in better shape than six years ago, but the other provinces are much worse," she says. With the rise of the Islamic State in Iraq, Farah and Mahmmoud have become less hopeful of ever returning to Iraq.

Their daughter Dena attends second grade and is in her school's gifted program. Farah and Mahmmoud are excited for her future, and her chance to grow up in their new house. Although they want to keep her connected to Iraqi culture, Farah says they aren't pushing visits to the local mosque. Farah tells us, "I kind of want her to get her own ideas about religion. She's so young. The rights and wrongs are all the same for everybody. I want her to learn that first."

Refugee Hotel (2012), edited by Juliet Linderman and Gabriele Stabile, is a book of oral history and photography that documents the experiences of refugees first arriving in the United States, and then their adaptation to life in the States in the years after. Many of the initial photographs (by Stabile) were taken starting in 2007. Interviews conducted by Linderman took place in 2010 and 2011.

Pictured at right: Refugee housing in Erie, Pennsylvania

FELIX LOHITAI

AGE WHEN INTERVIEWED: 48
BORN IN: *Rokon, Sudan*
INTERVIEWED IN: *Erie, Pennsylvania*

Felix Lohitai is a Sudanese refugee who has been living in Erie for three years. Since his arrival, he's become a pivotal figure in the Sudanese community, working closely with Habitat for Humanity to facilitate home ownership for refugees. Felix was born in Central Equatoria in South Sudan, and served in the rebel army for nine years before fleeing first to Uganda, then to Kenya.

There is some confusion as to when I was born. 1964 was my year of birth, but of course refugees coming here don't have birth certificates because everything is lost. Everyone now says that the first of January is our date of birth.

Our tribes people were known as Langos in Sudan. I was born in Rokon in Central Equatoria, about fifty miles from Juba, the capital of South Sudan. But I lived in Eastern Equatoria for some time, because I traveled a lot with my father, who was a medical assistant. When I arrived in the United States I spoke five languages—Swahili, English, Kakua, Madi, and a little bit of Dinka.

The first war in Sudan, from 1955 to 1972, I remember only from my parents. The president came and made an agreement with the rebels to give South Sudan regional autonomy. Even though the North is primarily Muslim and the South is primarily Christian, there are lots of Muslims in the South, and Christians in the North; but the South Sudanese didn't want to be considered Muslim. Then, in 1983, the president decided to forget the whole agreement, declared a state of emergency and declared Sharia Islamic Law in South Sudan. A couple of military leaders decided to rebel, and that was the beginning of the war—people were disappearing, and politicians were being detained, arrested, killed, or exiled.

In September 1984, when I was almost twenty years old, I joined the rebel army. At that time, security forces were everywhere and there was an impending conscription. If I didn't join the rebels, I would have been drafted and taken to the North to be trained to fight against my own people. So I joined. I was a private, and I trained two divisions of 12,000 men each—24,000 men total. On September 21, 1986, I was promoted to second lieutenant and sent to war. It was all kinds of emotions—it's thrill, it's fear, it's courage, it's everything. I was part of the rebel army for nine years.

In 1993, I left the struggle when internal fighting broke out among the South Sudanese rebels. Like many guerrilla movements, there was a disagreement about leadership and power. Whenever the leadership splits, you find yourself on one side, without really knowing what side is the right side. There were two options—leave Sudan immediately, or be ready to die. There were three main warring factions already in South Sudan, and if one of them told me to join and I refused, I would have been killed. And I didn't want to take up arms and fight against my own people. I decided to leave, to go back to school, and so I went into exile. By that time, I had a wife and three kids, and I sent them to Uganda first. A few months later, I laid my gun and my uniform on my bed one night and left.

I walked to Uganda, where the Red Cross took me to the Agojo refugee camp. My family had been staying in a church in Uganda because my wife's father was a minister in Sudan, considered a bishop or a "chairman," and I brought them to the camp. But at the time, northern Uganda had its own guerrilla movement, and the guerrillas were killing refugees. There was famine and violence, havoc and ambushes. I had seen a lot in my life and I wasn't afraid. But I was scared for my family, so we took an overnight train to Kenya because we heard that the U.S. government was resettling refugees there. The Dadaab refugee camp in Kenya was worse than the camp in Uganda. Refugees were confined to the arid areas in the north and northeast of Kenya, where there is a lot of drought and the temperature was often over 100 degrees. There were close to 3,000 Sudanese refugees in Kenya living in shacks. My family was given a tarp to make our shelter. Over time, we built walls using mud and sticks. But I knew that there would at least be opportunities in Kenya for education, and if I could go to school, I could better help my family.

While living in the Agojo camp, Felix had met Mary Mason, a Church of the Brethren missionary from the U.S. who was working in rebel-occupied areas of South Sudan. Felix and Mary became friends. Felix says she considered him her "African son," and he considered her his "American mother," and they often wrote letters to each other. After Felix's arrival in Kenya, Mary helped him apply for scholarships to universities in the U.S., for which he was granted admission but was unable to attend after being denied travel clearance. Mary then facilitated Felix's admission to a university in Nairobi, Kenya, and paid $1,000 per semester for his education while his family stayed behind in Dadaab. In 1997, Mary was sent on a mission to Puerto Rico and the two of them lost touch. Felix returned to the refugee camp, unable to pay his own tuition. Then, in 1999, a pair of ministers called Phil and Louie Rieman contacted Felix. Mary had told them about Felix's situation, and they gave him the phone number of a top UNHCR official, instructing him to go to the UNHCR office the next day to discuss resettlement options. But in the months and years that followed, Felix's path to third-country resettlement would be repeatedly obstructed by unforeseen obstacles. At one point, his identity was stolen and used by another refugee to travel to New Zealand. After many false starts, he and his family eventually made their way to Erie.

On Louie's instructions, I went to the UNHCR office. I walked through the main door. Refugees are never allowed through that entrance, they have their own door. It was crowded with refugees and there were police everywhere—local Kenyans who would beat the hell out of anyone who misbehaved. In 1999, a UNHCR official interviewed me. At the time, New Zealand was accepting refugees, so she submitted my papers to the New Zealand Embassy.

After submitting my application, nothing happened. My family and I waited and waited for one year, until 2000, but we were never called, not even for an interview. The case for New Zealand just disappeared. I had friends in the United States who were pushing me to resettle in there. My friends had contacted a Joint Voluntary Agency, the JVA. The JVA worked with U.S. immigration to help resettle refugees. I was just a little person; they were big people in big offices, but they contacted me and I filled out the paperwork. My family had our first interview, and then our second, third, fourth, and finally we were accepted in 2001. Our itinerary was set. It was March 15, and we were ready to board a bus to the airport—I had my kids, my luggage, everything. Then, someone came from the International Organization for Migration, IOM, with a letter in hand. He asked me, "Are you Felix?" I said, "Yes." He said, "Felix, we want to see you in our office tomorrow. Your flight has been canceled." I felt like I'd been hit by a bus. If I were by myself it would have been no problem. But I was looking into the eyes of my kids and I just couldn't take it. My youngest was still in diapers, and my oldest was fourteen. Everyone was devastated. We had already given all our things away.

In the morning, I went to the IOM office and I was told that I must go to the U.S. embassy, that there was a problem with my name. They said someone with my name had already traveled to New Zealand. I knew nothing about this. I went to the office, and I contacted everyone I knew in the United States and had them write letters confirming that I was the true Felix. They wrote to senators, and the senators sent the INS letters. For two years I wrote the INS, one letter every week. I said, "This hand of mine, I will use this hand and this pen and I will get to the United States. If tonight my children go to bed with no food, I'll write it in the letter." Finally, in December 2003, I was called back to the INS. An officer there brought my file, full of letters—he had to wheel it—and he said, "You are indeed the real Felix, and you're determined to take your family to the United States. And you will."

Felix and his family were assigned to Grundy Center, Iowa, and in February 2003, they boarded a plane bound for the United States. Felix lived in Grundy Center for six months with his wife and children before moving to North Manchester, Indiana, where he enrolled in a peace and conflict studies university program. His wife and children eventually joined him there in 2005. When Felix graduated in 2009, he gave his wife the option of moving the family anywhere in the United States. She chose Erie: a small, quiet city with an African refugee community already in place.

When we got to Erie, we only knew one family. I saw a place where our community was not doing well, both in terms of assimilating to American culture and preserving our own culture. I know some people living here who want to go back home. Some of them have been here twelve years and they are not citizens, because of the position of the community. But now we are talking about the importance of becoming a citizen, of changing the mentality of never being sure where you are or if you belong.

So we started having meetings. In the camps, we had a community helping us, but in Erie, parents go to work in plastic factories and when they come home they're tired, and they don't know what their kids are doing. They speak Arabic; they can't help their kids with their homework. What these kids get is total confusion. And some parents want their kids to behave like Sudanese, but when they go to school, they are taught to be like Americans, and American culture is totally different. The parents feel out of place with their children, and there is always conflict.

At the time, most Sudanese refugees were living in public housing. When you live in the projects, you don't feel that you are really a part of

America. People live in the suburbs and come into Erie to work. Who is left actually living in the city? Minorities, in cheap housing in bad neighborhoods where children connect easily to the wrong people.

I've seen a difference during the time I've been here, since we organized. We contacted the Habitat for Humanity office in Erie to talk about housing. We can't live in government housing forever. Do you think we're ever going back to our country? No. This is our country now. We live here. We need to own houses. Most of the Sudanese refugees in Erie are working in plastics and earning minimum wage. So I told Habitat for Humanity, "We have a problem," and they started working with us.

The first refugee in our community to buy a house was a medical doctor from Sudan. Now, he owns his house. Pretty soon there was another who bought a house. Now there are seven refugees who own their houses. Owning a home gives you confidence. If I'm renting, it's not my home, it's someone else's home; I can pack up and leave and disappear and no one will care. If I have a house here, I know that this is home; it's an incentive to integrate into American culture.

I thought I knew a lot about America before I came, but my research was shallow.

Many things surprised me. There are a few people controlling everything, and misleading everyone. Food policy, domestic policy, criminal justice—the fact that America has more incarcerated people than China—those things disappoint me. Everyone has been affected by the economy. Without a job, you cannot feel stable, even Americans. But in this country, you can go as far as anyone can possibly go in education, and you can't do that anywhere else. I know with my education, I'll get a job somewhere.

This is my country now, and I will be a U.S. citizen. I will carry a U.S. passport. When I was first chosen to come here, one caseworker told me, "You are going to the United States. That is your country, and don't you ever, ever feel like a stranger." Everybody in America is a stranger when they first arrive. But in fifty years our grandchildren will be just like everyone else.

———————————————————

When we spoke to Felix at the end of 2014, he was thinking of moving from Erie. Budget cuts had led to his layoff from a job with United Way in 2013, and he still hadn't found work. He was especially interested in doing counseling work in an academic setting and he told us he was proud that both of his sons are in college. Felix obtained U.S. citizenship in 2013 and considered traveling back to South Sudan to work for an aid organization. But warfare between rival factions in the new country made that impossible. His brothers there warned him that former citizens who left and then came back were not looked on favorably. Felix wants to write about his experiences in Sudan, but other priorities come first. He tells us, "Many of us immigrants think we are so used to worrying, but in the U.S. we worry every day too, about bills, your landlord standing there demanding late fees, cars not running. It's wholly different from what we used to worry about."

High Rise Stories: Voices From Chicago Public Housing (2013), edited by Audrey Petty, includes stories of former residents of Chicago's iconic public housing high rises. The interviews for the collection were conducted starting in 2010, in the aftermath of Chicago's plan to demolish the high rises and diffuse concentrations of public housing. For many narrators in this book, the demolitions shattered communities, even if the buildings themselves were nearly uninhabitable.

Pictured at right: Cabrini-Green

DOLORES WILSON

AGE WHEN INTERVIEWED: *83*
BORN IN: *Chicago, Illinois*
INTERVIEWED IN: *Chicago, Illinois*

We first meet on a sunny day in March 2011, at a coffeehouse situated about a mile north of Dolores's new apartment in the Dearborn Homes high rise. Dearborn Homes is a public housing complex situated at the crossroads between Bronzeville (to the south), the McCormick Place convention center (to the east), Chinatown (to the west), and the Chicago Loop (to the north). Dearborn Homes was one of the Chicago Housing Authority's first public housing developments and remains one of the last standing—it now houses mostly senior residents. Dolores was relocated here last month after living in Cabrini-Green for the last fifty-three years, from 1958 until 2011. As we talk, Dolores is clearly distraught at the thought of her old building's scheduled demolition. "So many of my treasures are still there," she says. She goes on to catalog some of the valuables (family photos, trophies, clothing, books) that she had to leave behind during the hasty relocation process. Days after our conversation, 1230 N. Burling—Dolores's former home, and one of the last public housing high rises left standing in Chicago—was demolished.

THE STERILE WARD

I was born in Chicago in 1929. Cook County Hospital, Ward 32. I think that's the sterile ward. They had 31 and 32. If you're born outside the ward, your baby's un-sterile 'cause you could catch anything in the hallway.

After I got grown and got married and started having children, my mother told me the Cook County Hospital is the best hospital to go to. She said, "They have the best doctors." And I soon found out why, because it was like a charity hospital. You're not turned around. They can treat this, treat that, the doctors are learning all that they didn't get in school.

I had Chichi and Debbie at Cook County Hospital. Cheryl was born at Provident. Mike and Kenny were born at home. Those were the easiest births I had, Mike and Kenny. Chichi almost died because he was breech. Feet first. If the instrument that the doctors used to turn the baby had not been there, I would have died. But it was there when they needed it. I wrote my mother a postcard, and I said on it: "I almost died!" When I got home she said, "You don't never write nothing like that on a postcard where the mailman and everybody can read it!"

They had this nice sudsy water or some kind of solution and a swab, and they would just clean you afterwards. Couldn't nobody get an infection or anything in there. I loved the County. I don't know how it was after years went by. I hate that they're tearing it down. That whole hospital— they could have made it for the homeless. They had everything: toilets, kitchen, everything. All they had to do was just get security to make sure nobody was causing any problems. Now they gonna tear down Michael Reese Hospital too,[1] for some kind of high rise. Chicago is a capitalistic town, is all I gotta say. And that's why we're not in Cabrini anymore.

---

1. Michael Reese Hospital was founded on the Near South Side of Chicago in 1880. Its founding mission was to serve all Chicagoans without regard to race, creed, or nationality.

ONE OF THE FIRST FAMILIES IN CABRINI

I lived in Cabrini-Green for fifty-three years. My husband Hubert and
I raised five children there. When we moved there in '58 the oldest was
eight, the youngest were two and one, and we loved Cabrini. Where we'd
been living on South Side, on Sixtieth and Prairie, they were like fire traps.
The buildings were just deteriorating. The placement at the private real
estate office would charge us ten dollars to find an apartment, and at that
time ten dollars was a lot of money. But we paid it, and everywhere they
sent us were nothing but fire traps. They were no good, and some of them
said they didn't want children 'cause they throw rocks and break windows—like every child will throw rocks and break windows.

So I kept looking, and after a while I thought, *Well, Altgeld Gardens and
Cabrini was offered to us by the city.*[2] I wanted Altgeld Gardens, 'cause the
complex was made up of family homes, with little front yards and back-
yards, but the city buses near there ran on a slow schedule, and I didn't
want to be slowed down by anything. When I was ready to go out of the
house and go somewhere, 1 wanted a bus that was coming in the next
two minutes or something. So that's what made me ask directions all the
way to Cabrini-Green. And I loved the apartment. The apartment had
three bedrooms, and it was on the fourteenth floor. When I first stepped
off the elevators and looked out over the railing I thought I was going
to faint! I'd never been up that high. The cars below looked like little
toys. I didn't even try to look at anything. I just looked down to see how
high up I was. But after a while you get to liking everything. Just like
with people, I don't care what neighborhood you're in. I don't care if
it's a diverse area or what, after a while you get to love and know your

---

2. In the mid-1960s, the median Chicago Housing Authority family was working class and two parent.
Rents in CHA housing units were determined by building maintenance costs, not family income. Not
until the 1970s, with the passage of the Brooke Amendment at the federal level, was rent indexed to
25 percent of family income, then later 30 percent.

neighbors and everything and get along. That's the way it was with me and that fourteenth floor.

Me and Martha Williams, who is still my very good girlfriend, we were the first two families to move into 1117 Cleveland. She was on the second floor. After they started moving more people in on the floor, you get to have neighbors and all, and in the back of my mind I'm wondering, *How this heifer gonna be?* And I was thinking, *I don't want to be up here fighting nobody, telling me that they smell garlic.* I'm using that as an example, 'cause we did have Puerto Rican neighbors, like the Montanes, who cooked a lot of garlic. I can't stand the smell of a lot of garlic. Makes me sick. But they were wonderful people and even though they were young, my children always wanted to go to church with the Montanes. I was so happy to know that somebody on the same floor is taking time with my children. And they had about four or five of their own. Taking them to church. And they would cry, "Mom, I want to go to church with Miss Montanes! I wanna go to church with the Montanes!" My son Michael was the main one begging to go with them. And I'd be glad. The kids went with them all the time.

THIS IS A CASTLE

Ten years later, around 1968, we moved from 1117 because my husband's boss wanted him to be the assistant head custodian in one of the Green buildings, and that meant maintaining a whole building. My husband's boss was moving out, and he wanted my husband to take his place. I thought that was such an honor, but the assistant heads and the heads had to live in the building that they care for. That's why we had to move on to 1230 N. Burling. I was so mad that we had to leave our home. That's how attached you get to people. Ooohhh, I cried the whole time! My next door neighbor, Queenie, we were like sisters, and so she and her husband and her daughters and son helped my family move with some of the guys in the neighborhood. And when I got off from working at the Water Department that day, everything was in divine order cause I'd marked on the boxes, *This goes in this room, that goes in that room.* Curtains were hung and everything. I was on the sixth floor and we had four bedrooms and a bath and a half. I said, "Oooh, this is a castle." But I still was around strangers.

The move to Burling happened right after the '68 riots, after King was killed.[3] I remember my son Kenny, who was about twelve at the time, was heading out the door when the riots first started, and he said, "Mom, I'm going over to Pioneer." That was the grocery store nearest in the neighborhood. And I said, "Going for what?" They were rioting everywhere. And the police didn't care. They had the National Guard, but as long as you didn't go east across Wells, you would be safe. No harm would come to you. You could tear up everything else on that side, because the Chicago Police Department didn't care about the stores and businesses. And you know, most of the businesses didn't come back.

And I said, "What are you going out there for?" He said, "I'm gonna get a shopping cart." He wanted to join the looters. I said, "No you're not." And he said, "Everybody else is." I said, "You don't do what everybody else does. You do what I tell you to do."

WHERE'S THAT MUSIC?

After a while, my husband became head janitor. So we lived rent-free. I'm telling you, I could see myself with a home in the sky. But the more money you get, the more money you spend. But it was wonderful, you know. And everybody, they just loved our family. They really loved my husband. All he was supposed to do as head janitor was just work with a pen and paper. But he didn't know nothing about doing no easy work. He wanted to help push and pull the garbage, and help with everything.

They called him "Old Man." They said, "Old Man, we got this, we

---

3. Martin Luther King, Jr.

got this." So they would help him push the dumpster. That building was spotless. People loved my husband, so they wouldn't even throw anything down on the floor.

I would come home and he'd tell me about his day and I'd tell him about mine. I worked for the Water Department. It was a secretarial job in payroll, and it was nice. Office was in the Pumping Station over on Chicago and Michigan, on the Magnificent Mile. Across from the Water Tower. Then they moved us to the purification plant near Navy Pier.

When we were at 1117 Cleveland, my husband started a drum and bugle corps. And there were kids from 1117 and 1119 Cleveland, and kids from certain buildings in our area and across the street from the Green section. And they were in three or four Saint Patrick's Day parades. And they weren't even in full uniform 'cause they didn't have the money for uniforms. They would practice outside on the black top or Father Sebastian would let them come to Saint Joseph Church and practice in their school's gym. But then it at all changed after the '68 riots.

More people moved in from other places that had been really affected by the riots. We started seeing gang writings on the wall. Sniping at different buildings. Snipers were a problem for many years. These people would set up in a window of the towers and just shoot at anyone. Two police got killed.[4] I remember one day, a cop car was sent to my building because someone was sniping at them from the building facing my lot. And one young girl that I remember seeing, she had on a trench coat. She was really running across the lot. When she got to the building, the back of her coat had caught a whole lot of buckshot. It was a miracle she wasn't hurt.

The Eighteenth Police District, they sent Commander Brash and a man named Fred Rice—he passed recently—and they worked with us and they had officers patrolling in that area, so the kids in the drum and

---

4. In 1970, Sergeant James Severin and Officer Tony Rizzato were crossing a field when they were shot and killed by a sniper positioned in an upper-story of a Cabrini-Green high rise.

bugle corps were protected when they were coming to practice. They'd have patrols watching them coming and going. That's how they got safe passage from Saint Joseph's Church to our building.

My husband worked with kids for many years. He had a basketball team and a baseball team. Those teams won trophies. The drum and bugle corps got twenty-three trophies without even being in full dress. The kids played music by ear, and when they played that "Watermelon Man," boy, people would be looking. "Oh, where's that music coming from?" Especially in the Saint Patrick's Day parade. People be amazed. *Where's that music?*

They were called the Corsairs, my husband's group. My son Mike, he played that timbale, that's the three drums. Dolores, stop bragging! Okay. Can't help bragging. And all the gals liked him. There were the flag girls and the rifle girls. You know, the ones that twirl the rifles and the girls that twirl the flag. You know, all they say is: practice makes perfect. Beautiful! They were beautiful together. So when my husband passed away in 1981, one of the guys in the corps said, "Momma Wilson, what we gotta do is have a concert every May 11." That's the day my husband passed. He said we were gonna have a day to celebrate—a day for my husband. But it never came through because this one's living here, that one's living there.

GANGS THAT DIDN'T EVEN HAVE NAMES

I was the president of our Building Council for ten years after my husband passed away, from about 1983 to 1993. That's how I got into the Local Advisory Council and residents' management program. Every building had a Building Council, but in the late eighties, the residents in 1230 N. Burling started taking resident management courses. We pulled together and handled everything except the electricity and plumbing. The residents had jobs— work order clerk, janitors, maintenance men, secretary, treasurer, everything. We even collected the rent. Eventually our building was rehabbed after we went into resident management. All of the blinds, all of the kitchen, the refrigeration, double-pane windows, everything was brand new. I believe 1230 N. Burling was the first building in Cabrini-Green that went into resident management. The first President Bush, Daddy Bush, named us "a model for the nation." We met with Jack Kemp and then Henry Cisneros in Washington, D.C. And our building was incorporated in 1992.[5]

Back when I first got started, at my first meeting as president of the Building Council, there was a room of people—old, young, middle-aged—waiting to hear from me. I was so happy when I came in and saw all these people in there, but then I got so flustered I didn't even know what to say. "A dah-dah-dah-dah-dap. Uh-uh-uh dip-dip-dip-dip . . . we'll have a striptease next week!" I didn't know what to say, you know, all the different ages, waiting to hear from me. People with little babies and guys in there that belonged to gangs. Everyone was giving me suggestions. *We can do this with the building, we can do that with the building.*

But what really took off was working with the little kids. The grown folks, the older ones, they would make their appearances at meetings for maybe a few months, but the little kids, they're the ones that kept working with me, improving the building, picking up trash. "You better pick! Ooh, I'm going to tell Miss Wilson you threw that paper on the floor." They'd pick up that litter and throw it in the garbage. I'd put homemade paper badges on the kids saying they're elevator monitors, so that folks don't get on and leave trash. I'd have two on at a time and they worked those elevator buttons. They didn't even want to get off.

The older kids—the boys—they didn't join gangs because they wanted to, but in the eighties, with other gangs moving into the neighborhood, this made them form gangs in response, for self-protection. Gangs that

---

5. Jack Kemp was Housing and Urban Development Secretary under President George H. W. Bush, from 1989–1993 and Henry Cisneros was Housing and Urban Development Secretary under President Bill Clinton, from 1993–1997. 1230 N. Burling was the first of Chicago's high rises to be granted resident management status, a designation applied nationally under the first Bush administration to provide Federal dollars directly to public housing residents to develop and manage their buildings. By 1997, seven Cabrini-Green buildings were under resident control, as well as parts of Dearborn Homes and LeClaire Courts.

didn't even have names. Even I wanted to carry a gun. There was so much slicing and shooting and carrying on. I said, "I'm gonna start shooting back," but I didn't have no gun. One lady was shot at who had a baby in the stroller. They were just sniping from that one building, I'm telling you. And 1150 and 1160 Sedgwick. One group just took over those two buildings, and guys that used to live in the building had to go along.

My very good girlfriend, she moved over there on Sedgwick, I guess 'cause she wanted a larger place, I don't know. But that made her son, you know, when in Rome do as the Romans do. So a lot of 'em had to be a part of that gang. Now, I'm so glad to know that this guy, he's into the Word. He sang at a funeral for a friend of ours and to hear him speak, you wouldn't ever think he had to pick up a gun. A lot of them, they have to join—either you shoot me or I shoot you.

The way our building was, if you come out one side you had to shoot, and if you came out the other side there was another gang waiting for you. Oooh, it was terrible. August 5, 1991, my son Michael was standing in front of our church at the corner of Hobbie and Larrabee, which is Holy Family Lutheran, the same church I've been going to now for forty-three years. And he got shot right there, standing there. The shot came somewhere from way up high. The bullet came straight through him. He died. He must have been forty years old.

A lot of folks knew who did it, and when the detectives came, I'm trying to tell one of the detectives who did it. He'd say, "Well, it's just hearsay, we don't know, we don't know." But I know. I heard who did it. I told him, "I want you to go up there." They wouldn't even go, 'cause a lot of times they don't even care. That's what bothers me.

IN CABRINI, I'M JUST NOT AFRAID

Not too long after my son got killed, must have been in the fall of '91, I was at a benefit dinner, something to do with my community work, and this reporter came up to me and said, "Aren't you Ms. Wilson?" When

I said that I was, he said, "Aren't you afraid of living in Cabrini with all this shooting and stuff?" I said, "No. I even leave out at night and go to the store," which I did. I said, "Only time I'm afraid is when I'm outside of the community. In Cabrini, I'm just not afraid." It's like I told my boss, "If I'm going to live somewhere all these years and be scared, I'm crazy."

In '93 I retired after nearly thirty years of service with the city. I got some congratulatory letters and tapes that people made for me. Janitors and clerks and everybody. Over the years on the job, so many people there wanted to ask me how I survived Cabrini. They had extreme ideas about what was happening there. I'd get to work in the morning and somebody would come up to me: "Ooh, Dolores. Did you get hurt? I read in the newspaper about this and that shooting." I'd say, "I don't know nothing about it." What got to me was the reporters didn't put down no address in their stories. Cabrini is a big neighborhood, from Halsted down to Sedgwick. But the news would just say, "It happened at Cabrini," and a lot of times, things would happen outside of Cabrini or nearby and they still pinned it on Cabrini. So folks wouldn't want to come up in there. Even my own brother. He would flat out refuse.

One day, I'm waiting on the bus in the dead of winter, to get to work. Waited so long I finally tried to flag a cab down. One guy stopped and said, "My boss told me not to pick up anybody in Cabrini, said if anything happen to me or this cab, my family don't get no compensation or anything." And then he said, "But I'm picking you up. You look like a nice lady." I said, "I *am* a nice lady." I could hardly lift my hands to shut the cab door, they were so frozen cold.

THEY MADE ME MOVE TOO FAST TO HOLD ON TO MY MEMENTOS

My building, 1230 N. Burling, is still standing. Supposed to knock it down in just a few days. When the last family was moving out, I felt so sorry for the lady who had just moved out of one building that they tore down. Everybody in that building had to move. You know, it's sad when you get a little age on you, you got your place the way you want it to be, and then they're talking about how you got to move.

When they told us that we had to leave, I'm thinking, *fifty-three years in Cabrini.* They gave us letters letting us know how many days. I think it was maybe 120 days, and I thought, *Oh, well I got time to move.* But I was still surprised. I thought that they were only going to tear down the buildings that were degraded and not working. It was such a rush to do this and do that. And it was hard for me. I was eighty-two years old when I moved. I didn't want to give up my apartment, and it was only two bedrooms. By then, I was on the eighth floor. Me and my youngest son, Kenny, we were the only ones still there, till he passed four years ago. But it was still my home and it held everything I owned since we were in 1117 Cleveland, including memories.

I had so many mementos and they made me move too fast to hold on to them. Now I cannot find my wedding pictures. I don't have one picture of me and my husband and my parents and his parents and our wedding cake that my aunt made. She had a bakery and I cannot find that one picture. I can't find a picture from one of our meetings with Bertha Gilkey. She was a public housing activist from St. Louis. Bush came. Daddy Bush. And he met with all the board, not all the residents. We met with Bush and he had his picture made with each one of us. I can't find that picture either. My husband and I went to Jamaica so many times. I don't have one picture from Jamaica. My sisters and I went to the Bahamas two or three times. I don't have a picture of that. It was in the house. I'd boxed it, and I'm trying to think 'cause things was happening so fast, and they were telling you you gotta get out by this that and other, you know. My husband's trophies are gone now. I didn't have the help to get those out of the closet, you know, and no boxes! I just had to leave them.

And I said, "Oh well." Now my stuff is probably off in some dump.

I got a brick from Cabrini, from our first building at 1117 Cleveland. And I got a brick from when I traveled over to St. Louis with Bertha and a group of public housing resident leaders; got a brick from where Pruitt–Igoe[6] once was. I saw the remains. Said it was gonna be a huge parking lot.

The last day I was allowed to be in 1230 N. Burling, I was so happy that the manager let me go back in there. Mostly I went in looking for my wedding picture. And three times she let me in. I thought that was so nice of her, 'cause I didn't think she had to. But I was still rushing and I just couldn't find that wedding picture. You see, I didn't have a pickup truck or anything to help me put stuff in storage—I couldn't afford it, and they didn't provide. They didn't give me nearly enough boxes! And I didn't find out there was storage for people who were forced out. Didn't learn that until the day the movers showed up. But, oh well.

A lot of people had to move. Everybody, you know, you look out the window, you see long trucks. This one moving, that one moving. Different ones were using different vehicles, pickup trucks or whatever. I just didn't have it together. They gave me and my daughter one long truck. We were each supposed to have one truck because she was moving to a new place, too, so I was rushing and I didn't pack what I needed. And if I didn't get out on time, I'd have to pay rent for both places.

Everybody was moving in all directions. The housing office kind of steered you to where they wanted you to go. I'd been interested in Hilliard Homes[7] and Parkside,[8] but they said those places weren't taking applications. Quite a few of us headed to the Dearborn Homes, where I live now. My daughter's right nearby. But we're not all in the same building. The people I've known from Cabrini are all in different buildings. And when we see each other, it's "Ohhh ahh!" Like we haven't seen each other for

---

6. Built in 1954, the Pruitt–Igoe housing development of St. Louis was one of the first high rise housing developments in the U.S., and also one of the first to be demolished.

7. A forty-nine-year-old public housing structure located on the Near South Side, it consists of two sixteen-story buildings reserved for elder housing and two eighteen-story buildings reserved for low-income family housing.

8. A mixed-use development of townhouses on the Near North Side, blocks away from where the Cabrini-Green high rises once stood.

a thousand years. And a lot of them, their sons come to visit, "How you doing, Ms. Wilson?" 'Cause I'm there by myself. "Are you all right? You being taken care of okay?" And they come back and keep checking. "You want anything from the store?" All times of day and night they stopping in, I can hardly rest, but I get up anyway and say, "Thank you for coming." Young guys, their mommas probably send 'em to ask me. That's the way it's supposed to be. That's family. That's what it is.

I'm still getting used to things at Dearborn Homes. It's like that song says, "a house is not a house, a home is not a home" until you live there. My new place is okay, but I'd really like to be in a larger space. I always joke that I can sit on my sectional couch and cook on my stove! It's okay. It's not Cabrini. It's funny—now I like to be up high! I like to see the sun set, but from where I am now, I can't see anything set. From my window, I see the building in front of me and the parking lot and a little bit of the street, and I can also see the playground. God is good all the time. You know, for a while I was so stuck on seeing the sun set. One night I saw the moon, and I got all excited and said, "Ooh, thank you, Father. Thank you, Father." He said, "Where have you been staring all these years?" I was stuck on the sun setting, and he said, "Look at the moon."

In 2015, Dolores continues to live in Dearborn Homes. "It's nice. I like it," she tells us. She mentions, however, that there are no stores near Dearborn Homes, and she has to take public transportation to buy groceries. She's working with a neighbor on a petition to bring a grocery store into the neighborhood. Still, she is less enthusiastic about building a community with her neighbors than she'd been when living in Cabrini-Green. Dolores doesn't like visiting the neighborhood where she raised her family. "That's all tears," she says. "It's not like home to me any more. Home is where you plant your roots, where you know everybody and everybody knows you. Everything there has changed. There's a Target now across the street from where I used to live, and they were going to build a high school there named after Barack Obama. That's nice, I guess."

High Rise Stories: Voices From Chicago Public Housing (2013), edited by Audrey Petty, includes stories of former residents of Chicago's iconic public housing high rises. The interviews for the collection were conducted starting in 2010, in the aftermath of Chicago's plan to demolish the high rises and diffuse concentrations of public housing. For many narrators in this book, the demolitions shattered communities, even if the buildings themselves were nearly uninhabitable.

Pictured at right: Aerial view of Cabrini-Green

YUSUFU MOSLEY

AGE WHEN INTERVIEWED: *61*
BORN IN: *Columbia, Mississippi*
INTERVIEWED IN: *Chicago, Illinois*

Yusufu Mosley was born Lonell Mosley in Columbia, Mississippi. Yusufu was a name first given to him by a Tanzanian minister who visited his family's church in 1967. The word itself is Kiswahili for "one who encourages." When he was eight years old, Yusufu's mother and stepfather moved the family north in order to provide more opportunities for their children. He lived in Cabrini-Green in the early through late 1960s. His experience of racism in Chicago politicized him and spurred him to travel back south to volunteer in the Freedom Schools.[1] As a young man, Yusufu became involved in organized armed resistance and violent activity. He says, "We thought the revolution needed to be fought with knives and guns rather than minds and hearts." In 1974, Yusufu was convicted of murder and attempted murder and was incarcerated in southern Illinois. He remained a dedicated student of history during his incarceration, and he enrolled in a college program through Roosevelt University and earned a bachelor's degree. During his imprisonment at Menard Correctional Facility, Yusufu co-organized a Black Cultural Coalition to bring

---

1. Freedom Schools were seminars designed to teach civic engagement. They were a feature of the Freedom Rides—campaigns to register Southern African-Americans to vote in the early to mid-1960s.

African-American scholars and community leaders from Chicago into dialogue with prisoners there. Since Yusufu's release in 1996, he has done extensive training and work in restorative justice, with a particular emphasis in mentoring young people. He is also an organizer for the prison-abolition organization Critical Resistance. When we make his acquaintance, Yusufu lives in a group home in Englewood. We meet for several conversations over breakfast at a pancake house in Hyde Park, where a teenaged Yusufu once worked as a busboy.

CHOPPING COTTON

We left Mississippi because my mother and stepfather didn't want me and my siblings to grow up to be sharecroppers like them. I had three brothers and three sisters at the time. I remember picking cucumbers, peanuts, and other vegetables as a child, and I remember being in the cotton field back in Mississippi. They don't call it picking cotton down there. They have another name for it, *chopping* cotton. I don't remember doing that kind of harvesting myself, but I remember seeing people I knew with the long bags walking row-by-row. And taking full sacks of cotton to the place where they'd pull the seeds out.

I remember the confusion a lot of the whites had toward my father and grandfather. Both of them refused to be called "boy." They wouldn't respond. This is where I probably got my sense of resistance. I remember white men's pursuit of black women. They hated everything that wasn't white, except black women, black horses, black cars. Black men—they hated them especially. That's what got me making inquiries about why they hated us so much. As a child, I asked my father first. He said, "Ask your mother." I asked my mother, she said, "Ask your father." When I kept asking, my parents finally said, "Ask your grandparents." My great-grandmother was still alive at the time and she's the one who would talk to me about racism. She said, "We came here as slaves from our home country in Africa. We worked to build the country for over two hundred-something years and then they freed us, but they never really liked us." And my ma's mixed blood—she claimed that she's Seminole Indian, and my great-grandmother told me how most whites really hated the Indians. "So this is your history," my great-grandmother said. "Let me show you what your great-grandfather used to do. He was a Pullman Porter." And she had pictures of them together, with him wearing his uniform and everything. He traveled all over the country. He died before I got to know him. My great-grandmother told me that she and my great-grandfather had both been in bondage in Florida. When she laid it all out, I was curious. It didn't feel good once she told me about my great-grandfather, about how he'd been nearly blinded as punishment after trying to escape once. But he and my great-grandmother had come far since then.

THEY DID THE BEST THEY COULD WITH WHAT THEY HAD

We traveled to Detroit from Mississippi with my parents and grandparents around 1960, when I was eight, and then we moved to Chicago about a year later. I lived on the West Side when we first got here. My grandparents took care of the four oldest kids when we first arrived. They did the best they could with what they had. I got my first pair of dress shoes from my grandfather. What we used to call "roach killers"—Spanish boots with the elastic in the middle and a inch-high heel. I got them one size too small. But I was cool. And that's what I wanted to be: cool.

After my stepfather and my mother split, my mother moved us to Cabrini-Green reluctantly. This was in the mid-sixties. I was in ninth grade then. My mother wanted to be a nurse, but there were a lot of us kids to tend to. Nine of us in all by then. And I was the middle one. The one who caught all of the flak from both sides. When the little ones messed up, I got blamed. When the old ones messed up, I got talked to like I was one of the old ones.

An early memory I have from Cabrini was seeing the first Daley, Richard M. Daley, visit for the opening of an outside swimming pool. Mayor Daley and some other city officials came over for the dedication and we met some of them directly. I never really questioned things politically or economically then. We watched the mayor give a speech that afternoon. He treated my siblings and me like good little kids.

At the time, I didn't know it, but I know it now: my mother, she had sold her vote to the Democratic Party. And they gave her, all of the people, little bitty envelopes and inside were two dollars. I do remember seeing my mother's name on her envelope. Two brand-new dollars. The local committeeman would distribute the envelopes. He'd have a meeting and call over to each person who had an envelope. *Here's yours, here's yours.*

WE CALLED RACISM "PREJUDICE" THEN

I had all kinds of jobs as a boy. For a while, I was up at four A.M. delivering papers—Chicago's finest, *Sun-Times.* We boys would go down to the branch with our wagons and get our paper load. I started off making $20 or $25 every two weeks. I also delivered bottles of milk from a little milk truck. Later, when I got to be a teenager, I'd work as a bag boy at the A&P.

The stepfather who came into our family's life when I lived at Cabrini was named William. I don't remember exactly when that was. He met my mother when she was working as a waitress at a lounge called the Outer Limits, right up on Sedgwick and Larrabee. She met my stepfather there and she brought him home and he had that look on his face, like, "All of these kids—oh my God, what did I just step into?" He didn't say anything, but you could tell. He had that stunned look and I thought that he was going to be gone. My mother had had other boyfriends, but not ones we saw— they would come and go. William was the first one that actually came in and at an appropriate time, like seven o'clock. We were watching a show on our color TV and he came in and all of us looked at him and, like I said, he had that look. And he stayed, he stayed, he stayed. He was a stand-up man.

I kept up with school very well back then. I'd had black teachers in Mississippi, so seeing all these white teachers in my schools in Chicago was still a novelty to me. I think it wasn't until fifth grade when Jesse White was my first black teacher at school here. My teachers took an interest in me; as much as I read, I read slow. But this one Asian teacher taught me how to read real fast, with some kind of machine that had a light across the page. You could increase the speed of the reader and at the end of each reading would be questions about comprehension. That helped me turn a lot of corners, 'cause now I can read three or four books at a time. One of my most supportive teachers was Mr. Koob. Mr. Koob was a white guy. Of course, Koob is *book* spelled backwards. And that's what he would always mention. "Anytime you see me you should grab a book." And my brother and sister were like, *Yeah, right. You know what you can grab.* But I would grab a book. Since Mississippi, I was reading as much as I could.

Jesse White—now the Illinois Secretary of State—he was our gym teacher. Jesse White was a very strong disciplinarian but he was also a community man The man went door-to-door to every building, asking parents, "What you want your kids ending up doing?" He inspired me to do community work. He got the kids together, playing sports.

I was also a Boy Scout, in Troop #146, and we went on camping trips to scout jamborees, where all of the scouts from across the country get together. There were other black troops coming from other places, and of course we gravitated toward them. And there were these little Girl Scouts there, and the brothers were, "I'm taking that one over there. And you talk to that one over there." And when we'd go to the campfire, we'd sit next to them. Some of the white girls were kind of liberal with the colored brothers, but the majority were apprehensive. Lots of white Boy Scouts were outwardly aggressive towards us. They said the N-word. They called us black SOBs. And said, "We're not gonna work with them." I don't know how they got any merit badges. My troop talked about it at our meetings. We called racism "prejudice" then, and my thing was to ask why. *Why is it they just don't like us?* People would make excuses. "You don't know what you're talking about. So-and-so said something to him and that's why he called him a nigger." But I'd noticed how things went down and there wasn't any real provocation. And we tried to sort it out, but Jesse tried to smooth over that people just disliked us.

LEAVING CABRINI AND
GETTING INTO REAL TROUBLE

Leaving Cabrini one day was when I got into real trouble. It happened when I was fourteen or fifteen. I was going over to my grandma's, like I did sometimes. She lived on the West Side and I'd have to cross over the Ogden Bridge to get to her. The walk there was problematic because it wasn't straight to the West Side. You had to go over a very long bridge and then pass through several different communities. You had to walk a little over a mile. If I remember correctly, one Polish, one Italian, and one Irish community. This one day as I was walking, I heard the fabulous words that some people used to like to speak in those days: "Nigger, what you doing over here?" And I turned around and I saw the man shouting at me and I gave him the finger. The man was a tall burly kind of white guy, looked like he'd been playing football. Muscular. He was blond-haired, blue-eyed and a little bit older than me, in his twenties. He was a big guy and I wasn't about to try to fight him, and when I gave him the finger he charged at me and pulled out one of those little itty bitty baseball bats they called Louisville Sluggers, and started swinging it at me. I was fortunate enough I ducked out of the way, and in ducking I started moving into the street, and in moving into the street of course I stopped traffic, and when I got into the street he was still out there literally swinging at me like he was trying to hit a baseball or something. And when I got out of the way one time it hit one of the cars that was stopped and beeping and telling us to get out of the streets and all that kind of stuff. And when it hit the car the guy jumped out the car and said, "What you doing, nigger, what the, you trying to destroy my car?" And I say, "It ain't me with the baseball bat, sir," and it just kept on kept on.

Finally some people, I guess they got tired of it, and they came over and tried to break it up. Someone had called the police. They came and instead of grabbing the guy that had been attacking me, they grabbed me. I asked, "Why are you grabbing me? He's the one who was trying to hurt me." "You in the wrong neighborhood, boy." That's what I was told. I snatched away from them and one officer pulled out his pistol and said, "You're coming with us."

They took me to the police station and they charged me with assault and battery. I think they later dropped it when they found out that I was a youngster, but they kept me detained there. They asked me questions. "What are you doing over there? Why were you going through that neighborhood? Where do you live?" The questions would come almost all at once. And they had me handcuffed to a ring in the wall. The handcuffs was probably as tight as they could be 'cause my hand started swelling up. The two who were questioning me were doing the good cop/bad cop kind of stuff and I guess that counts for something because the good cop would come and loosen them up a little bit.

What I remember most clearly from that day were the spectators. Me and that guy were almost in the middle of the street and these people were stopping their cars, getting out of their cars, and surrounding us, so that I wouldn't have too many places to go when I stepped back. And they were just standing there. Nobody trying to do anything, nobody saying nothing. Not, "That's wrong," or "What are you doing?" They just stood there like what was happening was an everyday thing. Spectators. I can say it now, I didn't do it then, but it was straight-out Mississippi racism, here in Chicago. I had walked that way many times before, had gotten called nigger, but nobody ever confronted me. This was the actual first confrontation. It's one of the experiences that got me involved in the Civil Rights Movement more earnestly.

MY POLITICS WERE GROWING
LITTLE BY LITTLE

My politics were growing little by little. There was a deacon in the local Catholic church. His name was Smith. I don't remember his first name, but he and his wife took a liking to me and they took me to one of my first operas. I was like, *What are they singing about? I don't know none of that stuff.* Something happened in the story and I said "Boooo," and Reverend Smith said, "You don't boo. You either clap your hands or snap your fingers; you don't boo." *Oh, okay.* And it was so horrible. Four acts and I had to sit there. I don't understand a word they're saying and they're singing at the top of their lungs. And the people are clapping and giving a standing ovation. And none of them look like me.

Back in '65, Reverend Smith convinced my parents to let me go back to the South on the Freedom Rides. Reverend Smith was always talking to us kids about rights and duties and all those things, and he asked if we were interested in the Civil Rights Movement. He convinced me to sit down and he talked to me about Dr. King. I was a hyperactive kid, but I guess I must've showed some sign of interest 'cause he kept talking to us about Freedom Rides. I didn't know what he meant at first: I just knew "riders" as passengers on the Greyhound bus. But Reverend Smith convinced me, and I went to talk to my mom and my stepfather and my mom said, "No. Hell no, I don't want you going down there. I ain't gonna open your coffin if they send it back." But I was my feisty self and my stepfather supported me. He said, "Why not let him go? He needs the experience, he needs to know this world, let him go." And they argued for two or three days before she finally agreed. She was scared half to death about my going back South. We were quite conscious of Emmett Till.[2] Reverend Smith had to convince my mother it was in my best interest. He told my mother that I was mature enough to make the trip and he told her I'd be traveling with a group and staying with good families. My mother kept

---

2. Emmett Till was a fourteen-year-old African-American from Chicago who was murdered in 1955 while visiting relatives in Mississippi. He was reportedly murdered for flirting with a white woman at a local grocery store. Days after his visit to the store, Till was kidnapped from his relatives' house and driven to a barn, where he was severely beaten and tortured, then shot and dumped into a nearby river. After his body was returned home, his mother insisted on an open-casket funeral. Photographs of his body were first published in Jet magazine and helped galvanize a national Civil Rights Movement.

reminding me of Emmett Till. She showed me the *Jet* magazine.[3] We saw the pictures. Wasn't no WVON[4] or Channel 9 covering it. We had the *Jet* and the *Defender*.[5]

I went back down South for a little more than two months. I lived with families and I worked to sign people up to vote. I also got to volunteer in the Freedom Schools, working with the elementary and high school students, helping to make the young folks more politically and socially conscious. It seemed like nothing had changed there since I moved away, but I had changed and I felt like I was doing what I had to do.

One of the highlights from being back down South was meeting Ella Baker.[6] She wouldn't have remembered me, but I was part of the audience when she spoke. Ella Baker was one of my heroes. I always use her model for organizing, as opposed to the Saul Alinsky model.[7] See, the difference between him and the kind of organizing I am talking about is that the Alinsky model relies on a leader to mobilize people and to challenge particular issues. Ella was talking about a whole structural kind of assault, and a paradigm shift, so we can look at things in a collective way. It's not about individuals. And that's why they obscure Ella Baker in history.

---

3. An American weekly magazine marketed toward African-American readers; founded in Chicago by John H. Johnson of Johnson Publishing Company in 1951.

4. A Chicago radio station that was founded by Leonard and Phil Chess (of Chess Records) in 1963 and which geared its programming toward an African-American audience.

5. A Chicago-based newspaper founded in 1905 for primarily African-American readers.

6. Ella Baker (1903–1986) was a leader of the Civil Rights Movement.

7. Saul Alinsky (1909–1972) was a leading community organizer who worked for decades to address concentrated poverty in Chicago and across the U.S. His influential book *Rules for Radicals* (1971) proposed organizing social movements around charismatic leaders, among other strategies. Alinsky's approach contrasted with that of Ella Baker, who avoided media attention. Unlike Alinsky, Baker believed that the most effective social movements are carried through broad public participation without figureheads or visible leaders.

DIDN'T MANY PEOPLE KNOW
ABOUT BLACK HISTORY

When I was around sixteen, in 1968, we moved within Cabrini. From 1340 to 1160 Sedgwick. My oldest sister got married and my two brothers eventually moved in with their own girlfriends, so we had reduced living space. If you ever saw *Good Times*,[8] the building that JJ and them lived in was the building we moved to. They'd show that building in opening credits. And so we lived there. We didn't have any Thelmas, but we had a lot of Willonas, and by that I mean we didn't have any special-looking ladies like Thelma. And I've seen the actress who played Thelma in more recent years at different events tied to Chicago public housing, and I told her just that, and she asked me, "What do you mean you didn't have nobody that looked like me?" And I had to tell her, "We didn't have no beautiful black women like you in the projects. We had your mom and your next-door neighbor; those were the people we looked at." If there'd been a Thelma walking around the neighborhood, there would have been a fight daily! When I told her that, she said she didn't believe it. And I don't believe it either, but it's kind of true. I saw that show with my mom a couple of times while we were living in 1160 Sedgwick. We didn't have JJs in the neighborhood neither. Let me tell you: JJ couldn't have survived in Cabrini; he was too foolish. That "dy-no-mite" stuff? JJ wouldn't have lasted there. He woulda been dynamite. Remember the character Booker, the building custodian? We had custodians like him, but their behavior wasn't comedic. They were trying to get sexual favors or whatever kind of favors, because 90 percent of the women were single.

Eric Monte, the guy who helped make *Good Times*, grew up in Cabrini. A lot of other famous people grew up in Cabrini-Green as well. Curtis Mayfield—he grew up there. And Ramsey Lewis was from the neighborhood.

---

8. A CBS sitcom that aired from 1974–1979. Focusing on the life of an African-American family, *Good Times* was set in a public housing development in Chicago. The series was produced by Norman Lear and co-created by Michael Evans and Eric Monte.

You could tell he was going to be something 'cause he was always playing the piano. His talent was remarkable.

But most of us didn't grow up understanding who we were or where we'd come from. Didn't many people know about black history. We didn't know about Langston Hughes or other great thinkers. There was Negro History Week: an upgrade from Negro History Day. We learned a little about Booker T. Washington and George Washington Carver. But we didn't learn much. We just thought of Carver as the peanut man. He was a genius. Little did I know this man had a skill for nature. I'm glad to have that fuller picture of him now, but it was good to have some exposure like that because we could imagine that our history was more than just slavery.

Once in school I wrote a poem about what the Fourth of July meant to me. I can't remember what I wrote, but I know it wasn't nice. They asked me to rewrite it. Something more appropriate that could be published in the community newspaper. I was a radical. And I was ugly. People looked at me and thought, *Either he's going to be dead or he's going to be way out so far they gonna never catch him.* I didn't even think about Cinderella or things turning around like that. But I was one of the smartest kids.

In 1974, Yusufu was convicted of murder and attempted murder, and he was incarcerated in southern Illinois. After his release in 1996, Yusufu became involved in restorative justice, an approach to mitigating the damage that violent crime causes to the larger community. Part of his work includes counseling young men who have recently been released from prison.

YOU DID THAT FOR ME?

For the past few years, I've been living on the South Side, doing training and working with young men through restorative justice. Troy Davis,[9] the brother they executed in Georgia, I was anguished about that. Troy himself

---

9. Troy Davis was sentenced to death in Georgia for the 1989 murder of a police officer in Savannah, Georgia. He maintained his innocence up until his execution in 2011 and won the support of numerous public figures and human rights groups.

showed a lot of dignity. He said, "Don't let this end with me." And I started wondering: how does one deal with a case like this through restorative justice? I talked about this last week at an event called *Englewood If.* How could things be different in Englewood? What if there were more resources in that community? What resources are most needed? People are looking for answers, but they're stuck in the same paradigm. People think they're getting something new, but it's the same thing repackaged.

I give credit to CeaseFire.[10] They're doing a great, heroic job, but you can't just stop violence, you have to stop the roots of violence. It's not the violent gang chief I'm worried about, but the mentality that produced it, where you have to use violence to get what you want. We're in a culture where violence is equated with manhood.

I've seen the distress in our communities. I've seen it when I was working in juvenile courts and the Community Justice for Youth Institute. Too much instability. I worked with a lot of kids whose moms were doing time in prison and whose dads were wherever. When those kids thought I was a probation officer, they'd tighten up, talk hard. I'd have to tell them, "You don't have to talk like that to me. I don't work for probation." It's something that tugs at your heart. *What can I do? I'm just an old guy working with the court.* I try to find the links that they need with welfare programs, but it's not enough.

Back when my mother was on welfare, I swore it would never happen to me. It created a dependence in her that was just heartbreaking to me. She never got off of it. And she passed away when I was in prison. Now I'm underemployed and I need assistance. When I first went to get my Link card,[11] I was in line like everybody else and the scene there is depressing, full of impatient people and people who are so down and out. When I got up to the table, the lady said, "Will you step over here?" And when

10. An anti-violence program and initiative, first launched in the West Garfield neighborhood of Chicago in 2000.

11. In Illinois, benefits for the Supplemental Nutrition Assistance Program (formerly Food Stamps) are provided on the Illinois Link Card, an electronic card.

I stepped over to the side with her, she said, "What are you here for?" I said, "I really don't know, but I'm supposed to get the Link card." She said, "Okay, you stay right here." She went to the back and took my application out the back and she said, "Come out of the line." She asked me to come back the next day.

When I got there the next day, I was the third person in line. She pulled me out of line and gave me the paperwork. She said, "You go back to that room right there and you'll get your Link card." When she came back to speak to me, she said, "You don't remember me. You helped me with my son a couple of years ago over at the juvenile center. I literally moved your name up on the list." I said, "You did that for me?" She said, "You talked to him and he's in college right now. And if it wasn't for your talking to him, he wouldn't be there." I said, "I thank you for that."

After years of moving from home to home, in 2014 Yusufu settled in a Chicago Housing Authority mixed-development high rise on the site in the Bronzeville neighborhood in the South Side. "They call this building a high rise—of course we called it the projects when I was young." Yusufu remains active in the restorative justice movement and also works with adults with disabilities through the non-profit Easter Seals. He feels that restorative justice as a means of healing communities is especially important following protests of men killed by police in Ferguson, Missouri and New York City. "It's getting close to the atmosphere of the sixties here," he says.

Invisible Hands: Voices From the Global Economy (2014), edited by
Corinne Goria, tells stories of human rights abuses throughout
the global economy, from exploitation of agricultural workers to
communities destroyed by industrial accidents. Interviews took
place mostly between 2011 and 2014 and spanned the globe.

Pictured at right: The collapse of the Rana Plaza factory

KALPONA AKTER

AGE WHEN INTERVIEWED: *38*
BORN IN: *Chandpur, Bangladesh*
INTERVIEWED IN: *Los Angeles, California*

We first interview Kalpona Akter in Los Angeles after she speaks to the local branch of the AFL-CIO.[1] *At the panel discussion, workers from different points along the supply chain for a major U.S. apparel retailer—from the tailors who sew the clothes abroad to the warehouse workers who supply them to stores—compare stories of forced overtime, uncompensated injuries, and retaliation for bringing grievances to management. When it's Kalpona's turn to speak, she describes her evolution from twelve-year-old seamstress to activist to prisoner. She explains that in Bangladesh, garment workers often enter the factories as children, facing superhuman quotas for piecework, harassment and physical abuse from supervisors, and a minimum wage that comes out to about 20 cents per hour, by far the lowest of any significant garment-producing nation.*[2] *Workers who try to organize face intimidation not only*

---

1. The American Federation of Labor and Congress of Industrial Organizations is the largest federation of unions in the United States, made up of over fifty-six national and international unions from dozens of industries. In all, the AFL-CIO represents over twelve million workers both in the United States and abroad.

2. This figure is based on the Bangladeshi minimum wage rate of 3,000 taka per month from November 2010 to October 2013.

from their employers but also from politicians who opine that they should be grateful to have work at all, regardless of the toll on their bodies and spirits.

Bangladesh has nearly half the population of the United States, yet geographically, it's smaller than the state of Florida. As densely populated as it is, the country still has a largely agricultural economy and, with a per capita income of under US$2,000 per year, is one of the poorest countries in Asia. Starting in the 1990s, however, garment production boomed as international clothing retailers began to take advantage of the country's inexpensive labor supply and the Bangladeshi government encouraged investment with tax incentives. Today, Bangladesh is second to China as a leading exporter of apparel. Around four million garment workers produce US$20 billion worth of clothing for export a year; this figure represents the vast majority of the country's total export earnings. Meanwhile, the garment workers themselves—mostly women—struggle to survive as wages decline compared to the cost of living, and abysmal working conditions lead to workplace disasters such as the Rana Plaza factory collapse in April 2013. For Kalpona and fellow labor activists, speaking out is not just a matter of achieving more favorable working conditions—it's a matter of life and death.

AS A CHILD, I WAS SO NAUGHTY

When I was around six and in my second year of school, my family moved from Chandpur to Dhaka, which is the capital of Bangladesh.[3] My first memory of Dhaka is of waiting with my four-year-old brother for my dad to come home from work in the evening. He worked as a construction contractor in the area around our home in Mohammadpur,[4] and he used to bring home treats after work. He might bring us sugarcane, or it could be cookies, chocolates, or some fruit. He would bring home something

---

3. Chandpur is a city of 2.4 million located sixty miles southeast of Dhaka, the capital of Bangladesh. The Dhaka metropolitan area has a population of over fifteen million.

4. Mohammadpur is a neighborhood in Dhaka that was first developed in the 1950s and experienced a construction boom in the eighties and nineties.

for us every night. Besides my brother, I had a sister as well at that time, but she was only a year old and still nursing.

As a child, I was so naughty. I used to talk back to my mom all the time, and I irritated her with a lot of questions. "Hey Mom—why is Dad late?" "Hey Mom—why is the sky blue?" "Hey Mom—why isn't it sunny? Why is it raining?" When she was cooking, I'd say, "I want to see."

My mother used to cook all the kinds of traditional food we have in Bangladesh: dahl, fish, she could do everything. I remember that we had an oven but we didn't have gas—it was a wood oven. We'd collect wood outside our house or buy it at market.

During that time our family had our own tin-roofed house, which is a common kind of house in Bangladesh. We had three bedrooms, two balconies. At the tin-roofed house, we had a backyard and front garden. We had guava and mango trees, and my mom also used to grow vegetables in the garden.

But we were forced to sell our house at a low price to a local politician. It was in a nice area of the city, and the politician put a lot of pressure on my dad to sell it. I don't know too many of the details. Later I tried to speak to my dad many times about the nice house, but he didn't want to talk about it. We bought a smaller house without as much outdoor space. My father changed parties and political views after that, though. He was really hurt and felt he'd been cheated.

I don't remember exactly when we lost our house, but I was still in primary school at the time. I loved school. There we learned Bangla, basic English, and math. There was a small playground at this school where I would go and run around with friends. Near the school playground, there was a bazaar, so sometimes my mom or dad would give me some money to have a snack or something cool to drink. I would buy fruits, ice cream, or some sour pickles—I was eating everything.

In Bangladesh we go to primary school until grade five, and then we go to high school. I passed the primary school and was put into grade six, at the high school. In high school up to the ninth grade, we studied Bangla,

English, math, social science, and then science and religion. Religion was the last subject I studied. Every religion had its own class. So if you were Hindu, you'd study Hinduism. Muslims, they had Islam.[5] All the students had other classes together, but we would split up for religion classes. We didn't pray much at home, and at the time, girls and women were not allowed in the mosque. So religion class was where I'd learn about the life of the Prophet and how to pray. We didn't have any choice of which subjects we studied, but I can remember that my favorite subject was science. I believe that I was one of the best students in my high school.

WHATEVER MONEY MY MOM HAD, IT JUST RAN OUT WITHIN A MONTH

Many people were building houses in Dhaka in the late 1980s, and my dad was a successful general contractor, or middle man—people would hire him to build the house, and then he would subcontract or hire others to complete the smaller jobs on the project. So he would often have a lot of money on him, because people would pay him the whole sum for the project and he would use that fund to pay other workers.

I have a cousin who was living with us and was also working with my dad. My dad started to entrust my cousin with the finances for the business. My dad would put the money in a bank account, and then my cousin could draw on it when he needed to pay subcontractors or other workers.

One day in 1988, just after I had turned twelve, my cousin took all the money my dad had entrusted him with and just disappeared. My family didn't hear anything from him for a couple of months—he was just gone. And then, one day, he showed up again. He didn't say he took the money, but he didn't deny it either. He just didn't take responsibility.

After the theft, my dad suffered. He had two strokes within two months,

---

5. The population of Bangladesh is nearly 90 percent Muslim and 9 percent Hindu. Though the country is predominantly Muslim, principles of secular government were written into the original constitution in 1972.

starting about a week or two after my parents learned that the money had been stolen. One stroke after the other. The whole right side of my father's body was disabled after the strokes, and he couldn't speak for many years. He had to be admitted into the hospital, and my mom really had a very difficult time during his illness. She had to pay all the hospital bills because, as far as I remember, we really didn't have health-care insurance or a health-care system in Dhaka back then. In any case, my mother had to find a way to pay all the medical bills herself. My father was back and forth to the hospital for maybe six months.

Whatever money my mom had, it just ran out within a month after my father's strokes. So then she had to sell our house. We moved to a rental house. The rental house had about six rooms occupied by three families. We had two rooms to ourselves, but we had a shared kitchen and a shared toilet and shower. It was a disaster. There were maybe eighteen people total living in this small house. The house had a small balcony off of our rooms, and that is where my father stayed mostly while he was recovering. He'd sleep on a bed out on the balcony. It was too hot inside, and we didn't even have a fan.

There was a lot of tension in our family at that time. My dad couldn't talk. He had lost use of one side of his body. He couldn't leave the bed, or even move. Within six months, we ran out of all the money we'd received from selling the house and all the other savings my parents had. We didn't have anything.

My mom decided to go to my father's other siblings to seek justice, or to have my cousin come and give us back the money he stole. But my cousin never came to our home at all. He refused to take responsibility. And it turned out that none of the other siblings wanted to help us. No one was helping us. There were six of us at home, or seven, after my littlest sister was born. We barely had enough food at home for my younger sisters and brother. And my dad needed to have his medicine.

My mom had never worked before—she had always been a housewife and we'd had a happy family. But because of everything that was happening, my mom decided she had to get a job. At the same time, Mom asked me whether I thought I should also work. I was twelve years old. And, because I saw what was going on in the family, I said, "Yeah, I want to work. But how I can get a job, Mom?" I didn't want to quit school since I was doing well. I was even class captain for many months, but I felt I had to help my mother and father if I could.

There were some garment workers who used to live next to our house whom we'd known for a long time. Mom spoke to some of them, and they said that they would speak to the midlevel management at their factory to see if I could get a job. About a week later, our neighbors came and told me that they could get me a job. So one day I went to school and the next day I went to the factory.

MY FRIENDS ARE AT SCHOOL, BUT I'M STUCK WORKING HERE

I didn't tell anyone that I'd left school. They began to worry after about two weeks, though. My teachers showed up at my house. They said that they wanted to award me some sort of scholarship to keep my studies going. But my mom said, "How can she go to school? There are still four other kids. They don't have any food. Kalpona has decided to work." My teachers kept insisting then that I should stay in school, that I should not work, but, you know, my mother had no other choice.

So I didn't go back to school. I went into the factory, and my mom did too. She got a job in a factory far from our house. It was about ten kilometers away from our home. But I got a job in a factory close to home, maybe one kilometer away. I could walk there.

The very first day I went to work in the factory—oh my gosh—it was a crazy experience. There was so much noise, more noise than I had ever heard before, and people were shouting all over the place. Midlevel supervisors were yelling at the workers all the time. We had two buildings in the factory and around 1,500 workers all together, and everything just seemed like chaos to me at first.

Every day, I'd walk to the factory along with my neighbors who had helped me get the factory job. The supervisors at the factory first gave me a job cutting the belt loops in pants. The loops were made of four or more layers of fabric. I had to scissor the four-layered fabric, and it was tough. When I cut the fabric layers, the scissors made my fingers and hands hurt. I must have cut more than a thousand a day. Except for a couple of breaks to eat, I'd be cutting nonstop for fourteen hours a day, from eight in the morning until ten at night.

After my first couple of days, it was like my skin had been rubbed away. When my hands started to bleed, I would bind them with some pieces of fabric from the production floor. It was unhygienic, but I had to protect my hands so I could keep working. You can see these black marks on my hands. The very first day I hurt these fingers. These scars I got from that scissoring. I stayed on the belt loops for four or five weeks, and then moved on to a different job with a different order of clothing.

It was painful for me to go to work because my factory and my old school were so close. We would often go to the rooftop of the factory to have our lunches, and from there I could see the playground in my school, and I could also see my friends playing. I mean, almost every day during the lunch hour I would cry, because I thought, *My friends are studying there at school, but I'm stuck working here.* But I also had a brother and sisters. And when I went home and saw them, saw their faces, it would remind me that I had responsibilities that I needed to take care of.

IT WAS A VERY SAD PART OF MY LIFE

When my mom and I started working at the factories, my mom would wake up early to cook something like rice, dahl, or vegetables for the whole family—that was food for the whole day. While we were at work, my brother, who was ten at the time, would take care of my youngest sister, who was a newborn baby, my other two sisters, and my dad, who was still sick from the stroke. Sometimes my mother and I used to take food with us to the factory; sometimes we wouldn't, because we didn't enough food to take with us. Sometimes we would work the whole day without any food. And sometimes when I came home from work, I would see there was no food at home either, so that meant that my mom and I wouldn't eat for two days.

It hurts sometimes to not have any food. It makes you weak. Still, when you see that your younger siblings do not even have food, you don't have any choice but to go without. My brother would not even eat the food we left for all of them in the morning. He would save this food for the two youngest and for my dad, because the two youngest used to ask for food all the time, so my brother would save his portion for them. So he was like a dad and a mom to them—he was raising them all by himself. He was ten years old.

After five or six months working at the factory, my mom got sick. She was dehydrated, malnourished, and the doctor said there was something wrong with her kidneys. She was so dehydrated that she couldn't breastfeed my baby sister. She had a pain in her kidneys and it became impossible for her to work.

After she quit the job at the factory, she started feeling better. So we decided that instead of my mom, my brother would go to the factory with me. Around this time I also changed to another factory. The new factory was farther away, but I could make a little more money there. At the old factory, I could get maybe 240 taka in base salary per month, and maybe 400 to 450 taka per month after overtime.[6] At the new factory, I could make a base salary of 300 taka per month and up to 500 taka per month with overtime, because I used to do the night shift as well.[7] If I made 500 taka a month, I could pay for much of our rent—which was a little under 500 taka a month—but not for food. That is why we decided my brother should work at the factory as well. So I took my brother into this new factory

---

6. In 1994, 240 taka = approximately US$3.80. 400 to 450 taka = approximately US$7.

7. In 1994, 300 taka = approximately US$4.75. 500 taka = approximately US$7.90.

and convinced my supervisor to give him a job. My brother got a job as a sewing-machine helper and started working in the building next to me.

There were other children working in the factories, too. The youngest child I saw in the new factory was a boy about eight years old. I think during that time I had been promoted to sewing-machine operator, and the eight-year-old was my helper. That eight-year-old boy used to cut the threads and pile up the clothes that I sewed. And I can remember he used to come in the morning and say, "Oh sister, I'm so sleepy."

Our factory work used to start at eight, so my brother and I needed to get out from the house at something like six thirty or a quarter to seven. Then we'd walk about one kilometer to get the bus to the factory area, and then we'd walk about a half kilometer to get into the factory. And that is what we would do for three or four years, the same routine every week.

The factory is not far from where I live today. The site still exists and some of the buildings are still there. So I can see the factory every day, twice a day sometimes. When I see it now, sometimes I laugh. Sometimes it gives me pain. Sometimes it gives me lots of things to remember. It was in this second factory, too, that I met my future husband.[8]

It must have been around 1991 or '92. He was in the embroidery section and he was a relative of the factory owner—I think a cousin or second cousin—so he'd gotten the job in a very easy way. I don't remember how I met him, maybe when I was on the bus to the factory. Or while going into the factory or coming out, I saw him. I was seventeen years old when we got married in 1993 and I moved in with him and his family. I was so young.

If I want to, I can remember that part of my life, but it's really painful for me. It was a very sad part of my life when I met him. The marriage was troubled from the start, and the factory workers were just beginning our fight at the same time.

---

8. Kalpona has asked us not to name her husband or use a pseudonym.

WE REALLY GOT ANGRY

I remember how the trouble started at the factory. Basically, we were working sixteen days in a row during Ramadan in 1993, right before Eid ul-Fitr, the breaking of the fast of Ramadan.[9] We were working day and night, and the Muslims in the factory were fasting for Ramadan. We would fast over the day and break the fast in the factory with little snacks, and we'd eat our dinner after sunset with the little money that the factory provided. And then working the whole night and getting food at around three a.m., before fasting again after sunrise.

When we worked overnight, we might work ten hours of overtime, and the custom was that the factory would give us an extra five hours of bonus pay. In 1993, after we'd already done sixteen days of overnight work, management announced they weren't giving out any bonus pay for overtime that year. They said they could not afford it.

And as I mentioned, it was before Eid, so when we were working those extra hours, we were planning to have the bonus money for the feast at the end of Ramadan. We really got angry. We didn't have much of an idea about labor law or our rights as workers, but some of the senior workers said to us, "We will not work ten hours overtime without the bonus. We will strike until they pay us the amount they owe us." I agreed with them.

I was one of the initiators of the strike. We had 1,500 workers in two units at the factory, so among the 1,500, it was 93 of us who called for a strike until the factory agreed to pay the bonus.

When I returned home the day we decided to strike, my husband had heard that I was involved, and he beat me. He was related to the factory owners, so he didn't support the idea of a strike. At the time, I was feeling very helpless. Very helpless. But the next day, the day of the strike, I told

---

9. For the month of Ramadan, observant Muslims fast from dawn until sunset every day. Eid ul-Fitr is a major feast marking the end of Ramadan and traditionally includes lavish meals and charitable giving. Depending on local tradition, the holiday may last from one to three days. In 1993, Ramadan began in February.

some of the other ninety-three who were protesting, and they said that they understood and would always support me, that they wanted me to always stand with them, and that I was one of the courageous ones. We continued with the strike, and after a single day the management agreed to give us the bonus money. But they made it clear that they would not pay the same bonus in the future, and we agreed. At the time, we didn't have any idea about the law.

After the strike, we factory workers went on holiday for Eid. After holiday finished we came back, and it was then we learned that twenty of my co-workers who had demanded the bonus money had been fired. The twenty fired workers were the ones the factory considered the main instigators of the strike.

The organizers decided they would not give up, and they started to look for an organization that could help them. And they found Solidarity Center. Solidarity Center is an international wing of AFL-CIO, the big U.S. union. The full name is American Center for International Labor Solidarity, but during those days, the branch we worked with was known as AAFLI: Asian American Free Labor Institute.[10]

The Solidarity Center had already begun helping a group of workers to form an independent union for just garment workers, the BIGUF, or Bangladesh Independent Garment Workers Union Federation. The new garment worker reps met with some of our leaders and said they would help us to sue the factory owner for retaliation. And at the same time, they said they had awareness classes where my co-workers could go and learn about labor law, and then they could better take on their management. So some of my senior colleagues, they went to the law classes and they found it really interesting. They came to work and encouraged some of us interested in fighting back to go to the classes.

---

10. The Solidarity Center, or American Center for International Labor Solidarity, was launched by the AFL-CIO in 1997. Its purpose was to help develop union representation for workers in developing economies, and it replaced earlier, regional AFL-CIO union-development organizations such as the Asian American Free Labor Institute (founded in 1968).

A SECOND BIRTH

It was around the end of 1993, and I was seventeen. I wasn't allowed to go anywhere without my husband, or I had to at least tell him where I was going. He was a very controlling man, so I didn't tell him the truth when I went to the labor classes at the Solidarity Center.

When I learned about labor law and rights, it was like a second birth for me. I thought, *Wow, we are working in hell.* So then I decided to commit to organizing. When I came home in the evening, my husband asked me where I had been. I told him the truth then, and he asked me, "Why have you been there? Did you get my permission?" I said, "No, I didn't," and so he beat me. But I was determined that I would not take a step backward.

So the next day, after realizing that there were all of these laws that were covering workers' rights in the factory, during the lunch break, I started telling my co-workers that I had gone to the Solidarity Center and had learned a lot. And I brought some of their booklets with me to the factory. It was risky, but I had to do it.

Some of us started to meet in a small room in a co-worker's house, which was quite close to my house. And we were also going to meetings sponsored by Solidarity Center for BIGUF. I had back-and-forth communication between BIGUF and the workers at my factory. The center was giving me guidelines for how I should organize. So I was really doing the organizing part and persuading our workers to sign the union application.

My husband was an anti-union guy. I didn't listen to him. But once he discovered the signed union forms that I had gathered from my colleagues, he tried to take them and give them to the factory owner. So then I went to some of the other union members working at the factory that day, some of the local people who were very close to my husband. I explained to them what happened. And they ran up behind him as he was taking the forms to the factory owner and told him not to do that.

I was beaten by him because of my involvement with organizing the union, because I was helping to organize workers in his cousin's factory.

Also, when I tried to give some of my wages to my family, he beat me because he wanted me to give all my money to him, whatever I earned. So he kept me from helping my family, even though my family was so needy during that time. They needed my support, but I couldn't help.

My husband had control of my life. But I felt like I couldn't leave him because of cultural expectations. If I got divorced or left him, it would be bad for my younger sisters. I mean socially, it would look bad. The culture expects that if the eldest sister got divorced, then she must not be from a good family, and no one would want to marry any other sisters. So I had to tolerate my husband.

We were together for about nine months and then we had something like a settlement: a partial separation. We were staying in the same house, but in two separate bedrooms. I started sharing a room with his sister. And I was with him for a couple more years like that.

"IF YOU WANT TO FIRE ME,
YOU HAVE TO TELL ME THE REASON"

I was eventually fired because of my work in helping to form BIGUF. It happened in 1995. Some of my co-workers, I think they whispered about me, or maybe my husband told the factory bosses about my organizing. However they found out, the bosses called me into the office several times to indirectly threaten me. And then after one meeting I was suspended for twenty days without any reason.

Finally, one morning just after I had started my work for the day, a co-worker approached me and let me know I had been called to the office. I went to the office room and the bosses told me I was fired. But they weren't just sending me home. They were offering me a good amount of money to leave. I don't know how much it was, but it was a big bundle right there in the office. And they said, "You're fired, you can take this money and go." And I said, "I will not take any money. If you want to fire me, you have to tell me the reason." And they said that they could terminate my employment anytime that they wanted. And I said, "I know that you have the right to fire me any time, but you have to tell me why I'm being terminated."

The company made a lot of drama. They wouldn't state officially why I'd been fired. I sued them in the labor court. My husband was angry. Many of our mutual co-workers supported me, though, so he was careful not to come out too strongly against me. But he let me know that he would not support me, and he would not spend any money to take the case to court, and he would not allow me to spend any of my money on the case. Instead, I got legal support through BIGUF.

During that time, my dad still couldn't walk much at all, but he got his voice back. So I explained to him, "I've lost my job and some difficult things are happening with my husband, and I need you to help me out." But my mom wouldn't agree with a separation or divorce because it would make it hard for my other sisters to marry. I hadn't told my mom that my husband was beating me, because I didn't want it to hurt her. So later I had to tell her that this was happening. I was like his slave, I told her. So then my dad said, "Okay. Move out."

So I moved to my parents' house. Six months after that, I divorced my husband. I had trouble getting work in other factories, because I had been blacklisted. I found work in two other garment factories, but I was quickly fired from both of those jobs. The owners of the factory I was suing, they informed those factory owners who hired me that I had sued them in the labor court. The bosses at one factory, they told me that I could continue my job at that factory if I withdrew my case against my previous factory owner, and I said no. So they fired me.

The BIGUF gained official union status in 1997, around the time I was being blacklisted, and so I checked in at the new BIGUF union office. I told them what was happening to me, and that I couldn't get a job anywhere. So at first they appointed me as an intern organizer for three months. And then they appointed me as a full-timer with the union up to 1999. That's when my court case was dropped, and the judge ruled that the company that had fired me owed me only my severance pay.

When I was working full-time at BIGUF, my task was to organize workers door-to-door. In the mornings before factory shifts started and in the afternoons during the factories' lunch breaks, I used to go to the areas outside the factories to organize workers, to tell them there's an organization where they can come and learn the law and their rights. And in the evenings, I had to do house visits, to go to the workers' houses and speak to them there. And on Fridays there were awareness-raising classes. During those classes, I had to give a lecture about basic law and rights, what I had learned coming to BIGUF, and my life before I joined them. My task was to educate workers.

ACTIVISM WAS IN MY BLOOD. I COULDN'T HELP MYSELF.

In '99, I quit the BIGUF. The problem for me was that the BIGUF would work only for garment workers; many other kinds of workers used to come to our union office to get support, but we couldn't help them. It was frustrating not to be able to help. So I quit, and I decided I wouldn't work for labor rights anymore. I'd had a bad experience: I'd lost my court case, I couldn't find work, and I couldn't help a lot of people who needed help. So I thought I would do something else, like set up a small shop selling food or other things close to my house. I thought, *I can survive with that.*

But you know, activism was in my blood. I couldn't help myself. Many workers knew my face, they had my contact info. The workers used to call me and ask for help, and I couldn't help them because I wasn't with a union anymore. Then, around the end of '99, one of my former union colleagues, Babul Akhter, contacted me. He said, "Let's do something ourselves!" So Babul and I started our own program that year through sponsorship of the international Solidarity Center, and we called it the Bangladesh Center for Worker Solidarity, or BCWS. The formal launch of the BCWS was in August 2000. I was about twenty-two years old.

We got funding from the AFL-CIO and also organizations like the International Labor Rights Forum.[11] Our whole philosophy was that our organization was going to be a long-term commitment to all workers. And we were going to work in an innovative way. If you talked about unions in Bangladesh, the factory owners would say, "Oh, unions are evil! They destroy everything." We wanted to change those perceptions, so that not just the workers but everyone else would have respect for unions and for workers' rights. Our focus was on providing information, so we made posters and pamphlets and met with workers to inform them about their labor rights. We wanted to train female garment workers to form their own organizations, to speak out themselves about their rights. So that was the beginning of the BCWS. We were pretty successful for the next few years. I think the BCWS was doing a great job achieving our goal of raising workers' awareness about law and rights, helping them to handle their grievances, giving them legal service, legal support. Helping them to grow their leadership capacity. Giving them educational programs, helping working mothers get educations. So that was really successful in the following years, after our formation.

We also wanted to form a kind of federation that could be a national voice for the workers, more of an actual union rather than just a source of information about unions and labor rights. So in 2003, we were able to do that. I helped found the Bangladesh Garment and Industrial Workers Federation, or BGIWF, of which Babul is the president. The two organizations work out of the same office, but they have different functions. BCWS is an non-governmental organization, and our mission is educating workers about their rights. Meanwhile, BGIWF is a union federation that has the legal power to help workers negotiate with their employers and assist other unions.

During this time I was still living with my family. Luckily, even though

---

11. The International Labor Rights Forum is a human rights organization that works with unions, faith-based groups and community organizations to demand dignity and justice for workers.

I had been divorced, two of my little sisters were able to marry. We remained very close after they moved out and started having children. My younger brother joined me in helping to grow BCWS as well. My brother has been a big source of support. My parents, too—my family has stuck by me through everything I've faced.

AT THE BCWS, WE DID NOT SUPPORT VIOLENCE

In 2006, there was a big uprising of workers across the country. The major issue, among other issues, was that there was a big gap between workers' wages and the cost of living in Bangladesh. The minimum wage of 950 taka per month was set in 1994. And factories weren't even complying with that standard.[12]

At the BCWS, our position was to support the workers and help amplify their voices on issues like a new minimum wage. During the uprising, some property was vandalized and damaged across the country. There was a lot of violence between political parties leading up to national elections as well. At the BCWS, we did not support violence and damage to property. None of us had any prior idea about this movement, or this uprising. It wasn't planned, it just happened. But the uprising had an impact. Afterward, the minimum wage was raised and better enforced.[13]

But it was also after that 2006 uprising that Babul and I began to feel that the government had taken notice of the BCWS. They started to follow our work around that time. They would visit our offices, follow our activities, and seemed to be watching us closely.

---

12. In 1994, 950 taka = US$18.

13. In 2007, minimum wage in Bangladesh was set at 1,663 taka a month (approximately US$23 per month) and then raised again in July 2010 to 3,000 taka a month (approximately US$43 per month at the time of the wage hike, but devalued to US$38 per month by the end of 2013 when wages increased to 5,300 taka a month).

Worker associations in Bangladesh such as Kalpona's BCWS and BGIWF made gains throughout the early 2000s, including the legalization of worker association groups within free trade export-processing zones and updates to minimum wage and worker safety laws.[14] *In 2006, a string of violent confrontations between political parties and a series of labor strikes effectively halted the nation's economy. President Iajuddin Ahmed declared a state of emergency and turned the government over to a military-run caretaker regime. The emergency resolution also suspended the right to assembly and granted police the power to arbitrarily detain citizens for any length of time. Though elections would be held again in 2008, abuses by police, including arbitrary detentions, continued.*

HIS TOES HAD BEEN BROKEN

In April 2010, we started hearing serious threats. Babul was approached by an NSI agent who told him that we needed to stop talking about labor rights with workers or the agency would take strong action against us.[15] Then, in June 2010, the Bangladeshi government decided to revoke BCWS's NGO status registration. This was a big deal, because if we wanted to have foreign funds to run our programs or activities such as educating workers, we had to have registration with Bangladesh's NGO Affairs Bureau. So all of the backing that we got from international organizations like the AFL-CIO was no longer legally available to us. The government stated that our registration had been revoked because we were doing antistate activity—which was not true. And they didn't give any proof or any evidence of that. We weren't sure what kind of work we were still legally allowed to do since our license was revoked, but we were meeting at the offices anyway. Now we no longer had any funding, and we were certain then that there was a campaign being waged against us.

And that's when we had our first confrontation with the NSI. It started

---

14. Export-processing zones are designated areas without export tariffs or taxes.

15. The NSI is the National Security Intelligence agency of Bangladesh.

when the chief inspector of factories with the Labor Ministry, someone we had worked with before to resolve worker conflicts, called us to come help settle a dispute between striking workers and their company, which was called Envoy. I reminded him of our registration issues and asked that he make sure we wouldn't have trouble with the government if we participated, and he agreed.

We sent one of our colleagues, Aminul Islam, to gather a group of Envoy workers as representatives to bring to the meeting at the Envoy offices. Aminul was an excellent negotiator and one of the most effective members of our staff at BCWS and BGIWF. He'd been with us since 2006. He'd been a worker in a garment factory as well, just like me and Babul, and he had been quite successful organizing in some of the factories in Ashulia, a big industrial zone just outside Dhaka.

So Aminul was able to gather about eighteen workers and headed off to the meeting. Babul and I were trying to get there as well, though we were running a bit behind Aminul. We were on our way to the meeting when we got a call. Another one of our colleagues who had arrived at the meeting said that men had stormed in and blindfolded Aminul and taken him off just after they'd arrived. Our colleague who was telling us this had gotten away himself, but he said that there were men waiting for us and that we shouldn't come.

We were shocked. First we called the chief inspector and demanded to know what had happened. We were really yelling at him, but he wouldn't tell us about Aminul or promise to protect us. He wouldn't say anything, really. Then we called every police force and security agency contact we had, but nobody would tell us anything about Aminul.

Early the next morning, June 17, another BCWS colleague got a call. It was Aminul. He was crying, terrified. He said he'd been picked up by the NSI and driven north of the city where he was interrogated and beaten. The NSI officers had asked him things like: Why did you stop the work at the garment factories? Who ordered you to stop the work? Why? Tell us his name. Tell us if Babul asked you to stop the work at factories. The persons who told you to stop the work at factories should be punished. If you just say that Babul and Kalpona asked you to stop the work at the factories we will set you free. We will arrest them in a moment and take them here.

Aminul had managed to escape in the middle of the night when they'd let him out of their vehicle so he could pee. We were able to get Aminul to a safe place and get him medical attention, but he was badly wounded. His toes had been broken and he had a lot of internal hemorrhaging from being struck with a stick across his back and head. He told us the NSI had tried to get him to sign confessions and implicate me and Babul in all sorts of antistate activities like inciting riots. We knew we were being closely watched, but eventually we got Aminul back to his home so he could be with his family.

WHEN THEY ARRESTED ME, MY HEAD WAS BLANK

Then the next trouble started with a demonstration in Dhaka on July 30, 2010, in which there was vandalism and property damage. The issue at the time was that the government was set to raise the minimum wage again, and on July 30 it was announced that the minimum wage would be raised to 3,000 taka a month.[16] Many worker advocacy groups had advocated for much more than that, because inflation was making the cost of living much higher very rapidly. So there were demonstrations on July 30 protesting the new minimum, and some vandalism took place five kilometers away from our main office. But we at BCWS weren't involved. I was at a staff meeting thirty-five kilometers away, and I didn't know anything about the incident.

While I was at the staff meeting, I heard about the demonstration and vandalism through a U.S. embassy officer that I knew. He was on vacation in Malaysia, but he texted me, and he told me that there was something

---

16. In 2010, 3,000 taka = US$43.

on television about an uprising going on around some of the garment factories in Dhaka. This embassy officer wanted to know whether we were
safe or not. So I started checking in with some people with BCWS, and
I called one person I know in the Dhaka office. He said he and some other
colleagues were in the office and had locked the doors and were all safe.

After that, I went home. In the middle of the night, maybe around
midnight, Babul called me and said that in the newspaper there was a
story about the demonstration. The story mentioned that six criminal
cases had been filed, and our names were there. The story claimed that
our organization had helped start the unrest. And I said, "What's going
on, it's crap! We weren't even there." I was a target, Babul was a target,
and so was Aminul, as well as a few organizers from other unions. They
were charging us with things like inciting riots and using explosives. Very
serious charges.

So the next day, a Saturday, we started calling my colleagues and our
lawyers and informing them about what was happening. We also started to
talk to those other federation leaders who had been accused in similar cases.

Soon the police started looking for me and began to bother my sisters
and their husbands, threatening and harassing them to try to find where
I was. That's when Babul and I went into hiding. We were able to stay in a
safe place we'd set up in some unused BCWS offices until August 13, when
the police finally found us. They stormed in early that morning. It was
still dark. When they arrested me, my head was blank. I couldn't understand what was going on. I wasn't sure what to do. They shined flashlights
in our faces, cuffed us, and took us to the police station.

Babul was sent to a cell. There was no cell for females so I was told to
sit on the floor in a tiny, dirty office room. They forced me to sit squeezed
behind a desk and a wall. The two-by-four-foot space was so small I couldn't
even lie down. That's where they kept me sitting, cramped for seven days.
I couldn't sleep the whole time. I would lean against the wall and maybe
nod off at moments, but I could never fall asleep fully. The whole experience was so scary. During this time, the police would take me out of the

space only for interrogation. They would interrogate me at any time of day for two, three hours. The longest session was something like eighteen hours in a row.

They would ask the same few questions over and over. Sometimes just to me or just to Babul, sometimes to both of us together. They would ask questions like: Who funded us? Was there any international organization or any specific country who was giving us funding to destroy the garment industry of Bangladesh? Who were the other organizations we worked with? Why did we start the recent unrest?

When we stated that we hadn't anything to do with the incident in July, they'd say, "Then tell us who is responsible, we have to bring them in." They wanted us to talk about our families, our international connections, to basically tell them about everyone we knew or had ever worked with. There were maybe a dozen interrogators who would take turns asking Babul and me the same questions over and over, thousands of times.

After a week of interrogation, we were brought to the courthouse for our initial hearing. We were charged with vandalism, arson, and inciting riots. I faced seven charges and Babul faced eight. After that, I was sent to central jail for another three weeks.

The central jail was like something from a century ago, except there was electricity, but we actually couldn't turn the lights off at night. I was with about 130 other prisoners. We could take showers only rarely, and when we did it was in an open courtyard in full view of everyone, including male prisoners held in another part of the same facility.

A couple of days after I was sent to central jail, my sisters brought their children for a visit. By this time I had a nephew who was about twelve and my nieces were about nine and five. The prisoners were allowed visits from family once a week, and we all gathered in a big room that was separated in the middle by two nets a couple of feet apart. It was loud, and the only way we could hear each other was by shouting. I remember my nephew and nieces just crying, asking why I was in this place and why they couldn't touch me. I remember one of my nieces trying to reach me through the netting. I was just crying the whole time. I couldn't even talk, really.

While I was in central jail, Babul was taken away to a police station in Ashulia, the industrial park where some of the vandalism and arson supposedly occurred. There he was severely beaten many times, usually with a stick against his back. It got so bad that Babul gave a fellow prisoner his wife's and lawyer's phone numbers and asked that he call them when he got out to let them know what had happened, because Babul didn't think he'd be leaving the prison alive. The worst was on August 30. He was assaulted by several non-uniformed persons who entered his holding cell, blindfolded him, and beat him with a thick wooden stick, inflicting injuries on his leg, hip, and groin. Babul's assailants also threatened him, telling him that he'd be taken from the police station and shot by police during a staged incident. The same threat that was made against Aminul when he was detained by the NSI on June 16.

After thirty days in jail, Kalpona and Babul were released on bail, along with their colleague Aminul, who had been arrested and sent to a different facility, where he had also been beaten. The three continued their regular worker training and organizing work while awaiting trial until April 4, 2012, when Aminul was kidnapped outside the BCWS offices, tortured, and killed. His body was discovered sixty miles north of the BCWS offices with broken toes and massive internal bleeding. Signs point to NSI involvement in the murder, but so far no perpetrators of the crime have been brought to justice. Lack of progress in the murder investigation quickly raised concerns of cover-ups to protect security forces. Meanwhile, labor leaders feared for their safety. Eventually, Aminul's death led to major international protests, including condemnation by U.S. Secretary of State Hillary Clinton on a trip to Bangladesh in May 2012.

I DON'T WANT TO BRING SOMEONE INTO THIS WORLD WITH THE STRESS THAT I'M FACING

I still live with my parents. They've been through so much stress. For years they were harassed by the police, security agents, anonymous calls. They've been through a lot, and I worry about their health. My siblings have suffered harassment as well. Still, we are a close family. My younger brother has worked by my side at BCWS. He's had a difficult time as well, but he remains so strong. And I'm very close to my nephew and nieces. I mean, they call me "mom." Yeah, sometimes my sisters get jealous!

My family has always been such a comfort for me. I have one memory of being picked up by the police in the courtyard just outside my house and put in a van to go to trial. My family was there, including my nephew. It was a very hot day, and I was sweating. After the van started to pull away, I heard my nephew running by the van, crying out to the police, "Where are you taking my mom? I want to give this to her!" The police asked me if he was my son, and I told them he was. So the police stopped and took something from him and handed it back to me. It was a paper fan. I was very touched.

I'm just crazy about babies. I want babies myself, but I can't figure out how that would happen. I don't have time to think about being a mother. And of course you need an appropriate person. You cannot have a baby with an irresponsible person. So this is another reason. And sometimes I think if I really do want a baby, why don't I try in vitro fertilization? So then I need to figure out who could be the donor for this. And he has to have a good soul, at least. I just don't have a lot of time to think about it all. This is another problem with having babies myself: I am doing too much work, there are too many stresses, and I don't want to bring someone into this world with the stress that I'm facing.

In June 2013, two months after the Rana Plaza collapse captured the attention of the world, the United States announced that it was suspending certain tariff-reducing preferential trade benefits with Bangladesh because of serious labor rights violations. Part of the Bangladeshi government's response included dropping the charges against Kalpona and Babul and formally reinstating BCWS as an NGO in August 2013. In November 2013, after it finished its investigation into the death of Aminul Islam, Bangladesh's Criminal Investigation Department filed murder charges against Mustafizur Rahman, a Bangladeshi security intelligence agent. Rahman had disappeared after he was suspected for involvement in the murder of Islam.

Kalpona continues her work with BCWS and speaks about her activism at events around the world. She toured extensively in the United States in 2013 and 2014.

Invisible Hands: Voices From the Global Economy (2014), edited by Corinne Goria, tells stories of human rights abuses throughout the global economy, from exploitation of agricultural workers to communities destroyed by industrial accidents. Interviews took place mostly between 2011 and 2014 and spanned the globe.

Pictured at right: Semiconductor assembly

HYE-KYEONG HAN

AGE WHEN INTERVIEWED: 36
BORN IN: *Chuncheon, Gangwon Province, South Korea*
INTERVIEWED IN: *Seoul, South Korea*

While manufacturing circuit boards for Samsung, where she had been employed since 1995, Hye-kyeong Han developed unusual symptoms that left her unable to continue working. After a string of visits to various specialists, Hye-kyeong was diagnosed with a brain tumor in 2004, leading her to undergo a number of surgeries and radiation treatments. She was twenty-six at the time. Although Hye-kyeong's cancer is currently in remission, the removal of her cerebellum (the part of the brain responsible for fine muscle movements and maintaining posture and balance) has made speaking and walking difficult. While Hye-kyeong is now able to walk for a few minutes at a time thanks to rehabilitation training, the road to recovery has been slow and difficult.

We first interview Hye-kyeong and her mother by phone in 2011. They had just arrived at a rehabilitation center in Seoul the day before our conversation. Hye-kyeong answers questions slowly and deliberately, and her mother takes over when Hye-kyeong is tired or unable to respond. Hye-kyeong speaks intently about her determination to hold Samsung accountable for the working conditions that led to her illness, as well as her wishes to prevent similar problems from befalling other young workers within the electronics industry. When we ask Hye-kyeong about her hopes for the future, she begins to sob as she shares her dreams to one day fully recover from her illness.

I WAS JUST AN ORDINARY GIRL

Hye-kyeong

I'm at the hospital right now, in Seoul. But I am originally from the suburb of Chuncheon, the capital of Gangwon Province.[1]

As a child, I was just an ordinary girl. I was healthy—I never had colds. My dream was to become a nurse, or an aerobics instructor, or a massage therapist. I enjoyed reading and listening to music—mostly ballads. I don't have many memories of my elementary school years, but in middle school and high school I had a good friend, a great friend who was like my own sister. Still today, she and I, we really are like sisters. I always think about her without even seeing her, or when I'm not calling her. I know she lives in my heart. I'm really proud of her.

One memory I have of myself as a young girl is from after my graduation from high school. My friend married early, so she, her husband, and I went on a trip to a tiny town called Wontong in the northeast. It was around my birthday, so my friend made breakfast for me, to celebrate. My friend made so much food—and put it all on one small table—so much food I was afraid that the table would break! This is a very happy memory for me.

IN ONE SHIFT WE MADE
SEVEN HUNDRED LAPTOP SCREENS

Hye-kyeong

I started working for Samsung a little before my high school graduation, in October 1995. I was eighteen. One day at school there was a job announcement posted from Samsung. It paid well and offered benefits, and Samsung was known as a good company. There were other companies posting offers but Samsung seemed to be the best. Since our class was

---

1. Chuncheon is a city of 275,000 about forty-six miles northeast of Seoul.

graduating and looking for jobs, a number of companies sent notices to us. They knew we had to get jobs, but other than Samsung there weren't a lot of good options.

I remember on my first day, I went to a training institute in Gangwon. Once there, we were shut up in a room for training and not allowed to even use the phone. It practically felt like a prison. Life at the training institute felt like total hell to me. We woke up early each morning and, if there was time, had a regular meal. We had to exercise each morning as well. We were taught about semiconductors and how they work, but also about living on our own and stuff like that. It lasted about a month.

The first day at the factory was astonishing. We wore a kind of dust-free apron, a mask, gloves, and special underwear to protect from radiation. Inside the facility it was like, "You go here, and you go there." That was how the foremen talked to us, the line workers. So we went wherever they told us to go. I was told to go to the SMT, the surface-mount technology line. So I went and there were four large machines with several parts and one person was running around doing the work. My first thought was, *So that's what I'm working with.*

We had to memorize the machine parts. The names of the parts were long, too, and there were several types. I would get confused after looking at them and trying to remember them later. At first I didn't have a clue what was going on, but soon it seemed there was no need to memorize anything. I just started to learn it all after going back day after day. In the beginning I just ran around, clueless. But my co-worker told me to look over the machine parts, so I would stand in the middle of the machinery and inspect the exterior of the first one, then do the same with the second, and so on; it was mind-numbing. The machinery was so long that you had to run from one end of it to the other. There was a small opening between two of the machines that we called a dog hole, which we had to crawl in and out of. It was fun but tiring work, and time just flew by.

The product I made was a kind of circuit board called a PCB, or printed circuit board. I'd have to glue lots of tiny wires and electronics parts onto a green board using solder cream. The circuit boards I was gluing together would then go into the backs of laptop computer screens. There must have been a quota, but we just kept working; we were never told a particular number we had to assemble. If we put together everything for one model, they'd change the model and we'd put a different one together. In one shift we made about seven hundred laptop screens.

On average we worked eight-hour shifts and usually did about four hours of overtime—so about twelve hours a day. You could work for six days, then have two days off. Or you could work for ten days doing nine-hour rotations and then get a day off. For bonuses, each individual employee was evaluated on a scale. I remember I got a fridge once. Everyone got one. At that time semiconductors were doing really, really well.

WE EVEN GOT TICKETS TO A THEME PARK

Hye-kyeong's mother

At Samsung, Hye-kyeong earned enough money so she could support herself and our family. We had no house of our own before, but after Hye-kyeong worked at Samsung for three or four years, we were able to buy a little apartment. We lived together in the apartment in Chuncheon—myself, Hye-kyeong, and my three sons.

There were other benefits, too. I went to the Samsung Seoul Hospital in Gangnam and got an endoscopy.[2] I got it for free by using a company coupon that Hye-kyeong gave me. I had blood tests done. At that time I just figured that since my daughter was working at a big company, this was just how they did things there. My friends were even a bit envious of me that I was now getting checkups through my daughter's work. Before that, I'd never had any kind of physical exam, and so I just thought that since my daughter worked at a big company, she could help her mother to

---

2. The Samsung Medical Center in the Gangnam District of Seoul boasts one of the largest cancer-treatment facilities in Asia.

live more comfortably. We even got four free tickets to Everland,[3] so Hye-kyeong, my son, my sister, and I went and rode the rides and ate lunch, all for free. At that point I just thought to myself, *Wow, Samsung really is a great company.*

Hye-kyeong

When we received health monitoring at Samsung, a bus would visit the factory from the hospital. Health personnel came to the factory to check our blood and urine and perform X-ray tests. They also tested our vision and hearing acuity. I had a health exam every year. After, I would get the results of the health monitoring, but I could not get an explanation of the results. The health personnel never told me that I was okay. They just said nothing.

LIKE THE SKY IS YELLOW

Hye-kyeong's mother

In 2001, when Hye-kyeong was twenty-three, she was sick all the time—it seemed like she always had a cold. She was so sick that she actually stopped working that year. Then, she started to notice that her menstruation was not regular. My daughter felt very strange all the time. She always had pain in her shoulders. So in 2004 I took her to a Chuncheon hospital to have her shoulder examined. They took an X-ray, but nothing showed up. We had absolutely no idea why she felt sick, and no one could tell us anything.

Hye-kyeong went to almost every kind of doctor. She saw gynecologists about her irregular periods. She went to different doctors because of the pain in her shoulders, and because of the cold or other illness she'd had for a long time. My daughter has been seen by doctors in every field and specialization. Finally, in October 2005, we went to a hospital to take an MRI. That's when we found out that Hye-kyeong had a brain tumor.

---

3. Everland is a theme park southeast of Seoul and is owned by Samsung Group.

When I heard the news, I was flabbergasted, shocked. In Korean, we say, "It looks like the sky is yellow." When the tests were over I stood crying at the sound of the words "brain tumor." Hye-kyeong didn't know how severe the disease was. She asked me, "Mom, what on earth is wrong with me?" I lied to her, saying, "You've got water on your spinal cord. You'll be all right once we can get that water out, just hold on until then." And the next day we went into surgery.

After the surgery, my daughter started chemotherapy. She had chemo treatments three or four times a week. She had radiation treatment forty-one times. In early February 2006, she began a rehabilitation program in Chuncheon. There was a person there who cared for Hye-kyeong, but I couldn't be with my daughter at that time because I was working at the restaurant I owned. Later that year, I had to close that restaurant so that I could be with my daughter.

After her surgery, Hye-kyeong became seriously disabled in speaking, walking, and in her vision. Those disabilities were so serious she had to get more rehabilitation treatment. But in Korea you cannot stay more than three months at any one hospital and have insurance continue to cover the cost of the stay. So we just moved from hospital to hospital.

Between 2006 and 2008, it was such a difficult time for us. We were traveling very far to each hospital. We had to go to faraway cities. We lived in Chuncheon but we had to go to Wonju City and other places to find a new hospital.[4] Later, in the autumn of 2007, we had to sell our apartment to make money for Hye-kyeong's treatments and our living expenses. Now we live with the support of SHARPS, but before we met SHARPS, we were just living on our savings.[5]

---

4. Wonju is a city of 310,000 located ninety miles east of Seoul.

5. SHARPS (Supporters for the Health and Rights of People in the Semiconductor Industry) is a coalition of labor unions and human rights groups that seeks to protect the health and worker rights of semiconductor manufacturing workers.

THEY ARE ON THE SIDE OF THOSE
WITH MONEY OR POWER

Hye-kyeong's mother

When we moved back to Chuncheon and were at the province's rehabilitation hospital, a social worker from that hospital told us about SHARPS
and recommended we contact them because she knew Hye-kyeong used
to work with Samsung. In this type of situation it's important to get your
story out there so I wrote some of it down and asked my son to post it
online. In less than three hours I received a call from an attorney with
SHARPS, Mr. Lee Jong-ran. And, in three or four days' time, attorney
Jong-ran Lee and another activist, Ms. Ae-jung Jung, came and found us
at the Gangwon Rehabilitation Hospital.

After we met with SHARPS, we applied for the Korea Workers'
Compensation and Welfare Service[6] in March 2009. The whole process
has been humiliating. KCOMWEL is supposed to be there to console the
worker, to take care of them, or at least that is what I thought; but what
I have felt from them is that the marble walls inside the building get
better treatment than we do. One time, KCOMWEL told me to bring
in writing whatever it was that I had to say, so I wrote it all down on a
piece of paper. When I arrived, they wouldn't give me an appointment
to talk with anyone, so I stuck my paper up on the wall. A woman from
KCOMWEL told me to take it down. I said to her, "My daughter can't
walk, and she can't even stand up, and I can't take down this paper. Why
do you want me to take it down?" Her response was that if I wouldn't
take it down then she would and that she'd stick it to my face. That is the
kind of treatment we received there. KCOMWEL has become a business.

At first we expected KCOMWEL to consider our case an industrial accident, at the very least. This type of cancer doesn't just appear

---

6. In Korean, the acronym is KCOMWEL. KCOMWEL initially refused to acknowledge a possible
link between circuit board manufacture at Samsung and cancer and thus refused to compensate cancer-
stricken workers with occupational compensation unless clear, causal links could be established.

overnight. There was no phone call or letter or anything from KCOMWEL. We learned our case had been denied from our attorney. Before that I went to KCOMWEL and spoke with one of the directors; I told him about Hye-kyeong's case and begged him to approve our case. This all happened as I cried on the stairs of the lobby. All that and then we heard only from our attorney about the rejection, and my first thought was, *Of course.* That was my first thought, but I had never actually been put in a position to feel the kind of power a company like Samsung has. Since being rejected on the industrial accident application I've come to realize just what kind of power there is behind money. I can't imagine how hard it must be on our attorney Lee Jong-ran every time he has to call and say that something hasn't been approved.

KCOMWEL refused to compensate us, without giving any reason or making any investigation. They just denied our case. The facility where Hye-kyeong used to work doesn't exist anymore, so frankly speaking, an investigation of her working conditions was not possible. I think something should be done, but the government denied our case. They just refused to compensate us. And I think it's because the government, themselves, are under pressure from Samsung. They are so afraid of Samsung themselves that they don't want to decide anything against them. When I heard the news, I felt like the government is not on the side of powerless workers, only on the side of those with money or power. We were so disappointed.

Hye-kyeong thinks there are probably still many workers who work as she did in similar facilities doing the same kind of work that Hye-kyeong was doing. The same environment that made her sick. KCOMWEL decided to investigate other facilities that were producing similar products to the ones produced in the facility where Hye-kyeong had worked. But these other facilities were new—they were totally automatized and they were completely different from the facility where Hye-kyeong worked. So the investigation did not have anything to do with Hye-kyeong's case.

Hye-kyeong

The first time we applied for compensation, I could not speak in public about my experience with Samsung. But later I began to speak in public when my mother and I made a protest visit to the workers' compensation agency, to meet the chairperson about our demands. This was the spring of 2009.

We went because, at some point, we realized that we had to fight this thing. It's natural. If I tell people about it, then the fight will go on. Even if it's not people who actually worked at the factory, if I just tell anybody on the street about it they'll see that Samsung is a bad company. I know since I worked there myself. I know when Samsung is lying and when it is telling the truth.

When I began speaking about Samsung, frankly speaking, I felt like I wanted to hurt Lee Kun-hee, the chairperson of Samsung Electronics. If there are other victims like me—even just one more—then Lee Kun-hee must be punished. I feel it's ridiculous they insist Samsung is such an excellent company; there is nothing good in that company. It's a shame to call Samsung a good company.

Hye-kyeong's mother

We started rehabilitation again in the fall of 2010. We went to the rehabilitation hospital in Chuncheon for three months before she was discharged. Next she went to the welfare center as an outpatient, then to the National Rehabilitation Center in Seoul for a month for occupational therapy, and then home, and now here. We will stay until the hospital says, "Okay, time to go back home." But this time the hospital is somewhat different from before. It's a special hospital for workers, so we might be able to stay longer than three months. Hye-kyeong's body seems to be getting better and so we'd like to stay here a bit longer. But she's worried that they'll ask her to leave soon.

Hye-kyeong's doctor says that the risk of the cancer recurring is not big because there is no evidence of change, so recurrence may not come. But function in the cerebellum—that was the site of the cancer so the

THE VOICE OF WITNESS READER

cerebellum was removed—can never be recovered 100 percent. For the future, this means there are some limitations in living alone and doing things by herself. She cannot walk on her own at all, she needs assistance.

Hye-kyeong

When I first started at Samsung, my dream, my hope, was just simple: I wanted to earn money and to learn about technology to buy a house for my family and support my younger brother in his education. I wanted to contribute to those things; I wanted to finish my work, then go back to my hometown and get a house where I hoped to live with my mother. That was my hope and my dream, but then I got this disease. In ten years, I want to walk again. I want to be normal again.

In 2013, Hye-kyeong continued to receive treatment for her disability while her family fought in courts to have KCOMWEL acknowledge the link between her illness and her former work with semiconductors. In 2013, KCOMWEL denied numerous other cancer-stricken workers' compensation claims on the grounds that establishing a causal link between possible carcinogens and specific cases of cancer was impossible. Out of nearly three dozen compensation claims against Samsung in 2013, only two claims were successful. Hye-kyeong's claim was denied in administrative courts in the spring of 2014.

In 2015, Hye-kyeong remains in remission, but is still partially paralyzed and she has difficulty speaking. However, Hye-kyeong's mother and other former Samsung employees are hopeful that Samsung might be willing to reach a private settlement over compensation claims.

Palestine Speaks: Narratives of Life Under Occupation (2014), edited by Cate Malek and Mateo Hoke, explores the lives of people who have grown up under military occupation in the West Bank and Gaza. Interviews were conducted between 2011 and the summer of 2014. Though most of the initial interviews took place during a time of relative calm, war in Gaza and unrest in the West Bank broke out in the spring of 2014, deeply affecting the lives of many narrators in this collection.

Pictured at right: Israeli military roadblock, West Bank

IBTISAM ILZGHAYYER

AGE WHEN INTERVIEWED: 54
BORN IN: *Battir, West Bank*
INTERVIEWED IN: *Bethlehem, West Bank*

During our dozen or more meetings with Ibtisam Ilzghayyer in her office, her black hair is either pulled back into a slick ponytail or falls to her shoulders in tight curls. She speaks with us in English, and she has a distinct accent influenced by her time studying at Newcastle University in northern England. When she stands, she adjusts a clamp on a knee brace in order to walk. This is due to a childhood bout with polio, which she contracted when she was two years old.

Ibtisam is the director of the Ghirass Cultural Center, which she helped found in 1994. Ghirass, which means "young trees" in Arabic, serves more than a thousand youth annually in the Bethlehem region through enrichment programs in reading, traditional Palestinian arts, and more. The center also provides literacy programs for women—generally mothers who are learning to read so that they can take a more active role in their children's education.

The walls of Ibtisam's office are decorated with awards and framed drawings by children who have passed through the center. Throughout her day, children stop by to share their successes—an improved test score or a list of books read during the month. Ibtisam takes time with each one to congratulate and encourage them, and to laugh with them. She spends most of her time at the center—she works five or six days a week, though she can often be found at the center on her days off as well. When she isn't at the center, she is likely to be at home with her elderly mother, tending a large garden of fruit trees, flowers, and vegetables.

ALL MY LIFE I HAVE LIVED
UNDER OCCUPATION

I was born in 1960, in Battir.[1] Life in the village was simple. Most of my neighbors were farmers, and when I was a child, people from Battir would all travel into Jerusalem to sell produce in the markets there. My parents had some land that they farmed, and my father was also a chef. When I was very young, he worked at a hotel in Amman, Jordan, and we'd see him on the weekends.[2] Then, after 1967, he began working as a chef at the American Colony Hotel in Jerusalem.[3]

My mother stayed home and raised me and my siblings—there were nine of us. We didn't have TVs, and there were no computers of course, and no plastic toys to keep us distracted. I think we were lucky to not have those things. Instead, we used nature. We'd play in the fields, climb trees, make toys ourselves out of sticks and stones. It seemed then like there weren't divisions then between neighbors, despite religion or other differences. We were all part of one culture in many ways. I remember my mother coloring eggs every Easter. It was something that had been passed down for generations—it wasn't a Christian thing or a Muslim thing, it was a Palestinian thing to mark Easter that way.

I must have joined in all the games when I was very young, but then

---

1. Battir is a village of around 4,000 people located four miles west of Bethlehem and three miles southwest of Jerusalem. It is a site of ancient agricultural terraces and was named a UNESCO World Heritage site in 2014.

2. Amman, the capital of Jordan, is a city of over 2 million residents. Jordan administered the West Bank between 1948 and 1967, and many Palestinians worked in Amman during this time.

3. The American Colony Hotel is a luxury hotel in Jerusalem. It was built in the 1950s on the site of a former utopian Christian community started by an American couple from Chicago in 1881. The hotel is well known as a gathering spot for influential people from diverse political and religious backgrounds.

I developed a disability as an infant. When I was two and a half years old, my mother was carrying me past a clinic in town one day. A clinic nurse stopped us and told my mother she should come in, that she should get me the vaccine for polio. So I was given a vaccine. That night I had a fever, and I couldn't move my right arm and left leg. Over the next few years, I was able to regain function of my limbs, but my left leg grew in shorter than my right. At age four, I started wearing a brace to help me walk. It was just bad luck that we walked past that clinic.

I had to get used to people treating me differently because of my disability. Even people's facial expressions when they first met me were different—they didn't react to me as if I were a normal child. When I was at school, I was excluded from physical education activities, and some field trips that required a lot of walking. That was really difficult.

I also had learning disabilities. My teacher beat me once in fourth grade because I was nearly failing all subjects. Education was important to my parents, so they were unhappy that I was struggling. My father had only gone through fourth grade, so he could read and write. My mother had never been to school. But they wanted more for their kids. Especially me. Because I had a disability, they wanted me to do well in school so that I'd be independent when I grew up, and not need to rely on anyone.

Then in the fifth grade, I succeeded on an exam, and the feeling was very strange. The teacher handed back the paper and said the work was "excellent." I couldn't believe I'd done anything that would make her say that. I couldn't believe that it was *my* paper that was excellent. I thought she'd made a mistake. I think that's common for children who aren't used to success—they don't realize it's their effort that leads to excellence. They think it's by accident. But I tasted success just that one time, and I realized I loved it. I just had to convince myself it wasn't a mistake! Then I continued to try hard at school, and I started to realize my potential.

In 1977, I was accepted into a boarding school in Jerusalem. It was actually right next to the American Colony Hotel, so I could see my father sometimes. I'd also go home on holidays. It was still relatively easy to travel into and out of Jerusalem then.

I did well enough in high school that I got accepted into the University of Jordan in Amman.[4] I started there in the fall of 1979, and I studied economics. I loved university, and I wasn't lonely there. Other than college students who became friends, I had a lot of family living and working in Amman. But I still felt homesick sometimes, and I started to understand what made Palestine feel special. In my last year at university, the Palestinian poet Mahmoud Darwish came to read at a theater on campus.[5] I got tickets to go, but when I arrived, the theater was absolutely packed. And the streets outside were full. There were so many Palestinians in Jordan, and we all wanted to hear this poet remind us what it meant to be Palestinian.

IT RAISED A LOT OF EMOTIONS FOR ME

I returned home in 1984, and I had one of the hardest years of my life. I had just spent many years working extremely hard to make something of myself, to become independent from my parents—economically, emotionally, socially—so that I wouldn't be a burden to them. Then I returned to Palestine and found I couldn't get a job. Because of my economics degree, I wanted to work in a bank, but there weren't any jobs in that field available, and I couldn't find any other sort of work. So I lived with my parents for a year and they supported me. I was very depressed during that time.

---

4. The University of Jordan is considered one of the most prestigious universities in the Arab world. It was founded in 1962 and currently serves over 30,000 undergraduates.

5. Mahmoud Darwish (1941–2008) was considered Palestine's leading poet and helped lead a movement to promote Palestinian cultural heritage. Darwish was also a political leader of the Palestinian liberation movement and part of the executive committee of the Palestinian Liberation Organization (PLO) from 1973 to 1993.

Then one day in 1985, I read a classified ad put up by the BASR.[6] They were offering to train workers in a field called community-based rehabilitation, which was about helping people with disabilities overcome them by working with the family—the whole community, really—to integrate the disabled into daily life. At first, I wanted nothing to do with that sort of work. I had an economics degree, and I had spent my whole life trying to get away from any limitations imposed by my own disability. I simply didn't want to think about disabilities. But I desperately wanted a job, so I applied.

I trained with the BASR for a year. It was hard. I worked with children who had hearing issues, blindness, mental health issues. The work brought up a lot of emotions for me, and it took some time to become comfortable around the children. But I kept receiving praise from my supervisors, and they made me feel like I was useful.

In 1986, I began working in some of the refugee camps in Bethlehem as well, and that helped open my eyes. I got to see some of the real trauma that was happening in the community. That same year, BASR opened a community center for people with mental health disabilities, and I helped to run it. It was a very busy time for me.

Then the following year, in 1987, the First Intifada began.[7] I remember it started just after I got my driver's license. I bought an old used car on November 30 of that year, and I was really proud of myself. I was starting to feel quite independent. Then I set out to drive to work for the first time on December 6, and I ended up driving through streets littered with stones and burning tires. It was the first day of the Intifada, and I couldn't make it to work that day—there was too much happening in the streets. So I spent the day listening to the news with my family.

---

6. The Bethlehem Arab Society for Rehabilitation (BASR) was originally founded in 1960 as part of the Leonard Cheshire Disability project, a major charitable organization in Great Britain dedicated to global disability care.

7. The First Intifada was an uprising throughout the West Bank and Gaza against Israeli military occupation. It began in December 1987 and lasted until 1993. *Intifada* in Arabic means "to shake off."

THINKERS BEFORE FIGHTERS

The idea of starting a community center came to me in 1990. It was the middle of the First Intifada, and the streets were dangerous places to play for children. Aside from the threat of getting caught in fighting, children were sometimes targeted by soldiers. Sometimes children threw stones at soldiers, but other times soldiers would find children simply playing traditional games with stones. Many children, even young children, were arrested by soldiers who saw them playing these games. So the idea of the center started as a way to give children a safe place to play.

Also, at that time many schools were frequently closed by military order, so children had to stay at home for long stretches of time. Sometimes the Israeli military would even use schools as checkpoints to control the area. The school in Battir was used as a military camp. These realities came together to make us want to start the center.

The BASR was able to complete construction on the Ghirass Cultural Center in Bethlehem in late 1993, early 1994. In the West Bank at that time, the school curriculum was Jordanian. In Gaza, it was Egyptian.[8] So when I went to school, I studied a Jordanian curriculum. We never studied anything about Palestine or its history. We never saw a Palestinian map. We studied the history of Jordan, of China, of Germany, of England— I remember learning about all the families who had ruled England—but nothing connected to our history, nothing connected to our geography, nothing connected to our culture.

When we started the center, we wanted to educate children about Palestinian culture, Palestinian music, Palestinian poetry. We have famous poets like Mahmoud Darwish, but it was forbidden for us to read from them or read other Palestinian writers. If the Israelis caught us with a book

---

8. Jordan administered the West Bank and Egypt partially administered Gaza until 1967. Textbooks developed during those administrations were used even during the Israeli occupation after 1967, but when the Palestinian Authority assumed administrative control of the West Bank in Gaza after the Oslo Accords, it developed its own educational texts.

from certain Palestinian writers, we might end up in jail. We couldn't have Palestinian flags, political symbols, anything considered propaganda for a Palestinian state—everything could get us into trouble. My family, like most in the West Bank, had a hiding spot at home. For us, it was at the back of the cupboard. When we heard there were going to be raids on houses, we'd quickly hide our forbidden books of poetry or flags or whatever behind a false wall at the back of that cupboard.

With these restrictions in mind, one of our first goals at the center was to provide a sense of Palestinian culture to children. We wanted the center to be inclusive, so we didn't allow any religious symbols or symbols of any specific political parties in the center. We had children from Christian communities and Muslim, urban and rural, from refugee camps and from relatively well-off neighborhoods. I also continued to work with children who had disabilities, but we integrated them with the other kids in the classroom, whether they were blind or hearing impaired or had learning disabilities. They were all integrated.

After working this way in the cultural center for some time, I even began to forget my own disability completely. I had other things to worry about or work on. One day, I saw myself in a reflection in a window while in the street, and I remembered I didn't walk as other people do—I had simply forgotten for a time that I had any disability at all. And I was happy for myself! Overcoming my own disability was no longer my focus.

In the center, I tried to make students thinkers before fighters. I did everything I could to keep them in the center, or make sure they went straight home to keep them from dangerous interactions with the soldiers. We lost some children—some had a strong feeling that they wanted to fight. It was very difficult. Of course, they didn't always understand what they were doing. But they weren't just imitating other people who were fighting in the streets, they were expressing their own anger from experiencing humiliation and violence.

Not long after the center was established and I had begun working there, I had the chance to travel abroad for the first time. I went with a friend to help her apply for a scholarship offered by the British consul to study in England. While there, I applied myself, sort of on a whim. But it turns out I won the scholarship. When I got the call that I had won, the consular office gave me two weeks to get ready for travel. So for the first time, I got to leave Palestine—other than my college years in Jordan.

I studied for a year at Newcastle University and learned administration and counseling. It was a good experience, even though it was hard. I felt homesick from the moment the plane took off. I was away from home from the fall of 1994 to the spring of 1995. I got to travel a lot throughout England, and that was interesting, but I wanted to go home the whole time. I remember I had very little money, and what I had I'd use to call my family. I'd spend hours asking my brothers about neighbors I barely knew—old men who hung out on the street that I never talked to, for instance—just because I wanted to know about everything that was happening at home. When I completed all my coursework, I was expected to stay for the graduation ceremony and some parties. But I told the school administration I didn't want any parties, I just wanted to go home and see my family!

CHILDREN SEE THAT THEIR PROTECTORS ARE SCARED

The Second Intifada began in 2000.[9] During that time, I had to get around a lot of crazy obstacles just to continue my work. From late 2000 to 2003, I used to practically live in this office because I couldn't always go back home. I remember the first time I tried to go home to Battir from Bethlehem in 2000, just after the Intifada started. It was just a couple of miles, and the checkpoint was closed. Nobody could cross to or from the five villages on the other side of the checkpoint. The soldiers refused to let anyone go back home. Children, old men, workers—imagine, all these normal people

---

9. The Second Intifada was also known as the Al-Aqsa Intifada. It was the first major conflict between Israel and Palestine following the Oslo accords, and it lasted from 2000 to 2005.

who wanted to go back home at four p.m., the end of the working day. Hundreds of people! We were surrounded by soldiers, and I remember thinking that nobody had any place to hide if shooting started. I waited that day from four p.m. to seven p.m. At seven p.m., I was so angry and depressed I started talking to myself. I said, "God, are you there? And if you are there, are you seeing us? And if you are seeing us, are you satisfied with what's happening to us?" Finally, after seven p.m., I gave up and came back to Bethlehem and stayed at the center.

Another time that same year, I tried to walk home past the checkpoint. The Israelis had blocked the road with large stones. I wanted to go around the stones, because I couldn't climb over them with my leg problems. It was also slippery, because it was wintertime. But a soldier, a man less than twenty-five years old, stopped me from going around. When I tried to explain, the soldier said bad things to me—nobody in my life has said these things to me. He called me a prostitute. I can't repeat all the things he said. I became angry and I started to argue, and at that moment, a young man, Palestinian, tried to calm me down and asked me to stay quiet. He took my hand and helped me pass the checkpoint. At that moment I couldn't talk. I passed the checkpoint, and my brother was waiting for me on the other side. He took me by my hand and led me to his car, where my nephews and nieces were waiting. Normally I would talk to them, but I couldn't say a word. I knew that if I spoke, I'd start crying, and nobody would be able to stop me. I reached home and I threw myself on the bed. I felt I was paralyzed completely.

I saw the soldier the next day. I had a feeling that if I'd had a gun, I would have killed him. You know, I can't kill an insect, but in that moment, I felt my anger was more than it's been at any time. When he saw me, he began swearing at me again. It was very humiliating. I saw that soldier many times—usually soldiers would stay one week or ten days before they changed the group of soldiers at the checkpoints. I had to see him every day. And every day I looked at him and wished that someone would kill him in front of me. I wanted him to suffer.

One more occasion stands out from that checkpoint during the Second Intifada—I'm not sure exactly when. I remember a little girl was crying. She needed to get to school to take exams, and the soldier wouldn't let her. It's not guaranteed that a child is able to go to school. And it's not guaranteed that the child will be able to come back. Of course, this kind of helplessness has a psychological impact on kids as they grow up. Many parents have told us that their children have nightmares, and they have achievement problems. Children look to us adults as people who can protect them, and when we can't—in many situations, we're scared! To see the child recognize that his mother is scared, his father is scared—it's not an easy thing.

When you move around Bethlehem, it's very restricted. We don't travel long distances. When you face a checkpoint or a wall, you might need to travel only a mile or two as the crow flies, but your destination is far away behind the wall. The children I teach don't have a good sense of distance because of the restrictions. They might say they live "far away," and I'll ask, "How far?" And it's a ten-minute car ride away, if not for checkpoints. That's far for them, because that fifteen minutes might actually be an hour or two most days.

Sometimes I try to put all the obstacles in the back of my mind—the checkpoints, the harassments—to try and keep up my energy for my work, to keep my optimism for the future. But when I'm waiting at checkpoints, I have to face the hard realities of our lives. And the children I deal with—they also have to face these realities, and before they're even fully grown they have to face them without guidance, without someone to protect them.

THE SIGN JUST SAID "OTHERS"

Back in 1994, just after we'd started the center, we used to take students to Jerusalem for trips, to spend the day in the city. It was possible then. Since the Second Intifada, it's not possible to take the class to Jerusalem.

I think this may be the first generation of Palestinians that isn't able to see Jerusalem easily. Now we only talk about Jerusalem. At the center, when we ask the children, "What is Jerusalem?" they only know about the Dome of the Rock. That's all Jerusalem is for them. They've never experienced the city—to see it with true senses, to feel it, to smell it. They only know it through photos. I think it's really demoralizing that this experience, something that used to be essential to being Palestinian, has vanished. I think the Israeli government wants other parts of Palestine— Gaza, Jerusalem— banished from our minds. The new generation, these children might never come to Jerusalem. After years, how will it be in their mind? They won't think of it as Palestine.

Here in the center, we try to keep our students connected with the different parts of Palestine, even if it's only through media like photos, movies, films—anything. For instance, I want our students to understand that Gaza is part of Palestine. This is my hope for all Palestinians in the West Bank, that if they have the opportunity, even if it takes a lot of effort, to go and visit Gaza. I think it's our duty. Many people have lost their lives to keep Gaza and the West Bank one land. I'm not losing my life, but I have put in some real effort to go there.

In 2011, I went to Gaza to facilitate an outreach program. I was with a German colleague who worked for a German NGO that addressed international development projects. The German NGO was trying to fund a cultural center in Gaza that used our center in Bethlehem as a model.

The Israelis keep a tight control on who gets into Gaza, so the permits to visit were not easy to get. I had to go through a lawyer and the court to get the permit. First, the Israeli military rejected my request for the permit, but I was able to appeal and get permission from the court to go for one night. It took me some time to get permission. But even then, I had to go through checkpoints—a checkpoint to get out of the West Bank, and then another checkpoint to get into Gaza.

To get to Gaza, we took the car of my German colleague. When Palestinian workers who cross every day into Israel talk about the checkpoint, you can't imagine—you hear about it, but you need to live the experience to understand it. We went through the checkpoint nearest Hebron, because from Bethlehem it is the most direct route to Gaza. It was the first time I was at that checkpoint. I can't imagine the mind that designed that checkpoint. It's a kind of torture. We tried to pass through the checkpoint in her car. We thought we might have an easier time in her car since she was an international. She passed right through in her car at first, but then a soldier stepped into the road and stopped us. They checked my ID, saw that I was Palestinian, and I was made to get out of the car and walk back to the checkpoint building—a fifteen-minute walk! It was difficult for me to walk all that way with my brace. When I got back to the checkpoint, I was put in line with the rest of the Palestinians. It was around seven a.m., so most of the people there were workers. We were herded in lines through cages, and all around us were young soldiers with guns. There were only three or four other women in line, and they all passed through with no extra delay. But not me.

All the Palestinians have to pass through metal detectors. I failed the detector because of my metal leg brace. The soldiers had to examine me personally because I couldn't just take off the metal and pass through the detector. Soldiers behind security glass told me that I'd need to be taken to a special cell. The whole time I was at the checkpoint, I hardly ever talked to a soldier directly—it was through microphones, since they were always behind glass.

I was taken to a cell with no chairs. The walls were all metal with no windows, and I couldn't see anyone. I stood waiting for half an hour. I thought they might have forgotten about me. Because of my disability, it's difficult for me to stand for long periods of time. I knocked, and nobody came. Later, I knocked several more times, to remind them that there was somebody here.

Then I was taken to another room, also like a cell—just five feet by five feet. Here there was a soldier behind security glass. She was young, in her twenties. Otherwise I was alone in the room. The soldier was dealing with me as if I didn't exist. She ignored me and didn't bother to explain what would happen next. She just sat there behind the glass. From time to time I would knock, or ask her to please search me so I could leave the cell, and she'd say, "I'm just waiting for someone to come." For an hour she left me standing there.

Then another soldier joined her behind the glass. They told me to undress. I said, "I can't, there's a camera." She looked at it and said flatly, "Yes, there's a camera in the room." Every checkpoint has a Palestinian mediator, someone to translate and do chores for the soldiers, and I made them get him for me. This took a long time. Eventually, he arrived and I talked to him. He put his jacket on the camera and then brought me something to put on. I got undressed and then the soldiers told me how to move so they could examine me. Then I put on the clothes the mediator brought while he took my other clothes for them to examine. More waiting. After everything was over, the mediator took his jacket and left, and then I was taken to pass through the metal detector again.

The whole time, my colleague was in the car waiting for me. It had been hours. Then, once we made it to the Gaza border, it was the same procedure. My German colleague was allowed to pass quickly through the checkpoint, while I had to go through procedures strictly for Palestinians, not for foreigners. At the Erez checkpoint, we were not in the car.[10] We had to park, and after you pass through the checkpoint, everyone has to walk through a mile-long tunnel to where the taxis are.

The tunnel was an open-air tunnel with fencing on both sides. It was narrow—not big enough for a car to drive through. Outside the fence was a barren, treeless security area. My colleague had waited for me so we could walk the tunnel together, but a mile is very far for me to walk. I had to sit on a luggage cart of another Palestinian who pushed me the whole way. It was a struggle for me. I like to think of myself as strong,

---

10. As of 2014, the Erez crossing is the only remaining crossing point between Israel and the Gaza Strip accessible to Palestinians. The crossing is tightly restricted since 2007, and special case-by-case permits granted by Israel are needed.

independent. I do things on my own. It's not easy for me to sit on a luggage cart and be pushed!

We finally made it to Gaza after many hours going through the checkpoints. We went directly to the organization because we couldn't waste time. They only issued me a permit for one day! It's ridiculous to not be able to visit your own country. We can move freely in other countries, but not in our own.

After I finished my trip to Gaza, I had to go back through screening at Erez. This time, at the start of the checkpoint, I saw the two signs—one for "Israelis and Foreigners," and the other just said, "Others." You know, it's like they want us to feel that we belong to nothing. They could write "Palestinians," they could write "Arabs," but "Others"?

Going through the tunnel, there were open-air cells along the way. They were more modern than the Hebron checkpoint, but the same principle. The soldiers were all on high scaffolding with guns. They looked down on us from up high and talked into microphones. They would say things like, "Open gate number 2. Open gate number 10." And they'd tell us to move along. The whole time, we could see soldiers on the scaffolding, but we could never see exactly who was talking to us and ordering us onward to the next cell.

The last cell had a ceiling and a grated floor. A soldier behind the glass was there. She asked me to take off my clothes. We negotiated what I could take off and leave on. I took off my trousers and my brace and put them on the conveyor belt. She checked them and then put my things back on the machine to send back to me. I waited for them to contact the people who got me a permit. It took a long time. I thought I had already negotiated all the permits I needed, so it would be fine, but no. They made me wait anyway.

I've spoken with some friends and some people at the Bethlehem Arab Society for Rehabilitation. They go through the same thing, the same conditions. They have the same procedure. It's not because of me—they target Palestinians anyway—but they could show more understanding. They could not make me wait so long, or bring me a chair to sit on, to be humane. I understand they need to check, but they could do it without humiliating people. If this were just about security, they wouldn't need to humiliate Palestinians and not others. It's to show that we're a lower class of people. The Israelis and foreigners are first-class, the Palestinian people fifth-class. And people don't understand why we are fighting. I want to be equal! Equality! Not one of us is better than the other.

Someday I want to go back to Gaza to keep working on developing a cultural center that is like Ghirass. But by then I hope I can find an easier way to get there than through the Hebron and Erez checkpoints as they are now. Still, I'm happy that I passed that experience, really. Now I know what it's like for Palestinians who have had to travel through the checkpoints day after day for work.

ALL THINGS INDICATE THAT
THE FUTURE WILL BE MORE DIFFICULT

I am very proud of being Palestinian, and I have never thought of living in another country. I've traveled across Europe, but I prefer to live in Palestine. When I was abroad and something bad happened in Palestine, it would be very difficult for me to sleep. If people I love die, then I want to die with them; if they live, I want to live with them. If they face a difficult situation, I want the same thing to happen to me. I want to be a member of this society. When I think of Palestine, I think of the struggles we've had. We have to keep struggling for our rights, and there's no end to the struggling for me—some days it's for rights, some days it's to improve education. We are all fighters. When I do work with the children at the center, that's fighting. When I work to improve their quality of life, that's fighting. And working against the occupation, that's fighting as well.

Day by day, it becomes more and more difficult. All things happening in Palestine indicate that the future will be more difficult. Twelve years ago we did not have the wall, the settlements were fewer, the harassment was less. Everything bad is increasing. Usually I avoid going to the checkpoints, because it makes me sick—physically, emotionally, all kinds of sick. It usually takes me time to come back to normal.

My goal now is to expand the center—to extend it and spread it to other places. We're working on outreach programs, to reach schools and other communities that are struggling just to continue to exist. Some villages are surrounded by Israeli settlements and are cut off from important resources. We are looking to support these communities and improve the quality life through education. I believe a lot in education if you want to rebuild the nation.

At the cultural center, we try to keep our students as children as long as possible, to protect them. When they reach a certain age, we can't protect them anymore, they have to face the reality of the streets by themselves. And this is very sad. I can think of many times I've been out walking with my nephew, or with other young boys and girls who are nearing the end of childhood. Suddenly I would get very sad, because when they reach fourteen, fifteen years old, they are children under international and national law, but the soldiers don't think of them as children. They deal with them as adults. And it doesn't matter if they're following the law or not. How they're treated depends on soldiers' moods.

I use many strategies to manage. My strategy is that I love life. I want to protect my life, and the lives of others, as much as I can. Life, even with all these difficulties, deserves to be lived. And I like to look for nice things. Even the smile of a child, or flowers—I try to find something.

I'm not optimistic about the future for Palestinians. Israel is strong, and the Western powers give them their support. On the other hand, I don't think Israel can continue this forever. The world will not support Israel forever with all their behavior towards the Palestinian people. One day, changes will happen—history proves this. One day, sooner or later, the Palestinians will have their rights.

When the world looks at Palestine I do not think they see the full situation. If people want to see the reality of the situation, they will see. If they want to hear the reality, they will hear. But if they don't want to know the reality of the situation, they won't, even if it's right there in front of them.

When we speak with Ibtisam in January 2015, she says that it's more difficult to be happy in the West Bank now than it was in the past. She notices more hopelessness, especially among young people who are just graduating and unable to find work. There is a rise in suicide, which she says was almost unheard of in Palestine in the past. But she tells us that her work still helps her to manage, and that the children she is working with today will be the next generation of young adults. She says that having an influence on them gives her hope.

Palestine Speaks: Narratives of Life Under Occupation (2014), edited by Cate Malek and Mateo Hoke, explores the lives of people who have grown up under military occupation in the West Bank and Gaza. Interviews were conducted between 2011 and the summer of 2014. Though most of the initial interviews took place during a time of relative calm, war in Gaza and unrest in the West Bank broke out in the spring of 2014, deeply affecting the lives of many narrators in this collection.

JAMAL BAKR

AGE WHEN INTERVIEWED: 50
BORN IN: *Gaza City, Gaza*
INTERVIEWED IN: *Gaza City, Gaza*

During our 2013 trip to Gaza, we meet Jamal Bakr twice at the marina where the fishermen dock their boats. On each occasion Jamal is not fishing; instead, he is watching other boats with expensive nets, and the extensive manpower required to use them, as they bring in their hauls of sardines. Jamal has short-cropped gray hair and a trimmed salt and pepper beard. He has a small frame, and he wears black shoes and slacks even though he spends his days amid the muck of the marina.

Approximately 4,000 Gazan fishermen rely on access to the open waters of the Mediterranean to make a living, but the range in which they can travel by boat has been significantly restricted since Israel imposed a naval blockade on Gaza in 2007. Following the Oslo Accords in 1993, Gazans were permitted to travel up to twenty nautical miles in pursuit of large schools of fish. By the time of the Second Intifada in 2000, that range was reduced to twelve nautical miles, and in 2007, after the imposition of the blockade, the range was further limited to six nautical miles (and sometimes three nautical miles).

In 1999, Gazan fishermen harvested over 4,000 tons of fish, and their sale represented 4 percent of the total economy of both Gaza and the West Bank. Today, the fishing economy has collapsed, as Gazan fishermen have depleted schools of sardines and other fish in their limited range. Over 90 percent of Gazan fishermen are living in poverty and dependent on international aid for survival. To pursue fish beyond the permitted range means to risk arrest, the confiscation of fishing boats, or even shooting by the Israeli navy. Some fisherman report being harassed or attacked by the navy even within the permitted fishing zone. According to Oxfam International, an anti-poverty non-profit organization that works in over ninety countries, in 2013 there were 300 reported incidents of border or naval fire against Gazans, and half of those were targeting fisherman at sea.

When we meet, Jamal tells us that he comes from a very long line of fisherman, but that he now relies on international aid to support his family. Since the imposition of the blockade, he can't rely on catching enough fish to provide meals for his family, let alone catching enough to sell at market. He also shares with us the dangers of the Gazan fishing trade—a profession he has no plans to abandon.

MY CHILDREN ARE THE MOST IMPORTANT PEOPLE IN MY LIFE

I was born here in Gaza in May 1964, and I've always lived off of the sea and what it provides. My family takes its job from our ancestors—we've been fishermen since long, long ago. I first went out on a fishing boat with a brother-in-law when I was twelve. I loved it immediately and knew that was what I wanted to do with my life. My father taught me to fish when I was thirteen. I got my own boat when I was sixteen, and I fixed it up until it was in good enough shape to sail in the sea. I've fished now for thirty-five years. I've never done anything else.

I'm very close to the other fishermen. I've worked alongside them for decades, and we see each other more than we see our own families! But my children are the most important people in my life. It used to be that my parents were most important, and now it's my children. I've been married to my wife Waseela for twenty-eight years—we are cousins, and our parents arranged for us to be married. I have eight daughters and one son. We fishermen love to make more and more children because we want sons to help us on the boats. I think of having more children, God knows, but I have to convince my wife! My son Khadeer is eighteen, and he's a fisherman already. He left school after the sixth grade because he wanted to work with me. He's been a full-time fisherman ever since, but he's not old enough yet to be very reliable.

Before the blockade, my family used to go far out into the sea and get amazing amounts of fish.[1] We'd find mostly sardines, but also plenty of mackerel. I could make $500 in a single day sometimes. Fishing around Gaza City was actually better when Gaza was still occupied, since we had more freedom to travel throughout the sea then.[2] But things have been especially difficult with the blockade. Actually, things have been especially bad ever since Gilad Shalit was captured.[3] Before his capture, we used to have access to twelve nautical miles around Gaza City for our fishing boats. But since then, the restrictions have been much tighter. It might change a little, but whether it's three miles or six miles doesn't make much of a difference. We can't find much in those waters—only a few sardines. There are no rocks for bigger schools of fish to live around, since it's mostly only mud in the zone where we're permitted to fish.

When we go out on the sea, we're often in crews of at least three or four. Our boats may be about twenty feet long, with roofs and a closed compartment in the center that we fill with ice and use as a cooler for our catch. We have lights mounted to the roofs of our boats to spot schools of fish in the early morning and late evening, and we use GPS devices so we can return to the best available spots and also make sure we're not crossing the boundaries of the blockade. When we find fish, we have nets we use to bring them in. But these days, it's not so easy to find fish.

---

1. Israel's blockade of the Gazan ports began in 2007, partly in response to Hamas taking power in the Gaza Strip. Egypt also formally restricted its borders with Gaza at the time.

2. Gaza was fully administered by Israel from the end of the 1967 war until the signing of the Oslo Accords in 1993. Israeli settlers and the Israeli military continued to occupy parts of Gaza until September 2005, when Israel evacuated all settlers from the strip and withdrew military forces.

3. Israeli soldier Gilad Shalit was captured near Gaza in 2006. He was released as part of a prisoner exchange in 2011.

Since the blockade, most months I don't make a single penny. It's not only that I don't make money, I even owe the gas station money because it costs a lot to fuel up the boat. Then I don't make anything, so I can't pay. So at the end of the day, most days, I'm losing money. When I do catch fish, I take them to the market behind the marina. But most days there's nothing to sell, so I just sit at the marina with other fishermen. The Gaza seaport— the marina—is pretty much a mile-long strip of concrete where fishermen tie up their boats. There's a gate separating the marina from the rest of the city's shoreline, but not much else there besides a strip of concrete. Recently, a Qatari–Turkish-funded project added some tables and chairs where families can congregate on Thursdays and Fridays. When we get together at the marina, we mostly talk about the fish we found or didn't find out at sea.

But even when there's not enough fish to sell in the market, I feed my family sometimes with the fish I can catch. We eat a lot of sardines when I can catch them. Mostly for dinner, but sometimes for lunch as well if we've caught enough. We'll grill them or fry them, and always eat them with rice. The best kind of fish I catch is the *denees*.[4] That is a delicious fish.

EVERY SINGLE DAY I EXPECT TO BE KILLED

When I'm out on the water, I'm nervous about being shot. Shootings happen all the time on the water. I have a cousin who got killed a year ago, when he was just going out on the water for fun. He was nineteen, and he'd just gotten engaged. He went out on a Friday with his uncle, and, at the time, the fishing zone was limited to three nautical miles. They might have gone too far out. My cousin didn't do anything wrong, he was just a little out of the restricted area. There was no good reason why he was shot.

I probably see around three Israeli gunboats almost every day I go out. Usually, they are off in the distance, but sometimes they get quite close.

4. Denees is the gilt-headed bream, often called *dorade* in U.S. markets.

They are about forty feet long, with a crew of twelve or so. Sometimes they'll pull close to a Gazan fishing boat like mine and simply shout curses through a megaphone. When this happens to me, I just pretend like they aren't there. They couldn't hear me if I tried to say anything back, anyway. They have water cannons that they sometimes fire on boats, as well as rockets and machine guns.

Every single day, I hear that someone got shot at. Every single day, I expect to be killed. Whenever I leave my home in the morning, I'm not sure I will get home alive. That is what it's like to be a fisherman in Gaza. I don't know how to keep myself safe, because we don't have time to think of how to protect ourselves when the shooting starts. When the navy starts shooting, a fisherman doesn't even have enough time to put on a life jacket.

The soldiers often shoot for no reason at all. It doesn't have to be because someone went out of the restricted area, like my cousin. It could be because of something else that was happening in Palestine, or the mood of a soldier. Sometimes, if the soldier's girlfriend broke up with him, he comes and—just because he's angry—he shoots up the fisherman. They keep you guessing. I don't think soldiers who shoot always have a reason, really; they can just do whatever they want without fearing anyone.

In the middle of November 2012, I didn't work at all during the week of bombing.[5] After the cease-fire later in November, I started going out again, and so did my son Khadeer. As part of the cease-fire, we fishermen were supposed to be able to go out up to six miles, so we were all eager to see what we would be able to find in the waters we could now get to.

At that time I had two boats—my old boat that I got at sixteen, and a newer, nicer one with a new motor that I had saved up to buy. Three days after we started fishing again, on November 28, Khadeer went out early in the morning to fish with three of his cousins. They took my new boat out on the water. Later that morning, his cousins

---

5. Israel targeted Gaza with bombings during eight days starting on November 14, 2012, during what it termed Operation Pillar of Defense.

showed up at my house. When I saw them, I thought right away that my son had been killed.

My nephews told me that they were fishing out in the sea, about two miles from the marina. There were maybe twenty other boats around that were fishing in the same area. Suddenly an Israeli gunboat appeared a few hundred feet away. Without warning, the boat fired a missile at my boat's engine and completely disabled it. It caught fire. Nobody was injured, they just destroyed the engine. That was their introduction. Then an Israeli navy guy called to Khadeer and his cousins through a megaphone and told them to strip to their underwear and to jump into the sea, because they were going to blow up the boat. My son jumped in the water, and they hit the boat with another missile and it exploded. After the boat was destroyed, the navy guys began shooting in the water all around where my son and his cousins were swimming. They were all really scared. Then the Israeli boat pulled up and grabbed Khadeer out of the sea. His cousins watched him get handcuffed to the mast of the boat. He was in his underwear, and it was one of the coldest days of the year and very windy on the sea. Khadeer's cousins then swam to another fishing boat, got a lift back to shore, and came to see me.

That morning, I stayed home waiting for news of my son. I thought the police might call with news that he'd been arrested by the Israelis. At some point that morning, friends called to tell me that they'd talked to fishermen who had stayed for a while near the attack on my son. They said he was still okay, that he was aboard the Israeli boat. But I wasn't even focusing on what my friends were saying, because my heart was about to stop.

Then, a few hours later, around three in the afternoon, Khadeer came back. When I saw him, I felt that I got my soul back. The first thing he said was, "We lost the boat." I told him, "You shouldn't have to worry about the money and the boat. It's fine. As long as I didn't lose you." It soon became a big huge gathering of friends and family, and everyone was crying.

Later, Khadeer told me that he was handcuffed to the mast of the Israeli gunboat for three hours. Then soldiers refused to take him to shore, because they didn't want their bosses to know what they'd done to him. They didn't have a reason or excuse for it. While he was handcuffed, they fired on another boat. Eventually, they threw him in the sea and told him to get the nearest fishing boat to take him back to shore. Imagine if something bad happened to him—how could you throw him again into the sea without checking to see if he was close to freezing to death? I think if something bad had happened to him, none of them would have ever cared. Maybe they would have said, "It was by mistake."

I felt really lucky because when I lost the $10,000—the value of the boat—I felt like I'd lost money, but then I got compensated with millions of dollars by getting my son back. I told Khadeer, "Don't think of it. Don't worry about it. This just happens." I didn't want to let him feel too scared by the experience. He started fishing again after one week. By now, my family is used to the nature of this work. When we go to the sea, they know—my son and I are either going to be back home in the evening or we'll be killed. So we all live with this fact.

I feel really disappointed because my life is always in danger, and it's not even for any good reason. It's not for a good thing at the end of the day. Before the blockade, I used to face many hardships, but it was for something good, because I used to make a good income. But now I'm sacrificing my life for nothing. Now I have a dead heart. I don't care about shooting, or anything that comes to me. If anyone starts to feel a bit weepy about their lives, they shouldn't go out on the water.

The important thing is that I have Khadeer back, but the attack has totally affected my life, because the boat that we lost was the new one, and it had a good motor. Now I have only the older boat. Now I'm using my friend's motor because I don't have enough funds for my own.

Even this old boat is at risk. Another worry that fisherman have is boat seizures. The Israelis find all sorts of reasons to seize boats. Then they'll tell the fisherman that his boat will be returned, and it never is. Sometimes I think that Israel is financially fighting Palestinians in Gaza. Because they seize boats for reasons that have nothing to do with security issues, reasons that have more to do with fighting people and their source of income. Sometimes I think if they see a fisherman trying to haul in a huge amount of fish, they keep shooting until he leaves everything behind and runs. So the main target is to control what financial benefits people can get out of the sea.

It's really hard now to support my family through fishing. It's really bad. Before, I used to donate money to charity. But now I'm living on international aid. It's only because of this that I can survive. We get some support from CHF, but it's not money. It's just flour and oil.[6] I could make $500 a day before, and now I haven't made anything for a month. If I could make even $30 in a single day, that would be an incredible day of fishing. But I never feel discouraged. I'm always hoping for the best.

I owe a lot of money to a lot of people. I've borrowed from family and friends. People don't hassle me about it yet, but I feel the pressure whenever I see them. Since the incident of the boat, I don't sleep much, only two hours a day. I didn't sleep at all last night. How would I sleep knowing everyone wants money from me? And, more than this, I wake up in the morning and I'm not sure I'll be able to feed my children. So it's becoming complicated, and it's affecting me and my state of mind because I'm not feeling fine. Still, I never thought of getting any other job because I feel like I'm a fish. If I leave the sea, then I will die.

We catch up with Jamal at the Gaza seaport in January 2015 in the midst of a bitter cold snap. He tells us that the summer of 2014 was the hardest time he remembers in Gaza. "I didn't leave my house during the war, as no place was safe. I was relying on humanitarian handouts to feed my children, and my house was damaged by the nearby airstrikes." In July, four of his young cousins were killed

---

6. Cooperative Housing Foundation (CHF) is an international aid non-profit now known as Global Communities. Following the air strikes of 2012, Global Communities began distributing food to 47,500 Gazans in partnership with the United Nations.

in an airstrike while playing on the beach—a tragedy documented in international coverage of the conflict. Jamal's boat was also destroyed in strikes. "I bought a new one, but I can tell you that this war has totally changed my life for the worse." Still, on the day we speak to him, the January cold snap had brought schools of sardines closer to shore. His catch that day is the largest he remembers in some time, and he estimates that it will be worth enough to feed his family for three months.

UNIVERSAL DECLARATION
OF HUMAN RIGHTS

The Universal Declaration of Human Rights was drafted by the UN General Assembly on December 10, 1948. It is composed of thirty articles that set out international standards of human rights that apply to all peoples. The principles of the Declaration inform the work of Voice of Witness, and the document itself is a useful supplement to both our book series and educational materials. The following text was drawn from the United Nations Office of the High Commissioner for Human Rights website. For more information, visit www.ohchr.org/EN/UDHR/Pages/Introduction.aspx.

Preamble

Whereas recognition of the inherent dignity and of the equal and inalienable rights of all members of the human family is the foundation of freedom, justice, and peace in the world,

Whereas disregard and contempt for human rights have resulted in barbarous acts which have outraged the conscience of mankind, and the advent of a world in which human beings shall enjoy freedom of speech and belief and freedom from fear and want has been proclaimed as the highest aspiration of the common people,

Whereas it is essential, if man is not to be compelled to have recourse, as a last resort, to rebellion against tyranny and oppression, that human rights should be protected by the rule of law,

Whereas it is essential to promote the development of friendly relations between nations,

Whereas the peoples of the United Nations have in the Charter reaffirmed their faith in fundamental human rights, in the dignity and worth of the human person and in the equal rights of men and women and have determined to promote social progress and better standards of life in larger freedom,

Whereas Member States have pledged themselves to achieve, in cooperation with the United Nations, the promotion of universal respect for and observance of human rights and fundamental freedoms,

Whereas a common understanding of these rights and freedoms is of the greatest importance for the full realization of this pledge,

Now, therefore,

The General Assembly

Proclaims this Universal Declaration of Human Rights as a common standard of achievement for all peoples and all nations, to the end that every individual and every organ of society, keeping this Declaration constantly in mind, shall strive by teaching and education to promote respect for these rights and freedoms and by progressive measures, national and international, to secure their universal and effective recognition and observance, both among the peoples of Member States themselves and among the peoples of territories under their jurisdiction.

Article 1

All human beings are born free and equal in dignity and rights. They are endowed with reason and conscience and should act towards one another in a spirit of brotherhood.

Article 2

1. Everyone is entitled to all the rights and freedoms set forth in this Declaration, without distinction of any kind, such as race, color, sex, language, religion, political or other opinion, national or social origin, property, birth, or other status.

2. Furthermore, no distinction shall be made on the basis of the political, jurisdictional, or international status of the country or territory to which a person belongs, whether it be independent, trust, non-self-governing, or under any other limitation of sovereignty.

Article 3

Everyone has the right to life, liberty and security of person.

Article 4

No one shall be held in slavery or servitude; slavery and the slave trade shall be prohibited in all their forms.

Article 5

No one shall be subjected to torture or to cruel, inhuman, or degrading treatment or punishment.

Article 6

Everyone has the right to recognition everywhere as a person before the law.

Article 7

All are equal before the law and are entitled without any discrimination to equal protection of the law. All are entitled to equal protection against any discrimination in violation of this Declaration and against any incitement to such discrimination.

Article 8

Everyone has the right to an effective remedy by the competent national tribunals for acts violating the fundamental rights granted him by the constitution or by law.

Article 9

No one shall be subjected to arbitrary arrest, detention, or exile.

Article 10

Everyone is entitled in full equality to a fair and public hearing by an independent and impartial tribunal, in the determination of his rights and obligations and of any criminal charge against him.

Article 11

1. Everyone charged with a penal offence has the right to be presumed innocent until proved guilty according to law in a public trial at which he has had all the guarantees necessary for his defense.

2. No one shall be held guilty of any penal offense on account of any act or omission which did not constitute a penal offense, under national or international law, at the time when it was committed. Nor shall a heavier penalty be imposed than the one that was applicable at the time the penal offense was committed.

Article 12

No one shall be subjected to arbitrary interference with his privacy, family, home, or correspondence, nor to attacks upon his honor and reputation. Everyone has the right to the protection of the law against such interference or attacks.

Article 13

1. Everyone has the right to freedom of movement and residence within the borders of each State.

2. Everyone has the right to leave any country, including his own, and to return to his country.

Article 14

1. Everyone has the right to seek and to enjoy in other countries asylum from persecution.

2. This right may not be invoked in the case of prosecutions genuinely arising from non-political crimes or from acts contrary to the purposes and principles of the United Nations.

Article 15

1. Everyone has the right to a nationality.

2. No one shall be arbitrarily deprived of his nationality nor denied the right to change his nationality.

Article 16

1. Men and women of full age, without any limitation due to race, nationality, or religion, have the right to marry and to found a family. They are entitled to equal rights as to marriage, during marriage, and at its dissolution.

2. Marriage shall be entered into only with the free and full consent of the intending spouses.

3. The family is the natural and fundamental group unit of society and is entitled to protection by society and the State.

Article 17

1. Everyone has the right to own property alone as well as in association with others.

2. No one shall be arbitrarily deprived of his property.

Article 18

Everyone has the right to freedom of thought, conscience, and religion; this right includes freedom to change his religion or belief, and freedom, either alone or in community with others and in public or private, to manifest his religion or belief in teaching, practice, worship, and observance.

Article 19

Everyone has the right to freedom of opinion and expression; this right includes freedom to hold opinions without interference and to seek, receive, and impart information and ideas through any media and regardless of frontiers.

Article 20

1. Everyone has the right to freedom of peaceful assembly and association.

2. No one may be compelled to belong to an association.

Article 21

1. Everyone has the right to take part in the government of his country, directly or through freely chosen representatives.

2. Everyone has the right to equal access to public service in his country.

3. The will of the people shall be the basis of the authority of government; this will shall be expressed in periodic and genuine elections which shall be by universal and equal suffrage and shall be held by secret vote or by equivalent free voting procedures.

Article 22

Everyone, as a member of society, has the right to social security and is entitled to realization, through national effort and international co-operation and in accordance with the organization and resources of each State, of the economic, social, and cultural rights indispensable for his dignity and the free development of his personality.

Article 23

1. Everyone has the right to work, to free choice of employment, to just and favorable conditions of work, and to protection against unemployment.

2. Everyone, without any discrimination, has the right to equal pay for equal work.

3. Everyone who works has the right to just and favorable remuneration ensuring for himself and his family an existence worthy of human dignity, and supplemented, if necessary, by other means of social protection.

4. Everyone has the right to form and to join trade unions for the protection of his interests.

Article 24

Everyone has the right to rest and leisure, including reasonable limitation of working hours and periodic holidays with pay.

Article 25

1. Everyone has the right to a standard of living adequate for the health and well-being of himself and of his family, including food, clothing, housing, and medical care and necessary social services, and the right to security in the event of unemployment, sickness, disability, widowhood, old age, or other lack of livelihood in circumstances beyond his control.

2. Motherhood and childhood are entitled to special care and assistance. All children, whether born in or out of wedlock, shall enjoy the same social protection.

Article 26

1. Everyone has the right to education. Education shall be free, at least in the elementary and fundamental stages. Elementary education shall be compulsory. Technical and professional education shall be made generally available and higher education shall be equally accessible to all on the basis of merit.

2. Education shall be directed to the full development of the human personality and to the strengthening of respect for human rights and fundamental freedoms. It shall promote understanding, tolerance, and friendship among all nations, racial, or religious groups, and shall further the activities of the United Nations for the maintenance of peace.

3. Parents have a prior right to choose the kind of education given to their children.

Article 27

1. Everyone has the right freely to participate in the cultural life of the community, to enjoy the arts, and to share in scientific advancement and its benefits.

2. Everyone has the right to the protection of the moral and material interests resulting from any scientific, literary, or artistic production of which he is the author.

Article 28

Everyone is entitled to a social and international order in which the rights and freedoms set forth in this Declaration can be fully realized.

Article 29

1. Everyone has duties to the community in which alone the free and full development of his personality is possible.

2. In the exercise of his rights and freedoms, everyone shall be subject only to such limitations as are determined by law solely for the purpose of securing due recognition and respect for the rights and freedoms of others and of meeting the just requirements of morality, public order, and the general welfare in a democratic society.

3. These rights and freedoms may in no case be exercised contrary to the purposes and principles of the United Nations.

Article 30

Nothing in this Declaration may be interpreted as implying for any State, group, or person any right to engage in any activity or to perform any act aimed at the destruction of any of the rights and freedoms set forth herein.

EMPATHY AND INQUIRY:
THE VOICE OF WITNESS
EDUCATION PROGRAM

The educational resources offered in this section can be used by community and classroom educators, non-profits, advocates, journalists, arts and culture organizations, book clubs, libraries, and more.

The Voice of Witness Education Program connects classrooms and communities throughout the U.S. and around the world with the stories in our book series. We offer oral history workshops, training, school site visits, and Common Core-aligned lesson plans that engage participants with a more nuanced and critical understanding of contemporary history. We provide them with the tools for sharing their own, often unheard, stories, and connect them to the skills and practices of the oral historian: empathy, inquiry, listening, and a deep desire to understand the experiences of others.

From our experience, when students learn from the oral histories of living witnesses, something quite amazing happens: they're suddenly empowered with a different vision of history. They see the past not as a pre-determined series of events, but as a series of choices made by individuals and groups. It's a participatory vision of history that encourages them to discover their own voices. And through oral history training, they discover their capacity for authentic, compassionate listening, and their own relationship to issues in their communities and around the world. Jason Jeong, a former student from Oakland's Envision Academy, perhaps sums up the program best: "This is the type of project that just smacks you in the side of the head. I actually get this now—not to judge people. I need to look deeper into their stories."

Educational programming for Voice of Witness began in 2007, when we teamed with a small cohort of Bay Area educators to develop lesson plans that incorporated narratives from our book series and introduced basic oral history skills. In 2010, we partnered with Facing History and Ourselves to develop a pilot project for a broader classroom-based oral history curriculum. The curriculum that was generated during this time was instrumental in formalizing the Voice of Witness Education Program and laid the foundation for our book *The Power of the Story: The Voice of Witness Teacher's Guide to Oral History*. We've recently developed *Say it Forward*, a field guide for inspiring community-based oral history projects that will be released in 2016. Our books and curricula support our four program goals: fostering communication, literacy, critical thinking, and community engagement.

The following section offers a small sample of the oral history-based curricula that we've created around our book series. There are shortened lessons that have been adapted from our larger resources, and activities and discussion questions that have guided learners through critical and creative explorations of the narratives featured in *The Voice of Witness Reader*. Although primarily designed for the classroom, the material shared here represents the variety of ways that narratives in our book series are used by community and classroom educators, non-profits, advocates, journalists, arts and culture organizations, book clubs, libraries, and more. We've discovered in our trainings and workshops that these disparate communities have found countless ways to collaborate and learn from each other, and it is in this spirit of cross-pollination that we offer the following sample resources.

Cliff Mayotte
Education Program Director
Voice of Witness

For more information on our educational offerings, visit www.voiceofwitness.org

SURVIVING JUSTICE:
AMERICA'S WRONGFULLY CONVICTED
AND EXONERATED

Teachers at the high school and college level use *Surviving Justice* to expose their students to the complexities of the criminal justice system. Christopher Wendelin of Amos Alonzo Stagg High School in Palos Hills, Illinois, teaches sophomores *Surviving Justice* alongside *To Kill a Mockingbird*. Professor Susan Katz of the University of San Francisco says her students would read the book and "could vividly see—and even emotionally experience—real life examples of how men of color in particular are systematically targeted and tracked in the penal system."

Graffiti Wall Exercise

Time Needed: One to two class periods

Materials: Chris Ochoa's narrative (page 33) or Beverly Monroe's narrative (page 53); Poster-size sticky notes or large pieces of butcher paper; tape; large felt-tip markers

Objective: To encourage personal responses to contemporary issues through interpretation, analysis, and empathy.

Related Core Curriculum Standards: Reading History RH.9–10.2, RH.9–10.3, RH.9–10.4

Step One: Read selected excerpts of Beverly Monroe's or Chris Ochoa's story as a class or in small groups. Encourage students to practice active reading strategies (20 minutes).

Step Two: Hang large pieces of butcher paper or poster-size sticky notes on the wall. Have students post on the "Graffiti Wall" their feelings, responses, and questions related to the narratives, using individual words, quotations, questions, drawings, and symbols. If it is a large class, you can split into two or more groups for this part of the activity (10 minutes).

Step Three: Have the class silently "examine" the wall(s) (5 minutes).

Step Four: Facilitate a class discussion based on what the wall communicates about students' personal responses to the narrative (15 minutes). Possible prompts include:

- Do any themes emerge (inequality, oppression, anger, confusion, etc.)?

- Are there any contradictions?

- Is there anything missing?

- Does oral history personalize the issues represented on the wall? If so, how?

VOICES FROM THE STORM:
THE PEOPLE OF NEW ORLEANS ON
HURRICANE KATRINA AND ITS AFTERMATH

Voices from the Storm requires students to reflect on the roles of citizens and government in the face of vast humanitarian crisis. Students studying these narratives from survivors of Hurricane Katrina are challenged not just to empathize with the storytellers, but to also consider the responsibilities of the government towards its citizens, as well as the responsibilities of citizens towards each other. Jennifer Moore of Mission San Jose High School in Fremont, California, uses the book in a lesson about the biases and discrimination of mass media. "We read stories from *Voices of the Storm* and compared those stories to the pictures of people 'looting versus finding' food and other necessities. Students immediately understand how the media can manipulate our reactions to news events."

Multiple Perspectives Fishbowl Discussion

Description: A "fishbowl" is designed as an inclusive, participatory group discussion format that encourages all participants to share their opinions and listen respectfully to the opinions of others. It can be used and adapted for classrooms, community groups, book clubs, and more. This iteration of the fishbowl format is focused on a discussion of multiple perspectives from Dan Bright's narrative (page 85) in *Voices from the Storm*.

Set Up: The basic set up is to create a circle of chairs (usually between six and ten) for discussion participants, and another circle of chairs (numbers can vary) outside of the circle for observers/listeners of the discussion. During the activity, each participant will be able to engage as a discussion participant and also as an observer/listener.

For "Multiple Perspective" Discussion Participants:

- Discuss Dan's story from the perspective of his arresting officer on the night of Saturday, August 27.

- Discuss Dan's story from the perspective of one or more members of his family.

- Discuss Dan's story from the perspective of a guard at Orleans Parish Prison on Sunday, August 28, and a guard on the Broad overpass from Monday, August 29 to Thursday, September 1.

- Discuss Dan's story from the perspective of one of the "older guys" in the prison during the storm.

- Discuss Dan's story from the perspective of one or more of his fellow prisoners, in both Orleans Parish Prison and the Broad overpass.

- Discuss Dan's story from the perspective of an inmate and a guard at Hunt Correctional Center.

- Discuss Dan's story from the perspective of Dan Bright.

Discussion Agreements and Format: Before the discussion begins, classes or groups should review any group agreements regarding respectful discussions. Participants may find it worthwhile to respond to the prompts in writing before the activity begins. The observers/listeners should have specific tasks explained beforehand, such as taking notes, active listening, questions to pursue, emergent themes, etc. They might also take notes on the nature of the discussion itself, describing the details of what they feel constitutes a "good discussion." The discussion participants begin their conversation, and after fifteen minutes, the facilitator calls "switch." The listeners/observers then move into the inner circle to become the discussion participants, and the discussion participants move back to the outer circle to become the listeners/observers.

Activity Debrief: In addition to discussing the content covered and questions it raises, all participants should have a chance to comment on their experience as listeners/observers, and discussion participants—reflecting on takeaways from the overall experience as well as strategies for improving future discussions.

UNDERGROUND AMERICA:
NARRATIVES OF UNDOCUMENTED LIVES

Eileen O'Kane of Lick-Wilmerding High School in San Francisco tells us, "In my senior seminar immigration course, I use stories from *Underground America* to create a lesson on the daily challenges faced by undocumented immigrants." Students in O'Kane's class then read source material from *Underground America* and articulate their own responses and insights into these powerful stories.

Examining the Myths and Facts of Immigration

Time Needed: Two class periods

Materials: Lorena's narrative (page 107) or Mr. Lai's narrative (page 127); the American Civil Liberties Union's "Myths and Facts About Immigration" (2008); *They Take Our Jobs! and 20 Other Myths About Immigration* by Aviva Chomsky (optional); butcher paper or poster-size sticky notes; markers

Objective: Through reading, analysis, and discussion of first person narratives, students will develop critical thinking skills to deepen their understanding of U.S. immigration issues.

Related Core Curriculum Standards: Reading Literature 9-10.1, Reading History 9-10.1, RL 9-10.2, Speaking and Listening 9-10.1, SL 9-10.3, SL 9-10.4

Essential Questions:

- Do the stories from *Underground America* complicate your thinking about immigration issues? How so?

- What are the origins of myths about immigrants in the United States? Who benefits from the perpetuation of them?

- Where does the story of the "American Dream" come from? What are its sources?

Preparation: Download and photocopy "Immigration Myths and Facts" from the ACLU's Immigrants' Rights Project for students (www.aclu.org/immigrants-rights/immigration-myths-and-facts). Another excellent resource is *They Take Our*

Jobs! and 20 Other Myths About Immigration by Aviva Chomsky (www.beacon.org/ They-Take-Our-Jobs-P638.aspx).

DAY ONE

Step One: Hand out copies of "Myths and Facts About Immigration" and read it as a class (10 minutes).

Step Two: Divide the class into groups of six or eight, and assign each group either Lorena's or Mr. Lai's narrative. While students are reading their assigned narrative, they should copy three to six direct quotes from their narrators that seem to align with or contradict the myths and facts of immigration (40 minutes).

Step Three: Instruct the groups to discuss the quotes they wrote down. Each group should assign a facilitator and be prepared to discuss the following (10-15 minutes):

- Why quotes were chosen and how they specifically connect to particular myths and realities of immigration.

- How chosen quotes helped students empathize with the personal experiences of the narrators.

- How chosen quotes enhanced students' understanding of immigration issues.

DAY TWO

Step One: On nine poster-size sticky notes or large pieces of butcher paper, write each immigration myth at the top and the corresponding fact at the bottom. Hang them up in various places around the room. Have several markers placed near each "station." Ask students to get out the quotes they wrote down while reading their narratives on Day One. Give students time to move around the room, writing their chosen quotes directly on the particular myth/fact of immigration that it relates to (15 minutes).

Step Two: Once all the students have contributed their quotes, ask them to walk around the room, in their groups, silently examining the quotes at each station (7 minutes).

Step Three: Circle of Voices: Students return to their seats in the groups. Each group should consider their responses and reactions to what they've just viewed at each myth/fact station. Each group member then has ninety seconds of uninterrupted time to talk about his or her responses, reactions, and questions. Once the first ninety seconds is up, the second group member begins his or her ninety seconds. After everyone has had a chance to speak, members of the group may react, comment, and discuss for the final ninety seconds (15 minutes).

Step Four: Class Discussion. As a large group, consider the following questions (20 minutes):

- Where do you think these myths come from?

- Who benefits from these myths?

- In your opinion, is there any "gray area" between the myths of immigration and the facts? If so, can you give examples?

OUT OF EXILE:
NARRATIVES FROM THE ABDUCTED
AND DISPLACED PEOPLE OF SUDAN

Out of Exile examines the civil war and humanitarian crisis in South Sudan. Students explore issues of civil conflict, human displacement, and the role of the international community in addressing humanitarian crises.

Discussion Questions

1. In his introduction to the book, editor Craig Walzer recounts an experience with a narrator named Mary who was critical about the positive change her story would bring about for the Sudanese people. She said, " I have heard these questions before, and nobody has come to our help. We have never been helped. They say money will go to building schools and hospitals. We have been told about this all the time, and nothing ever happens." Walzer's reply was, ultimately, "I'm sorry, I don't know what to say." What are some of the factors that may have influenced her response, as well as his inability to articulate a clear outcome?

2. At the beginning of Achol Mayuol's story (page 147), she recounts witnessing the destruction of her village when she was three and being abducted for slavery when she was six. How did hearing this at the start of her narrative impact you? What does your reaction say about our struggle to, and the importance of, bearing witness to traumatic stories?

3. How would you describe the main themes in *Out of Exile* (as well as Achol's story) and what do they communicate about the people of South Sudan?

4. Achol's story is full of hardship and struggle. What are some of the sensory details from her narrative that make it possible for you to connect or empathize with her?

5. Achol talks about being treated and sold like cattle, shouted at, and repeatedly reminded that she is *abeeda*, a slave. In what other ways did her captors attempt to de-humanize her, and what was her response to these attempts?

6. Achol recounts how she was forbidden to speak her native language or practice any aspects of Dinka culture. She was also forced to learn Arabic and the Koran. What do you imagine was the impact of this on Achol and others in her situation?

7. What role does religion play in the ongoing crisis in Sudan?

8. Is the situation in South Sudan an "internal dispute," or a crisis that the global community has a responsibility to respond to? What actions have been taken so far and what has their impact been?

9. What challenges (internal and external) does an exiled person or refugee face?

10. How many examples of "internally displaced" exiles or refugees within the United States can you think of? What do you know about these people or groups?

HOPE DEFERRED:
NARRATIVES OF ZIMBABWEAN LIVES

The narratives in *Hope Deferred* are studies in the ways citizens manage to adapt and survive under brutal dictatorships. These stories of life under the rule of Robert Mugabe in Zimbabwe demonstrate the remarkable capacities of the country's citizens to fight for their lives and their dignity even when the state they inhabit has failed.

Zimbabwe's Collapsed Economy

Time Needed: One class period, meeting, or group session

Materials: Pamela and Themba's narrative (page 187)

Objective: Through inquiry, collaboration, and partner interviews, participants will explore the personal, economic, and political context of contemporary Zimbabwe.

Step One: Working in pairs or small groups, participants explore any prior knowledge about Zimbabwe through discussion of the following suggested questions. If desired, participants can write their ideas in a journal or notebook before discussing (10 minutes):

- What do you know about the history of Zimbabwe and where did you learn it?

- Have you read any books or seen any films or other media related to Zimbabwe?

- What is your understanding of "black market" economies? Why and how do you think they emerge?

- How does the U.S. black market impact society and communities?

- Do you have any personal experience with Zimbabwe?

- What are you curious to know about Zimbabwe?

Step Two: Participants silently read Pamela and Themba's story (10 minutes).

Step Three: After reading the story, each participant writes five or six questions for a post-reading interview with a partner. The goal is for the interview process to deepen each other's understanding about the ongoing crisis in Zimbabwe. Questions should reflect observations about the content of the story ("What contributed to Zimbabwe's economic collapse?"), reflections about the impact of oral history ("Does a personal narrative impact your understanding of the crisis in Zimbabwe? If so, how?"), or reference specific themes ("How did Pamela and Themba cope with the struggle to acquire basic goods and services, and how has it affected their emotional state?") (7-10 minutes).

Step Four: Pairs conduct their post-reading interviews (15-20 minutes).

Step Five: All participants come together to reflect on the reading, the activity and how it impacted their understanding of the political and economic crisis in Zimbabwe (10-15 minutes).

NOWHERE TO BE HOME:
NARRATIVES FROM SURVIVORS OF
BURMA'S MILITARY REGIME

Nowhere to Be Home is an excellent tool for helping students understand the challenges of life in a police state, especially through the experiences of narrators who must face arrest and repression for simple acts of political expression.

A *"Living Sculpture"* Activity

Time Needed: Two class periods.

Materials: Kyaw Zwar's narrative (page 195); journals or notebooks; Living Sculptures handout (downloadable on our website: www.voiceofwitness.org/sample-curricula/); the *New York Times* online Myanmar (Burma) Country Profile: www.topics.nytimes.com/top/news/international/countriesandterritories/myanmar/index.html); Human Rights Watch: "World Report Burma, 2013" (www.hrw.org/news/2013/02/01/burma-rights-abuses-endanger-reform)

Objective: To bring oral histories physically to life in order to deepen student empathy and facilitate a detailed, nuanced understanding of the lives of youth in Burma.

Related Core Curriculum Standards: Reading History RH.9–10.1, RH.9–10.5, RH.9–10.7, Writing, W.9–10.3, W.11–12.3, Speaking and Listening SL.9–10.1, SL.9–10.2

Overview: Borrowing techniques from theater arts training, this lesson will enable students to develop their empathy skills through direct physical and emotional engagement with narrator Kyaw Zwar from *Nowhere to Be Home.* Through creative collaboration and analysis, students will engage with his story, allowing them to experience "walking a mile in someone else's shoes."

Essential Questions:

- How can I use arts-based skills to critically explore and connect with stories from Burma?

- Does this process enable connection and empathy between youth in Burma and my own life, community, and country?

Advance Preparation: Take some time to become familiar with recent Burmese (Myanmar) history. Among other sources, the *New York Times* Country Profile of Myanmar is a good place to start. Human Rights Watch: "World Report Burma" is another good resource. This information can be compiled into a one-page Burma Fact Sheet for students.

DAY ONE

Step One: Hand out Burma Fact Sheet. Present an overview of Burmese history, focusing on the period of the military coup (1962) up to the present. Provide details as to what defines a police state and specifically how it may affect the lives of youth (10 minutes).

Step Two: Introduce *Nowhere to Be Home* and break students into cooperative learning groups of four. Each group will read pre-selected, sequential excerpts from Kyaw Zwar's narrative. Encourage them to read aloud and employ active reading strategies (10 minutes).

Step Three: Share the Living Sculptures and Inner Monologue handouts. Introduce the activity by announcing that groups will be "walking a mile in their narrators' shoes." They will be reenacting pivotal moments from the narrator's life by creating a series of "living sculptures." Providing a definition of "empathy" may be useful (see discussion questions). Show examples of sculptures to help students visualize the activity. Also introduce the Inner Monologue activity and definition. If needed, provide literary or film/video examples of inner monologue or "subtext" (10–15 minutes).

Step Four: Students get into their groups and put together their four living sculptures, which include supporting quotes for each sculpture and an inner monologue paragraph ("Sometimes I feel"). Groups will need consensus about the four "impactful" moments as well as the physical composition of each sculpture. Each group member will also need time to compose his or her inner monologue for the sculpture in which he or she represents the narrator (15-20 minutes). During this work session, the following suggestions or "side-coaching" may be helpful for students:

- What are the details of your quote? How can you physically tell the "story" behind the quote?

- Allow your entire bodies to be expressive!

- You may find it helpful to write the "Sometimes I feel" paragraph after you have created each sculpture. Your body language will give you ideas about what your narrator is feeling.

DAY TWO

Step One: As a warm up, give groups time to do a final "rehearsal" before their presentations (10 minutes).

Step Two: Groups present their sculptures. Sculptures should be presented in chronological order of Kyaw Zwar's story. Some students may be testing their comfort zones, so remind everyone about any "class agreements" that are in place (15-20 minutes).

Step Three: After each group has presented their sculptures, facilitate a debrief/ class discussion that enables students to respond to the activity. It may be useful to begin with each group describing their experience (10-15 minutes).

Possible Discussion Questions:

- Did creating physical sculptures to represent your narrator's experience allow you to better understand his or her life? If so, how?

- The dictionary definition of empathy is "being aware of, and sharing another person's feelings, experiences or emotions." Did this activity enable you to do that? If so, how?

- "Police State" is a basic term that describes a complex situation. How can you apply the term outside of Burma? In the United States?

PATRIOT ACTS:
NARRATIVES OF POST-9/11 INJUSTICE

"Students in my three-week storytelling class read a narrative from *Patriot Acts*—this provided a platform for discussing issues of injustice, labeling, and stereotyping, and gives students an opportunity to reflect on ways that they have experienced or witnessed injustices in their own lives." —Lauren Markham, Oakland International High School

Civil Rights and Security

Time Needed: One class period

Materials: Adama Bah's narrative (page 221), list of civil rights (see below)

Objective: To analyze U.S. civil rights and security issues through the lens of personal narrative.

Related Core Curriculum Standards: Reading History 9-10.3; RH.9-10.4; RH.9-10.9, Speaking and Listening SL.9-10.1, SL.9-10.5

Step One: Examine and discuss the list of civil rights. The teacher should address any clarifying questions about the list before moving on to Step Two. You may find it helpful to refer to specific examples of these rights (10 minutes).

The following is a list of basic civil rights in the United States:

Your First Amendment rights—freedom of speech, association, and assembly; freedom of the press; freedom of religion.

Your right to equal protection under the law—protection against unlawful discrimination.

Your right to due process—fair treatment by the government whenever the loss of your liberty or property is at stake.

Your right to privacy—freedom from unwarranted government intrusion into your personal and private affairs.

Step Two: Introduce and read Adama's story from *Patriot Acts*. Based on your class's needs, students can read individually as silent, sustained reading or aloud in groups (20 minutes).

Step Three: Compare the list of civil rights with Adama Bah's narrative.

Discuss the following questions. If desired, have students respond to the questions in writing before the discussion (15-20 minutes):

- Were the civil rights of Adama Bah violated? If so, which ones?

- If these rights were violated, was it justified for the sake of security? Can civil rights and security be at odds with each other? If so, how?

- Adama Bah's experience was related to the passage of the USA PATRIOT Act in 2001. Can you think of other related examples from U.S. history?

- In times of upheaval or crisis, is it necessary to suspend some of our civil rights in order to maintain security? Why or why not?

Step Four (Homework/additional class activity): Persuasive essay or class debate. Take the remaining class time to assign a persuasive essay or to introduce a class debate for the next class meeting using the following question (5-7 minutes):

- What is your opinion of heightened airport security (body scans, searches, etc.) and increased national surveillance? Are they necessary precautions or a violation of an individual's right to privacy?

INSIDE THIS PLACE, NOT OF IT:
NARRATIVES FROM WOMEN'S PRISONS

According to Amy Crawford from the Communication Arts & Sciences Academy at Berkeley High School, *Inside This Place, Not of* It is an important tool in a unit she teaches on "models of justice." "My students find Ashley Jacobs's story powerful and her voice one of strength and optimism in the face of injustice, which inspires them to speak to members of their own families and communities about formerly taboo subjects."

Body Stories

Time Needed: One to two class periods

Materials: Ashley Jacobs's narrative (page 245) and Theresa Martinez's narrative (page 261); butcher paper; markers

Objective: Through reading oral history narratives, students will think critically about the physical, emotional, and psychological impacts of incarceration, and deepen their group communication skills.

Related Curriculum Standards: Reading History 9-10.1, RH 9-10.5, RH 9-10.7, Speaking and Listening 9-10.1, SL 9-10.2

Essential Questions:

- What are some of the long-term impacts of trauma on people's bodies and minds?

- How does one's position of power, or lack thereof, impact his or her ability to remain safe?

Step One: Divide the class into groups of four or five students. Assign each group either Ashley Jacobs's story or Theresa Martinez's story from *Inside this Place, Not Of It.* Based on your class's needs, students can read individually as silent, sustained reading or aloud in groups (25 minutes). If desired, students can read the assigned narrative for homework the night before the lesson.

Step Two: With butcher paper and markers, each group should draw a life-sized outline of a body, and imagine it as the body of their narrator. Using the following questions, encourage each group to fill it in according to how their narrator was affected by prison. Groups should also create five or six questions of their own (20 minutes):

Body

- How is _____ treated by doctors and nurses?

- Does _____ receive the medication she needs?

- Does _____ have all the knowledge she needs to best take care of herself?

- How is _____'s body different after prison?

Head

- What kind of privacy does _____ have?

- How is _____ treated by guards and wardens? How does that affect her?

- Does _____ receive any counseling or therapy?

Heart

- Does _____ feel comfortable expressing her feelings in prison?

- Does _____ have many friends in prison?

- Does _____ receive visitors? What is the visiting process like?

- If _____ has children, how has prison affected her relationships with them?

Step Three: Each group presents their narrator to the rest of the class, explaining how they filled in their body and why. They should be able to refer to specific passages in the narrative as evidence for why they filled in the body as they did, and how their choices about the same narrators differed from other groups. If time, or by extending the lesson into two class periods, students can reflect in writing (followed by a class discussion) on the following suggested prompts (15-30 minutes).

- What are some of the long-term effects of incarceration on people who've served time in prison or jail?

- Do these women's story complicate your thinking about the U.S. justice system? If so, how?

- Do these stories and this activity complicate your thinking about gender equality? If so, how?

THROWING STONES AT THE MOON:
NARRATIVES FROM COLOMBIANS
DISPLACED BY VIOLENCE

Throwing Stones at the Moon is a collection of narratives that challenge students to think about the ways civil war can affect the lives of everyday citizens, including the toll taken on those displaced by civil conflict.

Critical Reading Log
Time Needed: One homework assignment and one class period

Materials: Sergio Díaz's narrative (page 275); copies of the Critical Reading Log (page 428)

Objective: To build reading comprehension and critical thinking skills through personal student reflection on first person narratives.

Related Core Curriculum Standards: Reading History 9-10.2, RH 9-10.4, RH 9-10.10

Preparation: Assign students to read Sergio Díaz's narrative from *Throwing Stones at the Moon* the night before class. Make sure that all students have read the narrative before beginning this lesson.

DAY ONE
Step One: Hand out Critical Reading Logs. Ask students to write a 150 word summary of the people and/or events that occurred in Sergio's narrative (20 minutes).

Step Two: Instruct students to select two quotations from the reading that they feel are important or interesting, and write the quotations on their Critical Reading Log sheets, making sure to explain why they chose each quotation (10 minutes).

Step Three: Students are to make a connection/reflection between what they have read and what they have seen, experienced, heard about, or read in another book, film, newspaper, etc. Ask them to address the following questions:

- What did it remind you of?

- Why is this story/account important?

Remind students to write about both parts of the connection—something specific from the oral history narrative (Sergio's story), and something specific from outside the narrative (20 minutes).

Step Four: Students create 3-5 oral history interview questions they would ask Sergio Díaz if they were to conduct an interview with him. Encourage them to "strive to find the holes" of the story and ask questions that can help clarify his story and experience (10 minutes).

Critical Reading Log Format

Name:

Class/Period:

Date:

Title of book/story/narrative:

Author:

Summary:

Quotations:

Explanation of Quotations:

Connections/Reflections:

Oral History Questions:

REFUGEE HOTEL

Often Voice of Witness narratives work well as readings with simple discussion questions to follow. *Refugee Hotel* is a book of text and images that ask students to empathize with those who have come to the United States to escape violence or persecution.

Discussion Questions

1. Farah Ibrahim (page 283) speaks of "living in fear" during the Iran-Iraq war. How could living in constant fear of being taken away by the government impact a person's character?

2. Farah gives examples of the concrete, physical impacts of the war: they didn't have basic food supplies like sugar; they had no electricity in the 115 degree heat. What do you think were some of the emotional and psychological impacts of war?

3. Analyze this statement: "We knew if Saddam was the bad guy, the United States couldn't be the bad guy."

4. How might a refugee's ideas of "home" shift and evolve during and after resettlement? Mahmmoud (page 283) says that "home is where you feel safe." Do you agree or disagree with that statement? Why or why not?

5. Are American perceptions of refugees different from perceptions of immigrants who choose to come to the United States for better opportunities? If so, how?

6. Felix Lohitai (page 293) describes horrific conditions in the refugee camps he lived in. Can you think of more human responses, programs, and ways to shelter people going through forced displacement? Are there specific challenges to these responses? If so, what are they?

7. Farah, Mahmmoud, and Felix all discuss the solidarity they find in the refugee communities in the American cities to which they've been relocated. How might this camaraderie and support make the refugee experience more navigable?

8. Felix says that his ideas about America were vastly different than the realities he found when he arrived. How do you think "the American dream" is portrayed across the globe? Discuss the myths and realities of acclimating to life in America.

HIGH RISE STORIES:
VOICES FROM CHICAGO PUBLIC HOUSING

High Rise Stories is used by teachers to address issues of city planning and fair housing, and to explore the ways human relationships and community can be as critical as the need for secure shelter.

Concepts of Home

Time Needed: One class period

Materials: Dolores Wilson's narrative (page 301); copies of the Chicago Public Housing Fact Sheet; large butcher paper; colored markers; index cards

Objective: Students will explore the ideas of home and community through oral history narrative, and evaluate their opinions and findings through a short critical reflection.

Related Core Curriculum Standards: Speaking and Listening SL.9-10 1, SL.9-10.5. Language L.9-10.5. Writing W.9-10.3. Reading History RH.9-10.2, RH.9-10.4 Language L9-10.1

Essential Questions:

- Do you believe the government should provide housing to those who can't afford it? Why or why not?

- In your opinion, is public housing offered fairly in our country?

- How does an outsider's opinion about a neighborhood or community differ from an insider's?

Step One: Students respond to the following written prompt: (5 minutes)

- What does "home" mean to you? Is it defined by a place, a family, a feeling, a community? Something else? Explain.

Step Two: Read Dolores's narrative. This can be done as a class, in small groups, or as individual silent reading. Alternatively, the lesson can be adapted and students could have read the narrative the night before for homework (20 minutes).

Step Three: Journaling activity. Write the following prompt on the board, and ask students to spend 10 minutes free-writing (10 minutes):

- Think about Dolores's emotional journey throughout her narrative. Can you identify with her feelings of loss, grief, or displacement? What would it feel like to be forced out of the home where you've lived for over 50 years?

Step Four: Pair share. Ask students to find a partner and discuss their answers to the journal prompt (5 minutes).

Step Five: To prepare students for the Pro/Con chart, hand out the Chicago Public Housing Fact Sheet (downloadable on our website: www.voiceofwitness. org/sample-curricula/) and read it together as a class. Check for understanding and answer any questions students may have about public housing (7-10 minutes).

Step Six: Pro/Con chart. On the board, create a T-chart with PROS on one side and CONS on the other. As a class, brainstorm the pros and cons, or benefits and potential risks of public housing. Encourage the class to cite specific examples from Dolores's story. Examples may include: sense of community, shelter for people who otherwise might not be able to afford it, violence in the Chicago high rises, dilapidated buildings, low motivation for the city to make changes (10 minutes).

Step Seven: Exit cards. Allow students to anonymously respond on index cards to the following prompts (5 minutes):

- What do I know about public housing?

- What questions do I still have about public housing?

- What have I learned about definitions of home and community?

Student responses should be collected and used for further class discussion, readings, and an exploration of public housing in their community.

INVISIBLE HANDS:
VOICES FROM THE GLOBAL ECONOMY

The lessons that Samantha Wainwright of Moreau Catholic High School in Hayward, California, adapted for narratives from *Invisible Hands* "created a great opportunity for [her] students to practice empathy and not only understand an injustice happening in another part of the world, but feel it for themselves and have a deeper appreciation for the undervalued in our global economy."

Human Rights Abuses in the Electronics Industry

Time Needed: One class period

Materials: Hye-kyeong Han's narrative (page 357); paper and pens/pencils

Suggested Book Pairing: *Factory Girls: From Village to City in a Changing China* by Leslie T. Chang. (Spiegel & Grau, 2009). A look into the everyday lives of the migrant factory population in China.

Objective: Through reading oral history narratives, students will weigh the various financial and ethical choices that employers and management must make. Students will think critically about where their electronics come from and under what conditions they are manufactured.

Related Core Curriculum Standards: Reading History RH.9-10.2, RH.9-10.4, Speaking and Listening SL.9-10.1, SL.9-10.5, Language L.9-10.3, L.11-12.3a

Essential Questions:

- Is it possible to pay workers fair wages and also keep the cost of products affordable? Why or why not?

- What are the long-term effects (on individuals and cultures) of people moving from place to place trying to find steady employment?

- What responsibility, if any, do we have as consumers to ensure that the workers who manufacture our goods are treated and compensated fairly?

- What potential problems arise when corporations are funded by the government?

Step One: Students respond to the following written prompt (5 minutes):

- 1. Make a list of all the electronics you use on a weekly basis.

- 2. Where and how do you think these electronics are made?

Step Two: Ask for five volunteers to share their responses with the class (5 minutes).

Step Three: Distribute copies of Hye-kyeong Han's narrative. Based on your class's needs, students can read individually as silent, sustained reading or aloud in groups (20 minutes).

Step Four: Divide students into groups of four or five. Instruct groups to discuss Hye-kyeong Han's narrative and collaborate to answer the following questions on paper (20 minutes):

- Describe your narrator's situation.

- What specific human rights crisis did your narrator face?

- In what ways could this crisis have been prevented?

- What can be done to prevent this type of crisis from recurring?

Step Five: Draw a Venn Diagram on the board. On the left side, write "Business/Financial Concerns." On the right side, write "Moral/Ethical Concerns."

Ask students to imagine they are in charge of a manufacturing corporation. What concerns would they have about both business and ethics, and are there places where these concerns intersect? Brainstorm as a class. Before leaving, students should copy down any text from the "intersecting" portion of the Venn Diagram (10 minutes).

Step Six (homework): Using text and ideas from the intersecting portion of the Venn Diagram, students should write a one-page "proposal" to the CEO of Samsung, describing in detail how they would create a business model that would successfully merge the health/ethical concerns with the business/financial concerns of the company (30 minutes).

PALESTINE SPEAKS:
NARRATIVES OF LIFE UNDER OCCUPATION

Palestine Speaks raises issues of citizenship, demarcation of boundaries, and legal personhood. Aside from the deeply important topic of the Middle East peace process, the narratives in this book help readers grasp concepts of legal citizenship.

Demarcation and Boundaries

Time Needed: One class period

Materials: Ibtisam Ilzghayyer's narrative (page 369) and and Jamal Bakr's narrative (page 387); Lit Circle handouts (downloadable on our website: www.voiceofwitness.org/sample-curricula/)

Objective: Students will learn critical thinking skills through analyzing first person narrative and considering the role of power in creating boundaries and demarcations, and will practice collaborative learning and inquiry through Literature Circles.

Related Core Curriculum Standards: Speaking and Listening SL.9–10.1, SL.9–10.5. Writing W.9–10.3. Language L.9–10.5. Reading History RH.9–10.2, RH.9–10.4

Essential Questions:

* Who decides the boundaries of cities/states/countries, and how does this relate to power and oppression?

* What are some of the impacts of restricting people's freedom of movement?

* What are the impacts of being stateless?

* What is the relationship between boundaries and security?

Step One: Students respond to the following written prompt (5 minutes):

* What is the purpose of dividing land into countries, states, cities, and counties? Who decides where the boundaries are?

Step Two: Pair Share: Students partner with a neighbor and discuss their answers to the written prompt (5 minutes).

Step Three: Split the class into two groups, assigning one narrative to each group. From these two groups, create smaller Lit Circle groups of five (5 minutes).

Step Four: Distribute Lit Circle Handouts with job descriptions for Discussion Director, Vocabulary Builder, Illustrator, and Connector. Each group should determine individuals' roles, read their narrative or excerpt (taking turns reading aloud in their Lit Circle groups), and fulfill duties according to their jobs (30-35 minutes). Note: Allow approximately fifteen minutes for the groups to read the story, and fifteen minutes for group members to complete their Lit Circle duties on their own pieces of paper.

Step Five: Lit Circle groups share/present their work (10 minutes).

ACKNOWLEDGMENTS

Thank you to our partners past and present, including The Abundance Foundation, The Akonadi Foundation, Amazon.com, The California Arts Council, Cal Humanities, Dominican University, Facing History and Ourselves, The Flora Family Foundation, The Fred Gellert Family Foundation, The Geraldine R. Dodge Foundation, The Germanacos Foundation, The Hemera Foundation, The Hull Family Foundation, The Isabel Allende Foundation, The Joyce Foundation, The Kalliopeia Foundation, The Kimball Foundation, The Lambent Foundation, The Lannan Foundation, The National Endowment for the Arts, Not On Our Watch, The ONEXONE Foundation, The Open Society Foundations, The Panta Rhea Foundation, Proteus Fund, The Rex Foundation, The San Francisco Arts Commission, The San Francisco Foundation, The Skees Family Foundation, The Tin Man Fund, The Trellis Charitable Fund, The Valentino Achak Deng Foundation, The Weissberg Family Foundation, The Weissman Family Foundation, The Whitman Institute, and The Zeitoun Foundation.

We would like to thank the Voice of Witness Education Program Advisory Board: Rick Ayers, Nishat Kurwa, Katie Kuszmar, Bill Ayers, and Gerald Richards. We would also like to thank The University of San Francisco Human Rights Education Program, Aim High, The Oral History Association, Lisa Thyer, Steven Mayers, Trevor Gardner, Eileen O'Kane, Jeanne Barr, Shanti Elliot, Facing History and Ourselves, 826 Valencia, and 826 National. Thank you to the countless organizations and individuals whose advice and volunteered efforts have made our book series possible. And our deepest gratitude to the individuals who have allowed us to share their stories with our readers.

ABOUT THE EDITORS

SIBYLLA BRODZINSKY is a freelance journalist who has spent more than twenty years writing about Latin American politics, human rights, and social issues. She is based in Colombia and contributes regularly to the *Economist*, the *Christian Science Monitor*, and the *Guardian*.

DAVE EGGERS is the author of many books including *The Circle* and *A Hologram for the King*. He is the co-founder of 826 National, a network of writing and tutoring centers. He is the co-founder of Voice of Witness and ScholarMatch, a college access organization serving low-income students around the U.S.

CORINNE GORIA is an immigration attorney and author who lives in San Diego, California.

MATEO HOKE studied journalism at the University of Colorado-Boulder and The University of California-Berkeley Graduate School of Journalism.

ANNIE HOLMES was born in Zambia and raised in Zimbabwe. She has taught high school, run a book editing department, made documentaries and television, and led communications for feminist organizing and health research in the U.S. and UK. She now lives in London, but Zimbabwe is always home.

MAGGIE LEMERE is a multimedia storyteller and oral historian whose projects focus on social and environmental issues.

ROBIN LEVI is a consultant working in the field of human rights, and she is the former human rights director at Justice Now. While a staff attorney at the Women's Rights Division of Human Rights Watch, she documented sexual abuse of women in U.S. state prisons.

JULIET LINDERMAN is an Associated Press reporter based in Baltimore, Maryland. She has also worked as a reporter for the New Orleans *Times-Picayune*.

ALIA MALEK is an author and civil rights lawyer. She is a Senior Writer at Al Jazeera American, and her reportage has appeared in the *New York Times*, *Granta*, *Foreign Policy*, and others.

CATE MALEK is a freelance writer and teacher in Bethlehem. She previously worked as a reporter, receiving multiple Colorado Press Association awards.

PETER ORNER edited *Underground America* and co-edited *Hope Deferred*, and is the author of four books of fiction, including the novels *The Second Coming of Mavala Shikongo* and *Love and Shame and Love*. His most recent book, *Last Car Over the Sagamore Bridge*, was a *New York Times* Editor's Choice and named a Favorite Book of 2013 by the *Wall Street Journal*.

AUDREY PETTY has been published in the *Massachusetts Review*, *Callaloo*, *ColorLines*, *Saveur*, and *Oxford American*. She teaches with the Clemente Course in the Humanities and for the Prison + Neighborhood Arts Project.

MAX SCHOENING is the Colombia researcher for Human Rights Watch. He has written extensively about human rights issues in Colombia, including forced displacement, transitional justice, and abuses against Afro-Colombians.

GABRIELE STABILE is an Italian photographer who is based in New York City. His photography has appeared in the *New Yorker*, the *New York Times*, and the *Wall Street Journal*.

LOLA VOLLEN is a physician and human rights activist. She is a co-founder of Voice of Witness as well as The Life After Exoneration Program.

AYELET WALDMAN is the bestselling author of *Love and Other Impossible Pursuits*, *Daughter's Keeper*, *Red Hook Road*, *Bad Mother*, and, most recently *Love and Treasure*. She has also written for the *New York Times*, *Vogue*, the *Washington Post*, and the *Wall Street Journal*.

CRAIG WALZER co-founded and operates a bookstore on the island of Santorini in Greece, Atlantis Books, and a bookstore in Madrid called Desperate Literature.

ZOË WEST is a writer and researcher who works in the areas of labor, migration, and human rights.

CHRIS YING was formerly the publisher of McSweeney's and the managing editor of Voice of Witness. He is now the editor-in-chief of *Lucky Peach*.

SURVIVING JUSTICE

America's Wrongfully Convicted and Exonerated

Compiled and edited by Lola Vollen and Dave Eggers

Foreword by Scott Turow

"Real, raw, terrifying tales of 'justice.'" —*Star Tribune*

These oral histories prove that the problem of wrongful conviction is far-reaching and very real. Through a series of all-too-common circumstances—eyewitness misidentification, inept defense lawyers, coercive interrogation—the lives of these men and women of all different backgrounds were irreversibly disrupted. In *Surviving Justice*, thirteen exonerees describe their experiences—the events that led to their convictions, their years in prison, and the process of adjusting to their new lives outside.

VOICES FROM THE STORM

The People of New Orleans on Hurricane Katrina and Its Aftermath

Compiled and edited by Chris Ying and Lola Vollen

"Voices from the Storm uses oral history to let those who survived the hurricane tell their (sometimes surprising) stories." —*Independent UK*

Voices from the Storm is a chronological account of the worst natural disaster in modern American history. Thirteen New Orleanians describe the days leading up to Hurricane Katrina, the storm itself, and the harrowing confusion of the days and months afterward. Their stories weave and intersect, ultimately creating an eye-opening portrait of courage in the face of terror, and of hope amid nearly complete devastation.

UNDERGROUND AMERICA
Narratives of Undocumented Lives
Compiled and edited by Peter Orner
Foreword by Luis Alberto Urrea

"No less than revelatory." —*Publishers Weekly*

They arrive from around the world for countless reasons. Many come simply to make a living. Others are fleeing persecution in their native countries. But by living and working in the U.S. without legal status, millions of immigrants risk deportation and imprisonment. *Underground America* presents the remarkable oral histories of men and women struggling to carve a life for themselves in the United States. In 2010, *Underground America* was translated into Spanish and released as *En las Sombras de Estados Unidos.*

OUT OF EXILE
The Abducted and Displaced People of Sudan
Compiled and edited by Craig Walzer
Additional interviews and an introduction by
Dave Eggers and Valentino Achak Deng

"Riveting." —*School Library Journal*

Millions of people have fled from conflicts in all parts of Sudan, and many thousands more have been enslaved as human spoils of war. In *Out of Exile*, refugees and abductees recount their escapes from the wars in Darfur and South Sudan, from political and religious persecution, and from abduction by militias. They tell of life before the war, and of the hope that they might someday find peace again.

HOPE DEFERRED
Narratives of Zimbabwean Lives
Compiled and edited by Peter Orner and Annie Holmes
Foreword by Brian Chikwava

"Hope Deferred might be the most important publication to have come out of Zimbabwe in the last thirty years." —*Harper's Magazine*

The fifth volume in the Voice of Witness series presents the narratives of Zimbabweans whose lives have been affected by the country's political, economic, and human rights crises. This book asks the question: How did a country with so much promise—a stellar education system, a growing middle class of professionals, a sophisticated economic infrastructure, a liberal constitution, and an independent judiciary—go so wrong?

NOWHERE TO BE HOME
Narratives from Survivors of Burma's Military Regime
Compiled and edited by Maggie Lemere and Zoë West
Foreword by Mary Robinson

"Extraordinary." —The Asia Society

Decades of military oppression in Burma have led to the systematic destruction of thousands of ethnic-minority villages, a standing army with one of the world's highest numbers of child soldiers, and the displacement of millions of people. *Nowhere to Be Home* is an eye-opening collection of oral histories exposing the realities of life under military rule. In their own words, men and women from Burma describe their lives in the country that Human Rights Watch has called "the textbook example of a police state."

PATRIOT ACTS
Narratives of Post-9/11 Injustice
Compiled and edited by Alia Malek • Foreword by Karen Korematsu

"Important and timely." —Reza Aslan

Patriot Acts tells the stories of men and women who have been needlessly swept up in the War on Terror. In their own words, narrators recount personal experiences of the post-9/11 backlash that has deeply altered their lives and communities. Patriot Acts illuminates these experiences in a compelling collection of eighteen oral histories from men and women who have found themselves subject to a wide range of human and civil rights abuses—from rendition and torture, to workplace discrimination, bullying, FBI surveillance, and harassment.

INSIDE THIS PLACE, NOT OF IT
Narratives from Women's Prisons
Compiled and edited by Robin Levi and Ayelet Waldman
Foreword by Michelle Alexander

"These stories are a gift." —Michelle Alexander

Inside This Place, Not of It reveals some of the most egregious human rights violations within women's prisons in the United States. In their own words, the thirteen narrators in this book recount their lives leading up to incarceration and their experiences inside—ranging from forced sterilization and shackling during childbirth, to physical and sexual abuse by prison staff. Together, their testimonies illustrate the harrowing struggles for survival that women in prison must endure.

THROWING STONES AT THE MOON
Narratives of Colombians Displaced by Violence
Compiled and edited by Sibylla Brodzinsky and Max Schoening
Foreword by Íngrid Betancourt

"Both sad and inspiring." —*Publishers Weekly*

For nearly five decades, Colombia has been embroiled in internal armed conflict among guerrilla groups, paramilitary militias, and the country's own military. Civilians in Colombia have to make their lives despite the threat of torture, kidnapping, and large-scale massacres—and more than four million have had to flee their homes. The oral histories in *Throwing Stones at the Moon* describe the most widespread of Colombia's human rights crises: forced displacement. Speakers recount life before displacement, the reasons for their flight, and their struggle to rebuild their lives.

REFUGEE HOTEL
Compiled and edited by Juliet Linderman and Gabriele Stabile

"There is no other book like *Refugee Hotel* on your shelf." —*SF Weekly*

Refugee Hotel is a groundbreaking collection of photography and interviews that documents the arrival of refugees in the United States. Evocative images are coupled with moving testimonies from people describing their first days in the U.S., the lives they've left behind, and the new communities they've since created.

HIGH RISE STORIES
Voices from Chicago Public Housing
Compiled and edited by Audrey Petty • Foreword by Alex Kotlowitz

"Joyful, novelistic, and deeply moving." —George Saunders

In the gripping first-person accounts of *High Rise Stories*, former residents of Chicago's iconic public housing projects describe life in the now-demolished high rises. These stories of community, displacement, and poverty in the wake of gentrification give voice to those who have long been ignored.

INVISIBLE HANDS
Voices from the Global Economy
Compiled and edited by Corinne Goria
Foreword by Kalpona Akter

"Powerful and revealing testimony . . ." —*Kirkus*

In this oral history collection, electronics manufacturers in China, miners in Africa, garment workers in Mexico, and farmers in India—among many others—reveal the human rights crises occurring behind the scenes of the global economy.

PALESTINE SPEAKS
Voices from the Occupied Territories
Compiled and edited by Cate Malek and Mateo Hoke

"[These] are heartrending stories. . ." —*New York Review of Books*

The occupation of the West Bank and Gaza has been one of the world's most widely reported yet least understood human rights crises for over four decades. In this oral history collection, men and women from Palestine—including a fisherman, a settlement administrator, and a marathon runner—describe in their own words how their lives have been shaped by the historic crisis.

THE POWER OF THE STORY
The Voice of Witness Teacher's Guide to Oral History
Compiled and edited by Cliff Mayotte
Foreword by William and Richard Ayers

"A rich source of provocations to engage with human dramas throughout the world." —*Rethinking Schools Magazine*

This comprehensive guide allows teachers and students to explore contemporary issues through oral history, and to develop the communication skills necessary for creating vital oral history projects in their own communities.